COLONIAL MIGRANTS AND RACISM

Also by Neil MacMaster

SPANISH FIGHTERS: An Oral History of Civil War and Exile

Colonial Migrants and Racism

Algerians in France, 1900–62

Neil MacMaster
Lecturer in the School of Modern Languages and European Studies
University of East Anglia
Norwich

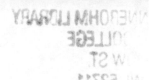

First published in Great Britain 1997 by
MACMILLAN PRESS LTD
Houndmills, Basingstoke, Hampshire RG21 6XS and London
Companies and representatives throughout the world

A catalogue record for this book is available from the British Library.

ISBN 0–333–64466–2 hardcover
ISBN 0–333–68700–0 paperback

First published in the United States of America 1997 by
ST. MARTIN'S PRESS, INC.,
Scholarly and Reference Division,
175 Fifth Avenue, New York, N.Y. 10010

ISBN 0–312–16501–3

Library of Congress Cataloging-in-Publication Data
MacMaster, Neil, 1945–
Colonial migrants and racism : Algerians in France, 1900–62 / Neil
MacMaster.
p. cm.
Includes bibliographical references and index.
ISBN 0–312–16501–3 (cloth)
1. Algerians—France—History—20th century.   2. Immigrants–
–Government policy—France.   3. France—Emigration and immigration–
–History—20th century.   4. Algeria—Emigration and immigration–
–History—20th century.   5. Racism—France.   6. Algeria—History-
–Revolution, 1954–1962—Influence.   I. Title.
DC34.5.A4M33   1996
305.892'765044'0904—dc20   96–32471
                                                                    CIP

This book is printed on paper suitable for recycling and made from fully managed and
sustained forest sources.

10   9   8   7   6   5   4   3   2   1
06   05   04   03   02   01   00   99   98   97

Printed and bound in Great Britain by Antony Rowe Ltd, Chippenham, Wiltshire

Contents

List of Maps, Tables and Figures

Maps

Tables

Figure

Acknowledgements

A generous grant from the British Academy enabled me to carry out archival research in the summer of 1988 in Aix-en-Provence and Algiers, just prior to the beginning of the crisis that has since made Algeria inaccessible to Europeans. I owe a large debt to the numerous librarians who have helped me in so many ways in Britain, France and Algeria, but in particular to the ever friendly staff of the Inter-Library Loan service at the University of East Anglia, Ann Wood, Sue Julier and David Harris. Without them this book would not have been possible. Phillip Judge of the School of Environmental Sciences at UEA designed the maps with his usual professionalism. David Seddon kindly read the manuscript in its entirety and made a number of valuable suggestions for its improvement. Needless to say any remaining flaws are entirely my own.

Last but first comes Mary MacMaster for her tireless support and humour when faced with the routine anti-social eccentricities of the researcher and writer.

NEIL MACMASTER

Introduction

During the last fifteen years immigration, the integration of ethnic minorities, and racism have become central issues in French politics. A 1990 opinion poll found that immigration was the second most important domestic concern after social and economic inequality.[1] The intense political debate as to the future position of ethnic minorities within France, whether they will gradually merge with the host society or constitute an indigestible enclave which threatens the integrity of the nation 'one and indivisible', has invariably centred on the position of the 'Arabs', the North Africans.[2] Among the minorities of Maghrebian origin or descent, the Algerians stand out as a particular object of hostility, the group that is perceived to epitomise all that is most alien and threatening to French identity. The racist targeting of North African immigrants or their descendents, the 'second generation' *Beurs*, in incidences of abuse, assault and murder is higher than for any other minority group.[3] In recent years, particularly after the right-wing Charles Pasqua became Minister of the Interior in 1993, the *Beurs* have been a constant target of police harassment which has generated explosive tensions and rioting in the huge, run-down council estates of the outer suburbs.

Two explanations are generally offered to explain why 'Arabs' have been a particular object of hatred and discrimination. Firstly, there exists a widespread dislike of cultural difference and in particular of Muslim identity, a dislike that found expression in the extraordinary debate over the '*foulards*' affair of 1989 when three girls were suspended from school for wearing headscarfs.[4] Recently anti-Arab feeling has reached new heights because of the fear attached to Islamic fundamentalism and the bombing campaign of the Armed Islamic Group (GIA) in France. A second cause of French hostility is the historic legacy of the Algerian War. At the end of the war in 1962 about one million European settlers, the *pieds noirs*, were 'repatriated' to France while over two million French soldiers had seen service in Algeria. The mass exodus of the settlers and the return to civilian society of armed forces personnel who had a first hand experience of bloody colonial war and

1

defeat injected a particularly virulent strain of racism into French society. This in part accounts for the hard-core element of extreme-right militants and activists that have been so prominent in the rise of the Front National, a party led by the ex-paratrooper Le Pen.[5] For many the Algerian presence on French soil was the ultimate insult: the former colonial subjects, perceived as inherently inferior, had not only been the victors but were now colonising the land of the 'civilised' masters.

One of the purposes of this book is to argue that the processes through which Algerians became a target of racism and discrimination originated well before the War of 1954–62 in an earlier phase of colonialism. On the outbreak of the Algerian War in November 1954 migration to France had already existed for half a century. The history of this early phase of labour and military recruitment to serve the needs of the metropolitan economy and armed forces provides an insight into the genesis and growth of racism, the processes through which European society began to categorise non-European migrants as inherently inferior outsiders. This early colonial development, which was already under way in 1910–20, established deep-rooted patterns of stereotyping, marginalisation and discrimination that have continued to leave a deep imprint on French society.

One reason for the relative neglect of non-European immigration into Europe before 1945 is that it has often been assumed that the arrival of 'Third World' migrants dates essentially from the period after 1945 when labour shortages and dynamic economic growth led to the recruitment of Afro-Caribbeans, North Africans, Asians and others. In recent years, however, specialists have begun to recognise not only that there was an earlier immigration but that the position of minorities in Europe cannot be properly understood without reference to an earlier phase of colonialism. Scholars have begun to turn with increasing interest to the *longue durée* of immigration into Europe to uncover the roots of contemporary racism and ethnic marginalisation.

In a general European context the two societies with the most significant history of early colonial immigration were Britain and France, the two outstanding imperial powers at the turn of the century, which together controlled enormous territories and their potential reserves of labour.[6] A growing body of research on Britain has centred on the 'hidden' history of colonial minorities prior to the Second World War.[7] However, before 1945 by far the largest presence of colonial workers in Europe was that of the North Africans, particularly Algerians, in France. In inter-war Britain colonial minorities concentrated in the seaports of Cardiff, Liverpool and London, probably numbered no more than a few thousand.[8] In comparison the Algerian migration to France took place on a much larger scale and their numbers rose from about 13 000 on the eve of the First World War to 130 000 in 1930. Very few people within Britain had any direct contact with colonial minorities, since the latter were geographically restricted to a few seaport enclaves.[9] In interwar France, on the other hand, a much wider population had contact with North Africans since they moved rapidly inland from Marseilles into the major urban conglomerations, particularly Paris and Lyons. The scale of the 'Arab' presence led to a far more significant popular response and has left a much richer historical documentation.

The roots of Algerian emigration lay in a complex interaction between 'push' factors, the processes that created a pool of rural misery and hunger in the colony, and 'pull' factors, the growing demand for a supply of unskilled labour in the metropolitan economy. The colonisation of Algeria between 1830 and 1900 had an enormously destructive impact on the traditional economy and society, through massive appropriation of lands, the uprooting and dislocation of tribes, the collapse of artisan industry, and the creation of an impoverished peasantry which was constantly subject to disease and hunger (see Chapter 1). The colonial system generated a large reservoir of underemployed and desperately poor peasant-labourers which could be readily tapped after 1900 when the metropolitan economy faced a labour shortage.

France was unusual among European states during the period from 1900 to 1939 in the extent to which it was confronted with an unprecedented shortage of labour. This situation arose because the French practised birth control on a wide scale, and an unusually low fertility rate was compounded by the enormous losses of the First World War.[10] Without an injection of foreign labour French economic growth would have been severely impeded. The response of the government and private industry was to elaborate the first system in modern Europe for the large-scale recruitment of foreign labour. By 1930 France had the highest level of foreigners in the world, 515 aliens to every 100 000 French citizens compared to the next highest, the United States, which had 492 aliens to every 100 000 nationals.[11] The 1931 census indicated the following nationalities, in descending order of size: Italians (808 000), Poles (507 800), Spaniards (351 900), Belgians (253 700), North Africans (102 000), Swiss (98 000), Russians (71 900) and Germans (71 700). The 2 890 000 foreigners constituted seven per cent of the total population of 41 800 000.[12] The Algerian mobilisation was just one part of a much larger-scale phenomenon, a drive to man the low paid, physically demanding and often dangerous work in mines, foundries, chemical works, refineries, tanneries and docks that the French refused to do.

Algerian immigration represented a relatively small statistical percentage of the total immigrant population at 3.5 per cent. However, Algerians concentrated in the urban/industrial zones of Paris, Marseilles, Lyons, Lorraine and elsewhere, living alongside much larger communities of Poles, Italians, Spaniards and Belgians, aroused a degree of public attention out of all proportion to their numbers. During the period 1912 to 1954 there was a veritable avalanche of publications, newspaper reports and official inquiries on the Algerian migration: economists, jurists, Islamic specialists, doctors, journalists, priests, novelists and politicians produced an almost ceaseless flow of books and articles on the 'Arab problem'.

The reasons for this public concern with the 'Arab' presence which are the subject of Chapters 7, 8 and 9 can be summarised as follows. Firstly, prior to the First World War, European society had generally defined its own identity over and against the image of primitive or barbarian peoples that lay spatially distant, out **beyond** the borders of Europe in 'Darkest Africa', Asia and the Americas.[13] However, the relatively large-scale movement of 'colonial' soldiers and workers into France from 1905 onwards meant that metropolitan society was for the first time compelled to define itself in relation to an immediate, visible minority presence which was perceived as threatening, a barbaric intrusion into the heart of Empire. Arabs were no longer experienced as rare individuals, oriental carpet vendors, snake-charmers, and exhibits in fairs and colonial exhibitions, but as workmen in the street of the *quartiers populaires* of Paris, Lyons and Marseilles.

Much of the inter-war journalistic reportage on Arabs showed a fascination with this exotic presence, as with the investigations of Father Paul Catrice who in 1929 visited, rather in the style of a missionary plunging into heathen Africa, the infamous North Africa shantytown of 'Les Grésillons' at Gennevilliers.[14] But the academic and specialist press was concerned with more substantive issues: particularly the question of whether migrants from a non-European racial stock and socialised into an alien way of life, culture and religion (principally Islam) could be assimilated into the French 'melting-pot'. There was a widespread fear that Arabs, inhabiting slum enclaves and organised in 'tribal' groupings that were impenetrable to police surveillance, would remain 'encysted' like indigestible foreign bodies within the urban tissue.

Secondly, underlying the sheer volume of official investigation and press reportage lay a more important **political** question. Although Algerian migrants made up only 3.5 per cent of foreigners in France, they constituted a much larger percentage of the total population of colonial Algeria. Most Algerian migrants were 'target' workers who came to France for one or two years with the aim of accumulating savings before returning to their home villages. The massive rotation of labour across the Mediterranean meant that some 500 000 Algerian males had some experience of life in France during the inter-war period. This was one in five of all men of working age, or between one tenth and one twelfth of the total population.[15] In areas of high emigration like Kabylia, there were some villages in which seventy per cent or more of all males had some experience of life in France as workers or soldiers. It was the consequences of this emigration from the point of view of the **colonial** society that was a particular cause of concern.

Settlers (the *colons*) were concerned that migration to France would seriously deplete the supply of native labour to European farms and drive up wage levels. But of far greater concern to colonial ideologues was the fact that migrants could escape the repressive and hegemonic constraints of Algerian society, symbolised by the 'Native Code' (*code indigène*), for the more open and liberal atmosphere of France. It was feared that the simple and illiterate peasant migrants would lose the paternalistic protection of their colonial masters and in the advanced industrial society come into contact with the French working class and be infected by Communism, trade unionism or currents of émigré Algerian nationalism. These subversive influences would then be brought back into every Algerian village by returning migrants and set in motion forces that would subvert and finally topple the whole colonial edifice.

One of the central problems faced by those interests that wished to counter these perceived dangers and to control Algerian emigration arose from the unique status of the colony. The early implantation of a French and European settler population gave rise to demands for full assimilation of Algeria to France, and the declaration of 4 November 1848 proclaimed Algeria as French territory, in principle an extension of French soil. The colony had a system of administration, with departments, prefects, communes and mayors, identical to that of the metropole. However, any colonial theory of assimilation (or later 'association') which implied the eventual extension of full citizenship and equality to indigenous Algerians was bitterly resisted by the *colons*.[16] The Senatus law of 14 July 1865 made a distinction between citizens and subjects. As subjects Algerians had no political representation, were denied access to public office, were subjected to heavier 'Arab' taxes, to special repressive laws and tribunals, and restrictions on freedom of movement.

A profound contradiction existed within the dualistic society of the colony between the Republican values of universal equality and the principles of the French Revolution (reserved for the settlers), and the inferior status of the natives.[17] The Paris government tended to mollify Algerian reformist pressure through a 'progressive' discourse which held out the promise of an eventual assimilation of natives into the French social and political order. However, this was dependent on an eventual acquisition of French culture and civilisation that was distant, often stated as 'centuries away', and entirely nebulous. The discourse which extended republican *égalité* to the Algerians, extolled their eventual entry into the *cité*, was a smokescreen which enabled the government and senior administrators to uphold the universal principles of the Rights of Man and to legitimate the colonial presence, while in reality denying the natives the most basic rights.

From 1900 onwards the proto-nationalist movement of the *Jeunes-Algériens*, led by an educated and Francophile élite, campaigned for an assimilationist policy which would extend full political rights and equality to all Algerian subjects. The government found it increasingly difficult to resist nationalist pressures for concrete reform and a serious move towards assimilation, particularly as it served its purpose to demand that Algerians, as 'Frenchmen', should face the same duties as every other citizen, including conscription and the ultimate 'blood tax' of sacrifice for the *patrie*. The government made some timid gestures in the direction of reform and the principle of assimilation through a series of piecemeal acts, one of which was the freedom to emigrate to France (Law of 15 July 1914). This act opened the way to what Gallissot has termed a single 'espace franco-algérien': in principle there was no frontier between France and Algeria and metropolitan industry could as readily mobilise labour in the colony as it could from Brittany or the Auvergne.

Throughout the period 1912–1962 the debate over foreign immigrant labour, or from the Protectorates (Morocco, Tunisia), was quite different from that of Algerian 'immigration' which – in strict legal terms – was no immigration at all, but a movement within the same nation-state. This meant that metropolitan industry and the state (in its military functions) could mobilise Algerian manpower without restriction and in a way that was not possible in the case of foreign labour. On the downside for the capitalist employer and the state was the fact that Algerians, as French subjects, could claim (or try to) claim) the same rights as citizens to equal pay, welfare, and social security. In principle (the reality was rather different) Algerians could not, during economic recession, simply be expelled as were unemployed foreign workers, particularly the Poles. The position of the Algerian migrant worker in France was shot through with ambiguity, and became the site of a crucial political and ideological struggle between the newly emergent nationalist movements and French imperialism.

The problem facing *colon* interests was how to halt or severely control Algerian migration once freedom of movement had been ensconced as a fundamental right and a symbol of French commitment to assimilation. Throughout the period 1914–1962 the French government refused to give way to colonial pressure to remove the basic right to free movement. To have done so was regarded as politically explosive, particularly at a time when nationalist movements were rapidly increasing in strength. A solution was sought by the *colon* lobby, with the tacit support of government, to hinder movement by the imposition of **administrative** hurdles. Through this means the government was still able to pay lip service to the principles of Republican *égalité*, while imposing *de facto* restraints. In this way the Algerian migrant was in a worse position than the foreign worker. Foreign migrants, particularly Italians, were frequently protected in their interests by their national governments, but Algerians were caught between the collusive force of metropolitan government and powerful colonial interests, including the *Gouvernement Générale*, and subject to demands like military service.

Chapter 8 explores in detail how a colonial lobby campaigned to subvert the law on free movement of 1914, and the basic tenets of assimilationism and Republican *égalité* through the administrative imposition of severe controls and an apparatus of police surveillance. One tactic employed was to influence French public opinion and the government through the systematic criminalisation of Algerian migrants. By creating a climate of opinion which came to fear 'Arabs' as violent and lubricious barbarians the self-serving lobby was able to emphasise the dangers of immigration to **metropolitan** society. The 'invaders' were also portrayed as vectors of dangerous microbes, particularly syphilis and tuberculosis. The proliferation of such stereotypes, particularly through the press, played no small part in the creation of a climate of racism which was to continue into the post-colonial period.

Since the settler lobby was unable to bring about a total halt of Algerian migration it campaigned, as will be shown in Chapter 9, to establish a neo-colonial system of policing and paternalist surveillance which would keep track on Algerians in France and their links to dangerous political movements. The establishment of specialised 'welfare' institutions aimed solely at North Africans, worker hostels, medical centres, evening classes, official mosques and even a Muslim hospital, was closely linked to a policing apparatus which aimed to collect intelligence and to segregate North Africans from the dangerous influences of the host society. This police and welfare apparatus was both designed and manned by Europeans from Algeria who introduced into the metropole colonial attitudes and techniques of control.

Thus while most immigrant nationalities, the Italians, Poles, Spaniards and others, aroused xenophobic responses in the French public during the inter-war years, the targeting of the relatively small group of North Africans was far more intense and sustained. These processes tell us much about the construction of racism, and how racial categories emerged and developed within a specific historical context.

While one purpose is to examine the political reactions to the Algerian migration within the colonial-metropolitan field, another is to provide a **social** history of the migration and its transformations through time. The Algerian movement provides a revealing case-study of the process of international migration, of how and why migrants set out for particular destinations, the problems they faced of finding work and accommodation, and the ways in which they coped with and adapted to living conditions in an advanced urban/industrial society.

However, in order to make sense of this process it is important that appropriate weight be given to an examination of both the society of **emigration** and of **immigration**. Studies of immigration into Europe have centred overwhelmingly on the position of minorities within the 'host' society, a Euro-centric perspective which explicitly or implicitly examines integration or assimilation by the degree of adaptation to the values and structures of European society. In recent years it has been increasingly acknowledged that the situation of migrants in Europe can only be properly understood through a better understanding of the society of emigration.[18] How migrants adjusted to or coped with life in European urban/industrial society requires an understanding of the values, customs, social practices and particular intentions which they carried with them. In practice few historians or sociologists have adopted this approach or they have made do with a rapid and shallow sketch of the conditions in the zone of emigration before passing on quickly to concentrate on the European scene.[19] In this study considerable attention is given to the long-term causes of emigration, the impact of colonialism, the socio-economic conditions in the zones of departure, and the influence of remittances and return migration in generating further departures. The constant interplay of contacts between the countries of emigration and immigration is particularly important in the Algerian case since migrants, only twenty-four hours away by ship, were engaged in an incessant circulation or *noria* that generated a continual dynamic interrelationship between the sending and host societies.[20]

Migration specialists have been much interested in the way in which, through time, particular streams of migration tend to pass through a regular cycle of change. The most common model has been that of a three stage process in which single-male, temporary migration changes to a second phase of more permanent emigration, marked by family reunification, and eventually to a third stage of community formation.[21] One problem faced by researchers of migration in trying to reconstitute the pattern of historical change is one of evidence. Some of the most interesting work on migration has been carried out by social anthropologists in the rural zones of emigration.[22] However, such field work investigations, based on interviews, generally locate mobility at one point in time and it may prove difficult to uncover a picture of earlier historical phases in migration and the longer term transformations taking place.[23]

This is where the historical sources that exist on the Algerian migration are particularly rich and valuable. Because of the high level of government and colonial concern to investigate and police the Algerian migration there exists a very extensive and detailed body of documentation that spans a long period of time. This evidence makes it possible to build up an unusually detailed picture of change. Official investigations of migration were carried out in 1912, 1914, 1923, 1928, 1937–8, 1949, 1950 and 1954, much of this involving the collection of data in both Algerian communes and in metropolitan French departments. Of all the major 'Third World' migrations into Europe during the twentieth century, that from Algeria has both the longest history and the most detailed historical record.

However, this massive documentation, despite its great volume, presents some particular problems of interpretation and use. One possible objection to a study which is based largely on sources produced by the dominant colonial élites, administrators, soldiers, police officers, doctors and others, is that this can only really tell us about the mind-set of the European observer. The world of the migrant is invisible, and cannot be known. In recent years a lively debate has centred on the issue of colonial discourse, and what, if anything, can be known about the colonised 'Other'. Gayatri Spivak argues that the 'planned epistemic violence of the imperialist project' was so absolute that it is near impossible to recover the voice of the colonised, the 'silent subaltern'.[24]

In what follows, part of my purpose will be to look at the discourse and ideology of French officialdom and colonial interest groups, and in particular how it generated racialised categories. The sources are, self-evidently, suited to this purpose. However, I would argue that official sources can also be used to construct a fairly detailed picture of the universe of the migrant worker. In spite of their inherent bias and Euro-centric perspective it is possible to glean from official and élite sources a great deal of information about the migrants' experience. For example a large number of French administrators of the *communes mixtes*, the backward rural zones where natives predominated, lived for years in close contact with the local Arab population and wrote numerous reports which are a mine of information on the endemic poverty which led to emigration.[25] The problems of interpretation of such materials are little different from those faced by the social historian who attempts to probe the lived experience of the nineteenth century European working class, most members of which were illiterate and left the barest fragments of direct evidence.

In addition there is a significant range of materials that enables a closer, or insider view of the migrant experience. This includes photographs, documentary films and letters from Algerians in France, all of which have been imaginatively used by Gilbert Meynier for the First World War.[26] There also exist a number of autobiographies that recount the inter-war experience of migration, most notably that of the nationalist leader Messali Hadj, as well as several important novels by Algerian writers. Where, unfortunately, there still exists a significant gap, is in the failure of French and Algerian historians to make a systematic and sustained use of oral sources, although there is a scattering of oral evidence in some of the best sociological work on emigration, particularly in that of Abdelmalek Sayad.[27]

A further barrier to understanding the Algerian migration experience stems from the fact that most natives were profoundly wary, and quite justifiably, of French officialdom. The appearance of colonial administrators in the rural communes was automatically associated with a long process of interference and spoliation: the imposition of heavy taxes, the survey and appropriation of land, the levy of forced labour, and repressive legislation. One response of the Algerian people to such interference was to create a façade that would protect the indigenous society as a secret zone that was impenetrable to the gaze of the colonial master. But it is possible, as J.C. Scott has demonstrated, to delineate some of the features of the 'hidden transcript' and to uncover important fragments of the reality underlying the subterfuges of resistance.[28]

An understanding of the culture of resistance in colonial Algeria has implications for the position of immigrants in French society. One of the central and most intriguing features of the Algerian presence in France has been the extremely slow process of integration. The fact that the Algerians have remained marginalised within French society, in spite of such a long history of migration, can be in part attributed to the degree to which they have been a target of racism. However, a number of other factors helped to ensure the separation out, the apartness, of Algerians. Firstly, migrants did not begin the process of contact and adjustment to French society when they first disembarked in Marseilles since Algerians had already lived in contact with the French for a century. In response to colonial domination and exploitation Algerians had constructed a range of defensive mechanisms, including the maintenance of social and cultural boundaries that were radically defined. For example, the degree of intermarriage between Algerians and Europeans – one of the most sensitive indicators of ethnic boundary maintenance – was almost non-existent. These socio-cultural practices which had developed over the course of a century were carried over into the metropolitan context.

One process was to live apart, segregated within a micro-society founded on kin, village and 'tribal' structures. The 'encysted' nature of the Algerian community, its resistance to absorption into European society, was further sustained by the circulatory pattern of migration. Workers constantly moved between France and their home villages. Migrants from the Nedroma region of western Algeria, for example, returned every year in time to help with the harvest.[29] The ease of rotation ensured that the migrant kept his roots in the peasant community and continually replenished the sources of tradition. Throughout the first half of the twentieth century the Algerian migration remained 'archaic' in the sense that the Algerian labourer was still fundamentally a peasant whose function was to procure external resources to sustain the traditional Kabyle society.

The long cycle of male rotation began to give way from about 1948 to a process of family reunification and settlement in France. However, this 'second age' of migration was just getting into its stride (1948–54) when the Algerian War of Independence broke out. One major consequence of the War was to continue, or even deepen, the isolation of Algerians within French society. A dual process was at work. Algerians in France became the target of police actions, public hostility, and racist violence. But the migrant community was increasingly controlled from within by the sophisticated and all-embracing organisation of the *Front de libération nationale* (FLN). The extremely tight and sometimes bloody 'encadrement' of the émigré community, the aim of which was to counter the influence of the French police and Messali Hadj's *Mouvement national algérien* (MNA), as well as to maximise fund raising for the war, further isolated the Algerians. Even with the end of the war in 1962 the newly independent Algerian government tried to retain a tight rein over its nationals in France, especially through the apparatus of the FLN's *Fédération de France* and its successor, the *Amicale des Algériens en Europe*.[30]

It is through this long history of colonial migration that we can begin to understand why Algerians, more than any other ethnic group, maintained their distinctiveness and continue to be the target of the highest levels of discrimination.

THE PATTERN OF MIGRATION: AN OVERVIEW

The remaining part of this introductory chapter will provide an overview of the statistics and general pattern of Algerian immigration between 1900 and 1962. This will provide a general framework for the more detailed discussion and analysis in later chapters.

One problem faced by the historian of Algerian migration is that contemporary sources frequently used a terminology which makes it difficult for the historian to distinguish between Algerian, Moroccan and Tunisian movements. For example, the Maghrebians as a whole were frequently referred to in official sources as 'North Africans' and '*Français-musulmans*'. In the streets of Paris and Marseilles Maghrebian workers appeared to the westerner identical in dress, language and physical looks and the tendency to treat them as an undifferentiated body was reflected in popular terminology, 'Arabs' and '*sidis*' and the more racist '*bougnoules*' and '*bicots*'.

Some historians, like Larbi Talha, recognising the similarities between the migration from Algeria, Morocco and Tunisia, have treated it as a whole.[31] An approach which treats migration from the Maghreb as a unitary field does make sense when the purpose is to analyse, often from a neo-Marxist perspective, the general **economic** features of capitalist penetration and exploitation of North Africa. However, in this study I have opted to concentrate on Algeria for a number of reasons. Firstly, as a colony Algeria had a quite special legal and political status. Through a juridical fiction it was held to be, quite literally, an extension of French soil, a status that marked it off from the Protectorates of Tunisia (established 1881) and Morocco (1912). Not only was the Algerian migration the largest in scale but the relative freedom of movement of its *sujets françaises* across the Mediterranean created a quite specific problem of control and policing for the French authorities. Abdelmalek Sayad has provided an extended analysis of the unique features of the Algerian migration which he calls 'exemplary', in the sense that it constituted a movement that generated a deeper level of state concern and of thorny political and ideological issues than for any other immigrant nationality.[32]

A generalised interpretation of Maghrebian migration would obscure the specific features and unique dynamic of Algerian mobility, while at a more practical level an adequate investigation of Morocco and Tunisia would require an additional volume. However, in what follows there will inevitably be some references to North Africans in general, particularly in relation to the situation in France where journalists, investigators and the public often viewed them as a single entity. Many of the texts which describe the situation of Algerians do so in terms of the general features of the North African community in the lodging houses and 'Moorish cafés' of Paris or Lyons. There is also the interesting question of the way in which Algerians and Moroccans, the second largest Magrebian minority, related to each other on French soil, how far they associated socially and politically, or maintained boundaries based on language, culture and proto-nationalism.

Official data on the flow of Algerian migration to and from France between 1900 and 1962 is inadequate and presents some thorny issues of interpretation and treatment. Luc Muracciole, in one of the best investigations of the statistics, noted that,'It is impossible to obtain anything else than approximations and estimations which vary from one to four'.[33] For the Algerian migration there exist, apart from a number of official surveys carried out in 1914, 1923, 1928, 1937 and 1948–54, all of which were seriously flawed, two principal sources of data. Firstly, the five-year census returns (*Recensements quinquennaux*) for 1921, 1926, 1931 and 1936 which indicated the number of 'North Africans' resident in France, registered somewhere in the region of 50 to 75 per cent of actual numbers. The returns failed to locate illegal migrants, but more seriously the census relied on the **voluntary** returns of the Algerians many of whom were illiterate, highly suspicious of French officialdom, and constantly on the move between different places of work and between temporary lodgings in overcrowded slums. In addition the census was too infrequent (those of 1916 and 1941 did not take place because of war) and too widely spaced to provide a data-series which can be linked to fluctuations in the economic and political sphere.[34]

By far the most useful statistics are the official records of Algerians leaving and returning via the major ports, which were compiled on both a monthly and annual basis between 1914 and 1942, and then resumed after the war, from 1946 onwards.[35] The statistics, listed in Table A1 in the Appendix, show a high level of both **departures** and **returns**. This reflects a crucial feature of the Algerian migration until the Second World War, that this was essentially a movement of constant circulation or *noria*. Migrants departed for France for periods which varied, generally from eight months to one to four years.[36] On return to Algeria many individuals, after a period of recuperation, would once again take the ship for France. The perpetual rotation across the Mediterranean meant that the Algerian community in France was in constant flux, with new workers arriving as others departed (see Figure 1). The geographical proximity of Algeria to France facilitated this circulation and explains in part why Algeria became the first 'Third World' labour reserve for the European economy.[37]

The total number of Algerians located in France at any one point in time cannot be accurately measured, but the trend can be established by adding year by year the accumulative balance (see Appendix, Table A1). The cumulative total probably underestimates the real numbers: for example, a large number of clandestine workers entered France, particularly after restrictive controls were introduced from 1924 onwards. On the other hand an untold number of migrants died in France from disease due to poor diet, appalling housing or industrial disease and accidents.[38] To this picture can be added information from other sources, for example an official investigation of immigration carried out in 1914 by a team headed by Octave Depont indicated a pre-war migration that began about 1905 and had reached about 13 000 workers on the eve of the War.[39]

The broad features of the fluctuations in Algerian migration between 1900 and 1962 can now be identified. The first wave of labour migration began in 1904–5 with the liberalisation of controls on Algerian emigration. However, it was the mass mobilisation of colonial labour and soldiers during the First World War which marked a crucial watershed. In all some 300 000 Algerians crossed to France during the war, 173 000 as soldiers and 118 000 as workers. In proportion to total Algerian population this represented an enormous mobilisation, about one third of males of working age.[40] Although the French authorities rounded up and repatriated all but about 5000 Algerians at the end of the war, this was followed by an unprecedented peace-time influx between 1920 and 1924.

There were four basic reasons for this post-war 'take-off'. The demand for labour in France was enormous because of the need to reconstruct the war-damaged zones and to man sectors of heavy industry, particularly metallurgy and mining.

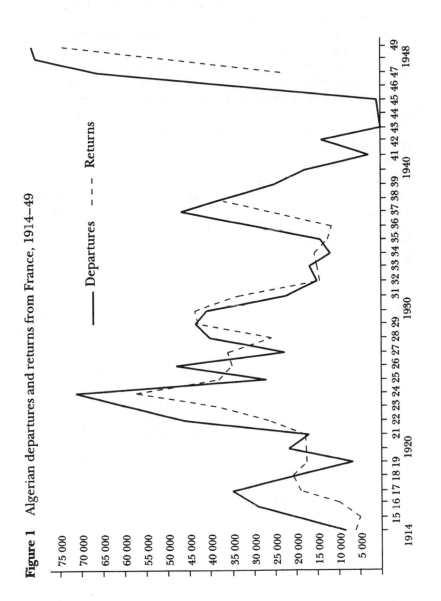

Figure 1 Algerian departures and returns from France, 1914–49

Secondly, the experience of a war-time 'command economy' had led to the elaboration of the first foreign labour system in Europe and encouraged massive post-war recruitment. Thirdly, at the supply end, the colonial socio-economic system was entering a phase of deepening crisis: settler appropriation of land and the erosion of the natives' basic level of subsistence ushered in a major famine in 1920–1. Yet at the same time tens of thousands of Algerians who had war-time experience of life and work in France knew at first-hand the higher wage levels, and felt confident about finding their feet in an alien urban environment.

After reaching a first peak in 1924, Algerian migration in the remaining fifteen years of the inter-war period went through a series of oscillations. Two major determinants were at work. Firstly, economic downturns in 1925, 1927, and 1930 followed by the Depression of 1931–5 led to unemployment, in which Algerians were the first to be laid off, and to growing xenophobia from French workers and unions. The higher level of port registered returns over departures in 1925, 1927 and 1930–1 indicate how sensitive the Algerian *noria* was to fluctuations in the French economy.[41] However, during the Depression many thousands of Algerians, even those who were unemployed, appear to have preferred to ride-out the crisis in France rather than to go home, where conditions were even worse. A degree of economic recovery during 1936–9 led to a further climb in departures to France: in 1936, for example, the powerful iron-masters, the *Comité des Forges*, recruited thousands of Algerians into the iron and steel industry of Lorraine.

The second determinant of the inter-war pattern of migration were changes in government controls on entry to France. After the First World War all Algerians, unlike other North Africans, were for the first time allowed complete freedom of movement to France under a law passed on 15 July 1914. However, the campaign by the colonial lobby and other interests succeeded in persuading the Minister of the Interior to impose strict controls on migration by administrative decrees issued in August and September 1924. Apart from a brief moment between 17 July and October 1936 when the Popular Front government removed all controls, the period from late 1924 until the outbreak of the Second World War was one during which a significant degree of restraint was imposed on

Algerian mobility. As will be shown in Chapter 8 the crucial reasons for initiating a system of controls which were intended to strangulate migration were political rather than economic. The block to Algerian labour migration, as with the British Commonwealth Immigration Act of 1962, which was also tailored to arrest the free movement of colonial minorities into Europe, arose from a fundamentally racist politics that had little if any economic logic. The dramatic fall in Algerian departures to France after September 1924 was a consequence of this policy.

The Second World War placed a further brake on the strong pressures to emigrate. During the early part of the War first the French government and then the German authorities recruited several thousand Algerians as workers, but the Allied landings in North Africa led to an almost total halt on movement between November 1942 and the end of 1945.[42] During this three-year period tens of thousands of Algerians were blocked in France and the total freeze on remittance payments was sharply reflected in the poverty experienced by zones of high emigration, particularly in Kabylia.

The Second World War marked a watershed in the qualitative and quantitative nature of migration. The last seventeen years of the colonial régime (1945–62) saw a dramatic and unprecedented growth in migration. Departures in 1947 (66 234) were higher than for any inter-war year apart from 1924 (71 028) and then continued to climb to 159 786 in 1954. The total number of Algerians in France increased from about 100 000 in late 1945 to 250 000 in 1950 and 350 000 in 1962.[43] As Figure 1 indicates, post-war emigration was marked by a significant shift into second gear. Firstly, with the Liberation came a series of measures, an ordonnance of 1944 and the law of 23 September 1947, which restored to Algerians complete freedom of movement.[44]

The sudden considerable increase in the number of migrants can also be explained by changing conditions in Algeria. Until the mid-1930s emigration had been mainly from Kabylia, where peasant Berber-speakers predominated, but from that period the zone of departure began to spread in an 'oil-slick' effect into the plains where Arabs were predominant. Emigration began to affect a class of landless proletariat which had weak ties to the land and was more prepared to emigrate permanently. The considerable potential for migration from the plains was however not fully realised because of the impact of the Depression and the Second World War (1931–45). During this period the crisis in the colonial régime was deepening and poverty increasing and when freedom to emigrate was restored the effect was like a dam bursting under the pressure of intense demographic pressures. As Omar Carlier notes,'The sheer power of this migratory liberation can in part be explained by the compression of migration from 1930 to 1945'.[45]

At the same time the underlying structure of emigration began to shift towards family reunification. Circulation did not end entirely but the periods during which individual migrants stayed in France became longer and longer. A crucial indicator of the transformation in the nature of emigration was the increase in departure of wives and children from an almost nonexistent level to a general phenomenon: by 1956 out of a total of 330 000 Algerians in France about 26 000 were women and children.[46] The entire *raison d'être* of the first phase of emigration, to seek external resources for the extended peasant family group, was radically undermined as migrants took root in France, settled permanently and invested wages in the needs of the nuclear family (housing, consumer goods).

The rapid increase in the scale of migration had just taken off when the Algerian War began. It might have been expected that such a savage colonial war, followed by the creation of a newly independent Algerian state, would have disrupted and then halted emigration to France. The war did temporarily reduce the rate of departure from 1956 onwards (Table A1), but even before Independence in 1962 large scale emigration had resumed. The war massively disrupted the colonial society and economy. In particular the huge transfer or *regroupement* of one third of the peasantry from villages into temporary camps led to a permanent dislocation and uprooting and to an eventual acceleration in emigration (Chapter 11).

Nor did the arrival of peace bring a counter-flow of return migration to the newly independent state. The FLN government inherited an underdeveloped economy, weakened by colonial neglect of the mass of rural and urban proletariat, and sabotaged by the departing *pieds noirs* who had also provided the professional cadres. Faced with enormous demographic pressures and massive underemployment and poverty the government had little choice but to allow emigration to continue since it acted as a safety valve and remittance payments were too valuable to the economy. While official FLN policy was that all emigrants, as citizens of the new nation, should eventually return to Algeria in reality the transition towards permanent settlement in France was already underway. By 1973, a decade after the war, when Algeria finally stopped all further primary migration there were some 800 000 Algerians living in France, the single largest minority group.

1 Colonial Destruction of Algerian Society

Colonialism, in association with the corrosive impact of capitalism, was an almost universal determinant of 'Third World' migrations into Europe in the twentieth century. Algerian migration to France shared many of the general features through which military conquest and the economic dislocation of traditional pastoral and agrarian societies led to the impoverishment and displacement of peoples.[1] However, each society of emigration had its own quite specific and historic characteristics. What distinquished Algeria was the unusual degree of violence involved and the systematic and premeditated way in which the French set about the radical dislocation of tribal society and the massive appropriation and transfer of land to European settlers. The removal of the economic independence of the peasantry and its reduction to a condition of endemic poverty, created a semi-proletarianised class which was compelled to sell its labour power first to the *colons* who had seized their lands and, eventually, to metropolitan employers. The impact of French colonialism was far more profound in the case of Algeria, for example, than for the neighbouring Maghrebian societies of Morocco and Tunisia and in part this explains the larger scale of emigration from Algeria.[2] However, it must be emphasised that colonialism was a necessary but not sufficient cause of emigration. As will be seen later the huge undermass of hungry Algerians could have remained bottled up in the North African colony; it required crucial legal-political measures by the metropole to open the 'doors' to emigration.

This chapter provides a brief introduction to the basic characteristics of pre-colonial Algeria, the enormous impact of colonialism, and those processes which eventually led to emigration. The general features of economic and social dislocation, impoverishment and proletarianisation are here discussed for Algeria as if it constituted a single, homogeneous space. Later chapters (2, 10) will examine in more detail the remarkable internal variations between zones of high and low emigration. Contemporary historians have tended to neglect these spatial differences which, I shall argue, hold an important key to the way in which colonialism/capitalism utilised indigenous labour and resolved the tension between *colons*, seeking to monopolise internal migration, and metropolitan employers, keen to develop emigration.

Algeria today constitutes a vast territory of 2.4 million square kilometres, nine tenths of which is Saharan desert. In 1830 the Algerian population, as today, was largely situated in the northern area or *Tell*, consisting of the Mediterranean littoral plains and the rugged mountain extensions of the Atlas, interspersed with river valleys and high plateaux. This zone extended like a long east-west ribbon, sandwiched between the coast and the Sahara. In this littoral band, which was only one to two hundred kilometres wide, the crucial life-sustaining level of rainfall declined rapidly towards the Saharan fringes.

At the time of the French invasion (1830) Algerian society was essentially rural. Of a total population of three million only ten per cent was urban and the major towns like Algiers, Constantine, Tlemcen, Oran and Bône were essentially market-trading, craft and administrative centres serving the rural hinterland.[3] French colonial geographers and historians divided rural society into two basic types based on the juridical distinction of *arch* and *melk* lands, a categorisation which is still useful to a general analysis.[4] The agro-pastoral tribes living on the huge open spaces of communal *arch* lands, situated mainly in the river plains and steppe-like high plateaux, made up some sixty per cent of the rural population. These tent-dwelling nomads relied on livestock (sheep, goats, camels, cattle) and temporary grain cultivation. French colonists, impressed by the huge open spaces that appeared to be thinly populated and under-utilised, wrongly assumed that there was plenty of room for European farming. However, given the harsh climatic conditions (low and unreliable rainfall), poor soils and thin vegetation, extensive pastoralism and grain cultivation was efficient and may have achieved an optimum balance between population density and the environment.[5] In 1859, Lestibourdois, criticising the forceable relocation of tribes and the seizure of their lands, remarked that the nomadic population was, 'Already developed to the furthest possible limit in the climatic conditions under which they live . . . It is not possible to suddenly resettle in strictly confined geometrical zones these people who need the Sahara in winter, the plains of the *Tell* during the spring and the harvest season, the mountain and littoral forests during the summer drought'.[6]

In contrast to the nomadic tribes the sedentary peasants of the high mountain zones lived in permanent village settlements built of stone or adobe. These peasants (*fellahin*) worked small plots of land intensively and produced a wide range of vegetable and tree crops (figs, cherries, olives) while livestock was grazed in the forests and on the higher mountain slopes. The system of intensive polyculture enabled such societies to reach population densities of one hundred or more people to the square kilometre, compared to levels of under ten among the nomads (see Chapter 2). *Melk* land was similar to European private property in that it was clearly demarcated by walls or boundaries, was owned by particular families, and could even be bought and sold.

The importance of the distinction between nomadic (*arch*) and sedentary (*melk*) societies is that the French colonisers found it easier to appropriate the land of the former, through both military force and legal methods. The dense mountain populations of the *melk* zones, with their pre-existing settled occupation of 'private' land, proved highly resistant to colonial penetration and occupation. However, the juridical distinction between *arch* and *melk* should not obscure the fact that normally there was no market in land: property was basically inalienable and was controlled or owned by the group or the community, whether the patriarchal family, or the tribal fraction.

The tribes, which numbered about 650, varied greatly in size from the smaller units of the mountains (a few thousand people) to the enormous groups of the plains such as the Abdennour (25 000 members) and the Harakta (30 000). Algerian society can best be understood as pyramidal in shape and operating from the base upwards. The elemental and most cohesive social unit, both in nomadic and sedentary societies, was the patriarchal, extended family, frequently located in a shared household. The family group regulated marriage alliances, collective property, and overall production and consumption. Families were united into a small structured community, the fraction or *ferqa*, shared the same common ancestor (real or mythical), and in Kabylia and the Aurès corresponded to the village settlement. The *ferqa* were in turn integrated into a much larger but less cohesive unit, the tribe. The tribe was a mainly 'political' organisation which sprang into action only spasmotically to defend its interests against any external threat from other tribes. This kind of society has been defined as segmentary, in that communities existed alongside each other in quite distinct groups that had restricted interrelationships.[7]

In order to understand the process by which the French set out to dominate and dismantle the traditional socio-economic order and to appropriate its key resource, the land, it is useful to divide the colonial period into three phases, 1830–70, 1871–1920, 1921–54.[8] The third period, which will be examined in detail in Chapter 10, was one of deepening crisis in the colonial economy and a dramatic increase in the Algerian population which helped fuel the pressures to emigrate. Here we are concerned more with the first two periods.

The first period, from 1830 to 1870, was marked by a long period of military conquest and consolidation, notable for the seventeen year war against Abdel Kader and the last major insurrection led by El Mokrani in 1871. During the 1840s the French began to plan and implement a *colonisation de peuplement* or settler strategy, the purpose of which was to introduce as many French as possible.[9] In order to make land available to the *colons* the colonial administration seized land through a 'right of conquest', by the appropriation of 'public' and 'vacant' estates, and by *cantonnement*. The latter policy involved the forceable compression of tribes into a small part of the territory which they had previously occupied, usually the most infertile, hilly and arid zones, or relocation in the 'empty' spaces which were supposedly under-utilised by other tribes. For example, the colonial settlement of Jemappes was created in 1848 on 2800 hectares of the most fertile land belonging to the Radjettas. By 1858 the peasantry in the district had lost 30 000 hectares of the total 50 781 hectares available and in 1861 it was decided to remove all of the remaining Radjettas southwards onto the territory of the Zardezas tribe. However, this area was already over-populated by 11 000 people who had themselves lost 4000 hectares of their most valuable land in the valley of the El Hammam Ouled Ali and been displaced into deeply ravined and infertile hilly country.[10]

Colonial discourse legitimated the process of *cantonnement* on the grounds that agro-pastoral tribes would benefit from settlement, become 'civilised' and through the adoption of European farming techniques succeed in making a higher return per hectare (*plus-value*). The reduction in the total surface area of tribal lands was not therefore damaging to their standard of living. In 1857 Jules Duval justified the *resserrement* or squeezing of those, 'Arabs who wander through an immense expanse of uncultivated land showing the indolence of pastoral and nomadic peoples'. In 1861 a Constantine newspaper claimed that through *cantonnement* and the transformation of land into private property the tribal zones would pass, 'immediately from the state of potential value (*valeur morte*) to a state of actual value (*valeur réelle*); millions will spring forth from nothing'.[11]

Until 1870, despite the violence of the methods used to dispossess the Algerian tribes, the total area of land taken by the Europeans was relatively limited and concentrated in certain valley or plain zones like the Chélif and Mitidja. Colonial settlement was fragile and insecure because of low population, high mortality, isolation, native attacks and the lack of infrastructures like modern roads, railways and water supplies.

The second stage of colonisation, from 1871 to 1920, was marked by a massive increase in land appropriation and the radical dislocation of the pre-colonial socio-economic system. The Algerian peasantry was struck a series of devastating blows. A major famine in 1866–68 led to the death of one fifth of the population of eastern Algeria and 'softened-up' the tribes to settler advance.[12] During the 1860s the government of Napoleon III moved towards a policy of protection of Algerian society from the worst excesses of settler greed and land appropriation. The protective strategy, symbolised by the operations of the military *bureaux arabes* which placed a firm paternalist hand on the rural communities and restricted settler inroads, generated enormous anger among the *colons*. The sudden fall of the Empire in 1870 brought to power the *colons* Republicans who eagerly set out to demolish the *bureaux arabes* and the protective policies of the so-called *Royaume Arabe* and to accelerate the ruthless dispossession of the natives. The first opportunity was provided by the insurrection of El Mokrani in 1871. A cynical decree of 15 July 1871 set out to punish rebels through the juridical ploy of 'collective responsibility'. This enabled the government to sequester one fifth of the land and capital of entire collectivities or tribes, regardless of the degree of individual involvement in rebellion. In the Province of Constantine, the main zone of conflict, 181 tribes lost 529 817 hectares and thirty million francs in fines, some seventy per cent of their total capital.[13] The Governor General wrote of the tribes of the Oued Sahel, 'We should not be deterred by the difficulties which they will face in paying the war fines within the time limit; the rich lands which they own in the Oued Sahel will enable them to pay off their debts by surrendering lands which will be a precious asset for colonisation'.[14]

A series of major forest fires in 1872, 1873 and 1881 was also used as a pretext to dispossess those tribes which were crucially dependent on the forests and scrub for grazing of livestock, charcoal burning and cultivation of clearings. The law of 17 July 1874 introduced collective responsibility for fires and sequestration of one fifth of the land or property of 'guilty' tribes. For example, after a fire in 1877, the Beni Salah lost 4199 hectares or fifty-two per cent of their total arable lands in the Sybouse Valley and were fined 280 082 francs.[15] A second forest law of 1885 brought a virtual halt to all further customary rights of grazing, wood gleaning and cultivation, and reduced numerous tribes that were crucially dependent on these resources to a state of desperation.[16]

However, the single most powerful mechanism for dispossession arose from the destruction of communal landownership through the imposition of a European legal system that recognised private, individual property rights and the sale of land. As long as extensive grazing lands were held in common, it had been almost impossible for settlers to buy up land. There were no recognisable fields or areas demarcated by boundaries which carried property titles that could be transferred through sale from one individual to another. The *Senatus Consulte* of 1863 broke up the tribes into smaller units called *douars*, and tied them down into specific territories which were surveyed so that clearly demarcated plots could be allocated to particular groups or families. The Warnier Law of 1873 and a further act of 1887 then made it possible for any one individual to seek to withdraw their 'share' of property from the collectivity, a procedure that was used by French speculators to

smash through the protective carapace of communal posses-
sion. An old tribesman was fully aware of the consequences of
this legal *machine de guerre* when he told Captain Vaissière:

> The French have defeated us in the plain of the Sbikha and
> killed our young men; they have imposed war indemnities
> upon us. All this is as nothing; wounds can heal. But the
> establishment of individual property rights and the power
> given to each person to sell lands which will be allocated as
> their share, this is the death sentence of the tribe and twenty
> years after the introduction of these measures the Ouled
> Rechaich will have ceased to exist.[17]

The privatisation of land through legal change would on its
own have had little impact on the traditional order as long as
Algerians refused to sell their property. However, a number of
factors conspired to force Algerians to alienate land on an
increasing scale. The pre-colonial economy was one based more
on exchange in kind than on cash transactions, a remarkably
stable system that was regulated by a set of customary ratios
between commodities. This situation was undermined as commercialisation and the widespread development of petty com-
modity production forced peasants into the circuit of monetary
exchange and into increasing debt. Under Turkish rule taxes
had been relatively low and were paid in kind. The French
retained the so-called *impôts arabes* but greatly increased their
burden, levied them more effectively in the interior regions,
and converted payment into money.[18] Between 1852 and 1859
alone the taxes more than doubled and this was a major cause
of a deterioration in the standard of living of the peasantry.
Since they were forced to pay their taxes within a two-week
period in the autumn the peasants often had to sell grain
immediately after the harvest, when prices were at their lowest,
but were compelled by hunger to buy back corn from speculators later in the agricultural year when prices were high.
  Throughout the colony there was a deepening penetration
of market relations based on the cash nexus. European middlemen, livestock hagglers, corn, hide and wool dealers, began to
operate deeper into rural society, buying up any surplus which
they could locate and funnelling it towards the ports of Oran,
Algiers, Bône and Bougie for export. The development of

modern roads and railways accelerated the process. Traditionally the tribes had protected themselves against famine and grain speculation by storing surplus harvests in underground pits called *matmora*. During periods of shortage, as General Martimprey remarked in 1860:

> The poor cultivator could find wealthy men in the tribe whose silos were always full and who would make them readily available for loans of grain without interest in accordance with custom and religion. The borrower paid back the loan in kind at harvest time. Today there are no longer reserves of grain in the silos of the rich: commercial progress has penetrated into the ways of the native and big grain surpluses are drained away as exports. The small cultivator himself sells any surplus grain in a good year and no longer keeps a reserve for the bad years as he used to do. Sometimes, forced by the need for cash and harassed by speculators, he even sells his harvest while it stands in the field.[19]

The peasants and pastoralists, forced by *cantonnement* onto a much reduced area of the most arid, infertile and hilly land, hit by fines and sequestrations for acts of rebellion or forest fires, and subject to heavy taxes paid in coin, were reduced to a level of poverty and hunger that forced them into increasing debt. However, loans were generally made by lenders at almost extortionate rates (120 per cent per annum was a common charge) and trapped small borrowers into a further cycle of indebtedness.[20] In desperation peasants were forced to mortgage or sell their most precious asset, the land itself. However, the land laws of 1863, 1873 and 1887 were at the same time creating the mechanisms through which property, previously indivisible, could be alienated. A host of unscrupulous speculators began to spoliate the tribes using every possible 'legal' swindle. For example, through the process of *licitation* speculators were only required to find one individual in a collectivity willing to sell their land, individuals who often did not even understand the nature of private property rights, and they could enforce the dismemberment of the entire *douar* through costly court actions.[21]

The dramatic increase after 1870 in the area of land occupied by the settlers is clear from Table 1.1. Van Vollenhoven estimated that Algerians lost some two million hectares or a

Table 1.1 Total hectares owned by *colons* and number of settlements created or expanded

Date	Colons *land,* hectares	Colon *centres*	Algerian *population*
Stage 1			
1830–50	115 000	126	3 000 000
1851–70	765 000	106	2 300 000
Stage 2			
1871–80	1 245 000	264	2 400 000
1881–90	1 635 000	107	2 800 000
1891–1900	1 912 000	103	3 500 000
1901–20	2 581 000	199	4 000 000
Stage 3			
1921–40	2 445 000	67*	5 000 000
1941–51	2 726 000	nil	6 500 000

* Figures for 1921–33: the last centre was created in 1928.
Sources: M. Bennoune, *Contemporary Algeria*, pp. 48–50, Tables 2.2 and 2.4. Population figures are the approximate average for the first date in the period. See J. Augarde, *La Migration Algérienne*, p. 44.

quarter of their landed property in the last two decades of the nineteenth century.[22]

The period from 1871 to 1920 was one during which the colonial economy entered a phase of dynamic capitalist growth. The building of large-scale projects, railway lines, docks, roads, irrigation schemes and urban centres, proceded apace. Vine cultivation, which was the motor of the colonial economy (forty per cent of exports by value in 1913), increased from 40 000 hectares in 1880 to 400 000 hectares in 1940.[23] Farming bifurcated into a dualistic system. On the one hand the farms of Europeans and wealthy Algerian aristocrats became concentrated in ever-larger units, on average over one hundred hectares in size, with high levels of investment in mechanisation and irrigation.

Alongside this dynamic, agrarian capitalist sector existed a vast number of small farms which were becoming increasingly subdivided and which depended on inefficient traditional

methods. In 1901 small peasant landowners and their dependents numbered 1 768 000 individuals, fifty-five per cent of the
agrarian population. An area of ten to thirty hectares, depend-
ing on fertility, was the minimum area needed to support a
family of six persons. André Nouschi has estimated that in the
Province of Constantine in 1914 about 54.7 per cent of the
peasants worked under ten hectares, 19.5 per cent from eleven
to twenty hectares and 12.4 per cent from twenty-one to thirty
hectares. Thus three fifths of the peasants cultivated an area of
land that was below the level for basic subsistence.[24] Increasing
numbers of small owners were forced to sell their land and
sank down into the lower social category of the share-croppers
or *khammès*, a group which traditionally received only a fifth
share of the crop.

The share-croppers and their families numbered just over a
million people before the First World War and made up thirty-
one per cent of the agrarian population. Their plight was even
worse than that of the small owners and they lived tied to
landlords in a state close to bondage. They usually worked an
area of five to ten hectares, inadequate for survival, and most
had to find supplementary income by labouring for *colons*.
The *khammès* therefore shaded over into the third and fastest
growing category, that of the rural wage-labourers, who increased from 356 000 in 1901 to nearly 600 000 in 1914. The
problem facing the labourers was not only the low level of
wages, about 1.5 to 1.75 francs per day before 1914 on *colon*
farms, but severe under-employment so that many could only
find sixty to one hundred days work in a year.[25]

The huge mass of rural poor lived in the most abject poverty. They were described at the turn of the century by European observers as working endlessly from dawn to dusk in the
full heat of the day and without pause. Their meagre diet
consisted of wheat or barley griddle cakes, whey and a few
dates or figs and, on rare occasions, couscous and meat. In
years of harvest failure they scoured the countryside for edible
grass, bitter roots (*talghouda* and *tafgha*), and wild fruit. Worn
and patched clothing provided inadequate protection, particularly in the bitterly cold winters, and natives eagerly sought
after European cast-offs or army blankets to make capes. As
sedentarisation of nomadic tribes took place they increasingly
abandoned the tent for primitive thatched huts (*gourbis*) which

were dark, squalid and unhealthy. In 1906 the peasantry was described as:

> Living in huts built with thin reeds, exposed almost without any protection to the seasonal changes in climate, dressed in a burnous full of holes when they possess one or in a greasy gandoura. They subsist on feast days on a coarse galette made with pounded barley that even the dog of a city dweller would refuse to touch and, on normal days, on wild grasses and fruits.[26]

The deepening crisis of rural society is reflected in the statistics of agricultural production. Grain production fell from a per capita average of 6.1 quintals in 1876 to 4.3 in 1886 and 3.24 in 1911. After subtracting the quantities used for seed, animal feed and export, the amount left for human consumption fell from 2.5 quintals per capita in 1901 to 1.87 in 1906 and 1.75 in 1911. Livestock also declined: for example sheep fell from 3 per capita in 1887 to 1.5 in 1900.[27] As the nutritional base declined the rural population became increasingly exposed to the vagaries of climate, harvest failure and to famine as in 1905, 1908, 1912 and 1920. In those years thousands of hungry peasants, as in the subsistence crises of *ancien régime* Europe, flocked towards the colonial towns and settlements in search of charitable relief and the pickings of abattoir offal and rubbish tips.[28]

The increasing dispossession of the Algerian peasantry had, by the turn of the century, created a large and growing reserve of labour which was utilised by the colonial economy. From about 1905 onwards this supply of cheap labour was also increasingly tapped by French metropolitan industry and armed forces. The long term destructive impact of colonialism on Algerian society created those conditions which dislodged pastoralists and peasants from the all embracing structures of the traditional socio-economic order, and ultimately made them available as a source of labour to the settlers. As in so many other colonial contexts in Africa, Asia and the Americas, the object in seizing huge areas of native territory was not only to gain unimpeded access to the land, for farming and mining, but also to destroy the traditional subsistence base of the natives so that they would be compelled to offer their labour power to the *colons*. It was frequently the case that Algerian tribes that were forced by *cantonnement* to abandon their most fertile lands and unable to survive in the infertile zones on the periphery of the new European settlements, were compelled to return to work as share-croppers and labourers on the fields that had once belonged to their fathers.[29]

This chapter has examined the general processes by which colonialism undermined the fabric of Algerian society, dislocated the traditional pastoralist-agrarian framework, and created an impoverished mass. However this overview has deliberately neglected the fact that within the huge space of Algeria there existed a complex patchwork of different ethnic or tribal groups, with distinctive languages and cultures. The differing nature of these groups, which long pre-dated colonialism, had an impact on the ways in which they interreacted with the colonial system.

The next chapter looks at the Kabyle people, the first to move to France, and what it was about this society that facilitated overseas migration.

2 Kabylia and the Migrant Tradition

Throughout the first half-century of emigration (c.1905–1950) there existed a remarkable variation between zones of high and low emigration. The great majority of Algerians in France were Kabyles, the mountain-dwellers of Berber descent, who inhabited the sedentary peasant villages of Greater and Lesser Kabylia to the east of Algiers.[1] This predominance was reflected in the title of the first official inquiry into Algerian emigration carried out in 1912–14, *Les Kabyles en France*. Kabyles were estimated to have constituted 84 per cent of total Algerian emigration in 1923, 75 per cent in 1938 and about 60 per cent in the early 1950s.[2] These figures should be treated with caution since there was no accurate way of identifying who the Berber/Kabyles were, since many had historically, and continued to be, absorbed into surrounding Arab peoples. However, the figures provide a reasonable measure of Kabyle predominance.[3] Since Kabyles made up about 21 per cent of the total Algerian population, but up to 84 per cent of all emigrants in 1923, Kabyle men were sixteen times more likely to migrate than Arabs. The remarkable geographical concentration of the regions of emigration is shown in Map 1 for 1949.[4]

Colonial sociologists and administrators were intrigued by the striking spatial distribution of zones of emigration and their transformations through time, and thought, quite correctly, that it held an important key to an understanding of the socio-economic and cultural roots of migration. This approach was best represented by Robert Montagne, a leading scholar of Maghrebian society in the first half of this century.[5] At the time of his death in 1954 he was the director of a team of specialists who were carrying out a detailed geographical and socio-economic survey of zones of emigration in Algeria and their links to specific areas of settlement in France.[6] Since Algerian independence in 1962 French and Algerian specialists have largely overlooked or neglected this spatial evidence. However, the failure to take account of the great variations in the geographical distribution of emigration presents some

Map 1 Regions of Algerian emigration to France (1949)

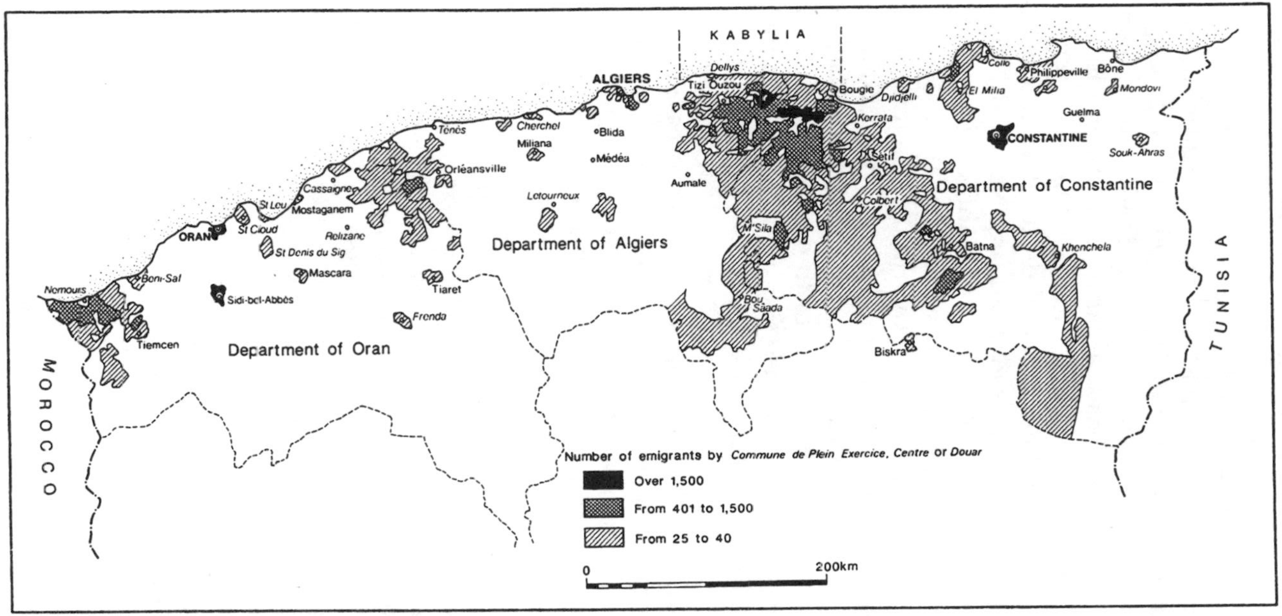

Source: J.-J. Rager, *Les Musulmans Algériens en France* (1950).

major problems for their analysis of the causes of migration to France.

Most post-colonial studies have located the source of emigration in the overall features of colonialism and capitalism impacting on the traditional society, an approach that has been followed in Chapter 1 above. However, this predominantly neo-Marxist school has tended to treat Algeria internally as a homogeneous and undifferentiated entity. The general model used is one which links colonial destruction to land dispossession, which in turn provided an impoverished class of casual labourers desperate to emigrate. Mahfoud Bennoune, who is quite typical in this respect, writes that the '. . . rapid deterioration of the material life of the rural communities induced an increasing number of paupers to cross the Mediterranean in search of employment in Europe'.[7] If the neo-Marxist analysis is correct one would expect to find that the zones of emigration would correspond to the areas of maximum colonial penetration, in which land dispossession, dislocation of traditional socio-economic structures and proletarianisation was most intense. The very opposite was the case: the zones of maximum colonisation and capitalist penetration were the areas of very low emigration in the half century up to 1950.[8] The question that has to be answered is why most emigrants came from the mountainous zones **least** penetrated by *colons*, and in which the pre-colonial socio-economic structures remained relatively intact. The equally important issue of why emigration was initially so feeble from the regions of intense colonial settlement and farming will be examined in Chapter 10.

Colonial conquest of Algeria was not a simple one-way process in which the indigenous people were the passive victims of brutal destruction and moulded to the economic and military needs of European society.[9] Rather the settlers were faced with a complex and heterogeneous map of local societies with varying structures and customs. In the complex interreactions between colonial and native peoples, the Europeans certainly set out to destroy and uproot the pastoral tribes of the plains, but in the mountains of Kabylia they were confronted with pre-colonial structures which were not only more resistant to domination but which the *colons* were prepared to adapt or channel to their particular needs. In particular the Kabyles had been engaged in an ancient system of internal migration which the settlers captured or redirected to supply labour for their farms.[10] At a still later date the internal labour migration became in turn redirected towards metropolitan France.

When French invaders first penetrated into the mountains of Kabylia they were immediately struck by the close resemblance between the densely inhabited villages, strung out along the crest of high ridges, the pantiled stone houses surrounded by orchards, and the hamlets of the Midi. Kabylia did share many of the features of the mountain regions bordering the Mediterranean: places like Grenada, Provence, Corsica, Tuscany, and Albania, in which from early times population was concentrated in the healthy uplands rather than in the plains which were zones of marshland, flooding and deadly malaria.[11] In the 1930s some Kabyle communes reached densities of 200 to 400 inhabitants to the square kilometer compared to ten to twenty in the plains below.

This extraordinary density in an area of deeply incised mountains was made possible through a combination of factors. The typical Kabyle peasant household worked minuscule plots of land and lived an extremely frugal existence. However, regular rainfall (800 millimetres per year) and an intensive cultivation of vegetables, cereals and tree crops (figs, olives, cherries, edible acorns) assured a diverse diet. Herds of sheep, goats and cattle were grazed in the higher mountain forests and pastures. The altitude of villages at about 800 metres assured a more temperate climate, an abundance of fresh water and the absence of malaria. The Kabyles also engaged in a number of artisan industries which included soap-making, tanning, pottery, cloth and metalworking (knives, guns, plough shares, coins and jewellery) and these products were traded in the plains and urban centres.[12] The striking resilience of the Kabyle economy and its ability to sustain a poor but dense population that escaped subsistence crises was shown during the terrible famine of 1867–8, when it was able to receive thousands of starving vagrants from the plains below in which twenty per cent of the people died.[13]

French specialists writing between 1930 and 1954 on the causes of Kabyle emigration ascribed it, quite simply, to demographic pressure. Legislation which allowed free movement to France after 1913 meant that Kabyle society, bursting at the seams, could dispatch its young men to the high-wage industries of the metropole. This simplistic explanation was plausible but misleading and the emphasis on demographic growth alone can be linked to a colonial discourse which accounted for population increase by the benign impact of colonial 'civilisation', in particular the termination of bloody wars between tribes and the introduction of European medical practice.[14] In this chapter I shall argue that Kabyle society had for many hundreds of years found a solution to demographic pressure through seasonal or long-term migration, a pattern of mountain to plain mobility that was found throughout the Mediterranean basin.[15] This pre-colonial system of migration was utilised by the French to supply labour to the colonial economy and prepared the ground for a later stage of emigration.

Pre-colonial Kabyle migration, which was uniquely male, was of three types: i) military recruitment by the ruling Turkish authority; ii) circulation by peddlers and traders; and iii) seasonal movement by labourers and farm workers. All three forms continued under the French throughout the nineteenth and early twentieth centuries.

Under Ottoman rule (1519–1830) the Kabyle tribes known as the Zouaoua were a source of mercenaries, a pattern which was continued by the French and which gave its name to the term Zouaves.[16] Kabyle soldiers played a prominent role in the Crimean War, the Franco-Prussian War, the conquest of Madagascar in the late 1890s and the pacification of Morocco after 1907. Their numbers in the infantry regiments and cavalry (*spahis*) fluctuated at around seven to eleven thousand men in the last twenty years of the nineteenth century.[17] Although relatively small in scale, military migration provided the first significant Algerian experience of French metropolitan life and developed in the Kabyle tribes that were to become the first suppliers of labour emigrants. The recruitment of colonial soldiers was a major factor in the origins of Algerian international labour migration as it was throughout the French, British and Dutch Empires.[18] Chapter 3 will show how mass recruitment during the First World War provided a great boost to the growth in labour migration to France after 1918.

The second form of mobility concerned Kabyle peddlers and traders who operated throughout the towns and villages of Algeria, Tunisia and Morocco. Trade involved the exchange of Kabyle products (olive oil, wax, leather, jewellery, guns, etc.)

against goods in short supply in the mountains (grain, livestock, textiles, metal) or the peddling of small items like perfumes, henna, mercery, medicines and dyes, carried on foot in sheepskin sacks. Most Kabyle traders would depart in this way for two to three years, leading an incredibly frugal existence so they could maximise their savings.[19] Peddlers required a special licence to travel and in about 1868 in the commune of Fort-National, later a major zone of emigration, some eight to ten thousand permits were issued annually.[20] The great scholar of Algerian society, Emile Masqueray, on a visit to the Kabyle tribe of the Aït Bou Akkach in about 1866, was struck by the contrast between the infertility of the land, the dense population of seven thousand people, and the relative well-being of the inhabitants:

> The villages were fine and well kept; one could see regular streets and many white washed houses. External trade was the sole cause of this extraordinary prosperity. You would meet there, from spring to autumn, only women, old folk and a prodigious number of children. All the able-bodied men were away.[21]

After 1870 the customary trade was increasingly undermined by the availability of cheaper, French mass-produced goods which reached the interior through improvements in road and rail communications. Faced with crisis, Kabyle traders eagerly turned to the new opportunity opened by freedom of movement to France and in the first decade of the twentieth century they were among the first to establish a bridgehead in the metropole (see Chapter 3).

The third type of traditional migration involved seasonal labour. The advantage of this system was that peasants could depart during the period of slack employment in the agricultural cycle, before or after the harvest, and bring back much-needed external resources in cash or kind and, simply through their absence, temporarily remove hungry mouths. Kabyle labour migration into the plains has been recorded as early as the fourteenth century and was sustained throughout the Turkish period. After the initial period of military conquest and disruption of Algerian society (1830–1850), French farmers, in desperate need of labour, began to revive and capture the pre-colonial flows of seasonal migration. Kabyles were reported as early as 1841 working on *colon* farms and during the good harvest year of 1854 farm owners sought them in the hiring fairs at two francs per day.

By the 1870s teams of harvesters, totally 15 000 to 20 000 men, descended annually from the mountains.[22] In 1903 Van Vollenhoven commented that harvest gangs operated under a leader who would negotiate a price with a farmer for a particular task:

> At the time of the grain and grape harvests, once the Kabyles had finished work on their gardens, they form groups of fifteen or twenty workers and meet up at the nearest railway station. They stay two or three months with the same *colon*, more or less in the same region where they worked the year before. In this way they cross right over the Mitidja plain, disperse en route from local stations, and in the department of Constantine spread beyond Sétif.[23]

The migrants, distinctive in their leather aprons and huge straw hats, lived in huts which they built themselves or in small limewashed sheds where they cooked frugal meals of vegetable stew or pancakes on fires of vine roots.

From 1880 there was a dramatic modernisation of the colonial economy: ownership of land was concentrated in large estates at the expense of small *colons*, investment increased and commercial exports grew dramatically. Vine cultivation, which increased from 40 000 hectares in 1880 to 400 000 in 1940, was ten times more labour intensive than cereals. The same period saw the rapid extension of mining (iron-ore, phosphates, lead, zinc) and large-scale construction projects like railways, roads, irrigation schemes, docks and urban building, all of which required large numbers of unskilled labourers. In an initial phase of this expansion there was a heavy reliance on skilled European migrant labour, especially from Spain, but following a series of crises in the Algerian wine industry after 1893 the *colons*, faced with a decline in demand and lower prices, tried to retain profitability by substituting Algerians whose wage-rates were in general about half that of the Europeans. Algerian workers moved into the more skilled tasks like pruning, grafting and cellerage work that had been monopolised by Spaniards. By 1908 three quarters of the total wage bill on the vineyards of the Mitidja went to native workers.[24] The seasonal employment of Kabyles continued to expand: by 1934, when the most detailed census was taken, 100 000 men were involved.[25]

Specialists in 'Third World' emigration have paid little attention to the relationship between patterns of internal labour mobility and emigration, whether for example the former prepared the way for the latter, or whether they were located in quite discrete areas which specialised in internal or external movement. In the Kabyle case the long-term process of integration into the colonial labour market certainly prepared the way for eventual recruitment into metropolitan industry. Kabyles migrants descended regularly into the plain where they often returned to the same farms, built up a position of trust with the *colons*, picked up skills on the job and some experience of wage-labour and capitalist work practice (clock-time, regularity). The *colons* began to form a generally favourable image of the Kabyle as an indefatigable and reliable worker, a stereotype which was reinforced by the 'Kabyle Myth'.[26]

However, French colonialism did more than simply tap into the pre-colonial patterns of traditional migration towards the plains but actively sought to protect Kabyle society as a reservoir of labour. Claude Meillassoux argues that 'the agricultural domestic community, through its organised capacity for production and reproduction, represents an integrated form of social organisation which has existed since the neolithic period, and upon which still depends an important part of the reproduction of the labour-power necessary to the development of capitalism'. With the advance of capitalism such zones of self-sustenance could only be preserved more or less artifically during a critical transitory period.[27] These peripheral areas of reproduction were to be found throughout the colonial and neo-colonial world, but Kabylia provides a particularly clear-cut example of this relationship.[28] The hard-working, abstemious Kabyles, flowing outwards from their base in the domestic economy of tiny mountain farms, were able to labour at rates which acted as a downward pressure on wage levels in the colonial zones. As the jurist Boyer-Banse noted in 1906, 'the situation of waged labour in the colonised regions depends ultimately on the general economic state of the natives massed in the non-colonised regions'.[29]

French colonialism reinforced the Kabyle domestic community and at the same time integrated it into the capitalist circuit, in spite of restricted European settlement, through 'protectorate' policies, education and the ideology of the 'Kabyle Myth'. These three factors will be examined in turn.

French military conquest of Kabylia came late and when the region formally surrendered to General Randon in July 1857 he recommended that a kind of protectorate should be established along with a clear commitment to bolster the strong traditional administrative and judicial institutions. In spite of punitive raids (*razzias*) and the crushing penalties imposed after the 1871 rebellion, the Europeans left the basic pre-colonial socio-economic structures intact.[30] This was made possible because of the relatively weak pressures from *colons* for the appropriation of native lands. Settlers were little interested in the densely populated mountain zones, which offered few opportunities for commercial agriculture, while the *melk* lands, similar in form to private property (see Chapter 1), could not be easily appropriated through legalistic subversion of tenure systems. Van Vollenhoven, an expert on land policy, stated in 1903, 'There is a single region in the colony where native property forms an invincible obstacle to the penetration of colonisation: Kabylia . . . In these mountains colonisation has never, and will never, penetrate.'[31]

As late as 1926 the arrondissement of Tizi-Ouzou, the zone of maximum emigration to France, had the lowest percentage of European settlement of any arrondissement in Algeria, with the exception of the Sahara, at 1.8 per cent of total population.[32] The relative absence of aggressive settler interests, unlike in the *communes de plein exercice* of the heavily colonised zones, meant that more protectionist *indigénophiles* administrators had greater freedom to implement paternalist policies of the kind that had been associated with the old *bureaux arabes*.

The survival of the traditional social structures, especially of the extended family as a unit of production, consumption and reproduction was important to emigration as it provided a solid foundation for the group to delegate one or more males to seek external resources through emigration. The aim of the migrant was not to earn money to satisfy his own individualistic purposes, or if he was married, the needs of his wife and children alone, but rather to aid the wider domestic unit which might include his parents, brothers, sisters-in-law, and their children. The strongly integrated domestic community, controlled by a patriarch or elder brothers, was bound by solidarities that were essential to group survival. This included the common ownership of land and property, the joint working of the farm, and sharing food and resources. There was no place in this society for a western style individualism: as one Kabyle migrant remarked, 'Each works for all, for the household (*maison*), and the household for all; there are no "smaller houses within the house".'[33]

This customary group solidarity carried over into the ability to sustain male emigration. The domestic community, with a tradition of internal migration which had existed for centuries, had evolved customary practices for initiating and coping with male departure, including group 'cover' for the temporary loss in labour-power and, in the case of those who were married, the care and protection of wives and children. The weak colonial penetration of Kabylia and the survival of traditional society left intact the structures which sustained internal migration and, at a later stage, emigration to France. By contrast, colonial settlement of the plains was accompanied by massive land appropriations, the dislocation of tribal society, and the reduction of families to a level of destitution and disintegration that made emigration difficult.

The French 'special relationship' to the Kabyles found a powerful ideological expression and reinforcement in the 'Kabyle Myth'.[34] From the 1840s onwards army officers, administrators, and other specialists portrayed the Kabyles as a racially distinct people who were ideally suited to act as partners with the French in the process of colonisation. The 'Myth' can be broken down into a number of key elements. The Kabyles, it was claimed, descended from an ancient, pre-Arabic people whose distinctive physical appearance (facial shape, blue eyes, blond or light hair) showed that they were European in origin, possibly Celts, Vandals or Romans. The Kabyles' attachment to private property (*melk*), their natural penchant for commerce, and their hard working, entrepreneurial spirit meant that they were ideally suited to function within a European market economy. Since, it was thought, the Kabyles, in their mountain retreat, had resisted Arab domination and Islamic indoctrination they had retained their democratic traditions, symbolised by the village council (*djemâa*), and were inherently disposed towards secular Republican values, unlike the 'fanatical' Arabs.

For every positive feature that existed for the intelligent and enterprising Kabyles there was a corresponding Arab negative. Van Vollenhoven's comments on Arabs are typical of the standard colonial discourse. He saw them as stupid, with a 'limited intelligence and completely apathetic', and riddled with vices, 'such as dissimulation and dishonesty, distrust and lack of foresight, love of sensuality, lechery and revelling'. A Social-Darwinist logic suggested that such an inferior people could legitimately be swept aside by a superior race. 'Intellectually superior, morally superior, economically superior, the *colon* will drive out the Arab, only leaving him those lands which he judges to be too poor to make use of.'[35] One of the underlying functions of the manichaean image of Arabs and Kabyles was to establish a policy of divide-and-rule, and to target the Kabyles as the most readily assimilable population which would promote the long term goals of transforming Algeria into a pure embodiment of French civilisation.

The 'Kabyle Myth' helped to reinforce the policy of protectionism towards Kabyle institutions and social structures. It also helped diffuse an image of the Kabyle as an astute, hardworking and trustworthy individual and encouraged both settlers and metropolitan employers to favour their recruitment. Lastly, the positive image of the Kabyles played a significant part in the location of numerous French schools in the region, a factor which in turn proved to be an advantage in emigration.

From 1873 onwards the Jesuits, soon followed by the Pères Blancs, opened a number of schools in Kabylia. However, the major expansion in education followed from reports by Emile Masqueray, published in 1876 and 1880, on the development of primary education in Kabylia and which influenced the Minister of Education, Jules Ferry. During 1882 Masqueray, under instructions from the Minister, carried out a tour of inspection in Kabylia which led to the establishment of schools at Beni Yenni, Tizi Rached, Mira, Djemaa Saharidj and elsewhere.[36] As Fanny Colonna has shown in detail, French school provision for Algerians was concentrated in Kabylia: in 1892 the arrondissement of Tizi-Ouzou which had 8.9 per cent of the total Algerian population had 22.7 per cent of all classes.[37]

The tribes which showed a remarkable and successful adaptation to French schooling, like the Beni Yenni, the Beni Iraten, the Aït Fraoucen and the Beni Oughlis, were also those which became prominent in the early phase of emigration.

The links between education and emigration were more complex than would appear at first sight. When Kabylia as a zone of high emigration is placed under a microscope it can be seen that there existed a remarkable variation in levels of emigration from one village to the next. A *douar* or village in which there was no emigration could be located a few miles away from one in which the entire male population had spent some time in France.[38] It might have been expected that the experience and example of emigration would have spread more uniformly through contact. The highly localised mosaic of emigrant zones can be explained through the contrast between what I shall term 'open' and 'closed' village communities.

When Masqueray travelled throughout Kabylia to select those villages which would be best suited to the establishment of schools he was inevitably drawn towards those tribes which showed quite distinctive socio-cultural features which made them receptive towards French education and western values. The Beni Yenni, for example, were famous for the manufacture of guns, jewellery, coins and knives. A high level of artisan skill, entrepreneurial links and a relative degree of prosperity predisposed them towards schooling. Lacoste-Dujardin noted similar characteristics in the metal-working village of Taourirt-n-ait Zouaou which had the first secular school in the area of her field-work and the oldest pattern of emigration.[39] Some villages followed a tradition of sending sons, trained in basic literacy in Muslim schools, to work as clerks with merchants and shopkeepers in the towns. They welcomed French schools as an opportunity to gain qualifications that could lead to employment as teachers or within the lower ranks of the colonial administration as post-men and clerks.[40] The 'open' village was also one in which Islamic cultural resistance to infidel European ways was weak, either because of the absence of traditionalist religious leaders (*marabouts*) or because the children of this caste monopolised the Koranic schools and excluded other groups who were quite keen to make use of secular schools.[41] These more dynamic communities were also relatively better-off, through industry and trade, a necessary precondition for families that could afford to send children to school.

The 'closed' villagers tended to be much poorer, peasant based communities that were highly resistant to colonial influence.[42] Frequently powerful hereditary castes of religious leaders, the *marabouts*, strongly opposed French culture in order to retain their hold over local people. The Republican school was seen as a particularly dangerous *machine de guerre* for the subversion of Muslim society.[43] A Kabyle who trained as a teacher in 1895–98 commented, '. . . a fifth of the people in our village belong to *marabouts* families, but they say to us, "Our ancestor the saint forbade us to teach the Kabyles in the Koran". They say that in order to keep their privileges and to be the only ones to make [magical] amulets and to say prayers for the dead.'[44] In the village of Tifrit resistance to French institutions led to a long delay in the establishment of a secular school and even when open a pupil explained the difficulty of attending in the face of local hostility. 'We went to school in spite of them. Our parents were frightened that we would become atheists, without roots . . . they did nothing to help us.'[45] The 'closed' village, impoverished, resistant to western values, and locked into a traditional way of life and subsistence farming that was entering a phase of deepening crisis, was incapable of seizing the opportunities offered by emigration.

The zones of resistance can also be mapped through the strong localised opposition to the introduction of universal military service in 1908–12 and conscription during the First World War. In the most conservative Muslim regions the volunteer soldier had a bad reputation as a debauched and strongheaded individual, who drank wine, neglected his prayers and showed no respect for the *caïd*. The introduction of conscription created a wave of bitter opposition in the form of large demonstrations in the administrative centres, dessertion, open rebellion and mass emigration from Algeria into the haven of other Arab states, particularly from Tlemcen in 1911.[46] The underlying reason for opposition, particularly by parents, was the fear that sons would be forceably removed from Algerian soil and made to live in the corrupt and hated world of the Christians, the *dar-el-harb*.[47] 'It was a rejection', notes Meynier, 'of any insertion into the foreign body; a fear that the family and tradition, for which the soldier stood as a living negation, would be destroyed; in a word a total repugnance to become French'. This mode of assimilation was perceived as, 'a crime against the collective identity'.[48] At El Kantara in May 1912, when soldiers had to be called in to control a crowd of protesting parents, a mother shouted, 'No, no, he'll be butchered. I cannot allow that my beloved son, my support, my pride, should go and swell the number of traitors, the impious, the alcoholics, and the polluted.'[49] It was in those villages in which such religious and cultural values were strongest, concentrated mainly in the West of Algeria, but some of them located within Kabylia, that opposition to emigration also occurred.[50] Where these societies did engage in migration, as with the highly conservative Mozabites, there is good evidence to show that they preferred internal migration within the confines of Muslim society, the *dar-el-Islam*.[51]

A further factor which tended to block the diffusion of emigrant practices from one village to another was the highly segmentary structure of Kabyle society. Each village constituted a self-contained community, sealed in upon itself, and in which group identity was defined by traditional hostility towards neighbouring factions (*çoff*). The lack of inter-marriage, of commercial exchanges and other contacts between villages located close to one another meant that a 'closed' hamlet would be highly resistant to follow the example of emigration in a neighbouring 'enemy' group.[52]

In general terms it can be seen that the variations in the density of the zones of emigration, both at the regional level, as well as at the micro-level of the village or hamlet (*douar*), cannot be explained without taking into account the diversity of the pre-colonial socio-economic and cultural structures.

For those villagers that dynamically embraced French secular schooling, there remains the question of the ways in which education aided emigration. To some extent employers, first in the colonial settlements and later in France, may have favoured Kabyle recruits because of their competence in French and their generally higher levels of education. One Kabyle teacher commented that educational reforms carried out in 1898, 'Were aimed to form workers for the *colons*, **workers who understand**.'[53] In 1913 when the Algerian authorities established apprenticeships in the skilled work of vine dressing the first recruits were sought among pupils from Kabyle schools.[54]

At about this time, according to Ageron, a knowledge of French had spread througout Kabylia. 'To the astonishment of French employers **all** the immigrant Kabyle workers spoke French; nearly a half could read and write it. During the war, correspondence with families was carried out in French.'[55] This estimation is certainly too high. The level of schooling for Algeria as a whole rose from only 2 per cent in 1889 to 8.9 per cent in 1930. Kabylia had more schools than other region but even so these were still quite rare, underfunded and rudimentary and only benefitted a minority of boys in any location.

It would be a mistake perhaps to assume that metropolitan employers, in seeking to procure Algerian migrant labour, were primarily influenced by the 'Myth' of Kabyle intelligence and capacity for hard work and their competence in French. Employers did speak in terms of 'Kabyle' labour but the term was widely used up until about 1925 to denote **all** Algerians and most were probably incapable of identifying Algerians by regional or ethnic difference. An official inquiry of 1923 found that Paris manufacturers were sending agents to recruit Algerians as they descended from the boat in Marseilles, without any regard to their ethnic origin.[56] Studies of migrant labour in Europe have shown that employers, in a time of labour shortage, are frequently quite prepared to take on immigrants regardless of their inability to understand or communicate in the language of the host country. Some companies have preferred to use large teams of illiterate 'colonials' for low-paid, physically demanding and unpleasant work (foundries, chemicals, tanning . . .) since they can be more readily exploited, segregated in shifts apart from European workers, and controlled through bi-lingual 'native bosses' or overseers.[57]

However, even if it did not greatly influence employer preference, the relatively higher levels of competence in French and in basic schooling in Kabyle villages did favour the process of emigration in other ways. For peasants from isolated rural communities the early phase of emigration presented a formidable challenge: the barriers that had to be crossed included the procurement of official documents (identity cards, medical certificates, work contracts), negotiating the route to Algiers, acquiring a boat ticket, and – most challenging of all – finding the way by bus or train in a new, hostile and often terrifying urban environment towards particular destinations. Pioneer migrants lacked the network of contacts and support from older, experienced workers that shaped chain-migration in later years. This is where those Kabyles who had received even a modest education in French schools and were partly acculturated into western values held a distinct advantage. They were able to steer their way through the complex labyrinth of metropolitan society, seeking out the best opportunities available in the job and housing market. Significant numbers were sufficiently enterprising to become self-employed, owners of lodging houses, cafés, small hotels, shops and taxis.

Once the Kabyles had established an early beach-head in France they were able, as will be shown in the next chapter, to deepen the movement of emigration and to establish a monopoly over the most 'desirable' employment and housing which made it difficult for later-arriving Arabs from the plains to gain a foothold.

3 Emigration: The Early Years, 1905–18

The destruction of colonial society and the resulting impoverishment and demographic pressure were not sufficient causes of emigration to France. The neo-classical theory of the free movement of labour from zones of low wages and surplus labour (the colony) to zones of high wages and labour shortage (the metropole), like water finding the same level between two interconnecting tanks, is entirely inadequate. It fails to take account of the fact that international migration is usually regulated by political and legal measures that can open or close the valves of ingress and egress according to the needs of the European economy.[1]

While colonialism and deepening poverty prepared the ground for emigration, two interrelated factors account for its more specific growth after 1904. One was the demand factor, the serious shortage of labour in the metropolitan economy, and the second the introduction of new measures which, for the first time, allowed Algerians to travel relatively freely to France.

Before 1904 very few Algerians, with the exception of soldiers and a few élite *caïds*, travelled to France because of the draconian *code de l'indigénat*. Under the *code*, which dated from 1874, Algerians could not travel outside their own *douar* or commune without a special pass or *permis de voyage*. In addition those few Algerians who were allowed to travel to France required special authorisation from the *Gouvernement Générale* and had to pay a deposit to cover any costs of repatriation.[2] The function of internal controls under the *code* was to prevent the movement of vagrants, large groups of bandits and 'criminals' (the *armées roulantes*), and subversive Islamic agitators. The *permis* were also used by the *colons* to discipline and control Algerian labour: they were issued freely to Kabyles so they could move on a seasonal basis to work on European farms, but were severely restricted in the zones of settlement so as to exploit a captive pool of low-waged labour or to extort bribes (*bakhchîch*).[3]

The regulation of movement, as well as the wider special powers of the *code* which gave mayors and local administrators arbitrary and despotic powers over locals, such as arrest and imprisonment for petty infractions, began to be challenged at the turn of the century by liberal *indigénophiles* politicians. Albin Rozet, deputy for the Haute-Marne, and Victor Barrucand, editor of the Algiers journal *L'Akhbar*, led a campaign from 1903 onwards for the freedom to emigrate, part of a broader political programme for the assimilation of Algerians as French citizens with full rights.[4] During 1904–5 Jonnart, the Governor General, who was generally favourable to a reform of the repressive *code*, responded to this pressure by issuing an administrative order on 28 January 1905 which allowed certain categories of Algerians, including Kabyle drovers, to travel to France.[5] Rozet continued to press for the abolishment of the *permis de voyage*, and in spite of opposition from administrators of the *communes mixtes* who feared that this would, 'weaken the source of their authority over the natives whom they would no longer be able to control', he achieved his goal with an order of the *Gouvernement Générale* (18 June 1913) which was confirmed by the law of 15 July 1914.[6]

The liberalisation of the controls on migration after 1905, although initiated by progressives who wished to extend equal rights to Algerian *sujets*, provided an opportunity which was eagerly seized upon by French employers to recruit colonial labour. Until 1905 most labour immigration involved the unregulated cross-border movement of so-called *frontaliers* from Belgium, Germany, Italy and Spain.[7] During the period 1905–1912 employers, faced with grave labour shortages in agriculture, coal mining, chemicals and other sectors of low-paid, dangerous and exhausting work, which both French and *frontaliers* refused to do, began to develop a radically new system of labour recruitment. This was a precursor of the state-controlled recruitment schemes that became generalised in Europe after 1945.[8]

Among the first Kabyles to migrate to France were itinerant peddlers, who travelled on foot to sea-side resorts and spa-towns selling oriental carpets and trinkets.[9] A second group was made up of Kabyle drovers who after January 1905 were allowed to travel freely on livestock ships to Marseilles where they stayed on to graze animals in preparation for the market.

Some of these men began to settle permanently in Marseilles and to find employment in local industry. The number of Kabyles in France increased rapidly from about 4000 in 1910–11 to 13 000 in 1914.[10]

In Marseilles much of this immigration was initiated by companies as a means of breaking strikes. In 1909 Italian workers in the oil-refining company of *Maurel et Prom* went on strike and a French foreman, who had lived in Tizi-Ouzou, used his contacts in Kabylia to bring over strike-breakers.[11] During 1910 a number of Marseilles oil and sugar refineries, *Rafinnerie de la Méditerranée, de Saint-Louis, Trois Mathildes,* and *Frisch* all recruited Kabyles to break strikes by Italian immigrants who had become unionised and militant. Tensions ran high and there was fighting between the two groups.[12] Similar employment of Kabyles in the merchant navy led to further conflict in 1910. In late March French stokers on a number of ships refused to work alongside Algerians and came out on strike. Rivelli, the President of the Marseilles seamen's union, attacked the use of 'foreign natives' [sic] to displace 'our nationals'. *L'Akhbar* proposed a massive recruitment of Kabyles to break the strike, showing that liberal *indigénophiles* were quite prepared to prioritise colonial economic interests.[13] In 1912 the Minister for the Navy set out to break the monopoly which registered French seamen held on merchant ships. He gained a ruling from the Council of State that colonial natives who were French *sujets,* a category which applied to Algerians, could be employed under the French flag.[14]

The early use of Algerians as strike-breakers confirmed the analysis of the political left and of trade unions that capitalists were quite prepared to utilise oppressed colonial peoples as a weapon against the European working-class. Employers resorted to divide-and-rule tactics which utilised Kabyle peasants who had no experience of trade unionism, who would work for low wages, and were easily divided from French, Italian and Spanish workers by language and ethnicity. The first phase of Kabyle immigration was already marked by a climate of French and European migrant hostility to the 'primitives' from overseas.[15]

Employers elsewhere in France became aware of the potential offered by Algerian immigration from about 1910 and recruitment spread rapidly into a number of regions, particularly Clermont-Ferrand where the *Michelin* tyre company had forty Algerians by 1912, the coal mines of the *Compagnie de Courières* in the Pas-de-Calais (400 men in 1912), the Mauberge basin of the department of the Nord (80 men), and in the Paris region (sugar refining, transport, chemicals, construction, and hotel work).[16] The migration appears to have taken place through a combination of organised employer recruitment in Kabylia and, increasingly, free individual movement.

In the first decade of the century large numbers of Kabyles had found employment in the rapidly expanding mining operations of Tunisia (Sfax-Gafsa). Regarded as excellent workers compared to Arab recruits from other regions, they were poached by French companies, to the annoyance of the *Comité des Mines de Phosphates de Tunisie*.[17] Several leading capitalists, like Edouard de Billy and Albert Galicier, had interests in both French and Maghrebian mining and metallurgy and would have known the labour resources available in North Africa.[18] Larbi Talha has emphasised the extent to which the migration of Kabyles into the advanced capitalist sectors of the colonial economies of Algeria and Tunisia prepared the way for the development of a migration chain that was eventually to carry them into France.[19] In 1913 the director of the National Office for Agricultural Labour in the Ministry of Agriculture began to plan for the recruitment of Kabyle workers and in December of that year a Deputy, Doizy, informed parliament that an *Agence générale de l'Afrique du Nord pour l'emploi de la main-d'oeuvre indigène* was operating from the Rue Bruce in Algiers to recruit both agricultural and industrial workers.[20]

Once a handful of pioneer Kabyles had found employment with a particular company in France further recruitment took place mainly through a snowball effect as migrants, by word of mouth and letter, encouraged new departures from their home villages. The mining *Compagnie de Courrières*, for example, in the Pas-de-Calais first employed several Kabyles in about 1910 and the management, pleased with their performance, then took on a few more. The news soon spread to Kabylia and triggered a much wider migration. The company was eager to take them on as it was facing a severe labour shortage which had been made worse by the sudden departure of several hundred Belgian miners following an amnesty granted on the accession of King Albert.[21] The number of Kabyles increased dramatically from 435 men in November 1912 to 935 in March

1914. Kabyle workers in Marseilles likewise encouraged friends and relatives from Tizi-Ouzou, Azzefoun, Michelet and Azazga.[22] This chain migration established a pattern which was to continue for the next fifty years by which men from a particular *douar* or locality were to 'colonise' or create a monopoly in particular companies or sectors of industry and to form, close to the factory gates, tightly knit micro-communities.

By 1911–12 the Kabyle migration was already on a sufficient scale for the colonial administration to take a close interest. In 1911 the Director of the *Office d'Algérie*, a Paris based outpost of the *Gouvernement Générale*, wrote a report in which he recommended the need to plan and control the increasing migration of 'nos indigènes'.[23] In 1912 the *Gouvernement* carried out the first of many surveys of immigration by requesting all Prefects in France to report on the number, location and occupation of Algerians. The returns, which were made from fifty-one departments, located 3297 migrants, although it was estimated that the real number was probably four to five thousand. In forty departments there were very small numbers of peddlers or small traders. The main industrial locations were in the Ain (cement works), Aveyron (mining), Bouches-du-Rhône (2000 in soap-works, refineries, docks, and casual labour), Meurthe-et-Moselle (steel works), Nord (mining), Pas-de-Calais (400 miners and dockers), Puy-de-Dôme (40 with *Michelin*), Seine (600 in sugar refining, transport, and chemical industry) and the Var (mining and casual labour).[24] The heavy concentration in Paris, Marseilles and the mining regions established, with the exception of Lyons, the basic pattern of immigrant settlement for the next fifty years.

, In a session of Parliament in December 1913 a socialist deputy, Henri Doizy, made a long speech in which he attacked numerous abuses under the *code de l'indigénat*, the resistance of colonial administrators to the new right of emigration established by the order of 18 June 1913, and the terrible conditions under which Kabyles were working and living in France.[25] In particular he used evidence supplied by a journalist from *L'Humanité* to expose the appalling housing conditions in the mines of Courrières. The company, he claimed, was failing to apply the law of 1898 on industrial accidents and a number of injured men had been sent back to Algeria without receiving any legal compensation. He asked the government to intercede with the powerful companies which were employing, 'these wretches and take advantage of their ignorance'.[26]

This attack immediately stung the *Gouvernement Générale* into action and within a matter of weeks it had despatched a three-man Commission to investigate the situation of Algerian migrants in France. The report which they produced, *Les Kabyles en France*, provides a fascinating and detailed account of pre-war immigration as well as an insight into the early attitudes of the colonial administration towards emigration.

The Commission was composed of De Costigliole, the deputy director of the *Office de l'Algérie* in Paris, Octave Depont and Ahmed Aït Mehdi. Aït Mehdi, *Caïd* of the Beni-Menguellet tribe in Kabylia, was a wealthy landowner, an influential member of the conservative native élite which supported French colonialism, and president of the Kabyle section of the *Délégation Financières*, a quasi-representative body of colonial interests.[27] In 1899 he had published a booklet, *En Kabylie: le colporteur et l'ouvrier*, in which he presented a case for a removal of the restrictions on internal migration by peddlers and, using the language of the 'Kabyle Myth', promoted 'the services which these hardworking and intelligent mountain people could make to metropolitan industry.'[28]

Octave Depont, who was to become the leading colonial expert on Algerian migration between 1914 and 1930, played a pivotal role in the formulation of policy in the inter-war period. Although born in France, he entered the Algerian administration in 1880 at the age of eighteen and after a ten-year period as an administrator in the *communes mixtes* became the *Chef de Cabinet* to the Governor General Lutaud and eventually the *Inspecteur générale* of the *communes mixtes*. An Araba-phone scholar, he wrote extensively on the political dangers presented to the colony by religious confraternities and expressed a strong fear of Pan-Islamism that was later to be transferred to the dangers of Bolshevik subversion.[29]

The three commissioners arrived in Arras on 16 January 1914 and after consultation with the Prefect and the Chief Engineer of Mines proceeded to an inspection of the mines of the Pas-de-Calais, before moving on to Paris and Marseilles. The conclusion of the Commission report, which was almost certainly written by Depont, provides an insight into the official position of the *Gouvernement Générale* on the eve of the

First World War. In general it was favourable towards labour migration to France. It found that the Kabyles were adapting well to French 'civilisation', were welcomed by the population, benefited from full rights to welfare and social provision, including accident insurance, and gained equal wages to the French. Employers were appreciative of the Algerians willingness to work hard and learn. Accommodation was inadequate, especially in the Nord, but was seen as a temporary problem which employers would soon rectify. There was no threat to French labour and wages since there was a severe labour shortage.

Most of this was a whitewash: the optimistic summary was contradicted in numerous places by the reports' own detailed findings. Clearly, the commissioners were determined not only to rebut Doizy, but to legitimate a process of emigration which they saw as in the interest of the French Empire. The French economy was highly dependent on cross-border migration by Belgians, Italians, Spaniards and others and, during a period of growing international tension, there was some anxiety that this presented a danger to national security. Kabyles could be used to replace these foreigners and, as French subjects, would provide a patriotic force in the frontier departments which would be liable to conscription.[30] In addition, Kabyle remittances, unlike the savings of foreign workers, would remain invested 'on a French territory'.

Emigration would also serve the purposes of assimilation, the fundamental colonial ideology by which Algeria and its people would gradually be absorbed culturally, politically and economically into the French Republic. The Report noted the high level of remittance money which was already flowing into certain Kabyle regions: in the first half of 1913 the post-office of Fort-National had paid out over 880 000 francs. Through contact with 'our civilisation' Kabyles were beginning to develop new needs, a taste for European clothing and food, that would increase French exports to the colony. Migrants would also learn new skills in mines and factories that would benefit the Algerian economy.[31]

The Report is revealing of a nascent division between the imperial concerns of high ranking colonial officials, for whom emigration should serve the higher purpose of France, and the more narrowly defined interests of the settlers. The commissioners rebutted a number of concerns of the *colons*, anxieties which were to assume major dimensions after 1918. The *colons'* fear that remittance money would be used by Algerians to buy back land from the settlers on such a scale as to undermine colonial domination was, they claimed, unfounded. Secondly, the fear that emigration would create labour shortages and raise wages in Algeria was also largely without substance. The departure of Kabyles was only temporary and did not present a permanent loss of manpower to the colony, but more importantly there were such huge reserves of labour in Kabylia, the Aurès and elsewhere that emigration offered no real threat to the colonial economy.

The final and most important recommendation of the Report was that the Algerian migration should be more regulated. The commissioners were undoubtedly influenced by the system of foreign labour recruitment that had already been initiated by French employers in Poland and Italy between 1906 and 1912. As Gary Cross has shown, the first bi-lateral agreements with the Polish and Italian governments, through which recruitment agencies operated in the zones of departure and oversaw the selection, medical inspection, and transport of workers under contract, marked an entirely new form of organised labour that departed in a radical way from the older nineteenth century liberalism that had allowed the spontaneous immigration of *frontaliers*.[32] The Report recommended that mining companies should establish their own recruitment agencies in Algeria or, along with French farmers, rely on a single organisation with offices located in Kabylia and Algiers. An organisation could also be established in Paris that would centralise employers' demands along the lines of the existing *Société Nationale de Protection de la main-d'oeuvre agricole*.

The rationale of the commission was that an efficient match should be made between the specific labour requirements of the French economy and the supply of a strong and healthy labour force that would be subject to medical inspection and selection. However, central to the idea of control was also a colonialist paternalist concern that 'our natives' constituted a child-like and vulnerable group which should be provided with, 'discrete protection and moral guidance', a concern that was to assume considerable importance during the inter-war period.[33]

The Report of the Depont Commission and its recommendations were, however, to be rapidly overtaken by events. The outbreak of the First World War led to a massive recruitment of both Algerian soldiers and workers on a scale and with a greater degree of regulation than the commissioners could ever have thought possible.

LABOUR MOBILISATION AND THE FIRST WORLD WAR

The European empires of the nineteenth century had made widespread use of native labour and military recruits, but manpower had been moved mainly **between** colonial zones while deployment into the European arena had been quite limited in scale.[34] The huge and unprecedented manpower requirements of the First World War gave rise to the first large-scale mobilisation of colonial or non-European forces into the metropolitan heartland. The French economy, because of low natality and labour shortage, had become dependent on immigrant workers well before 1914. The outbreak of war meant that the major sources of foreign labour, in Italy, Poland, Spain, Belgium and elsewhere were cut off or disrupted at the very moment when French males were conscripted into the armed forces. Between 1914 and 1918 the government tried to fill the gap by mobilising over three quarters of a million colonials made up of 222 000 workers, mainly Algerians and Indo-Chinese, and 535 000 soldiers, mainly Senegalese (181 000) and Algerians (170 000).[35] Algerians constituted by far the largest national group and if is added the 13 000 'free' workers who were already in France on the outbreak of war, as well as clandestine workers who migrated outside the normal recruitment channels, then in all about 300 000 Algerians crossed to France during 1914–1918. This represented about one third of all Algerian males of working age, a massive recruitment in relation to the size of the total population.

Although Algerian labour migration was already under way before 1914 the First World War marked a decisive stage in the development of the phenomenon, just as the Second World War was to do later for Afro-Caribbean emigration to Britain.[36] The remaining part of this chapter examines the impact of military recruitment in initiating Algerians into an experience of life in France that was to generate peacetime emigration after 1918. The situation of soldiers and workers in France was quite different and will be looked at separately.

ALGERIAN SOLDIERS IN FRANCE

Up until 1912 the recruitment of Algerian soldiers was voluntary and on a relatively small scale. However, as international tensions deepened between European states, the French government prepared to gain access to the manpower reserves of colonial Algeria by passing a highly controversial decree on 3 February 1912 which for the first time introduced a system of three-year conscription for *indigènes*. This was also the outcome of a long debate on conscription as a mechanism for the assimilation of Algerians into the 'patrie'.[37] Settler interests were bitterly opposed to the measure since it would lead, it was claimed, to the granting of full citizenship to Algerians and also train them in the use of weapons that could be turned against the Europeans. 'You are going to teach every wog (*bicot*) how to use a rifle!', warned *La Dépêche algérienne* in 1907.[38] The 1908 campaign of opposition to conscription led by the mayors, the natural leaders of the *colons*, was symptomatic of a deeper conflict between settler and metropolitan interests for the ultimate control of colonial manpower. It prefigured a similar mayoral campaign of 1923–4 in opposition to labour emigration (see Chapter 8).

In spite of the 1912 law the army preferred to recruit volunteers rather than impose conscription during the early years of the First World War (1914–16). It was thought that unwilling conscripts would make poor soldiers, while the use of volunteers would prevent opposition and rebellion in the conservative tribal zones (particularly dangerous when the army was tied down in Europe) and at the same time undercut the political campaign of the *Jeunes Algériennes* reformers for French citizenship as recompense for the ultimate blood sacrifice. During 1917–18 however, the huge losses at the front led to the eventual conscription of the entire 'classes' for those years and in 1916–17 a serious revolt broke out in the south Constantine region.[39] For the entire period of the war there were more 'volunteers' (87 519) than conscripts (82 751) and it is likely that the majority of soldiers came from the zones of labour migration, particularly Kabylia, and reinforced the pattern of emigration that had already emerged in the pre-war years.[40]

The impact of French life on soldiers was far more restricted than in the case of the workers in the war industries, mainly because of the segregation from French civilians imposed by barrack discipline or location at the front. Algerian infantrymen were organised in special regiments where, for political reasons, they were placed under French officers and inter preters who imposed a particularly strict control. Even when Algerians were not at the front they were located or trained in special barracks which were generally in small towns like Agde, Lodève, Casteljaloux or Carpentras, well away from the 'corrupting' influence of the major cities. Life in the barracks was regulated to prevent Algerians establishing contact with the local population. When on leave they were not allowed to stay with French families but only in special rest centres, while in 1916 French female nurses were removed from all hospitals with wounded Algerians to prevent relationships developing. The highly distinctive 'Arab' style of the Algerian uniform meant that soldiers could be easily recognised and intercepted by the military police.[41] This was all part of a general strategy aimed at separating Algerian soldiers, as far as possible, from contact with the 'dangerous' influences of the French working-class.[42]

However, in spite of such segregation, the experience of France and life in the army had an enormous impact and was to influence many thousands of ex-soldiers to return in later years as labour migrants. Algerian soldiers were impressed by the contrast between the highly racialised, repressive and segregationist structures of colonial society and the far more open and often friendly attitudes of the French. With the exception of highly localised pre-war hostility to Algerian strike-breakers in Marseilles, the majority of French people, as yet, showed little sign of anti-Arab racism, and colonial troops were welcomed as living symbols of the unity and power of the French Empire, the *Union Sacrée*. A young Algerian school-master wrote home in 1914 to describe his regiments arrival in France: 'Everywhere the little "turcos" are received with open arms. The children follow us and welcome us, the mothers and fathers make us a thousand gifts, while the young girls hug us and shower us with flowers.'[43] In spite of severe discipline many Algerian soldiers experienced the paternalist and even sentimental attachment of French officers to 'their men' as far more humane and egalitarian than the harsh and oppressive manner in which they were treated in colonial society. Infantrymen in letters home often referred to French soldiers as their 'brothers'.[44]

Algerian soldiers also, through their military training, introduction to modern weapons and technology, as well as the experience of western values and culture (clock-time and discipline) were also prepared for urban life and industrial practice. An old soldier, interviewed in 1974, remarked that he had returned from the front, 'absolutely transformed, both in his way of dressing and of thinking. He was forward looking, planned and showed an enterprising attitude towards his land. He had been impressed by the technical power of the French.'[45]

ALGERIAN WORKERS IN FRANCE

The impact of the French experience on Algerian workers recruited into the war industries was even more important in establishing a later pattern of labour migration. On the outbreak of war many Kabyle miners located in the northern coalfields moved south to Paris where they were housed in a camp in the Bois de Boulogne and eventually repatriated. However, the recent law of 15 July 1914 had given Algerians the right of free movement to France and about 20 000 so-called 'free' workers migrated before restrictions were reimposed on 12 October 1915. The deployment of colonial labour into the war economy was placed on a systematic basis with the establishment of the *Service de l'Organisation des Travailleurs Coloniaux* (SOTC) by the Ministry of War in January 1916.

The SOTC liaised with other ministries, centralised the demand for labour in both state and private industry, and regulated the contracts which guaranteed, at least in principle, fair wage rates, accommodation and conditions of work.[46] French administrators in the Algerian communes organised recruitment drives and the transit of men to 'collection centres' in the ports, where they were formed into militarised labour units under the command of army officers. On arrival in Marseilles the men were housed in a huge camp of wooden barracks, given medical inspections, photographed for identity cards, and organised into work detachments before being despatched to their destinations throughout France.[47]

A para-military command structure was organised at regional level to administer the colonial labour barracks which were established close to the war-industries, powder and munitions factories, chemical plant, foundries, quarries, gas works, and docks. The labour brigades, in most cases numbering several hundred men, were accommodated in spartan and often appalling conditions which led to high levels of illness and death. At Sète for example nine hundred Algerians lived in the sheds of a saw-mill which were without floors, water supply, toilets or cantines.[48] The work camps were policed by agents recruited among former soldiers of the Army of Africa or administrators of Algerian communes. Selected for their knowledge of Arabic, Berber and 'native customs', they reproduced the 'native management' techniques of the colonial régime (*encadrement*), a mixture of paternalism (respect for Muslim diet and religious practice) and harsh discipline, including the use of solitary confinement on bread and water.[49]

The SOTC officials gave various reasons for the *encadrement* of colonial workers: the need to maximise productivity among a backward labour force that was thought to be inherently inefficient and lazy; to overcome language difficulties; and to protect naive and primitive 'natives' from the moral dangers of urban society (alcoholism, prostitution, gambling).[50] However, the paramount consideration was to segregate colonial labour from contact with the general milieu of the French working class, trade unionism and subversive political ideas, and to prevent sexual relations with French women. In practice it proved impossible to maintain an impermeable barrier. Algerians travelled daily from the barracks to work where they inevitably came into contact with French and European migrant workers. They also had some freedom of movement during their leisure time to visit town centres, although many barracks were deliberately located far out in the suburbs to make this difficult.

There was, however, one group of workers which escaped from the control of the para-military barracks and these were the *ouvriers libres*, mainly Kabyles, who managed to enter France individually before the decree of 12 October 1915 put a halt to uncontrolled movement. Although numbering about 30 000 or one quarter of all Algerian workers during the war they played an unusually important role in establishing the later pattern of post-war emigration.[51]

Their main centres of location were in Paris, Lyons and Marseilles where they were attracted by unregulated high wages. In the big cities they became spatially concentrated in micro-ghettos or enclaves, particular inner-city sectors or streets in which cheap lodging houses or *garnis* and café-restaurants were run by North Africans for their compatriots.[52] Although the number of militarised workers increased from forty-five per cent of all Algerian labour in late 1916 to sixty-two per cent in late 1918, there was a continuous 'leakage' of clandestines from SOTC camps. These workers travelled on forged identity cards and *cartes de circulation* into the safe haven of the urban enclaves where they could easily avoid police detection, often with the complicity of employers who were desperately short of labour.[53]

In many instances Algerians settled in enclaves alongside or close to the major factories in which they were employed. Before the war several hundred migrants were employed in the sugar refineries of *Say* in Paris, found lodgings close by and socialised at a North African café located at 128 Boulevard de la Gare.[54] Such early Paris locations grew in size and number during the war and by 1918 Algerians were especially dense in the 13th, 15th, 18th, 19th and 20th arrondissements. Small North African *cantines* played a crucial role in the social and political life of the émigré community, such as the cafés situated in the Avenue du Pont d'Epinay in the industrial suburb of Genne-villiers close to the lodging houses of Algerians who were employed in the gas works. In April 1918 the Paris police reported the existence of fifty-four such cafés in the city of Paris and they were subjected to frequent raids because of gambling at *ronda*, alcoholism, prostitution, harbouring of deserters and frequent knife-fights.[55]

A similar pattern of dense settlement had developed even earlier in Marseilles where before the war there were already some twenty *cafés maures*, seven of them located in the Rue des Chapeliers. At the *Prado* in the Rue de Cassis a friendly society,

La Solidarité Algériennes, was established as early as October 1912.[56] During the war the constant arrival and departure of soldiers and workers through the port led to the appearance of distinct Algerian enclaves:

> It was during the war that the Algerian sector of Marseilles, Saint Martin, began to take shape near the Porte d'Aix, around the streets of Sainte Barbe, Chapeliers, Puvis de Chavannes, the Pénitents Bleus and the arab market of the Avenue d'Arenc. The life of Saint Martin was lived more and more on the margins of that of European Marseilles. It withdrew into an autonomous refuge located in the cafés or the overcrowded rooms rented out by French or Algerian landlords at exorbitant prices. The cafés, the brothels and the back-rooms of shops, where dominos and *ronda* was ' played, constituted the meeting places of an excluded and essentially masculine population.[57]

Saint Martin, like the Algerian *quartiers* of Paris and Lyons, became a natural point of arrival and reception for post-war immigrants and consolidated a pattern of enclave formation which has survived down to the present.

The continuity between wartime and post-war patterns of settlement was further reinforced by the tendency for Algerian workers to return after 1918 to the factories and mines in which they had been employed during 1914–18. For example in 1916 Algerians were first employed in the coal-mines of La Grande-Combe and this opened the way to their continuing recruitment by the company after 1918.[58] The existence of SOTC barracks in the Lyons suburbs of Venissieux, which in 1916 housed six hundred Algerians employed in the local chemical industry, led to the post-war growth of one of the biggest Algerian communities in France.[59]

Larbi Talha has demonstrated how the enforced militarisation of Algerian workers during the First World War was a decisive step in the brutal indoctrination of migrant Algerian peasants into the work-patterns of industrial capitalism. Algerians were astonished to find that work was precisely regulated by the clock and that the division of labour led to an uninterrupted routine with each worker tied to the same exhausting and mind-numbing tasks. War production of vehicles and armaments provided an opportunity for companies like Renault to introduce Taylorist methods of assembly line production that had been resisted by skilled French labour before 1914. This radical reorganisation of work practices and deskilling involved a significant recourse to North African labour, a pattern that was continued after the war by Renault and Citroën. Frequently Algerians cracked under the physical and mental strain and quit without notice, causing employers to complain about their ancestral 'nomadic' ways.[60]

A final major impact of the First World War in generating emigration after 1918 was through the experience of higher levels of wages and social benefits than could be gained in Algeria. For soldiers, both volunteer and conscript, the benefits were minimal. They were paid a joining-up bonus that averaged under one franc per day, a fixed daily payment of 0.22 francs and a family allowance of 1.25 francs, with a later addition of 0.50 francs per child.[61] A married man with one child received a daily total of just under three francs, a very low amount compared to the wages procured by workers either in France or in Algerian towns and one which was further eroded by the increase in basic prices during the war. In addition life in the army was exceedingly harsh and dangerous and over 25 000 Algerians were to lose their lives. For this reason, where military conscription was enforced outside the major zones of labour emigration like Kabylia it was to have little impact in initiating post-war emigration.

Far more influential was the impact of wage-labour. The contract workers recruited by the SOTC gradually improved their levels of pay. Initially promised by recruiters in Algeria a wage of 3.50 francs per day they found on arrival in France that 1.50 francs was deducted for food. Eventually the government agreed in September 1916 to pay the same rates as for French workers or a minimum of five francs for a ten hour day, although 1.50 francs was still subtracted for upkeep. Eventually in February 1917 a minimum wage of 4.50 francs was guaranteed with no deductions. Since workers in para-military organisations were generally classified as unskilled labour in order to depress wage levels, they rarely moved into the higher paid categories.[62] In general, however, the SOTC workers had an experience of France that prepared them better for post-war emigration than it did in the case of the soldiers: wages were fifty per cent higher and they gained a first-hand knowledge of industrial labour and urban life.

The most favourable conditions were those experienced by the 'free' workers. In all they numbered about 30 000 men, predominantly Kabyles, and they earned a daily wage of about seven to nine francs in 1917 and twelve francs or more in 1918. They constituted a kind of labour aristocracy within the emigrant community and a few were able to move into skilled categories, like the lathe-turner whose rate increased from twenty to twenty-seven francs per day in 1918.[63] Letters written home by this group, usually in French, were most enthusiastic about the opportunities to be found: 'France', stated one, 'is the land of work and money.' There was optimism about the chances for making savings and investing in the home village, especially in land.[64] Ageron estimates the total flow of wages and benefits during the war at some 240 million francs and this was on a sufficient scale to enable many Algerians to buy back lands that had been lost to French colonisers.[65]

The First World War, and the recruitment of some 300 000 Algerian soldiers and workers, marked a crucial stage in the development of emigration to France.[66] However, this huge mobilisation did not initiate, as might have been expected, a pattern of post-war migration that was evenly spread throughout Algerian society.[67] This can be explained by the fact that most recruitment, both military and civilian, was still voluntary or 'free' and came from the areas within Algeria, particularly Kabylia, which were most 'open' to western influences or already involved in patterns of labour emigration before 1914.

4 Departure and Employment

During the first forty years of emigration (1910–1950) the structure of the *noria*, the rotation of single males, remained essentially unchanged. In this and the following two chapters I shall provide a composite picture of the experience of the 'typical' migrant. This chapter looks first at the social context in which the decision to migrate was taken, the underlying strategies involved, how the difficult journey to France was undertaken and the way in which destination, the particular urban and industrial locations of Algerians, was determined by the geography of employment. Chapter 5 goes on to explore housing conditions, the social life and organisation of immigrants within the enclave, and their degree of integration and acculturation into the values of French society. Chapter 6 takes a closer look at the issue of adaptation through a study of the most sensitive indicator of identity, Islamic belief and practice. The chapter closes by showing how the gradual impact of emigration on the sending village was to subtly transform the traditional socio-economic order and cultural values, thereby inevitably undermining the structures that gave rise to temporary departure.

Individual Algerian migrants, with a few exceptions, were engaged in a constant circulation between their home villages and periods of French employment. The migrant, even after periods of twenty or thirty years in France, still regarded himself as primarily a member of his home community. Even as he toiled in mines or on car assembly lines, or collapsed exhausted in over-crowded dormitories, the inner landscape of the migrant, his *imaginaire*, was essentially that of his native village, the particular fields, trees and houses of home. Historians and sociologists have had some difficulty in classifying this working-class type. The migrant who had spent most or all of his adult working-life in a French foundry, car plant or coal-mine would appear to be a classic proletarian, but his fundamental project was to maximise savings in the shortest time possible so as to return to his family and to invest in the peasant domestic economy, in land, livestock and debt redemption. His psychological state in France was always that of the transient, everything in his life was 'provisional', and he was in essence most like the European peasants who, in the early phases of industrialisation, travelled daily by foot from their farms to work in mines and factories.[1] Claude Liauzu refers to Algerian migrants as a 'semi-proletariat'; a better term would be 'peasant-worker'.[2]

THE JOURNEY

At the end of the First World War the military authorities immediately shipped back to the various colonies all the soldiers and SOTC workers under their command. A large number of Algerian and Moroccan workers managed, however, to slip through the police nets. During 1919 the Ministry of the Interior organised police operations in Paris, Marseilles and elsewhere to round up all those who had avoided compulsory repatriation as well as 'free' Algerian workers who were unemployed. During June 1919 two separate convoys of about one thousand men each were shipped back to Algeria on the cargo vessel, the *Jabatoa*.[3] In June 1920 the Governor General was still complaining that 4000 Algerian contract workers were unaccounted for, while French authorities were beginning to protest about the presence of unemployed North Africans, like the Prefect of Seine-et-Oise who noted these, 'disreputable subjects who live from pilfering and sustain on the banks of the Seine the ways of the outback (*bled*)'.[4]

In the haste of various ministries, especially the Ministries of the Interior and the War Office, to expel **all** Algerians from France the law of 15 July 1914, which guaranteed freedom of movement, appears to have been overlooked. The police in many instances acted illegally in arresting and deporting Algerians and this led to strong protest, particularly in Marseilles where a North African petition was addressed to the Prefect in January 1921.[5] In spite of police harrassment and strong pressure from the Governor General Abel to introduce strict controls that would remove the provisions of the 1914 act, the government was powerless to stem a rapid increase in Algerian emigration. In a circular of 19 January 1920 it was compelled to remind administrators of the right of free movement and departures from Algerian ports climbed rapidly from 21 684 in 1920 to 71 028 in 1924.

Most emigrants came from rural societies in which a shortage of land, heavy taxes, low wages, debt and massive unemployment or underemployment meant that most peasants were living in abject poverty. The situation after the war was particularly precarious as severe drought in 1920 ruined the grain harvest and decimated livestock. During the famine of 1921, the worst since 1866–8, hordes of starving peasants laid seige to European farms and towns and tens of thousands of corpses lay scattered along the highways. One eyewitness reported:

> At this moment there are Algerian provinces where the natives are dying from hunger quite regularly, in broad daylight, on the roads, within sight of everyone; it's absurd, horribly distressing, but that's how it is . . . the people look incredible because they are walking mummies.[6]

The appalling conditions in Algeria in the immediate post-war years were a major precipitant of the large-scale emigration.

Migrants, when interviewed, invariably gave economic reasons for their departure: typical is the statement made by one Algerian to a Paris journalist in 1926:

> Back home in the mountains I had long flowing robes made for me of white cloth, a house, a bit of land. But soon, no means to live: the taxes, famine, the rod of iron of the administrators and the *Caïds* who made us sweat blood (*'font suer le burnous'*). I came here leaving my wife, my mother and four children and sent them back a bit to keep alive. I then returned home and wanted to stay there, but we would all have starved to death. I had to come back to France.[7]

When formulating the first decision to migrate, on what sources of information could the peasant depend? Did he have a reasonably sound idea of the job prospects, the level of wages, and living conditions and could he estimate his likely saving capacity and length of stay? Some migration was organised by professional recruiters who may have impressed naive peasants with glowing but false accounts of the golden opportunities in France. In 1914, for example, a mining company in Epinac-les-Mines sent a Kabyle overseer called Oauli Said Ben Arezki to recruit directly in his *douar* of origin in Akbou: he was still active in 1929 when his target was fifty recruits.[8] In a novel of 1938 Marcelle Marty described the propaganda of such a re-cruiter: 'To the youth the orator would promise amusements, women, lights, promenades, something to satisfy all the appe-tites; to the more serious-minded, he presented a picture of them coming home with savings . . .'[9] Colonial experts, obscur-ing the roots of emigration in European conquest, often emphasised psychological instead of economic factors and portrayed Algerians as childlike primitives who were dazzled by the lure of France as an Eldorada.[10]

In reality most prospective migrants had fairly accurate information about France. Firstly, recruiters played a quite minor and declining role in organising emigration. An invest-igation in 1929 by the *Gouvernement Générale* into the activities of recruiters showed low and diminishing levels of activity.[11] The great majority of emigrants gained their information through letters sent from France by relatives or through the accounts of men returned to the village. Oral evidence sug-gests that returning migrants, for reasons of honour and sta-tus, did often exaggerate the wonders of France while remaining silent about the extreme levels of hardship and degradation they had suffered. The first migrant from El Akbia, Abdlraham, returned after eighteen months with two large suitcases con-taining new suits, shirts and shoes and boasting of his affairs with beautiful women. His second cousin, Rabah, followed him out a year later only to find that he had been totally misled; there was no housing, no decent work, and 'I realised quickly that no beautiful French girl would go out with an Algerian worker unless he was well-dressed and educated'.[12] But while some villagers could see quite readily through this veneer, the psychological attitude of most was to engage in a willing sus-pension of disbelief in order to sustain an image of France as a place of relative opportunity compared to the grinding pov-erty of the *bled*. What counted most for the young men was the sight of those who returned on vacation: 'We saw them return, well dressed, their suitcases stuffed full, money in their pocket, which we saw them spending without a thought; they were handsome, well-fed . . . we admired them.'[13] A further indic-ator of quite accurate 'feed-back' into villages as to work oppor-tunities in France is shown in the sensitivity of migration flow to the phases of growth and slump in the French economy.[14]

Once an individual had decided to emigrate he still had to overcome some quite formidable hurdles. Firstly, he would have to find the cost of the passage. In 1913 the passage to France cost 90 francs at a time when the average urban wage was 1.25 to 3 francs per day.[15] This represented the income from thirty to seventy working days, an average which remained constant during the inter-war period.[16] The problem for peasants was the difficulty of finding any regular waged labour, and most raised cash by selling land, animals or, in most cases, borrowing at high rates of interest from village userers.[17] Secondly, after new controls were introduced in 1924, 1926 and 1928 (see Chapter 8) migrants had to incur the cost and overcome the bureaucratic hurdles to obtain an identity card with photograph, a medical certificate, a work contract, a certificate guaranteeing a clean judicial record and deposit money to cover the costs of repatriation. In communes in which administrators were opposed to emigration on the grounds that it depleted the availability of cheap labour, applicants could find themselves seriously impeded.[18] A combination of cash, savoir-faire and initiative was required by the migrant. Thirdly, the migrant had to be sure that his family could cope with the tasks of the farm in his absence and survive an unknown period of time until his first remittance payments arrived. In the most conservative villages there could also be high levels of family and community resistance to departure from the *dar-el-Islam*, the community of Islam, for the dangerous *dar-el-harb*, the house of unbelief.

As I have argued in Chapter 2 Kabylia, with a long 'tradition of migration', was better able to overcome the impediments to emigration than most other peasant societies. Contrary to the impression given in numerous studies of Algerian and other 'Third World' international migrations, it was not the poorest and most hungry strata that made up the first phase of male departure, but a middling rank of relatively better-off peasant families. The anthropologist Lacoste-Dujardin, in a study of a group of Kabyle villages, found that it was the *grandes familles* that had the oldest traditions of emigration, 'powerful lineages, long established landowners and rich in men'.[19] As Robert Montagne, Abelmalek Sayad and Pierre Bourdieu have insisted it was the traditional, extended Kabyle family, often 'rich' in adult males, which decided as a group to delegate one of its members to seek external resources to be invested in land, livestock, food and debt repayment.[20] If the emigrant was married his wife and children became the responsibility of male kin, fathers, uncles or elder brothers. Such *grandes maisons* had a better chance of raising the money for the journey and possessed the level of education or cultural capital to cope with the intricacies of French bureaucracy.[21] By contrast, Lacoste-Dujardin describes other families caught in a poverty trap that prevented emigration. Often this occurred where a man had a large, young family which prevented early migration; a factor which in turn led to further births (seven to eight children) and a life of extreme hardship.[22]

Once the first 'pioneer' emigrants from a particular village had established a foothold in France then it was quite usual to see a rapid acceleration in the number of departures through chain-migration. Information as to work opportunities and contact addresses were dispatched by letter, migrant workers frequently used part of their savings to fund the voyage of kin, and brothers often migrated in sequence, passing on the same employment. In a typical example, from the Kabyle village of Aït-Ziri, the oldest of four brothers first emigrated in 1921. He was replaced by the second oldest brother in 1924, who stayed for a period of four years and sent savings to help his two younger brothers invest in the farm (purchase of two cows) and to pay for the passage of the third brother who relieved him in 1928. He in turn was followed by the fourth and youngest brother.[23] The 'old hands' on vacation acted as guides to the young men departing for the first time on the difficult journey to Europe.

The Kabyle community/family sought to protect itself against the dangers of migrants going astray in France through a number of strategies. The fear was that young men would fall prey to the infidel fleshpots, fritter away money on alcohol or, worst of all, settle down with a French woman, thus failing in their primary task to maximise savings and even cutting off all links to the family.[24] Families would select a male who held the trust of the group: he must preferably be married, not too young, and have a certain experience and maturity of character. As one emigrant remarked, '. . . you don't send somebody who is going to cheat you: he'll come back empty-handed . . .'.[25] Frequently, before departure, arranged marriages were entered into through the *fatiha* ceremony, an unconsummated alliance with a young bride.[26] The aim was to reinforce the migrants' moral and symbolic links to the community of origin and to limit the danger of relationships with foreign women. Within the same logic was the refusal of the family or community to allow married women to accompany their husbands since this would pose the danger of emigrants settling permanently abroad.[27] However, as will be seen in Chapter 5, the most important control was that exercised by male relatives and village associations and networks in France.

Once a decision to emigrate had been made most men timed their departure to coincide with the agrarian and religious calendar. Most left in August–September, after the heavy physical work of the harvest was over. Very few men departed during the religious festival of Ramadan, the date of which changed yearly.[28] In societies in which emigration was a relatively new phenomenon the moment of departure could be an emotionally traumatic and even shaming experience. Migrants frequently departed in the dead of night to avoid observation, often concealing their European clothing outside the village or sending it ahead to a local town. One emigrant who first went to France during the 1930s recounted:

> I knew the time when to emigrate to France was something evil, shameful. One didn't shout it from the roof tops as now: 'look at me, I'm going to France or I've come back from France': one left silently. Word must not get about that such-and-such was quitting his plough ... Everything was done in secret, often at night. At nighttime everyone is asleep; in the house that prevents tears; outside it avoids words of pity.[29]

The sadness of departure and the grieving of mothers and wives was reflected in numerous traditional Kabyle songs.[30]

> Black train, black as a bee,
> You scream in the stations,
> Come and climb towards me;
> You carry away loved ones,
> Into a joyless exile,
> O train, go slowly.

As Khellil and others point out, emigration was experienced as an 'exile' (*el ghorba*) and a feeling of foreboding surrounded it, denoted by the word *lyerba*, meaning darkness and gloom.[31]

The ultimate fear of the migrant and his family was that he might meet his death and be buried in the land of the infidel, the *rumi*.

The main zones of emigration in Kabylia, in spite of its mountainous and rugged terrain, was only one hundred miles from the port of Algiers and most migrants could make their way there on foot and by train or increasingly by bus after the construction of metalled roads during the 1930s. The ferries like the *Ville d'Alger* and *El Mansour* which plied between Algiers and Marseilles usually made the crossing in about twenty-four hours, the migrants crowded into the steerage, segregated from the European passengers. The French travelling in First and Tourist classes could gaze down on the crowds of labourers:

> Down below on the vast decks of the '4th', a crowd of 'muslims', young men, most of them at the peak of their strength, poorly dressed in European style, almost all of them with a beret or fez, sometimes wrapped in yellow robes, and piled up in the middle wooden suitcases covered with bright paper and parcels rolled up in a blanket which the army picturesquely calls 'Senegalese packets'.[32]

Others, the clandestines, had a much more perilous crossing. The imposition of strict regulations after September 1924, controls that involved much higher costs, led numerous migrants to stow away or to resort to criminal networks that specialised in the supply of forged documents or arranged for illegal passage through payments to dockers and sailors. The most numerous and desperate group were Moroccans who had no legal right of entry to France. Many hundreds crossed on foot into Algeria only to fall victim to every kind of confidence trick in Oran and other ports. Many died on the passage, the worst incident being in August 1926 when ten Moroccans were found dead, asphyxiated in the holds of the *Sidi Ferruch*.[33]

In Marseilles the migrant workers were disembarked separately from French passengers and treated in a humiliating way that contrasted, in the memories of ex-soldiers, with the fanfare reception of the First World War. As a Kabyle noted in 1926, 'On disembarkation the humiliations began: the "superior" race got off first; as for us, the "inferior" race, we were kept back until the customs officers and police had searched us in a revolting manner'.[34]

For many new migrants the experience of arriving in the bustle and confusion of Marseilles was one of disorientation and fear. Some found their way by heading for the 'Arab' quarter or were picked up by the *Comité d'Assistance aux Indigènes Algériens*, a semi-official organisation funded by the *Gouvernement Général*, which housed them in the squalid reception camp that had been used during the First World War for workers and soldiers in transit.[35]

For most immigrants Marseilles was a temporary stop; from there they fanned out in search of work, mainly east towards the mines of Languedoc, or north towards St Etienne, Lyons, Paris, Lorraine and the Pas-de-Calais. Some were picked up at the docks by recruiters operating for Paris companies who took them in charge and paid their journey against future wages. Other migrants had paid every last penny on their passage and were forced to tramp across France, sleeping in barns and begging for food, running the risk of arrest for vagrancy and forced repatriation.[36]

Other migrants arrived in Paris, 'having exhausted all their resources, wandering about in groups looking for shelter, and making a painful impression on the public'.[37] Most Algerians, however, eventually made their way, either under the wing of a re-emigrant or clutching a scrap of paper with an address, to the door of brothers, uncles and village contacts. The solace of finding kin or fellow countrymen in such a foreign environment was negated however by the shock of the contrast between the new arrivals golden preconception of France and the harsh reality of filthy and overcrowded slums.

> I shall never forget the picture of my arrival in France, the first thing that I saw, the first thing I heard: we knocked at a door, it opened onto a little room which gave out a mixture of smells, humidity, a stuffy atmosphere, the sweat of sleeping men. How sad! What suffering in their looks, their voices – they spoke in a whisper – in their words. From that moment I came to understand what is solitude, what is sadness; the darkness of the room . . . the darkness of the street . . . the obscurity of everything French, because in the France that we know there are only shadows.

The men spoke about me to my uncle who had brought me with him: 'Why have you led him into this trap, why have you misled him, why have you offered him this snare?'[38]

THE LABOUR MARKET

The geographic distribution of Algerians within France remained largely unchanged throughout the period from 1912 to 1962 and was primarily determined by the opportunities for employment which were concentrated above all in the major industrial towns and mining basins.

Early attempts to organise the recruitment of Algerians into agriculture before and during the First World War had little success and this sector employed about 0.8 per cent of all immigrants in both 1926 and 1952. The North African dislike for farmwork arose from a number of factors: isolation from contact with fellow countrymen, lack of knowledge of western farming techniques, unusually low wages, and harsh treatment and exploitation by xenophobic peasant employers. Only during the desperate times of the 1930s Depression would unemployed Algerians fall back on seasonal agricultural work.[39] The low level of employment in agriculture is clearly reflected in the almost total absence of Algerians from the rural western half of France (see Map 2).[40]

A government survey of 1937 showed that about ninety per cent of all Algerians were employed in five key regions: the Paris basin (39.2 per cent), the Nord/Pas-de-Calais (5.9), the Lorraine basin (15.6), the Lyons-St Etienne region (11) and Provence-Côte d'Azur centred on Marseilles (19.2). This spatial distribution was stable throughout the first half of the twentieth century and was, with the exception of a decline in the northern mining regions, largely the same in 1968.[41]

Within these regions Algerians were employed in the low-paid, onerous and frequently unhealthy and dangerous work which the French refused to do.[42] After the First World War for example, large numbers were engaged in the extremely unpleasant task of clearing the old battlefields of shells, mines and débris.

The statistics of North African employment during the interwar period are highly unsatisfactory owing both to under-registration and vague or ambiguous classification of sectors or types of work.[43] The data for 1926 show that Algerians were particularly active in engineering and metal-working (mainly cars) (21 per cent), mining (9.1), chemicals, rubber and paper (11.3), iron and steel production (6.2), transport and

Map 2 Algerian workers in France (1937)

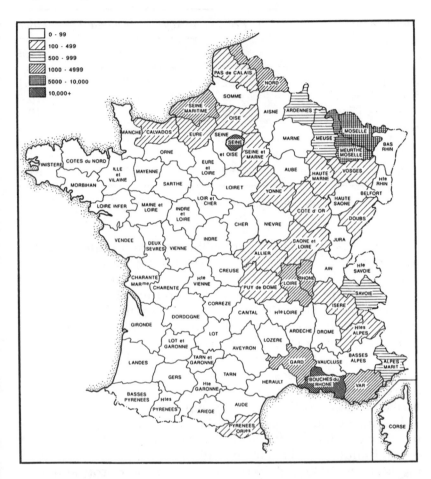

warehouse loading (9.3), construction (3.4), food processing (2.7) and glass/ceramics (1.9).[44] However, the bald data gives little idea of the extent to which North Africans were highly concentrated **within** companies in the most unpleasant, dirty and dangerous types of work. In coking and steel-works, for example, Algerians were found concentrated as furnace stokers in sectors of great heat, dust and noise and where accidents from molten metal and heavy machinery were frequent. Others operated in foundries as sand-moulders and metal trimmers, a job in which fine particles caused silicosis after three

Table 4.1   The regional location of Algerians, 1937–68

Major industrial region	Per cent of Algerian immigrant population		
	1937	*1955*	*1968*
Paris region	39.2	41.7	40.4
Rhône-Alps	11.0	10.3	16.8
Provence-Côte d'Azur	19.2	5.4	10.3
Lorraine basin	15.6	14.27	7.3
Nord region	5.9	9.9	6.8
Total for five regions	90.9	81.57	81.6

Source: M. Trebous, *Migration and Development*, p. 79.

or four years. The mixing of rubber involved high temperatures, poisonous fumes and high risks of saturnism as did the manufacture of electric batteries.[45] In 1932 at the works of *Moutin* in Saint-Denis all the workers in the galvanising sector, where 'hygiene and safety measures are unknown', were Algerian and many became ill from toxic vapours; the same was true at *Fulmen* in the section in which batteries were filled with acid.[46] Overall those types of unhealthy work which involved great heat, toxic gases, acids, dust, hot metals, and dyes had a predominance of immigrant workers among which North Africans made up the largest group.[47]

The incidence of industrial injury and disease (silicosis, respiratory problems, saturnism) was extremely high. At least six of two hundred workers from Taffraout died from lead poisoning between 1935 and 1938.[48] In the Lorraine iron and steel foundries Algerian accident rates were two to three times higher than for French workers.[49] The high incidence of accidents partly arose from the lack of experience among migrants of rural origin of industrial techniques and from poor understanding of French. But more often employers showed little inclination to give adequate training or protection to men whose lives they considered of low value. When Algerians protested on a building site at the death of a worker the manager retorted, 'What does it matter? He's only a *sidi*.'[50]

Other important forms of Algerian employment included

merchant sailors and dockers in the ports of Marseilles, Le Havre, Dunkerque and Rouen; taxi-drivers (some 300 in Paris in 1935); hotel and café workers; railway carriage cleaners and car washers. The major car-washing companies in Paris, *Citroën, Compagnie Générale, La Française* and *G7*, which together employed about 1400 North Africans, faced a series of major strikes during 1928–34 because of very low-paid night work in very harsh, wet and cold conditions and for shifts that lasted for fourteen to fifteen hours.

Although Algerians constituted only three per cent of the total immigrant population, they were highly concentrated in particular companies or sectors, a factor which explains their location in dense pockets of urban settlement. Some companies appear to have built up a tradition of Algerian employment that continued through many decades. The mines of *Courrières*, for example, employed 400 Kabyles in 1912, 935 in March 1914 and 982 in July 1923; *Renault* at Billancourt had 1500 Algerians in August 1923; while the sugar refinery of *Say* in the 13th *arrondissement* of Paris employed 250 Algerians in 1914 and 500 in 1923.[51] Once a company had employed a few Algerians, and was reasonably happy to continue with this source of cheap but unskilled labour, it could become rapidly 'colonised' by immigrants who frequently originated from the same village. This occurred because companies resorted to recruiters, trusted workers who were despatched to their home area. But, more commonly, established workers used their inside knowledge about vacancies and persuaded foremen, often through *pots-de-vin* (bribes), to take on relatives and friends.[52] Hence the spatial reinforcement of the apparent 'tribal' structures in many urban localities that so intrigued contemporary sociologists. Ray noted that, 'certain quarters, inhabited almost solely by representatives of two or three tribes, constitute reserves of labour on which local industrialists can draw, a fact which has produced, for example, a fortuitous concentration in several factories of members of the Oulad Jerrar and the Ida or Baqil'.[53]

Such a system could be in the managerial interest. Foremen were able to fill vacancies without having to search or advertise, and the Algerian putting in a 'good word' could be held answerable for the physical strength and reliability of a new recruit.[54] Companies also saw an advantage in recruiting men from the same region or ethnic background to work in teams. This overcame the problems of conflict that could often flare up between French, European and North African immigrant workers on the shop floor as well as between Algerian factions (*çoffs*) who engaged in traditional conflict.[55] Village or ethnic grouping also restricted contact with 'subversive' trade union influences and helped overcome language problems through the control of teams of workers by native overseers. The deliberate employment of numerous ethnic groups in the same plant also facilitated policies of 'divide-and-rule', made it easier to pay different levels of wages between French and Algerians, and made the chances of joint strike action less likely.[56] Some specialists like Laroque and Montagne also thought that recruiting 'tribal' groups, meaning immigrants from rural society, provided a better type of worker than the urbanised proletariat of the Algerian cities, tainted by alcoholism and 'physical or moral defects'.[57] Ethnic grouping could also benefit Algerians: for example many found the annual holiday too short to return home and they could often come to an arrangement with employers by which their job was transferred to a brother or friend. Another strategy was for a group of four related workers to share three jobs, each taking a period of leave in turn.

Algerians provided all the economic advantages to employers and to the French economy that have been analysed in such detail for post-1945 immigration.[58] A young male workforce, without family and aged parents, was geographically mobile and presented few social costs to employers or the state. This structure was reflected in the extraordinary high level of the inter-war employment rate: 95 per cent of all Algerians in France were in work, higher than for any other nationality.[59] In particular, the Algerians, as a reservoir of cheap labour, could be called upon during periods of economic expansion (c 1920–9) and then dispensed with and sent back to the colony during recession (c 1930–6). Those workers who were prematurely aged by exhausting physical labour, suffering from industrial diseases and accidents, or slowly dying from tuberculosis were discarded and the social costs born by their families and villages in Algeria.[60] An ageing migrant, who had first come to France in the mid-1930s, remarked: 'Here in France they throw you away like dross. The day that you are

affected by old age you are pushed aside, abandoned. A worker
... an Algerian, is like a lemon: they squeeze it, take the juice,
leaving the skin, which counts for nothing. Go back home now
that you are buggered, go and croak down there, die somewhere else, you're good for nothing.'[61]

While wage-levels paid to Algerians were in law identical to
those for French workers, in practice employers found numerous ways round this restriction. One argument, repeated ad
nauseam by employers, was that Algerians were mediocre
workers with levels of productivity that were generally claimed
to be 20 to 25 per cent below that of Europeans. While newly
arrived migrants from rural Algeria undoubtedly faced problems of adaptation to industrial labour, employers continued
to emphasise 'nomadism' and very low productivity as an excuse to depress wage levels. Even when migrants, after many
decades in France, had achieved work skills on a par with
those of French and European workers, they continued to be
categorised in the lowest levels.[62] As late as 1952–4 some 95
per cent of all Algerian workers were classified as unskilled or
semi-skilled workers (*manoeuvres* and *ouvriers spécialisés*), and
only 5 per cent as skilled (*ouvriers qualifiés*).[63]

Algerians, regarded as the most inferior of workers, were
the first to be laid off during recession, and were particularly
hard hit as industrial activity weakened after 1927 and then
collapsed in the Great Depression. By 1936 it was estimated
that nearly a quarter of all Algerians, some 19 000 men, were
unemployed.[64] However, there were two factors which, in spite
of this, worked in the Algerians' favour during the Depression.
Firstly, various laws passed between 1932 and 1935 protected
French labour during the recession by imposing quota limits
on foreigners in certain categories of work. Since Algerians
were French 'subjects', these restrictions did not apply and
employers seized the opportunity to substitute them for lost
foreign labour. Algerians were drafted into particularly noxious industries, like phosphorous production, glue works, and
tanneries from which other foreigners were now excluded but
which the French refused to do since these were 'the most
unpleasant or the lowest paid tasks'.[65] Those foreigners whose
governments were strong in protecting their nationals interests through bi-lateral accords and contracts (Italy, Poland,
Spain) no longer provided cheap labour compared to the

Maghrebians.[66] Secondly, after the government of the Popular Front introduced a forty-hour week, employers tried to retain their profit margins by taking on Algerian workers. The most dramatic instance of this practice occurred in 1936–7 when the industrialists of Lorraine organised a massive recruitment drive in the Algiers region, bringing in about 6000 men under an almost para-military régime that was reminiscent of the SOTC during the First World War.[67]

During years of recession the number of departures from Algeria declined considerably (see Appendix, Table A1), but many thousands of unemployed in France preferred to stay on waiting for an upturn in the economy.[68] These men survived through the group support of relatives in work, sleeping on floors and sharing their meals, or by claiming unemployment benefits which were higher than the lowest wages in Algeria. The French government responded to this situation by trying to enforce repatriation to Algeria, although this was strictly illegal (see Chapter 9). Since the enforced expulsion of other foreigners was legal – during the height of the Depression in 1934–5 about 140 000 were removed – Algerians retained an edge in the depleted job market.

Finally, there is one important category of employment which, although numerically small, had a political and cultural importance out of all proportion to its size, that of the self-employed, the élite of small proprietors of cafés, restaurants, hotels, and shops. Among the earliest Kabyle migrants into France were the peddlers and traders who went from town to town selling North African products which they had often imported from their home region. By 1928–30 this important trade was in decline, partly because of a heavy import duty on artistic products from North Africa, and these goods were replaced by 'oriental' carpets and jewellery made in Marseilles, false 'Moroccan' leather-work, and plastic combs. By the 1940s licensed street traders in oriental goods and fresh fruit and vegetables were increasingly organised in teams which worked for middlemen suppliers.[69]

While some petty traders eventually established themselves as shop owners or import–export dealers, the most numerous *commerçants* started as workers in industry who used their savings to open small canteens and lodging houses for a North African clientele. These astute entrepreneurs had often emerged as the 'strong men' in mines and factories whom employers relied upon as overseers and recruiters of labour (*marchands d'hommes*). Many gained a bad image in the French press as *marchands de sommeil* who charged exorbitant rents to migrants who were lodged in squalid and over-crowded conditions. 'Shrewd', noted one report, 'sharp, clever, they work in close harmony with European industry and commerce and maintain close ties with their co-religionaries'.[70] During the inter-war period many married French women who often helped to run the family business. In Lyons in 1931 of 31 small concerns identified by Massard-Guilbaud, 15 were café owners, 3 butchers, 2 bakers and an assortment which included a hairdresser, rag-merchant, locksmith, peddler and dealer.[71] In 1948 there were some six hundred café owners in the Paris region, thirty in Bordeaux and over a hundred in Lyons. The number of self-employed involved in all forms of commerce was about 11 000 in 1949 or five to six per cent of the total Algerian population.[72] Some of these café-hotel managers became quite wealthy and prestigious, but their crucial importance lay in their influence over Algerians workers for whom the North African café was the centre of social and political activity.[73] The next chapter takes a closer look at these social networks.

5 Life in the Enclave

A key feature of the social, political and economic organisation of the Algerians in France was their spatial location in dense 'micro-ghettos' or urban enclaves. This chapter will examine the position of migrants within the housing market, the processes of enclave formation, and the rich associational life of the Algerians which was centred on the North African café-lodging house. The organisation of the Algerians in introverted and compact kin and village groups located in spatially segregated zones is of particular importance to the question of weak integration and the low level of contact with the French working class. It also helps explain in part why French society came to develop a racialised stereotype of the immigrants as an alien, secretive and dangerous force lurking in the depths of the worst slums.

Housing existed in a variety of forms, from company barracks, government hostels, cheap lodging-houses and North African café-hotels to make-shift arrangements, shantytowns, abandoned railway carriages, and even tents. In general there were however two major forms of spatial location, that of the big company enclave and that of the urban enclave, each of will be examined in turn.

THE COMPANY ENCLAVE

The housing of North African workers by major companies was predominantly a feature of 'company towns', the centres of mining, steel works and heavy industry located well away from the major urban centres of Paris, Lyons and Marseilles. Company provision for North Africans was widespread in the coal-fields of the Pas-de-Calais and the Nord, in the iron and steel towns of Lorraine, St Etienne and Le Creusot, or in specialist centres of production like Clermont-Ferrand (*Michelin* tyres).[1] Because of their geographic location these companies faced serious problems of labour shortage and, without immediate access to the population reserves of the big cities, they tried to attract immigrants by providing accommodation.

Frequently these companies were also engaged in the direct recruitment of workers in Poland, Italy, North Africa and elsewhere. The powerful *Comité des Forges*, for example, introduced convoys of several thousand Algerians into Lorraine in 1936–7.[2]

Mining companies in the north of France which were dependent on immigrant labour from Poland, Italy, Belgium, Czechoslovakia and elsewhere were particularly keen to 'stabilise' and control their work-force. Single male migrants were regarded as particularly prone to indiscipline, alcoholism, and rapid turn-over. A key strategy of many companies was to encourage family migration, especially of Poles, and to provide them with good quality housing in estates or garden-cities. The formation of entire Polish communities, with their own 'villages', schools, clubs and Catholic priests, was also aimed to segregate the immigrants from contact with French Communism and trade unionism.[3]

However, enlightened paternalism rarely appears to have extended to North African migrants. Numerous surveys of employers during the inter-war period showed that they believed in a racialised hierarchy of worker competence and desirability. A typical survey carried out among managers in a Paris automobile plant in 1926 using a ten-point scale listed Belgians as top with an overall 9 for time-keeping, productivity, 'mental discipline', competence in French, and physical appearance, while below came Italians (7.3), Russians (6.6), Spanish/Portuguese (6.5), Poles (6.5), Greeks (5.2) and last of all the Arabs (2.9).[4] For most employers North Africans represented the lowest of the low, the group for which they reserved the most physically unpleasant and dangerous work which even other foreign workers refused to do, especially at the extremely low levels of pay which the Maghrebians received. This 'super-exploitation' of North Africans extended to company accommodation, which generally took the form of primitive barracks. Few companies were willing to undertake the higher social costs of 'stabilisation' of Algerian workers through family migration and decent housing: indeed the predominance of single males enabled employers to cram them in to the most 'cost-effective' buildings, sheds, ex-army barracks, and abandoned factory buildings.[5]

In some cases the companies continued the practises of para-military *cantonnement* that had been established by the SOTC during the First World War. Company barracks in the North of France were often placed under the control of former colonial policemen or soldiers who imposed a severe and disciplined regime. At *Michelin* in Clermont-Ferrand, for example, the early recruitment of Kabyles and their installation in company barracks was the initiative of the director of personnel, Commander Josse, an ex-army officer who had served in North Africa and in the Department of Native Affairs.[6] Josse established an elaborate system by which Algerians were 'rewarded' for good conduct and adaptation to company rules by being moved through four stages, each one corresponding to slightly improved conditions. After arrival in a reception hostel, migrants progressed first to large wooden huts which had outside washing and toilet facilities (but problems of vermin infestation), then to huts built with breeze-blocks which had inside toilets, and finally to barracks with slightly better amenities under the control of a *concierge* who provided morning coffee.[7]

A detailed investigation of living conditions in a company enclave in the mines of the *Compagnie de Courrières* in the Pas-de-Calais was carried out by Octave Depont's commission of inquiry in early 1914. The number of Kabyle workers in the mines had increased rapidly from 435 in 1912 to 935 in March 1914. The company selected only young, fit men aged from thirteen to forty years, who were subjected to a medical examination and then photographed and fingerprinted for an 'in-house' identity card. Most were employed in low-skilled and dangerous work as diggers, waggoners, hauliers and drivers. The company attitude towards the 'colonials' was paternalistic. For example, the employers went some way to meet the special religious needs of the Kabyles showing what the Chief Engineer referred to as, 'the *greatest tact* to avoid clashing with the fanaticism of this personnel'.[8] The time of the evening meal-break was delayed till after sunset during Ramadan and the company acquired a thirty-year concession on a plot of land as a Muslim burial ground. However, this concern did not extend to adequate housing, which consisted of overcrowded wooden huts. As the socialist deputy M. Doizy stated in his parliamentary exposure of the mistreatment of Algerians:

One of our friends from *L'Humanité* went to interview [the Algerians] at Courrières. He found nearly all of them housed in specially built huts, sleeping on bunk beds. The rent for these barracks is exorbitant. Some, with a cubic space less than 100 metres, house up to thirty tenants who pay 4 to 5 fr. per month.[9]

The commission found that housing conditions were indeed poor, but saw this as temporary and reported that the company was gradually improving matters by, for example, installing showers. However, it was noticeable that the company, as was the case elsewhere, preferred to reserve its best accommodation in the form of *corons* or small terrace houses for French and European migrant families, regarded as a more stable, docile and racially superior work-force.

The Kabyle miners at *Courrières* were increasingly drifting away from the company huts, which were deeply disliked for their regimented ambiance, for the greater freedom of private lodging houses and café-hotels. A typical doss-house and bar in Liéven had a French owner who employed a Kabyle called Jean to maintain order among the 45 Algerian lodgers, each of whom paid seven francs per month. The Commissioners visited one squalid *garni* in which they found young Algerians cramped two, three or four to each small room and shivering, 'huddled around the stoves'.[10]

In the 'company towns' the great majority of Kabyles, perhaps over ninety per cent, found accommodation in squalid lodging houses. Most companies prefered not to carry any social costs or responsibility for accommodation and were quite content to leave migrant workers to their own devices and to seek out their own lodgings in the private sector. The migrants were driven by a desperate need to optimise their savings from their low wages so that they could both feed their families in Algeria, accumulate some savings and return home as quickly as possible. This necessarily restricted them to the cheapest form of housing which they could locate, usually extremely overcrowded lodging houses run by French or North African racketeers or 'sleep merchants' (*marchands de sommeil*) who were able to make considerable profits.

Local health officials who inspected conditions in the steel towns of Lorraine in 1937 were shocked by what they saw. In Longwy, for example, at 44 Rue de Metz a single lodging housed between seventy and eighty men, of which 34 were located in a damp cellar with an earth floor and no proper lighting. The

first and second floors above had been divided up by rough
planking into five or six airless, windowless cells containing
fifteen beds, described as 'totally uninhabitable'. Even the roof
space, open to wind coming through the tiles, was rented out.
A small, greasy kitchen was heated by a broken coal stove
which presented the danger of asphyxiation by carbon mon-
oxide, a common occurrence in migrant lodgings. There was
only a single toilet in a courtyard, with no handwashing facilities and, 'numerous traces of urine and excrement can be
found almost everywhere in the courtyard and the corridor
giving off a disgusting odour'.[11] Nor were these conditions
exceptional: numerous reports describe similar conditions elsewhere in France.

   Although company attempts to house Algerians declined as
the problem of labour shortage disappeared during the depression of the 1930s, such practices revived with the frantic
search for foreign labour in the immediate post-Second World
War period. In the rapidly industrialising suburbs of Lyons in
1949 Algerians were housed in various barracks by the companies of *St Gobain* (glass), *Rhône-Poulenc* (chemicals), the *Fonderies
Prenat*, the *Tanneries Lyonnaises* and others. But the biggest concentrations were in the steel and coal towns of Lorraine. The
Charbonnages de Lorraine housed 2649 Algerians in three former
army camps. The biggest, the *Camp de Rosselmont* at Forbach,
included a grocer's shop, a butcher's, a hairdresser and a small
mosque.[12] An Algerian from the village of El Akbia recounted
his first emigration to Mulhouse in 1948:

> Upon arrival we went to the *caserne*, an old French military
> base, where the Arabs were living. This *caserne* was controlled
> by the *Société Alsacienne*. Abdlrahman knew some friends there
> from the Beni Khattab, they gave us some blankets and we
> slept on the floor. This place was not really suitable for
> housing; it was a run down building that had no heat and
> no running water. It was the winter and we were cold.[13]

THE URBAN ENCLAVE

In the conurbations of Paris, Lyons and Marseilles Algerians
were concentrated in dense pockets in close proximity to the

place of work. This was an age when low paid industrial workers avoided the costs of commuting by living under or close to the walls of the factory in the dense warren of the *quartiers populaires*. In the city of Paris, located within the present inner ring-road, the highest concentration of Algerians by 1926, about four thousand men in all, was in the 15th *arrondissement* close to the Citroën factory.[14] The next highest densities were in the 18th and 19th *arrondissements*, location of the Goutte d'Or, which has today become the archetype of the 'Arab ghetto'[15]. Many of those living in the central area were in the service sector or self-employed, taxi-drivers, hotel workers, petty traders, cleaners and so on.

After the First World War a dynamic growth in large industrial plant located in the suburbs of Paris meant that about two thirds of Algerian workers lived in the dreary 'smoke-stack' communes of north and north-west Paris, like Aubervilliers, St Denis, Asnières, Nanterre, Colombes, Puteaux, Boulogne-Billancourt and Argenteuil.[16] Among the major employers of Algerian labour located in the suburbs were automobile firms like *Citroën* (Levallois, Clichy, St-Ouen), *Renault* (Billancourt), *Donnet-Zédel* (Nanterre), *Hispano-Suiza* (Courbevoie) and *Amilcar* (St-Denis); metal-works like *Bimétal* (Alfortville) and *Gnôme-Rhône* (Colombes); and various chemical plant like *Rippolin* (paints at Issy), *Air-Liquide,* and *Compagnie des Eaux* (Gennevilliers), *Gévelot* (munitions at Meudon), *Fulmen* (batteries: Colombes) and *Goodrich* (rubber: Colombes).[17] A similar pattern of industrial location was evident in Lyons with Algerian settlement close to the chemical, glass, rayon, armaments and automobile plant of the Lyons suburbs.[18]

In the inner-city and suburban areas of Paris most Algerians found accommodation in overcrowded lodging houses of the type already described for Lorraine. However, a significant number lived either in official hostels for North Africans or in *bidonvilles*. The hostels, which were operated mainly by the SAINA, will be looked at in Chapter 9, but quite typical was one in the Rue Lecomte in Paris which was housed in an austere, reinforced concrete building, equipped with seventy-five military beds, and lacking in running water or gas.[19] Subject to strict control by ex-army officers most Algerians preferred to create their own social groups in squalid but less regimented lodging houses and shantytowns.

During the inter-war period the zones outside the line of the old Paris fortifications saw an extensive growth of ramshackle squatter camps with makeshift huts and jerry-built houses that were inhabited by poor French and immigrant groups alike. Georges Mauco provides an eye-witness account of his visit to these 'veritable colonies' made up of 'shacks built on a chaos of plots'. In a multi-ethnic colony at St-Ouen he noted, 'Squatting in a corner of a hut, five or six Arabs singing and clapping a monotonous rhythm.'[20]

The most investigated of the North African suburban enclaves was at Gennevilliers, the commune located inside the meander of the Seine north from what is now La Défense. This provides a good insight into the general conditions within a North African colony; what Joanny Ray called, 'a unique field of observation'.[21] In 1936 the commune was inhabited by ` about three thousand Algerians and Moroccans, the latter making up two-thirds of the total or one-sixth of all the Moroccans in France. In a detailed survey carried out in 1935–6 Ray was able to collect data on 848 Moroccans and 415 Algerians who were concentrated in the lodging houses of a small number of streets. Eighty-two per cent of all Moroccans lived in just twenty-one roads, eighty-nine per cent of the Algerians in fourteen. There was a considerable degree of spatial segregation between the two groups, with entire streets housing Moroccans only, but with a mixed zone as in the Rue Arsène-Houssaye with 168 men (101 Moroccans, 67 Algerians), the Rue Brenu with 127 (79 and 48), and Rue de l'Arbre-Sec 125 (77 and 48).[22]

Within the commune the most notorious area was a straggling shantytown known as 'Les Grésillons'. This *bidonville* first grew from a small nucleus of Moroccan workers who at the end of the First World War inhabited a large, isolated building known as 'Tagouidert' (the small fort) situated in an area of market gardens.[23] By 1927, when a commission of the Paris Municipality inspected the slum, Les Grésillons had grown into a warren of huts, concrete sheds and squalid courtyards traversed by muddy lanes which turned to dust in the summer heat:

In an area hardly larger than a hectare were makeshift shacks built with the debris from old huts and bits and pieces of rubbish, the whole often covered with tarred paper, and we stopped at the threshold paved with rubbish, requiring a strong stomach to confront the foul emanations that could be glimpsed. And in these antechambers of every disease live, crowded as in a rabbit hutch, nearly a thousand men.[24]

During the next decade, Les Grésillons became the favoured object of journalists and social commentators who wished to investigate conditions among the Arabs.[25] In 1928 and 1929 two Catholic priests, Paul Catrice and Georges Buchet, visited the slum, rather in the manner of the 'explorers' who plunged into the infamous rookeries of Dickensian London. They visited a typical Algerian hotel-restaurant, the decrepit walls decorated with bright posters of 'Mustapha Kemal, Zagloul Pasha, The Wonderful Journey of a Marabout to Mecca'. The owner had constructed around a muddy courtyard a number of dormitory huts made of tarred cardboard or breeze-blocks. In one of these, in a space eight metres by five, were fourteen broken-down beds, almost touching and covered with dirty mattresses. With no space for storage the room was pell-mell with old suitcases, opened tin cans, broken cooking pots and, hanging from the wall, the personal possessions of the migrants in woven baskets and knotted handkerchiefs. During the winter a smoking stove made the air almost unbreathable and teams of lodgers replaced each other every eight hours. For this they were each charged 50 francs per month, the equivalent of two days wages.[26]

The concentration of North African workers in Gennevilliers gave rise to a range of specialist services and activities that were typical of most enclaves. In his survey Ray located six lodging keepers and wine-merchants, ten halal butchers, five grocers, two hoteliers, three restaurant owners, five shopkeepers, a hairdresser, a tailor, leather-workers and a cake-maker (*chef-faj*).[27] Most of these self-employed men ran their small business with the help of their European wives or partners.[28]

The daily life of the typical migrant was a grinding routine of exhausting physical labour, the walk from decrepit lodgings to work and back, the consumption of a frugal meal before the collapse into a bed which, in many cases, had just been vacated by a friend. In this routine there was little time or money for leisure: what free time was available, particularly on

Sundays or national holidays, was experienced as a period of
enforced idleness and boredom that simply delayed the day of
return home.[29] In a perceptive article in *Le Populaire* in 1938
Magdelaine Paz described the soulless existence of the migrant, who suffered a profound sense of homesickness and
desolation:

> The Frenchman, and even the foreigner, has a family. He
> has a home, books, sometimes a wireless. At the *boules* ground,
> the stadium, the billiard hall, the club, and the cinema he
> can experience a kind of respite, a fleeting freedom. The
> African cannot. The hours he has available he kills for time
> more than he lives them, dictating a letter for his family to
> a friend who plays the role of public writer, doing his shop-
> ping, going to the baths or showers ... But it's above all
> through sleep and dreaming that he finds his means of es-
> cape. He is so weary, so poor and so alone! What else can
> he do with his 'leisure' than lie on his bunk or squat with
> his back to the wall, nose to his knees, and dream of distant
> horizons, loved faces and familiar voices.[30]

Few North Africans went to the cinema or listened to the
wireless because of the cost and difficulty in understanding
French, although some listened to Berber and Arabic broad-
casts from Paris or Algeria.[31] On the other hand they had a
passion for all kinds of games (dominos, *ronda*, lotto) and for
Arab music which they either listened to on gramophones or
played themselves. Moroccan migrants often brought musical
instruments with them and at gatherings or religious festivals,
'they play together on the *ghaïta* and sing some of the popular
songs of their native *bled*; or else a comrade, a fine storyteller
or celebrated mime, recites some verses or pronounces age-
old tales accompanied on a tambourine of various kinds (*tebbel*,
bendir, *goual*)'.[32] The nationalist movement, the *Étoile-Nord-
Africaine*, aware of this cultural need tried to extend its influence among the immigrants in Paris by organising numerous
popular cabaret-concerts at which itinerant Arab groups would
play. On Sunday 27 October 1935, for example, 350 migrants
attended an ENA 'Arab fête' at 28 rue Cavé in the suburb of
Levallois-Perret where an orchestra of Algerian musicians (pi-
ano, mandolin, violin and flute) and two dancers performed.[33]
In Lyons the police banned a nationalist concert by the famous

Algerian tenor, Mahieddine, because some pieces, 'Alennif', 'Phaquo' and 'Hadj Hlimat union of the unemployed' contained, 'scenes which compared and contrasted in a particularly exaggerated way French and Arab civilisation'.[34]

Only about two per cent of the North African population in France was made up of women, by far the lowest ratio of females to males of any immigrant group in France.[35] The Algerian enclaves held literally thousands of single males for whom the appalling hardship and degradation of emigration was compounded by the denial of normal sexual relations. The psychiatrist and novelist Tahar Ben Jelloun analysed in the 1970s the profound psychological problems faced by the North African migrants, a desolate *misère affective et sexuelle*, but the same factors were already at work in the inter-war period.[36] A Parisian journalist described in the 1930s the pitiful, 'anguish of the sexual problems' of the North Africans and the recourse to segregated brothels, operating 'at reduced prices, specialising in a native clientele, with silent groups before the door, each waiting patiently his turn, and clutching in his pocket the coin that was saved with such difficulty'.[37] Homosexuality was also said to be widespread in the cramped lodging houses and, according to Ray, was regarded by migrants as 'almost normal'.[38]

The traumatic lives led by immigrants, their brutal confrontation with a harsh capitalist system, regulated by the clock and competitive individualism, and far removed from the supportive framework of Muslim village society, meant that Algerians suffered from high levels of disease, stress and mental illness. By 1926 there were 580 North Africans in mental hospitals and on occasions they tipped over into psychotic violence, as with the notorious murders in the Rue Fondary in 1923.[39] The classic diseases of poverty and isolation, tuberculosis and syphilis, were endemic and were transmitted back into the home village with tragic consequences.[40]

French commentators almost inevitably viewed North Africans from the 'outside', as mute, passive objects. Numerous descriptions catch them for a fleeting moment like people in a snap shot, viewed at a distance in the street, as small groups of unhealthy looking, shabby men on their way to work, killing time on a street corner, or momentarily glimpsed through the door of a hut. However, there was one crucial sphere of

Algerian life which helped counter isolation and hardship, and revealed sophisticated forms of self-organisation, the network of kin and villagers. Within the bounds of the enclave there existed a remarkable degree of social cohesion which found a base in the North African café, the epicentre of cultural and political networks.

'TRIBAL' GROUPINGS AND THE CAFÉ-REFUGE

Throughout the period from 1918 to 1954 French observers showed an intense fascination with 'tribal' settlement patterns and this led to a number of sociological inquiries of which the most important were carried out by Massignon (1930) and Robert Montagne (1952–4).[41] Massignon, using statistics provided by the SAINA police, was able to map the links between the main Kabyle tribes and their locations in the Paris region. The Beni Yenni, for example, were concentrated at Boulogne, Billancourt and Puteaux; the Aït Yahya at Saint-Denis and Boulogne; the Beni Djennard in the eighteenth and nineteenth arrondissements and at Clichy and Nanterre, and so on. Montagne's much more exhaustive, but uncompleted project of 1950–4, likewise mapped links between particular tribal groups in Algeria and their concentrated settlement patterns in France. The term 'tribe', which was used by all those writing on North African emigration during the colonial period, should be treated with a degree of caution. Certainly men who belonged to the same tribe could be found grouped closely together, but it was not the loose membership of the tribal confederation that determined migration strategies, organisation and spatial location but kin and village affiliations. In this respect Algeria migrant grouping and solidarity was not much different from that to be found historically among European peasants in their move to cities, as with Bretons, Savoyards and Limousin in nineteenth century Paris, or of Spanish, Italian, Belgian and Armenian workers in the twentieth.[42] The widespread use of the term 'tribe' and sociological projects which focused on tribal patterns was part of a wider colonial discourse employed to emphasise the atavistic, primitive and exotic features of Algerian migration.

As has been noted earlier, dense groupings of men from the

same family or village were built up and sustained through time, in spite of rapid turnover because of constant departures and arrivals from Algeria, by the process of chain-migration. Once a handful of pioneer emigrants from a particular village had established themselves in France they were almost inevitably followed by a rapidly expanding number of men who arrived in the same locale. An excellent study of this process, based on oral evidence, has been made by Mahfoud Bennoune for El Akbia, a village located seventy kilometres north-west of Constantine. The first 'pioneer' emigrant called Abdlraham, an ex-soldier who had been in France from 1938 to 1945, was recruited in 1946 to work in Mulhouse on railway reconstruction. On his first return to the village in 1948 he impressed with his stories of life in France. Many village men wanted to return with him, but he acted as guide to only two, one of them a cousin who paid for his own and Abdlraham's journey by mortgaging a field and an orchard. A few months later in 1949 three more men departed with Abdlraham's address in their pocket and, within the short space of four years, there were forty-three men in France from a total village population of 690 people. All were located in north-eastern France at Mulhouse and in the Thionville area.[43]

Where Kabyle migrants differed from many European minority groups in France was in the unusual strength of the ties which bound them together. The strong cement which held the Algerian *douar*-group together in France was not based on a utilitarian or individualistic rationality but on the traditional values of mutuality which bound together members of the same extended family and lineage descent. The primary obligation existed towards those members of the extended family group, the *ayla*, a unit that could consist of three to four generations or twenty to thirty or even fifty individuals. A number of *ayla* constituted a larger social unit, the *ferqua* or fraction, which might be better described as a 'patriclan', in which members shared a common (or mythical) ancestor and were linked by inter-marriage, religious festivals, and various forms of reciprocal obligations such as collective labour during harvesting (*twiza*) and house construction. At a higher level of organisation a number of fractions, each spatially rather equivalent to a hamlet, were grouped into the tribe which was defined administratively by the French as a *douar*.[44] The *douar* of the Beni Hendel, for example, with a total population in 1965 of 5644 people in an area of 10 124 hectares was subdivided into twelve fractions varying in size from the Magtaa (170 people) to the Ouled Belkhefa (320) and the Metidja (740).[45]

Obligations and inter-aid among migrants in France was structured as a series of widening circles: strongest towards blood relatives, next to men from the same fraction or hamlet, and then to the tribal group, the region and nation. Reciprocal aid was a duty, a moral and religious obligation which if broken carried severe penalties of ostracism by the collectivity.[46]

Montagne's exhaustive inquiry showed that the typical 'colony' or enclave grouping might consist of two to three hundred men who originated from one large village of up to two thousand inhabitants, or of around one hundred men or less from a more dispersed *douar* population scattered in hamlets.[47] Frequently an original colony would, with growing numbers, subdivide and spawn groupings in new locations, a practice which helped insure the *douar* against overdependence on a single employer or sector which might face recession. All the 1800 men from the Douar Souhalier, for example, were in just three locations, the 14th and 18th *arrondissements* in Paris, with an offshoot of 400 in Metz.

Village or kin grouping was crucial to the ability of the migrant to survive within a harsh and disorientating urban environment. The supportive functions were various. Firstly, as we have seen, it provided an important point of contact for new arrivals, access to accommodation and to employment. By sharing crowded accommodation Algerians were able to pay the lowest possible rent, while in a system known as the *popote* cooking was often shared and made cheaper by group purchasing of foodstuffs.[48] Individuals, confronted with difficulties like illness or unemployment, would be supported by the group. During the Great Depression for example thousands of unemployed men stayed on in France, sleeping on the floor of relatives, while they waited for the economy to pick up. It was quite common for migrants to save money in a collective pool or to establish a form of friendly society to pay for the return home of the body of fellow villagers who had died. For a largely illiterate or semi-literate body of men the group was also important for the transmission of news about family and village matters, the writing and sending of letters or small presents, and carrying savings home.

Another function of group *encadrement* was to control 'deviant' behaviour which could threaten the basic objective of emigration which was to maximise savings on behalf of the peasant household. In the Kabyle village an assembly of all the adult males, the *djemâa*, dispensed an extremely detailed customary law (*qanun*), which regulated both criminal, moral and social behaviour. This could include proper respect for elders, prohibitions on gambling and consumption of alcohol.[49] Some of the functions of the *djemâa* were reconstituted in France and the 'elders' imposed fines and moral sanctions on deviants, particularly on the younger men who strayed from their duty by excessive personal consumption, a form of laxity which was a life-and-death issue for those starving in Algeria.[50] In practice group censure probably did not need to come into play very often since most individuals internalised the values of the home community, values which were continually reinforced by periods of return. In addition the 'encysted' nature of Kabyle groups, segregated from the host society, helped reduce contact with the seductive dangers of the French *quartier populaire*.

The only men who through time escaped the limits of the network were those who were economically successful, mainly self-employed *commerçants*; the broken men who had fallen into alcoholism, permanent unemployment and a beggarly existence; and a minority who had settled down with a European partner and cut all ties to their family.[51] When group controls had failed to prevent abandonment of familial obligations fathers would sometimes travel to France to berate delinquents (*imjahen*) or petition the authorities to intervene. In February 1925, for example, a lawyer acting on behalf of the parents of Saïd ben Mohamed Maouël, requested the Ministry of the Interior to force his return since:

> he is married according to Muslim law at Port Gueydon . . . He has four children and, in his status as oldest son he is, in addition, according to our customs, bound to look after his aged father and mother. But the said Maouël, at present completely unbalanced, has fallen in love with a women of easy virtue called Jolivet, with whom he cohabits, and she extorts all the fruit of his labour to the point that he no longer sends any payment to his wife, his children or his father.[52]

Wherever enclaves of North African workers developed entrepreneurs began to establish small cafés, usually in conjunction with cheap lodgings, and these came to assume a great importance as centres of social activity, leisure, contact and political organisation. The inquiry of 1913 found that such *cafés maures* were already in existence in the Nord, in Paris and Marseilles. In Paris one such café for Kabyle workers was located at 128 Boulevard de Gare close to the sugar refinery of *Say* which employed 250 North Africans. This café was the centre for a newly formed friendly society through which Algerians made regular contributions to support those who became unemployed.[53] In Marseilles in 1913 there were some twenty cafés-restaurants which served Turkish coffee and couscous. In the Rue des Chapeliers there were seven cafés and at 21 Rue de Cassis one which was the centre for another friendly society, *La Solidarité Algérienne* which grouped together both Kabyle and Arab migrants.[54] During the First World War the number of cafés in the city of Paris increased to fifty-four, located mainly in the 13th, 15th, 18th, 19th and 20th arrondissements, and these were subject to increasing police surveillance to clamp down on gambling and alcoholism.[55] In Lyons there were 52 North African cafés by 1934, mostly in the central enclave of Part-Dieu.[56]

The cafés served a great range of functions within the Algerian migrant community, as they had traditionally in North Africa.[57] Firstly, and most evidently, they provided a warm and inviting refuge from the harsh conditions of factory and squalid lodgings. A journalist in 1931 described workers leaving the *Say* refinery in the 13th arrondissement:

> . . . as night falls – the moment the sugar refineries spew their shifts onto the street – the Rue Henry fills with a swarm of swarthy men who in an instant are sucked into the small bars which are lined up in double file; there under the sparse lights, the North Africans crowd between the smoke-stained walls and, while a gramaphone begins to squeak a native song, the dominos line up on the wooden tables, the cards fly between the fingers: the *ronda*, the *bazya* begin their devilish dance . . .[58]

Algerian workers from the same *douar*, perhaps several hundred men, often lived in a number of separate lodging houses and rooms in the same street or sector and congregated in the evening and morning in a café owned by a man from the same village.[59] The café proprietors, relatively well-off by migrant standards, were a highly influential élite. These were in most instances migrants who had been long installed in France, worked their way up in mines and factories as overseers and recruiters of labour, and who had saved enough to open small cantines and lodging houses. Most of them were fluent in French, westernised in their life-style, and frequently married to European women who helped them run the business.[60] These hard-headed entrepreneurs served as the key fixers for their clienteles, as job-brokers, providers of information on unemployment benefits, money lenders, and negotiators with employers and police.

The central role of the café in the social life of the North African migrants was particularly apparent in the growth and organisation of the nationalist movement, the *Étoile-Nord-Africaine* (ENA). During the period from 1922 to 1926 the French Communist Party, under directions from the Comintern, was highly active in a drive to recruit and organise 'colonial' workers from North Africa and Indo-China. This initiative led to the founding of the ENA in June 1926, under the leadership of Messali Hadj and Hadj Ali Abdelkader, with the fundamental aim of, 'the total independence of each of the three countries: Tunisia, Algeria and Morocco, and the union of Northern Africa'.[61] Messali Hadj and his lieutenants, as migrant workers, had an intimate knowledge of the hundreds of tiny North African bars and their central role in the life of the migrants. The ENA penetrated this milieu by spreading propaganda, collecting funds and holding numerous meetings in the cafés in the enclave zones. Some cafés were owned by leading militants, like the Kabyle Youseef Kodja Ali, who had a restaurant at 66 Rue Gide in the suburb of Levallois. A 1934 police report noted: 'This Algerian enjoys among his clientele, which is uniquely North-African, a certain influence'. His café was a rendezvous for the ENA leadership. Another important centre of ENA activity was the café-restaurant, the *Hoggar*, owned by Si Ahmed Belghoul.[62] The ability of the ENA to organise in the cafés depended however on the support of their owners, many of whom had a conservative, petit-bourgeois mentality. This led Messali Hadj to organise a number of meetings in

1926 and 1933–4 to try and win over the proprietors, but not
with much success.[63] During the Popular Front in 1936 the
battle for control of the cafés hotted up when the radical ENA
leader Radjef Belkacem organised a campaign of intimidation
against uncooperative owners and even entered into direct
competition with them when he opened his own restaurant
at 14 Rue St Cloud in Boulogne-Billancourt as a centre of
nationalist activity.[64]

A last point to consider is the extent to which migrants, who
in Algeria would have had little contact with people from
outside their own tribe and locale, were able or willing to
intermix with men from other regions and even to forge a new
national consciousness as Algerians. There is some evidence
that the *douar* groupings were quite resistant to establishing
close links with men from other regions. One crucial reason
for this was economic: men from one village frequently
'colonised' a particular company or occupied a specialised
niche. Migrants from the *douars* of Idjeur and Akfadou in the
Haut-Sébaou Commune held a virtual monopoly in the Saint-
Louis refinery and docks of Marseilles; all one hundred of the
men in the *Francolor* factory at Villers-St-Paul in the Oise came
from the village of Amzeguère; the villagers of Aït M'Hammed
Saïd in the *douar* of M'Kira specialised in the cleaning of the
hulls of ships at Le Havre; the *douars* of Beni Flick, Oumalou
and Azazga held a monopoly of the car-washing jobs in the big
garages of Paris.[65] The retention of such monopolies involved
a degree of protectionism. After 1930 as emigration spread
into new zones of Algeria, like the Arab regions of the High
Plains near Sétif, the new arrivals found entry to these sectors
blocked by Kabyles, especially in the Paris region, and they
were forced either into the most low-paid work (navvies in
public works, sweepers . . .) or to colonise new sectors geographically further afield in Lorraine and elsewhere.[66]
Montagne reported that each work-place 'colony' showed
hostility towards other 'foreigners', meaning other Algerians,
and that 'the inner life of our companies is often, unbeknown
to the employers, secretly agitated by bitter struggle and ri-
valry'. Such oppositions could even reproduce the traditional
rivalries (*çoffs*) that divided village societies into warring factions. In Marseilles migrants from the *douar* of Akfadou lived
in two camps, those from the *çoff* of El Djar Alemasse were

grouped at 159 Rue Bernard du Bois, while the opposing *çoff* of Imesdouar was at 15 Boulevard Denis Papin.[67]

In time local particularisms were eroded as Algerians inevitably began to mix in cafés and elsewhere. The ENA, which was inspired by socialist concepts of proletarian solidarity, aimed to forge a new Algerian and even Maghrebian national identity and campaigned to eliminate regionalist patriotism. As its newspaper *El Ouma* noted in January 1935, 'Today . . . for us – whether in Algeria, in Tunisia or Morocco – there are neither Arabs, nor Kabyles, nor Mozabites: there is only one race: the Arab-Berber race'.[68] In practice the more politicised and educated militants of the ENA may have been able to overcome narrow localism, but they numbered only about four thousand men or less than three per cent of the North African immigrants. Frictions, particularly between Kabyle/Berbers and Arabs, continued to dog the nationalist movement down to the Algerian War and beyond.[69] However, Algerians would combine together when confronted with Moroccans. Joanny Ray in his study of Gennevilliers was able to show a high level of segregation between the Algerian and Moroccan zones of settlement: for example in ten streets lived 315 Moroccans but only nine Algerians.[70] In 1929 the priests Catrice and Buchet were guided by an Algerian through his zone of the Grésillons slum. When they arrived at 'the entrance to the Moroccan quarter . . . he absolutely refused to go any further, repeating as excuse these simple words: "here, Moroccans, me, Algerian"'.[71]

The social life of the Algerian migrants, the organisation in cohesive kin/*douar* groups that were spatially concentrated in North African lodgings located within micro-ghettos or enclaves, meant that they were significantly segregated from the surrounding French society. Although they frequently lived and moved among other poor workers, Italians, Portuguese, Russians, Spaniards and French, there was a very restricted level of contact. As will be shown in Chapter 7, the high level of antipathy and racism that existed among these other ethnic groups further drove Algerians back onto their own resources. As Sayad notes immigrants responded to French hostility by opting for 'auto-segregation' and quotes an Algerian informant. 'Racism, that has always existed, but it does not exist when we are together. Stay in your room, among your brothers, all the same as you, then you have nothing to fear; nobody knows

you, you know nobody.'[72] Although not institutionally complete until after the mass arrival of Algerian families in the
1950s, the enclave already provided a range of specialist services, from North African cafés to butchers, grocers, tailors
and hairdressers which enabled migrants to restrict daily contact to a circle of other Arab or Berber speakers. The next
chapter will examine further the degree of Algerian integration through two key aspects of identity, changing Islamic
practice and the relationship to the home society.

6 Islam and the Village

When French journalists and commentators peered from a distance at the shadowy world of the North African immigrant one of the questions which was uppermost in their minds was the extent to which they were assimilating to 'French civilisation'. This chapter looks at two key elements in the definition of Algerian identity and culture, first Islamic practice and then the relationship to the values of the home society, to assess the extent to which they were undergoing change during the period down to 1950.

MIGRATION AND CHANGES IN ISLAM

Muslim religious faith, custom and practice was the bedrock of Algerian identity, the fundamental cement in a society that still had a weakly developed sense of nationality. The key defining concept was that of the Muslim *umma*, the global community of all the faithful. Islam cannot be understood in this sense as a body of doctrine and religious observances, but as a total way of life, an integral part of all social, economic and cultural activity. As Guy Pervillé notes, even those Algerians who were entirely ignorant of Islam or even atheists were still 'Muslims' by birth and Islam, 'in giving shape to society in its totality, was dissolved and absorbed into it'.[1] It was adherence to Islam as a set of beliefs and practices that above all else enabled migrants to retain a sense of religio-ethnic difference that blocked assimilation into French society. It is not possible to assess the extent to which this Islamic culture and practice underwent change in France without some understanding of the traditional forms of religion in Algeria before emigration got under way.

During the nineteenth century the French had tried to repress and control Islamic practice, which they regarded as the crucial source of power and legitimation of the great tribal chiefs who entered into rebellion (Abdel Kader, El Mokrani), as well as the key to Algerian cultural resistance. The extensive *habous* lands which were endowed to fund religious institutions were appropriated by the state, hundreds of Koranic schools were closed, and 'official' religious leaders (*muftis, imams*) were appointed and funded by the government. However, the French were never able to gain effective control over Islamic practice which nearly all Algerians clung to with extreme tenacity as an expression of individual and collective identity which the European conquerors were unable to penetrate or dismantle.[2] A conclusive indicator of this allegiance to 'Islamic patriotism' was the tiny number of Algerians who agreed to take up French citizenship, in spite of its many advantages, since this was a step which involved renunciation of the *statut personnel* or legal status as a Muslim.[3]

In the rural areas of Algeria, the prime zone of emigration, religious life was controlled by a powerful caste of holy men, the *marabouts*, who claimed descent from a local saint or from the Prophet. Endowed with sacred powers (*baraka*) they retained a huge influence over the illiterate peasantry through their quasi-magical powers to cure illness, caste spells, or threaten revenge (rendering wives infertile, harming crops . . .). The *marabouts* often lived in or were attached to the *zaouia*, which were centres of religious activity, of teaching and of the great confraternities like the Qadiriya, Rahmaniya and Tiganiya which linked up in networks right across North Africa.[4] The Islamic faith of the rural population, in some ways similar to the Catholic practices of pre-Reformation Europe, could not be defined by a credo but more readily as a set of practices, rituals, festivals and semi-magical arts which were grounded in the concrete reality of village life, the harvest cycle, shrines, pilgrimages and recourse to the remedies of the *marabouts*.[5] This fixity of the religious in a specific locale, in particular holy tombs, village festivals, and landscapes, made it very difficult for emigrants to tranpose and restructure their Islamic practices in an alien, urban environment. But, despite all the obstacles, there is evidence to show that Algerians in France did retain the core of Muslim identity.[6]

The first migrants to France were particularly keen to try and observe the basic dietary regulations, the daily prayers and the fasts of Ramadan, in spite of their exile in the *dar-el-harb*, the land of the infidel. In 1917 a Tunisian conscripted worker, Mohammed Baccouch, wrote home:

Today I drank wine and ate pork. I intend to eat during the month of Ramadan, for we take our meals with Christians, and what's more the kitchen utensils which we use are soiled with pork and all that comes from it, grease, lard etc. I really don't know what to do, short of dying of hunger and thirst.[7]

Where large numbers of Algerians were gathered together in factories, mines, regiments or para-military work brigades the authorities were often willing to make some provision for religious needs. At the mines of *Courrières* before the First World War the Kabyle miners, who scrupulously observed their religious duties, persuaded the management to provide a Muslim burial ground, to delay evening meal-times to fit in with Ramadan, and to obtain a supply of halal meat from an abattoir.[8] Another mine in St Etienne provided a large room, 'arranged as a small mosque with carpet, mats, and *mirhab*. A central fountain allowed for ritual ablutions'.[9]

During the First World War officers noted with surprise that Koranic duties were more closely followed than in Algeria. Gilbert Meynier has shown in detail how one reaction to colonial domination in Algeria was a reinforcement of conservative religious practice so that by the turn of the century it was more strict and rigid than it had been fifty years earlier.[10] For the first migrants to France, where exposure to western society was far more intense even than in French Algiers, turning towards faith was a crucial psychological defence, a mean of preserving a sense of identity and personal cohesion.

The French authorities took steps during the First World War and after to make provision for religious practice. The army ensured that North African regiments were provided with correctly prepared food and prayer rooms in barracks and hospitals. The visit of *imams* was arranged and a wooden mosque was built at Nogent sur Marne.[11] Algerian soldiers showed little enthusiasm for such official provision because they recognised in it colonialist forms of paternalism and control. The army aimed, in part, to keep intact North African religious-cultural practices so that soldiers and workers would not be subverted by 'dangerous' western influences and reintegrate successfully on their return into traditional society. The government was also sensitive to the importance of pro-Islamic policy or propaganda to French imperial interests. During the First World War, Germany attempted to incite anti-colonial revolts in North Africa and military desertion in France by presenting itself as a defender of Islam and Ottoman Turkey.

After 1918 the French authorities continued to buttress religious practice as a means of social control over migrant workers. It was feared that weakening of Islam was leading to alcoholism, moral laxity, crime and corruption in an urban milieu.[12] French attitudes towards Islam were highly ambiguous. Commentators who were opposed to permanent Algerian settlement in France tended to present a highly negative image of Islam as 'fanatical', 'obscurantist' and incompatible with European civilisation. The same writers could defend the protection of Muslim religious practice within the logic of temporary migration, as a means to preserving 'native traditions'. Prestigious and lavish projects like the Paris Mosque, opened by the French President in July 1926, were also essentially an exercise in imperial propaganda. Pierre Godin, who initiated the project for a Muslim Hospital and cemetery in Bobigny, noted the important role they would play in presenting France, 'a great colonial power and a great Muslim power', as a champion of Islam.[13]

The Paris Mosque and the Muslim Hospital both came under fierce attack from the French Communist Party and the nationalist ENA, as an instrument of colonial propaganda.[14] The Communist journal *Al Alam Al Ahmar* linked the founding of the Mosque to French support for the 'marabouts and corrupt clergy', who kept the Algerian peasantry chained in ignorance, and reinforced imperialist 'sophistries' such as 'the motherland', 'France, muslim nation', 'France, protector of Islam' and other nonsense.[15] The avoidance of the Paris Mosque and other forms of 'official' religious provision was not a sign of declining religious faith but of political opposition to all manifestations of colonialism. For most immigrants religious practice was confined within the private spaces of the enclave, within lodgings and North African cafés. While some French commentators emphasised the extent to which migrants abandonned their religion,[16] there is evidence of a profound and resilient attachment. For example, under the conditions of industrial capitalism (assembly line work, fixed shifts) it was extremely difficult to say the five daily prayers or to fast for the twenty-nine days of Ramadan. However, most North Africans observed Ramadan, in spite of their exhausting physical labour, while Joanny Ray, visiting Moroccan lodgings, remarked that the workers were frequently to be seen, 'installed in their room on a mat, their slippers before them, facing towards Mecca (*Qibla*), dressed in a simple *haïk,* prostrating themselves, rising, and kneeling in the successive positions of the evening prayer (*maghreb* or, a little later, *icha*).[17]

While migrants did begin to break the taboo on consumption of alcohol, just as the urbanised proletariat was in the major Algerian cities, the level of alcoholism was much lower than suggested by French observers who wanted to exaggerate the moral dissolution and criminality of Algerians.[18] Many of the North African cafés were specifically geared for a clientèle which was more inclined to drink tea and coffee than wine. The cafés were also the location for most forms of collective worship or festivals. Migrants were occasionally visited by *marabouts* who travelled throughout France from one village group to another collecting religious dues (*ziara*).[19] One *mufti,* Bel Hadj Ben Maafi, from near Biskra, settled in Lyons in about 1927 as an official representative of the *zavuia* of Tolga, which belonged to the confraternity of the *Rahmaniya,* and of the *marabout* Hadj Ben Ali Ben Osman. He later acted as secretary to Azario, a police officer who was in charge of the surveillance of North Africans. His request to open a prayer room in 1933, although supported by the Mayor of Lyons and the Prefect of the Rhône, was turned down by the Minister of the Interior since:

> these pretended *mokkadems* seek, under the cover of religious proselytism, purely temporal advantages, notably gifts of money extorted from their Muslim coreligionists.[20]

The *douar*-groupings in France often established branches of the religious confraternities to which they were attached in their home village. The men from the Haut Sébaou affiliated to the *Rahmaniya,* those from Guelma to the *Ammariya,* from Mostaganem to the *Allawiya* and so on.[21] Emile Dermenghem, a specialist in Algerian popular culture, visited North African enclaves in Paris, and noted the activities of the various confraternities. 'Every week several workers from Citroën or the gas works gather to recite litanies, to sing the mystical verses of Ibn al Fâridh or of Hallaj and to abandon themselves to ecstatic dances.'[22]

Where the strong attachment to Islam showed itself in a fundamental way, even among those migrants who normally showed little concern for religion, was through the anxiety that they might die and be buried, without proper ritual, in the infidel soil of *dar-al-harb*.[23] This was a very real danger since during peacetime some ten per cent of immigrants died in France, mainly from tuberculosis and industrial accidents. During the First World War a circular from the Ministry of War (November 1914) noted the extreme concern among North African soldiers about proper arrangements for the dead and dying. Instructions were given that if a soldier was dying fellow Muslims should be called on to recite the *Chahada*, and the body must be buried in a shroud, never in a coffin, and facing Mecca.[24] However, workers would go to enormous lengths to ensure the return of a corpse to Algeria and the large sums of money required were usually raised through investment in friendly societies or collections among fellow villagers.[25] Where this was not possible, probably for the great majority, their countrymen would try and ensure that a proper ritual burial was obtained.[26] This was not very easy since the authorities dragged their heels on making land available and Paris did not open a Muslim cemetery until June 1936.[27] During the preceding years most immigrants had ended up in the pauper's grave (*fosse commune*) of a French cemetery. The graves of 101 colonial workers buried during the First World War in the cemetery of St Fons in Lyons were simply removed by administrative order in 1928 and, as Philippe Videlier comments, 'They have been expunged from the sites of remembrance.'[28]

Islamic faith and practice among migrants was not however a static traditionalism but subject to dynamic processes of change, as it was also in Algeria. During the inter-war years two key movements found a deep response among the migrants in France, the reformist *Oulémas* and the ENA-PPA.[29] The Association of the *Oulémas* founded in 1931 under the leadership of Ben Badis was opposed to *maraboutisme* and aimed to regenerate Islam by purifying it of all 'superstitions and false beliefs' and returning to Koranic sources. The Association attracted young modernisers and became suspect to the French as a subversive and proto-nationalist movement. By emphasising the pre-colonial history of Islamic Algeria and the restoration of Muslim dignity and Arab culture, the Association emphasised an Arab-Muslim identity that was fundamentally unassimilable to French 'civilisation'. In a famous declaration of April 1936 the *Oulémas* stated, 'This Muslim Algerian nation is not part of France ... it is a nation totally separated from France by its language, its customs, its ethnic origins, and its religion. It does not wish to be assimilated. It has a fatherland of its own ...'[30] During 1936–7 the *Oulémas* extended its organisation into the French émigré community through the establishment of 'Educational Circles' (*Nadi*) in the Paris suburbs (Saint-Denis, Gennevilliers, Clichy) and Lyons. At the height of its influence in 1937 some 1500 migrants attended classes in Arabic language and culture.[31]

Although the ENA-PPA entered into a struggle with the *Oulémas* for control of the migrant community, a battle which it won, it too was a fundamentally Islamic movement. Messali Hadj, who was raised in a highly religious family and educated in the confraternity of the *Derkaouas*, asserted the centrality of Islamic faith, culture and identity to the political movement for independence from French colonialism. After 1935 his style of leadership became one increasingly founded on that of the charismatic preacher and his discourse was suffused with appeals to the sacred nature of violence (*jihad*) and the spiritual and moral superiority of Muslims over the French.[32]

The nationalist movement in France owed its success to its ability to recognise and build upon the historic continuity and force of Islamic culture and identity among the Algerian peasant migrants. The *Oulémas* and the ENA certainly raised this often inchoate Algerian-religious identity to a new level of consciousness, but they could not have succeeded in their propaganda without the prior existence of this defining faith.[33] This was one crucial reason why the Communist Party with its secularist ideology was, despite considerable organisational effort among the North African immigrants, unable to gain any significant foothold among the Algerians in France. For the migrant workers faced with the psychologically traumatic and disorientating impact of French industrial capitalism and urban life religion became an anchor, a means of resisting depersonalisation, as it had for a century in colonial Algeria. This in turn acted as a barrier against those intermediary bodies, the PCF and trade unions, which were so important in the assimilation of European immigrants into French society.

IDENTITY AND THE VILLAGE

The regular circulation of migrants between the Algerian village and French mine or factory ensured that they retained a permanent footing in the home society and culture. The majority of migrants regarded themselves as first and foremost members of Algerian society who were only temporarily resident in France. Before the age of relatively cheap air travel, which only began after the Second World War, Algerians were unusual among 'Third World' migrants into Europe in their geographical proximity to France which allowed a *noria*, a regularity of contact, that was impossible for Asians, West Indians and other groups from distant colonies. The length of stay of migrants in France varied greatly, but a period of eighteen months to two or three years was quite normal, followed by a return to the village for three or six months of repose.[34]

What is unusual about this pattern of single-male rotation was the extent to which it remained largely intact for half a century, without making the 'normal' transition to permanent settlement. One reason for this was that acquisition of external monetary resources was harnessed initially to support and reinforce the **traditional** socio-economic order which was in crisis and may have otherwise collapsed. As Abdelmalek Sayad remarks, the first 'age' of emigration gave peasant society , 'the means to perpetuate itself as such'.[35] A number of studies of sub-Saharan Africa have shown similar links between emigration and the maintenance of tradition.[36] Also at work, as we have seen, was the extraordinary cohesion of family and kin structures which facilitated rotation. The failure of the Algerians to be assimilated readily into French society arose not from false perceptions of eventual reintegration or a 'myth of return', but from a very real temporary status. It is noticeable that after 1926 the ENA-PPA opposed family emigration, reunification being at cross-purposes with national independence and an eventual return from exile, and campaigned instead for greater ease of rotation, an end to controls on freedom of movement between Algeria and France, and for annual holidays of two and a half months to enable workers time to return to visit their families.[37]

However, in spite of the survival of rotation as the dominant mode of migration down to the 1950s, it did slowly and inexorably transform village life. The remaining part of this chapter will examine these processes, which eventually opened the way to definitive emigration. Firstly, the flow of relatively large quantities of remittance money into a subsistence economy in which there had been few opportunities for earning cash, and in which coins were at a premium, undermined the peasant economy. Remittance money sent home by post increased from 10 million francs in 1914 to 17 million in 1916, 38 million in 1918, 100 million in 1929 and 120 million in 1938.[38] By 1957 transfers came to equal a third of the total Algerian budget or a quarter of all earnings.[39]

Within Kabyle society this led to widening social and economic disparities which upset the relative equilibrium between families and their power and access to land. Those families which had the good fortune to engage in the very early phase of migration to France were in a highly advantageous position. With access to unprecedented quantities of money they could realise their ambition to buy land from other villagers or even from *colons* at low prices.[40] But in time as more and more men left for France and remittance levels increased land prices underwent rapid inflation.[41] Those men, generally from the poorest families, who migrated in a later phase were highly disadvantaged. Frequently they had to mortgage lands or borrow money at usurious rates from richer families, often those who had been among the pioneer migrants, to pay for the journey to France. Later migrants found the best jobs in France already monopolised by 'clans' or faced the prospect of unemployment during the 1930s Depression and the crippling burden of debt incurred to pay for their passage.

The process of saving money from mediocre wages became even more difficult and drawn out and even when targets were achieved men returned to their village to find that prices had in the meantime further escalated and eroded their ability to invest. Joanny Ray provided a detailed analysis of identical processes at work in Moroccan villages of emigration in the 1930s:

Slowly, step by step, a monetary economy penetrates the whole village . . . all prices climb equally high. *This is a major cause of emigration for the smallest producers,* for those who could not make themselves part of the clientele of emigrant families, dispensers of money . . . This produces a *monopolisation of the richest soils* by several émigré families, the first to return from France.[42]

Migrants, whose initial aim on departing from the village was to make a once-off journey to France, were almost inevitably drawn into a further round of departures. Typical was the letter of a Kabyle worker who in 1926 returned home to find, 'Here the cost of living is as high as in France. All my savings are exhausted and I have only bought necessities for my family. I shall be forced, to pay for my return expenses, to turn to the usurers who lend at a rate of 40 or 50 per cent.'[43] As each individual was drawn into a cycle of repeated migrations the period of stay in France gradually became longer, often culminating in settlement. The ENA militant Ahmed Chelbi, for example, from the *douar* Beni Aïssa near Fort National, first worked for *Berliet* in Lyons for one year from October 1924 to October 1925. After a return home for a year and a half he then departed for two further periods with *Berliet,* each time spending longer in France (2 years 3 months, 3 years), while the intervening home leaves became shorter.[44]

In time the economic survival of villages and entire regions in Kabylia became crucially dependent on a deepening cycle of emigration, a fact that was brought brutally home when all mobility and remittances stopped during the Second World War (1942–5). From the 1930s onwards French administrators began to note the progressive abandonment of agriculture and craft production like weaving. Rémond, the administrator of Fort-National, remarked: 'And here even the lower slopes are left uncultivated . . . Everywhere the land returns to its original condition.'[45] In 1937 in the *commune mixte* of Soummam, which had a total population of 125 000 people 20 000 men, all those of working age were in France. Since farming was left to women, children and the aged agricultural production had fallen dramatically. The *douar* of Beni-Curlis was no longer self-sufficient in grain as it had been twenty years earlier, artisan production had stopped, and absent men no longer bothered to return home for the olive harvest.[46]

These economic changes were accompanied by a gradual transformation in material culture and political values. One interesting indicator of change between the traditional village environment and France for which there is good written and photographic evidence relates to dress codes. Even before emigration to France began in about 1905 some Algerians were adapting to European dress. In 1891 F. Gourgeot described the daily increase in natives who wore French trousers, shirts and jackets, while remaining loyal to the fez, 'to show that the individual, while changing his clothes, means to remain a Muslim'.[47] He was undoubtedly referring here mainly to the small class of urban, westernised and educated professionals. But in the rural areas, the main zone of emigration, the great majority of peasants remained faithful to the traditional costume, a long ankle-length smock or *djellaba*, baggy 'sheep-tail' Arab trousers (*seroual*), and in winter a thick woollen cape or *burnous*, and a simple turban (*rezza*) or fez.[48] Only those who were in desperate poverty would wear cast-off European clothes and old military jackets. However, the first labour migrants adapted very quickly to European dress. The Depont Commission in early 1914 reported that Kabyles working at the mines of *Courrières* were wearing French neck-scarfs while over half of them had exchanged the fez, the last remaining symbol of Muslim identity to be abandoned, for the workman's cap. On Sundays some Kabyles, with a flare for style were, 'smartly dressed in matching jacket and trousers, sported a new fez or else a bowler hat and could not easily be told apart from the local inhabitants'. This Europeanisation of dress was even further advanced in the Paris region.[49] By 1950 the wearing of the fez had almost entirely disappeared.[50]

Since dress codes can be important signifiers of class and ethnic identity, did the Algerian abandonment of traditional dress represent a form of integration into the French working class? While some migrants, especially the youth, may have wished to blend in with French society and conceal their inferior status as 'Arabs', especially in the dancing halls, cafés and cinemas where they might meet French women, for the majority the change into overalls (*les bleues*) was a practical necessity. Those men who were recruited as 'colonial workers' during the First World War were issued, on arrival in Marseilles, with European trousers, shirt and cap and the same practice continued during the inter-war period when standard work contracts specified the issue of an overcoat, pullover, beret, boots and set of work-clothes.[51] For men who were engaged in extremely heavy physical labour, often in cold outdoor conditions, and requiring a frequent replacement of worn-out items, French clothing was the practical option.[52] North Africans in France sometimes reserved traditional dress for periods of leisure or for religious festivals, prayer and attendance at mosques. But in general migrants remained in European dress from the moment of departure until their return and, 'were little different from the factory crowds'.[53] When Messali Hadj, the nationalist leader, changed from European to Arab dress and a full beard in 1936 this was highly untypical of migrant workers, part of a calculated move towards the visible assertion of a more Islamic politics.[54]

Some French and colonial commentators, like Augustin Berque, thought the change in dress was superficial: 'The fact that the fez is replaced by a cap evidently does not suffice to transform their character and values.'[55] However, in rural society this was no small matter and the decision by departing migrants to conceal European clothing which was only put on away from the village was a sign of respect for the integrity of the traditional order. Conversely, until about 1936–7 it was a custom among returning migrants arriving by ship in Algiers harbour to throw French berets into the sea as a symbol of reintegration and then to replace their traditional Arab clothing before arrival back in the village. But by about 1939 the ritual was losing its meaning and berets and other forms of European dress were widely worn in Kabyle villages. As Rémond, administrator of Fort-National during the 1930s, reported of a return by ship:

> I waited expecting at any moment to see all these Africans throw overboard, as they used to do, with shouting, jeers and laughter, bottles, berets or hats, one of the symbolic gestures of rupture with European habits. But in vain: several worthless and worn objects, newspapers, a broken suitcase, a filthy headress were thrown into the sea, as if to cling on to a ritual ... Not so long ago no native dare disembark in European dress; one would have given a rough reception to anybody who returned to his village without the traditional fez.[56]

By the 1940s the wheel had turned full circle and returning migrants were proud to display their European suits, shirts and ties.

French commentators were fascinated by the increasing dependence on European goods within the Algerian village. The development of 'new needs' was interpreted as a sign of progress and assimilation to French 'civilisation'. Kabyles were beginning to buy European cooking pots, beds, Wellington boots, cottons in a 'false oriental style', food products like tea, coffee and sugar, and even bicycles and gramophones.[57] However, the most evident sign of this process and a symbol of the new status acquired through emigration, was the construction of two-storey houses in a European style which broke completely with the traditional form of the two-room stone cottage. Rémond noted in Fort-National as early as 1933, 'In the last twelve years European-style houses, with terraces, balustrades and balconics, have been springing up everywhere.'[58] This change in built forms marked a profound shift away from the enclosed and windowless space of the Islamic house and from the extended, patriarchal household towards individualism and a nuclear family unit.[59]

However, the most profound change of all, and the one which carried immense implications for the eventual destruction of colonialism, came from the shift in power and authority from the older generation of males, the traditional heads of family and of village assemblies, towards the younger generation of migrants. Pierre Bourdieu and Abdelmalek Sayad, in their classic anthropological study, *Le déracinement*, showed how wage-labour led to the demoralisation and despair of the traditional peasant farmer, the *bu-niya*, whose key values were those of stoicism and sobriety in the face of remorseless hard labour, and conservative dedication to the land which was received from the ancestors in trust. However, as migrants began to bring unprecedented sums of money into the Kabyle village they began to find a new status, while it was the ageing peasants bound to traditional forms of agriculture who lost in prestige. They were regarded as unenterprising *afenyan*, doomed to a desperately poor existence.[60] Departure from the village for France was no longer regarded as something shameful, to be carried out with stealth at night, but as a source of pride. It was through emigration that young males now demonstrated their courage, physical endurance, self-sacrifice and initiative rather than through the qualities of the *fellah*.[61] Young women began to show a marked preference for migrants as husbands.

At the level of the family the enormous power of the patriarch was eroded by the earning capacity of sons. Abdelmalek Sayad, during what he denotes as the 'second age' or phase of emigration, notes how migrants affected by wage-labour and a spirit of calculation became more individualistic. Resentful of the control exherted by the collective over their savings they broke away from the original purpose of emigration which was to assist the extended family, began to demand a greater control over investment of remittances, or in some cases ceased to send any money home at all. Aged patriarchs were no longer the source of all authority, to whom working sons were bound to defer in matters of group expenditure, but were reduced to the level of poor dependents, 'who "eat up" the labour of their children'.[62] Eventually in villages of emigration, where the majority of adult males may have been in France at some stage, the solidarities of the traditional extended family were undermined and younger married couples began to split away into separate households and even to divide up the land.[63]

The weakening of the authority of the traditional head of the household had wider implications for hierarchy and political power within the village. Returning or ex-migrants found a new prestige within the *djemâa*, the assembly of all the adult males, which made all major decisions concerning the community. The younger men had personal experience of French society and the modern world and access to forms of knowledge now regarded as superior to tradition which had valued continuity with the past and loyalty to the ways of the ancestors. The younger men knew how to influence local French administrators:

> Speaking French, natural intermediaries between his tribal brothers and the French authorities, reading newspapers, often having acquired a taste for politics and now understanding 'what it's all about', the how and why of things, they readily participate in the administrative *djemâa*, intervene with authority in the clandestine *djemâa* of the Berber regions and, in this role, clash with the 'elders' who are members.[64]

The impact of returning migrants was, in the longer term, to be particularly important for the diffusion of radical political and reformist Islamic ideas. The younger men, won over by the *Oulémas*, began to oppose the conservative *maraboutes*, an obscurantist élite which was seen now as an instrument of French colonialism intent on exploiting the peasantry through superstition.[65]

Within two years of its foundation in Paris in 1926, the nationalist *Étoile-Nord-Africaine* was beginning to spread its influence into the villages of Kabylia. By 1934 ENA groups were established in Tizi-Ouzou, Fort-National, Tlemcen, Sétif, Mostaganem and other zones of emigration.[66] Evidence of the early spread of the independence movement into rural Algeria is particularly clear for the Commune of Fort-National. Out of the leading seventy ENA militants identified by Benjamin Stora for the period 1933–6, no less than sixteen came from Fort-National, with a particularly strong presence in the Douar Oumalou (7 men) and Douar Oussameur (4 men).[67] These militants travelled to and fro between France and Algeria in increasing numbers after 1934, and eventually established the ENA headquarters in Algiers and in 1937–9 prioritised political work in Algeria over the metropole.[68] In early September 1934 police reports noted that a leading ENA militant, the taxi-driver Rabah Moussaoui, who was born in the Douar Oumalou in September 1904, had returned to his village where he was engaged in propaganda work and founded the ENA section of Fort-National.[69] Moussaoui wrote for the ENA journal *El Ouma*, which according to police sources was being distributed in 1934 in, 'the most isolated *douars*'.[70]

It was precisely the fear of the French authorities that migrants, through contact with working-class organisations, would transmit the germ of Communism, trade-unionism and nationalism into Algeria and subvert the colonial order. One response to this, the subject of Chapters 8 and 9, was to try and terminate or severely restrict emigration, a policy change that was justified through the racialisation of Algerians as a moral and criminal danger to French society. Before addressing this issue, however, the next chapter examines the response of the French working class to the Algerian presence.

7 Working-class Racism

The concepts of 'race' and 'racism' present notoriously thorny and controversial problems of definition. I concur with those who interpret 'race' as a social construct. Racial categories cannot be explained through a 'scientific' system of classification based on biological/genetic methods but are ideological constructs, forms of boundary definition between groups, that have evolved within specific historical and social contexts. ' "Races" are socially imagined rather than biological realities', notes Miles.[1] The dynamic process by which boundaries are delineated ('racialisation') allocates persons to particular groups by reference not only to supposed biological difference (usually phenotypical) but also cultural characteristics and other symbolic markers. 'Race' is chameleon-like, continually being reworked, and Stuart Hall has recommended an investigation of the 'different ways in which racist ideologies have been constructed and made operative under different historical conditions'.[2]

Sociologists and social psychologists in their investigations of racism have an advantage over the historian through their access to the living context (via direct observation, interviews etc.), but face a problem in that contemporary actors are born and socialised within a society in which racism is already constituted and reproduced (in language, laws, attitudes etc.). A key to an understanding of how and why particular groups have been targeted and racialised is to follow through the historical sequence of events, the 'phylogenesis of race'. The early arrival of Algerians within French metropolitan society, the first significant 'Third World' presence in modern times, provides a good opportunity for a case study approach to the genesis of racism.

The argument in the next three chapters is that the working class did show some initial hostility towards 'Arabs' but that racial prejudice was quite low-key and diffuse. It never became an issue of sufficient importance at grass-roots level to impact on local or national politics. A far more important role in the articulation of a racist discourse and anti-Algerian politics was played by decision-making élites. In this our findings concur with the argument of Teun van Dijk that élites are most responsible for the reproduction of racism. Élites have preferential access to and control over public discourse and persuasively pre-formulate the dominant consensus on ethnic affairs, in a top-down way. This is not to argue that there is no popular racism *sui generis*, but élites not only dominate the agenda (through access to power, the media etc.) but the *consequences* of their racism is more serious for minorities since they largely define and constrain their major life chances (access to employment, education, the political system, etc.).[3] An important consequence of this is that waves of racism do not, as is often claimed, necessarily relate to phases of economic crisis in which mass unemployment incite the working class towards xenophobia. Rather, élites can precipitate racism for political reasons that may bear little relationship to the state of the economy.

French working-class racism functioned significantly in terms of anti-Arab stereotypes – 'Arabs' as criminal, lazy, violent, libidinous etc. – that were generated and diffused by a colonial decision-making élite. This was composed of two interlinking interest groups. One was a colonial lobby made up of settler interests who feared the loss of cheap Algerian labour through emigration and who were supported by propagandists, most of them *Africains*, ex-administrators or soldiers from Algeria, who were active in Paris. Secondly, as Patrick Weil has argued, French immigration policy since the inter-war period developed within 'sectors' of the state, particular ministries and related interest groups, that were quite autonomous from electoral politics and public opinion.[4] Such a 'sector', 'with its own characteristics, its specialists and relative autonomy', was in the case of Algerian migration constituted by senior officials in the *Gouvernement Générale* and the Paris Ministry of the Interior, who were concerned with the political impact of migration on imperial security. Together, the lobby and the 'sector' diffused an extremely negative and racialised discourse that eventually impacted on public opinion. They also implemented policies that severely constrained Algerian migration and imposed repressive policing and paternalist segregationist practices. The aetiology of anti-Algerian racism was not one in which politicians responded to grass-roots hostility towards Arabs, but rather one in which élites acted almost independently of popular opinion. Our findings here coincide with those of Martin Schain for post-war immigration: decision-making élites in France (and the USA), 'for reasons that had little to do with links to mass opinion or reaction to immigration . . . developed understandings that defined a new wave of immigrants as different, and sufficiently different from those who had come before to be defined in 'racial' terms'.[5]

Before the First World War, and during the first two years of the war itself, most French working-class people showed a fairly tolerant attitude towards Algerian migrants. Up to 1914 the total number of Algerians in France, about 15 000, was very small and even where there were significant localised concentrations in Marseilles, Paris and the northern coal-fields there was little overt hostility. The Depont Commission, which visited these areas in 1914, found that the Kabyles had good relations with their 'French comrades' and 'are welcomed without hostility'. At *Courrières* the local French thought that the Algerians were unhygienic, which was not unsurprising when the mines failed to provide showers, but were impressed by their ability to speak French better than Flemish migrants. The French appear to have been intrigued and amused by the strange appearance and religious customs of the Kabyles. Kabyle miners at Billy-Montigny complained to the commission that the recent burial of a dead comrade according to Islamic rites, 'had caused such a gathering of curious onlookers that the progress of the funeral cortege had been impeded'.[6] They also protested at the abusive term 'tchouk-tchouk' used towards those who wore the fez, although this was quite mild compared to the colonial racist terms like *bicots* and *bougnoules* that began to appear in later years.

The greatest potential for conflict lay in the competition for jobs and in particular over the question of whether cheap Algerian labour would undermine wage-rates in general. During the early years the highest levels of tension were not between Algerians and French, since the latter were protected in the labour market, but rather between Algerians and **other immigrant** groups. Contact with French life, as Rager notes, was in reality 'often only contact with foreign life on French soil'.[7] During the period from 1910 to 1939 the Algerians never constituted more than about three to four per cent of the total immigrant population, which was made up from an incredibly diverse range of nationalities. In numerous work places throughout

France, Algerians were one small component of a multi-ethnic work force. The Anzin mines, which were quite typical, employed in September 1925 men of twenty nationalities, the main groups being Poles (7096), Belgians (1390), Italians (305), Spaniards (265), Czechs (125), Algerians (121), Hungarians (94) and Moroccans (72).[8] R. Blancard, working in the Alpine industries in 1924, noted,'When one rises in the morning, one encounters an odd assortment of swarthy men: some wear a turban or a fez; some are blinking Chinese; others, Spaniards with a blue chin or Russians still wearing the uniform of the Czar, all mixed in with French and Italian peasants'.[9] These different groups lived and worked alongside each other in the *quartiers populaires*, the inner-city slums and suburban shanty towns of Paris, Lyons and Marseilles.[10]

These ethnic groups were in competition for the same low-paid work, the jobs which the French refused to do, and tensions frequently spilled over into violence. At the *Courrière* mine at Fouquières-les-Lens in August 1913 twenty Belgians were dismissed after they had attacked newly arrived Algerians.[11] The Kabyles here, as elsewhere in France, complained to the *Gouvernement Générale* that as French subjects they should be given priority over foreigners like the Belgians and Italians. They also protested that European immigrant foremen favoured their own countrymen and tried to substitute them for Algerians by driving them out, 'by causing them a thousand difficulties'.[12] Some of the most violent confrontations occurred in 1910–12 between Italians and Kabyles in Marseilles. Although Italians, who numbered 100 000, were initially introduced by employers as a cheap labour force and as strike-breakers, by 1910 they were highly unionised and began to engage in a wave of strikes to increase wages. Companies began to counter this growing militancy by looking for new sources of more docile immigrant labour, turning to Algeria and Spain. In 1910 the oil-refinery of *Morel et Prom* recruited Kabyles to break an Italian strike, other companies soon followed suit, and much inter-ethnic brawling and intimidation ensued.[13] Kabyles even complained that Italians engaged in crimes disguised as Arabs, so as to bring them into disrepute.

On the eve of the First World War the majority of French people appear to have had a quite vague, but not particularly hostile image of the Algerian or, to be more accurate, of the

North African. In the factory or street the French working class had no way of distinguishing between the different national or ethnic groups from the Maghreb, mainly Algerians and Moroccans. Hence the use of generalised terms like 'Arab' and the sardonic 'Sidi' (meaning master) or the indiscriminate use of 'Algerian' for Moroccans and Tunisians.[14] Most working-class French derived their ideas about North Africa and its inhabitants from a diffuse range of sources, mass-circulation newspapers, illustrated magazines, World Fairs and colonial exhibitions, school text-books, popular novelists like Pierre Loti, the cinema and advertising.[15] In the *Exposition Universelle de Paris* of 1900, visited by over fifty million people, the Algerian pavillion, designed after the Mosque of the Fishermen in Algiers, stood alongside an Arab quarter with narrow streets and overhanging balconies where craftsmen were at work and` the delicacies of North Africa could be sampled.[16]

Such sources promulgated a popular orientalist image of North Africa in terms of romantic stereotypes: camel riding Touareg, dancing girls, and date-palms. But exoticism went hand-in-hand with an imperialist message of Arab inferiority, a backwardness which would recede as a benevolent France extended the benefits of civilisation. School children learnt through a text-book of 1913, 'France wants the little Arabs to be as educated as the little French children. This shows how our France is bountiful and generous towards the people she has conquered.'[17] As Lebovics argues, the great Paris exhibitions projected a vision of *la Plus Grande France* by wrapping native culture within the higher culture of European France, with its displays of advanced technology (dynamos, aircraft).[18] Messali Hadj noted that in all the factories and shops in which he had worked in Paris the French were almost totally ignorant of the real conditions of starvation and misery in North Africa.[19] Thus Imperial propaganda, even when not grossly racist but anodyne and paternalist, created the opinion among even the poorest of French that they were inherently superior to the benighted Arab.

The mildly positive but imperialist image of North Africa translated into strong popular enthusiasm for the Algerian and Moroccan troops who arrived during the First World War. The North African regiments of infantry and cavalry, dressed in their distinctive Arab uniforms, were seen as a concrete

symbol of imperial might and of 'our natives' love and ultimate sacrifice for the motherland. 'Who can forget', wrote
Depont in 1928,'those Parisian days, so burning with patriotism, when the whole population, crowding forward along the
main streets of the capital, applauded the long columns of
those magnificent regiments of Algerian, Tunisian and Moroccan infantrymen going to shed their blood for France.'[20] The
welcome which Algerian soldiers found in the French working
class and lower middle class was not only a reflection of patriotism but also evidence for the absence of anti-Arab racism.
Algerians were bowled over by the contrast with the colony,
where they were subjected to the highly repressive native code
and the entrenched racism and segregationism of settler
society.[21]

In France, by contrast, Algerians experienced a new freedom and unexpected warmth of friendship. A Kabyle worker
wrote home from Puteaux, an industrial suburb of Paris, to a
friend to come and join him. The pay was good and 'The folk
here shake my hand and we are mates.'[22] Many workers, as
well as soldiers on leave, were welcomed by French families
and taken in as lodgers. 'In Pau we were very well received by
the people; we were invited by the French civilians and we
taught them how to make couscous.'[23] In the shared hardship
and terror of army life Algerians found a strong sense of
comradeship and equality with French soldiers. Many Algerians workers and soldiers, to the horror of the military and
colonial authorities, established relationships with French
women. A military order of 1 June 1916 tried to put an end
to liaison by banning all female nurses from hospitals in which
wounded Algerians were convalescing.[24] Such relationships
suggest, as is argued later, that there was a degree of popular
acceptance of Algerian men.

The First World War, however, marked a significant stage in
the development of working-class racism towards Algerians and
other 'colonial' workers.[25] A major concern of the Confédération Générale du Travail (CGT) was that colonial workers,
while acknowledged as necessary to the war-economy, would
be used to force down French wage levels. The general strategy of the trade-union movement, as it was later during the
inter-war period, was to exert pressure on the government
to guarantee equal wages and social benefits for colonials.

Negotiations and agreement between union leaders and the government on these matters was not sufficient however to contain growing unrest among the rank-and-file workers. A particular cause for concern, especially in 1917–18, was that mobilisation of North African workers was enabling the release of Frenchmen from the economy so they could be sent up to the front. During 1917 a series of major demonstrations and strikes, which frequently deteriorated into violent attacks on North Africans, took place in St Etienne, Rennes, Clermont-Ferrand, Bordeaux, Brest, Lyons, Le Havre, and elsewhere. An attack by locals on an encampment of Arab workers in Brest led to a riot in which troops opened fire and killed five immigrants.[26] Some of these actions were led by women who found in North Africans a scapegoat for their anxiety at the conscription of husbands and sons. In Rennes women went on strike and marched through town shouting the slogan 'Give us back our soldiers!' and calling for the repatriation of colonial workers.[27]

This growing tension was accompanied by the rapid diffusion of racist stereotypes. The North African was regarded as a threatening and violent type, particularly prone to drunkeness, dirty and obscene, and a transmitter of disease. All these characteristics were summed up in the French fear of the Algerian as a sexually overcharged primitive, a rapist, molestor of children, vector of syphilis and a dangerous threat to the purity and honour of French womanhood. A miners' union in the Pas-de-Calais protested to the Ministry of Public Works on two grounds: '. . . one concerning questions of morality, given the close proximity of North Africans to working-class families whose heads are absent; one concerning . . . the possible contamination of the local population'.[28] The sexual fear of the migrant slipping into the bed of absent men was a topic of conversation in a munitions factory in Le Havre: 'If this continues there will not be any men left in France; so why are we fighting? So that Chinese, Arabs, or Spaniards can marry our wives and daughters and share out the France for which we'll all, sooner or later, get ourselves killed at the front.'[29] Everywhere Algerians began to run into signs of exclusion as in the restaurants in Clermont which displayed signs, 'Here we don't serve *Sidis*', or they were subjected to assault by soldiers and youth gangs.

At the end of the war anti-colonial racism subsided as workers and soldiers were repatriated, but the rapid increase in peace-time migration from Algeria during 1922–4, led to further xenophobia. The attitudes of the trade-unions in the interwar period towards Algerian migrants remained essentially unchanged from that of 1910–18; French workers should be protected from capitalist moves to cut wages and conditions by a guarantee of equal treatment for migrants. However, following the Bolshevik revolution and the founding of the *Parti Communiste Français* (PCF) in December 1920, the Communists and their affiliated union the CGTU sought to organise colonial workers in France, especially the Algerians, as part of an internationalist strategy of opposition to colonial oppression.[30] The militant P. Celor wrote in 1926 that the immediate task of the Communists was: 'to work to organise the colonial workers living in France to prevent capitalism using these native workers to lower the wages of the metropolitan proletariat and also to transform the power of the colonial workers into a revolutionary instrument'.[31]

The PCF established a *Commission Coloniale* in 1924, organised a first congress of North African Workers in Paris on 7 December 1924, published several newspapers in French and Arabic like *El Kasirna* and *El Amel*, distributed tracts in Arabic outside factory gates and through the Communist press called on workers to support their Arab comrades. However, despite considerable organisational effort, the PCF largely failed in its efforts to gain influence among the Maghrebians, one major reason being the latent racism or simple lack of concern among rank-and-file party and trade union members. A PCF report of 1926 noted 'In the factories the French Communists still have the widespread habit of considering the arabs as inferior'.[32] In 1924 attempts were made by the PCF to carry out a survey of North Africans, but of the ninety-three questionnaires sent out in the Department of the Seine only three were returned, and none from the Seine et Oise.[33] In 1923 the Paris Prefect of Police reported that in factories there were, 'some brawls often caused by the untimely mocking by the the men working with them'.[34]

During the inter-war period Algerians began to show a remarkable degree of union militancy and were involved in numerous strikes, some of which were carried out jointly with

French and European immigrant workers. But in most work places European workers were unwilling to support strikes by Algerians or they engaged in quite separate actions. In the bitter strike of 1928 in the big car-washing companies of Paris French taxi-drivers showed no solidarity and even washed their own cars, while Poles were brought in as strike-breakers.[35] The archives of the PCF are a testimony to widespread racism within the ranks of the party and to the general failure to counter these influences among the rank and file.[36] The most violent confrontations between the two sides occurred as employers organisations, usually with the support of the SAINA, utilised unemployed or inexperienced and newly arrived North Africans as strike breakers during the 1930s. Massard-Guilbaud argues that this, in leaving a permanent mark on the memory of the French working-class movement, may have blocked Algerian integration through association with left-wing and trade union organisations.[37]

Evidence of popular anti-Arab racism outside the work-place is largely confined to those urban areas in which there was a relatively high concentration of Algerians and Moroccans, in particular Paris, Marseilles and Lorraine. In Paris there was a concentration of Algerian workers in the thirteenth arrondissement where they worked in the sugar-refinery of *Say*. In early 1915 a delegation of women went to the commissariat to complain that 'Kabyles' had taken all available work in the sector.[38] However, most anatagonism related less to competition over work than to perceptions of Algerians as a criminal and sexual threat. On 7 November 1923 Khemilé Ousliman, an unemployed and mentally ill Kabyle, in a frenzied attack killed two women and wounded two others in the Rue Fondary. This street is located in the 15th *arrondissement* and at the time had the highest concentration of Algerians in the whole of Paris, about four thousand men, most of whom worked in the local Citroën factory.[39] The murders gave rise to an outbreak of popular anti-Arab violence: crowds quickly gathered at the scene and began to attack North Africans at random. One of them, Belhacem Lladi Mohammed, was lynched in an adjacent street, the Rue Frémicourt.[40] According to *L'Humanité*, the moral panic had been preceded by a growing fear of Algerian criminality: before the murders rumours had circulated that the *arrondissement*, 'is terrorised by the 'Arabs'. They have a 'lair', a 'headquarters'; they eat dogs, cats and rats. Soon they will be eating human flesh. When a crime, a rape, a theft, or any other offence is committed today or tomorrow, don't hesitate: get the Arab'.[41] The existence of this racialised fear of Algerians is confirmed by the statement of a neighbour of one victim. 'We are infested with Algerian natives, dirty, ragged, working little, often drunk. They go down the street searching interiors with their eyes, insolent, looting, obscene. They inspire such fear that nobody dare complain or chase them away.'[42]

The origins of such working-class racism cannot be identified with any degree of certainty, but the press played a key role in diffusing the stereotype of the Algerian as a primitive, 'instinctual' being who was prone to uncontrollable violence, particularly gruesome killings with the knife, and to sexual assaults on women and children. This function can be seen in the press reactions to the Rue Fondary murders. In spite of the fact that Algerian criminality was low and mostly involved minor infractions or assaults on other North Africans, *Le Matin* commented, 'the crimes and offences committed by Arabs are increasing . . . almost all the rabble which infests us is foreign'.[43] Haudos, the deputy for the Seine et Marne, wrote, 'thousands of natives are terrorising certain regions of France, certain quarters of Paris. They wallow in poverty, adding to the vices of the lower depths of the city those which they carry in a state of gestation. Libidinous crimes are on the increase, rapes, abductions, while armed robberies are beyond count.'[44] The enormous and racialised response of the popular press to the Rue Fondary murders illustrates how the stereotype of Algerians as sexual monsters was disseminated to a national audience.[45] The nationalist *Étoile-Nord-Africaine* was constantly aware of the role of the racist press which, 'in the pay of the colonisers, has hounded us with such rage that European public opinion is out of control . . . diseases, theft, murders, debauchery and immoral values are the terrible accusations with which we are freely credited'.[46]

Within the multi-ethnic enclave the reasons why North Africans were more targeted than other nationalities like Italians and Poles was due to a number of factors. Firstly, the Maghrebians had the lowest ratio of females to males of any immigrant group at two per cent, compared to the Portuguese (14 per cent), Poles (39) and Italians (42). The presence of large numbers of single North Africans males may well have generated perceptions of them as a sexually frustrated and threatening group. Certainly the Algerian recourse to prostitutes was quite visible and moves to open a segregated brothel for North Africans in the 15th *arrondissement* in 1931 led to a campaign of opposition by shopkeepers and the local press.[47]

However, evidence of extensive co-habitation and marriage would at the same time seem to indicate close social contact between Algerian workers and French working-class women in the factories, cafés, cinemas and dance halls of the *quartier populaire*. Of the 60 000 migrants in Paris in 1930 about seven hundred were legally married to French women, while five thousand were co-habiting.[48] Massignon's figures suggest that nearly one in ten Algerians were living in a stable relationship with a European woman by the 1930s, a level that is confirmed by a detailed study of Gennevilliers in 1936 which found that 14 per cent of Moroccans and 11 per cent of Algerians were married or co-habiting.[49] In many instances these women were in partnership with Algerians who had established a small business, usually a shop or café, and had begun to cut their ties to their home community. Many of the women were themselves of migrant origin (Belgians, Germans, Italians . . .) and some converted to Islam.[50] However, as Michèle Tribalat's research has shown a growing level of contemporary Maghrebian intermarriage has remained 'invisible' to the French population and not impeded racism.[51]

A second cause of tension in the enclave arose from competition over housing. Following the Rue Fondary murders one politician asked the Prefect of Police what he intended to do about hoteliers in Grenelle who were expelling French families in order to lodge Arabs. Unscrupulous *marchands de sommeil* were willing to replace French and other immigrant lodgers by North Africans since they could make larger profits by crowding them four or more to a room. Besombes, a city councillor, wrote to the Prefect of Police to ask what measures would be taken not only to guarantee, 'the safety of inhabitants against the nightime attacks for which Algerian subjects are responsible', but also to ensure, 'the application of the regulations of the housing inspectorate in the areas in which native workers live in large numbers'.[52] That housing and not just jobs was a cause of friction is shown by a letter to *L'Humanité*: 'People write fine things about the wogs (*Khouïa*), but as for the Parisian he hasn't a place to live, no work, only poverty ... Build houses for the large families, we'll take care of the *Sidis* later'.[53]

Thirdly, animosity targeted Algerians because of their alien presence and the anxiety that was primed by a lack of contact and understanding. At street level North Africans could usually be recognised by their worn clothing, their Arab-Berber features, and broken French. But beyond that they were a mystery to the French working class. The Algerian tendency to form closed groupings based on kin and village solidarities meant that the French had little point of contact either in the work-place, where ethnic teams were the norm, or in the café, street or lodging.[54] Such segregation was not conducive to the French gradually establishing a more informed and even sympathetic view of the Algerian. Not that building relations with the Algerians was easy: Abdelaziz Menaouer, a PCF militant responsible for trying to recruit Algerians into the trade union movement, noted the extreme suspicion towards all Europeans that these poor peasants carried with them from the oppressive colonial context. 'Illiterate, having a deep distrust of the European because of their experience in the colony, they have never been organised and know nothing about it ... Their ignorance of the French language prevents them from associating with their brother workers'.[55]

Social distance between the two groups helped generate and sustain a situation in which racial stereotypes, ignorance and fear could flourish. One finding of the Laroque Inquiry in 1938 was that, 'the tendency for North-African workers to withdraw into themselves, to live in very dense groups that are virtually impermeable, has always aroused the distrust of the populations with whom they come into contact, a distrust that is often exaggerated and generates fear ...'[56] When the priests Catrice and Buchet in 1929 visited the North African enclave of Les Grésillons in Gennevilliers they asked a local French worker for the direction and if there were many Algerians there:

The wogs (*bicots*)! But, my dear sir, there's piles of them! Look! Go down to the Grésillons. In five minutes you'll be right in Arabia. But take some care at least. You never know

with those types! . . . I never go to see. Us, we're from the
town aren't we. Down there it's the no go area. They fight
each other, murder each other, it's all the same to me . . .
These folk there, you have to watch out. Before you know it
they'll play you some dirty trick . . . if I was a big shot in the
government I would immediately send these types back to
their villages. We're fed up to the teeth with these evil wogs!
They're everywhere. All you hear in the street is the sound
of their gibberish. Look, at the sign of that grocer's, there
on the right, it's completely in '*sidi*'.[57]

This kind of working-class racism remained on the whole
diffuse and unfocused and only assumed a more organised
form where it was channelled by local petit-bourgeois interest
groups, shop-keepers, *commerçants*, and local councillors. In
Paris this frequently assumed the form of a defensive territ-
oriality the aim of which was to block the creation of any kinds
of special facilities for North Africans.[58] In November 1924 the
Municipal council of Gennevilliers, responding to public pressure, opposed the creation of a purpose-built North African
hostel. 'The town council considers that because of Algerian
customs, which are different from ours and might offend certain susceptibilities, that the establishment of this village [sic]
would be a nuisance both for the population and for social
work in the area'. The council felt that the hostel was really a
means to exploit 'these unfortunates' by lodging them five or
six to a room and, a tell-tale contradiction, that special provision was unfair and Algerians should be treated, 'on the same
and equal footing as the French'.[59] The Mayor wrote to the
Prefect of Police with a petition from 2749 residents opposed
to the hostel and requesting him to meet a delegation from
the *Comité de defense du quartier*.[60]

In Lyons a similar *Comité de défense* operated in the inner-city
locality of La Guillotière in which there was a dense Algerian
enclave. In its own newspaper, *La Guille*, the association attacked the spread of prostitution, while 'day and night rever-
berate the vociferations and varied shouts uttered by an
underworld composed mainly of Algerians'. All this was bringing 'the good name of our quarter' into disrepute and the
general image which it now evoked, 'is that of a pimp, his
controlled woman or a "Sidi"'.[61] The main impetus behind

such campaigning groups came from local conservative shop-keepers who were concerned with the impact of immorality and 'delinquent' Arabs on their business. When in 1931 the Prefecture of Police authorised a segregated brothel for North Africans in the 15th *arrondissement* there was opposition from local *notables*, a petition from shop-keepers, a campaign in the local newspaper *Le Vaugirard-Grenelle*, and a public meeting in the *salle des sociétés savantes.*[62]

The most interesting local campaigns were those in opposition to the building of a *Hôpital Franco-Musulmans*. A projected site on land owned by the city of Paris in the Rues Gassendi and Dauville was successfully opposed by inhabitants supported by the local councillor, Delsol. Similar opposition blocked location near council housing (HLM) at the Porte d'Orléans. The hospital was finally built on land in the communist municipality of Bobigny.[63] This decision was forced on the council of Bobigny in 1930, despite its opposition, by the conservative *Conseil Générale de la Seine* which was thus able to offload an unpopular project from central Paris into the 'red suburbs' where Communists would be caught in a trap between the principles of internationalism and the racism of its working-class constituency.[64] A further decision of 1932 to locate a Muslim cemetery in Bobigny was opposed by the town council as 'a calculated and tendentious manoeuvre aimed at the municipality of Bobigny itself'.[65] In this move by right-wing Paris authorities to deliberately decant or displace the 'social problem' and costs of North Africans into the left-wing suburbs, can be recognised the beginnings of a policy that continued for the next half century. The tensions which it generated in left-wing suburbs finally exploded in the unprecedented events of December 1980 in Vitry when the Communist Mayor was involved in a bulldozer attack on a hostel for Malian workers.[66]

Working-class anti-Arab racism during the inter-war period did not grow in a unilinear way, but varied in intensity from one locale to another and went through sudden surges of activity before declining into relative somnolence. Hostility was in part a response to the sudden 'visibility' of North Africans, a combination of both relatively large numbers (at the micro-urban level) and the **rate** of arrival.[67] Statistics of immigration from Algeria show a dramatic increase in arrivals during the period between November 1922 and mid-1923. It was the sudden arrival of these Algerians, a largely new and strange presence, in the popular *quartiers* of Paris which gave rise to xenophobia. The Laroque inquiry reported that after this initial wave of hostility, particularly strong just after the First World War, the two groups settled down into a pattern of mutual segregation and ignored each other.[68] However, confirmation for this 'rate-of-increase' reaction can be seen in Lorraine in 1936 following upon a massive recruitment of several thousand Algerians by the steel companies. This gave rise to a moral panic among the population of Moselle and Meuthe-et-Moselle. At Hombas, Laroque reported:

> distressing incidents have broken out in public dances; in Thionville the population uses the public baths, frequented by Algerians, less and less; the Tramway Company of Nancy has even considered putting in service on the Pompey line carriages reserved for North Africans; finally at Pompey the workers have requested and obtained from the managers of the steel works that the cantine where the apprentices live be separated from that of the native workers by a screen of strong wire netting.[69]

As in Paris local concern centred more on the perceived sexual and criminal danger of the Algerians than on their threat to French jobs. A rape at Homécourt, the murder of a child near Longwy and a 'lewd crime' at Knutange, were all blamed, despite the lack of any evidence, on the Algerians.[70] The Mayor of Longwy, Amidieu du Clos, wrote to the Minister of War calling for the expulsion from France of the Algerians: their arrival had coincided with, 'a growth in exhibitionism, the chasing of women and young girls in our lanes and footpaths, burgleries, assaults and even nocturnal rape'.[71]

France was the first European state to develop a regulated system of labour immigration. Gary Cross argues that the government was able to do this without creating strong opposition from the working-class by associating trade unions with the elaboration and implementation of policies which protected indigenous labour. A dual labour market developed in which immigrants were confined to the bottom of the job market while French workers moved up the occupational ladder. Immigrants seldom competed directly with French workers for jobs, while during periods of recession it was the former who were made redundant – providing a cushion against the dole queue. Immigration was not an electoral issue during the 1920s and French 'opposition to the immigrant was muted, sporadic and strictly localized'.[72] This analysis certainly fits in with the relatively low-key and sporadic opposition to North Africans in the work place, especially since even among immigrants they constituted the most expendable group. As Schor notes, 'Generally the French workers did not show hostility towards their maghrebian comrades, particularly as these latter, less skilled, were always laid-off first'.[73] Work-place tensions arose most frequently when the French objected to working in the same teams as North Africans whom they regarded as mediocre labourers of low productivity.[74]

Contrary to the interpretation of a number of historians, anti-Algerian racism in the working class was not primarily a response to economic competition during the Great Depression of the 1930s. Firstly, popular anti-Arab xenophobia appeared in its sharpest form during 1923–4, well before the Depression and during a period of unprecedented economic growth. This pattern is similar to the emergence of anti-black racism in Britain during the 1950s, also during a period of economic expansion and dependence on immigrant labour. This racism also had its origins in the decision-making élites of the Conservative Party.[75] Secondly, while trade union participation in the regulation of immigrant labour helped quell conflict, government and industry did almost nothing in relation to Algerian social problems. This may explain in part why racist hostility towards Algerians was centred less in the work-place than in the local community and was concerned less with job competition and wage-cutting than social issues like housing, crime, and sexual violence.

8 Élite Racism and the Colonial Lobby

The process by which Algerian migrants were targeted and categorised in racial terms reached a crucial phase during the period 1920–4 and was primarily the work of various colonial pressure groups. Their central object of concern was the liberal provision of the law of 15 July 1914 which had granted all Algerians complete freedom of movement to France. In the light of the later intense pressures to eradicate or cripple the working of the law it is curious that its passage through the legislature aroused little opposition. It appears to have been one of those 'blunders', common enough in the history of legislatures, in which potential opponents fail to recognise in time the radical implications of a new bill.[1]

Colonial opposition to the freedom of migration developed among two powerful groups, senior officials in the colonial administration, who were motivated primarily by political considerations, and settler organisations concerned with economic implications. These will be looked at in turn.

THE ADMINISTRATIVE LOBBY

Among the various departments of the colonial government it was the *Direction des Affaires Indigènes* (DAI) which played the crucial role in determining policy on emigration. The DAI appointed and controlled the administrators in the rural *communes mixtes* from whom it received a vast amount of information on the economic, social and political impact of emigration in the *douars*.[2] The various Directors of the DAI were powerful functionaries who carried sufficient influence with the Governor or with the Ministry of the Interior in Paris to shape 'Muslim policy'.[3] The DAI liaised directly with a specialist bureau in the Ministry of the Interior, the *Direction des Affaires Algériens* (DAA), regarding all matters to do with the regulation and surveillance of migrants circulating between the colony and Algeria.

The DAA, which was staffed with Arab specialists, many of whom had seen service in Algeria as commune administrators or officials in the *Affaires Indigènes*, shared the same background, formation and ideology as the colonial administrators. The *Direction* was strategically located within the Ministry of the Interior which exercised virtual control over the Algerian Governor and sent him instructions and decrees on every aspect of colonial government, in most cases without any reference to the French legislature. During 1918–24 the Paris DAA sympathetically received and amplified the anxieties of the Algerian *Affaires Indigènes* concerning the dangers of uncontrolled migration and eventually persuaded the Minister of the Interior, Camille Chautemps, to issue circulars in August and September 1924 which introduced major restrictions on the movement of labour.

Thus the overall administration of Algerian emigration, as well as the elaboration of legal orders that provided a regulatory framework, was fundamentally controlled by the joint actions of the *Affaires Indigènes* in Algiers and the *Affaires Algériens* in Paris. To all intents and purposes these two *Directions*, manned by administrators who shared an identical esprit de corps and world view, can be regarded as a single 'sector'.

This grouping, which I shall call the 'administrative lobby', found powerful support in a number of ideologues and propagandists, most of them ex-Algerian administrators, who were located in Paris where they were able to exercise a major impact on the press, public opinion and government. The most influential Paris-based voice of the administrative lobby was Octave Depont, an ex-administrator and inspector of the *communes mixtes*, who headed the 1914 Commission on migration. In addition to the 1914 Report he published extensively on Algerian emigration and during the 1920s was regarded as the authority on this issue.[4] Adolphe Gérolami, also an ex-administrator and inspector of the *communes mixtes*, a fierce opponent of emigration, was transferred from Algeria to the Ministry of the Interior to act as a specialist advisor to the Paris police on Algerian immigrants in the capital. In 1925, as will be seen (Chapter 9), he became the first head of the *Service des Affaires Indigènes Nord-Africains* (SAINA), the special police brigade concerned with the surveillance of North African migrants. He was accused by the left wing and nationalist political movements of behaving in a particularly brutal and despotic manner towards the Algerians in Paris.[5]

A third key member of the lobby was Pierre Godin who had entered the colonial administrative service in 1896. Like Depont and Gérolami he had been a native administrator and for five years acted as director of the Algerian security services. After filling various important administrative positions in France, including Prefect for the Hautes-Pyrénées in 1917 and private secretary to Clemenceau (1918–20), his career was divided between the *Cour des Comptes* (Revenue Court) and the Paris City Council on which he served for sixteen years.[6] During the period from 1923 onwards Godin was to campaign indefatigably within the Paris City Council to establish the SAINA and his son André Godin was later to succeed Gérolami as director of this police agency. The influence of this triumvirate extended out through a wide network of contacts with politicians, academics, government officials, and police officers who had a particular interest in North African affairs.[7]

From an early stage in the Algerian emigration to France the *Gouvernement Générale* was preoccupied by the danger which it was thought to offer to colonial security. In 1914 and early 1915 the Governor General was 'furious' to find that thousands of emigrants could readily avoid the habitual methods of control exerted by native administrators and colonial police and warned that military deserters, criminals and other wanted men were escaping to France. Under pressure from Algiers the French government eventually halted free migration in late 1915 and established the *Service de l'organisation des Travailleurs Coloniaux* (SOTC) which placed all recruits for the war industry under a strict military regime.[8] However, the *Gouvernement Générale* and the Ministry of the Interior continued throughout 1916–18 to be concerned with the 30 000 'free' workers who had emigrated prior to the establishment of the SOTC. In 1916 a special police unit, the *Bureau des Affaires Indigènes*, was created in the Hôtel des Invalides to identify deserters and clandestine workers. Under pressure from the Governor General, who was concerned at alcoholism, cannabis use, gambling, prostitution, and brawling, the Paris police organised a series of raids on Algerian cafés in March and April 1918.[9] The attitude of the *Gouvernement Générale* towards Algerians in France was identical to that of a foreign government concerned to exercise a close paternalist but authoritarian surveillance over what it regarded as its nationals.

The large-scale enforced repatriation of Algerian workers during 1918–20 was seen by the *Gouvernement* as a restoration of pre-war normality and colonial hegemony. However, the rapid return to France of ex-soldiers and war workers who acted as guides to a new and growing wave of migrants, gave rise to further anxiety in the colonial administration.[10]

The underlying logic of the colonial discourse which emerged so clearly during the decade 1914–24 was to present uncontrolled emigration as a danger both to **metropolitan** France and to the colonial order. Through this means the colonial élites had a greater chance of winning over the support of public opinion in France to the necessity of immigration controls. A racialised discourse presented the Algerians as naïve primitives, 'big and defenceless children', who really needed the firm, protective guidance of their colonial masters.[11] Unfortunately emigration to France placed Algerians in a context in which there was no support or restraint from native administrators or the *code de l'indigénat*. Exposed to a freedom for which he was not prepared, and transferred within days from a rural Muslim society that was still 'medieval' into the vast teeming French city with all its dangerous temptations, the simple migrant was vulnerable to every form of corruption and dissipation. This image of degeneration was undoubtedly rooted in a much older tradition of European thought which saw the city as a godless and evil environment which corrupted the good peasant migrant who became isolated from contact with godly Nature and the moral community.[12] Once Algerians were corrupted they began to reveal the more primitive and aggressive side of their 'instincts' for rape and violence.

A typical example of this racialised discourse was an article in *La Tunisie Française* in November 1923:

The Arabs who have come to France do not and cannot understand anything of our civilisation. Their essentially sexual nature naturally draws them towards the lower depths of this civilisation which has its imperfections and ugly side. The bistro, the brothel, the sleazy night-club, attract these frustrated and carnal beings . . . A bit at a time they lose the qualities of sociability and morality that the teachings of the

Koran and the mosque have inculcated in them. So for these illiterate minds a loss of faith – which is not replaced – gives way to all the instincts of an unchained beast ... A large number of them in the provinces engage in armed attacks, theft, pillage and murder ...[13]

Experts on migration emphasised continuously the high level of criminality of Algerians: Georges Mauco estimated it to be fifteen times higher than for the French population.[14] A close examination of crime statistics shows that there was no foundation to such claims and that the majority of offences for which Algerians were arrested consisted of minor infractions such as vagrancy, non-possession of identity cards, drunken behaviour, and petty theft.[15]

Yet the colonial lobbyists and right-wing media not only exaggerated the level of Algerian criminality but also its particular form and violence. The migrant was a primitive type, subject to uncontrollable outbursts of rage and quick to use the knife. But, above all, the Algerian was possessed of a hot-blooded and perverted sexuality which made him an extreme danger to all French women and children. Press reports helped build up a climate of fear in which Algerians figured as physically dirty, diseased and vicious types who lurked in the sinister lairs of the ghetto, ready to leap out and disembowel or rape innocent French citizens.[16] The anti-Arab racist discourse linked the concept of criminal invasion of a 'pure' French society with sexually charged images of irruption, penetration, and tainting. In particular the 'Sidi' was described as the transmitter of 'filthy' sexual diseases, especially syphilis, which it was claimed they carried in from North Africa. Benjamin Stora notes of this 'medicalisation' of immigration, 'The venereal phobia, spread by certain obsessional doctors motivated by a kind of growing fever, constantly revealed the fear of the other.'[17] Colonial medicine's symbolic demarcation of the 'unclean' and its regulation of native hygiene represented another form of control over the aliens body, a Foucaultian 'technology of domination'.[18] In his novel *Sidi de Banlieue*, Jean Damase implicitly criticised the ineffective medical checks on North African immigrants when they were described passing before an indifferent doctor: 'This doctor knew all too well that the pox and leprosy lay dormant beneath these yellow eyes, the ulcerated skin, the lousy hair and that these diseases would soon revive again ... in the interior, in the provinces, in the ghettos and wretched quarters of Valence or Paris'.[19]

By emphasising the dangers which Algerian migrants presented to **metropolitan** society colonial propagandists hoped to convince French public opinion that it was in its own interest to halt emigration. However, of far more central concern to the colonial lobby was the view that unregulated migration to France provided a transformatory experience that carried enormous potential dangers for North Africa. The Algerian worker enjoyed a degree of freedom that was unheard of in the colony, freedom to associate with French men and women on an equal footing and to become active in trade union, political and nationalist movements. The danger was that migrants, breaking free from the coercive native regime and the mental chains of colonial hegemony, would return to their villages with a radicalised experience and new ideas that would corrode and undermine the colonial order from within.

The nervous concern of the *Gouvernement Générale* for the politically and morally subversive potentialities of migration was shown as early as 1914. In August many thousands of Algerian miners in the north had witnessed the rapid German advance and defeat of the French army. The *Gouvernement*, worried that these men would return to their *douars* with stories of French vulnerability, asked the Paris government to prevent their return to Algeria.[20] An almost obsessive concern was shown with the extent to which the highly segregationist and racial hierarchies of colonial Algeria were blown asunder by the experience of life in France, particularly by the widespread prevalence of sexual relationships, co-habitation and marriage between Algerians and French women. As was almost universal in European colonies in the early twentieth century, the foundation of colonial authority was thought to rest on the strict maintenance of social distance between *indigènes* and their masters.[21] In 1916 the *Gouvernement* and the military authorities were so disturbed that the relationships that developed between convalescing Algerian soldiers and French nurses was leading to a loss of 'respect' for European women, and by implication French male authority, that all female nurses were removed from hospitals.[22]

The archives of the *Gouvernement Générale* show that during

1918–20 it kept a close eye on returning soldiers and workers and monitored their impact in the rural communes. In July 1919 the *Gouvernement* instructed local native administrators to carry out a thorough survey of 'the state of mind of the natives in the colony' and 'the moral and social impact of their stay in the metropole'. The administrators' returns provide fascinating evidence of the extent to which mass emigration during the First World War marked a crucial watershed in colonial history, the fracturing of French hegemonic power in Algeria.

The administrators' reports show a common set of concerns. Firstly, these Arab specialists had a barely disguised contempt for a French public which, ignorant of the 'reality' of native psychology and the need for a firm hand, treated them in the metropole as equals and unleashed a pandora's box of base instincts. 'The natives, particularly sensitive to the frequently exaggerated signs of friendliness and politeness that our compatriots, ignorant of their ways and beliefs, have shown them, come to think that the *colons* do not show them the respect which they merit.'[23] From French familiarity, 'they become vain and entertain too good an opinion of themselves'.[24] The most dangerous form of this was the readiness of some French women, usually dismissed as perverted nymphomaniacs, to enter into sexual relations with migrants, which led Algerians to think that all European women were prostitutes. This generated a 'lack of reserve towards French women'.[25]

Most worrying for the administrator was how this experience spilled over into a new-found spirit of insolence and independence towards his authority. The administrators, who exercised control almost single-handed over tens of thousands of tribesmen in the distant *bled*, were keenly aware of the fragility of their power and the extent to which it depended less on police or military strength (which was quite tenuous) than on their ability to command blind respect from 'their natives'. This was now in jeopardy. At Sidi Aïssa returning migrants, 'sometimes verge on indiscipline and insolence . . . they think that all is permitted and show no respect for decisions that have been made'. The same reports came from Djurdjura, 'very ominous for the future', and from Ténès where 'manifestations of independence' had forced the administrator 'to remind them of their sense of duty'. Finally, the administrators rounded off with the call to terminate the 'absolute liberty' of migrants since, 'given the actual mental state of the Muslim population, this ability to travel without control would appear to undermine the chances of security in a country that is still being formed.'[26] The officers were still able to cling to the myth of Republican equality and universality by simply deferring full freedom for Algerians into a distant future ('it will take generations yet before they assimilate to our way of thinking') when they would have abandoned their Muslim fanaticism and reached 'our level of civilisation'.

All these themes of native 'corruption', familiarity with French women, 'spoiling' by the French, inflated self-importance and an unleashed criminality found a clear synthesis in a newspaper article by Colonel Fabre. This is worth quoting at length since it contains almost every element of the colonial racialised discourse:

> In this way the native in France acquires deplorable habits: he, who only respects benevolent force and justice, finds himself treated with persuasive means as a 'model citizen'. He becomes vain, demanding and indisciplined . . . Through contact with the male and female population of the lower class (the only one he frequents) they become habitual drunks and learn to despise French women, who they respect in Algeria. When by chance they come into contact with the upper classes they are treated like spoilt children because of the unthinking attraction of the French for all that is exotic: the most humble of the 'Whatsit Tribe', finding themselves called 'Sidi' [Master], because the good people of Châlons-sur-Marne have heard that this is polite in Algeria, puff up with pride and accept the compliment. Also, when the native returns to work for the *colon*, who in spite of his benevolence has a different attitude towards him, he rebels. It's the *colon* who has to suffer. The native returns to France drawn by the memories of his stay and by the illusion of high wages . . . [but] in France you can't live off a watermelon or a few figs. So then he pillages, thieves and murders. When its not from need, its from passion that he kills: these impulsive beings, with their violent desires, far from their habitual ways and religious leaders, are suddenly dominated by savage instincts.[27]

By 1920 the Governor General Abel was increasing pressure on the Ministry of the Interior to introduce controls since migrants, 'contaminated by contact with certain unsavoury milieux of the major French towns . . . will present **numerous inconveniences for the maintenance of our domination of North Africa**.'[28]

During 1921–4 the concerns of the administrative lobby assumed a form that was less centred on moral subversion than on overt political dangers. After 1920 the survival of the Bolshevik state, the foundation of the French Communist Party at the Congress of Tours and the decision of the Communist International to build anti-colonial organisations generated a climate of insecurity and a fear of impending global revolution. At the same time Communists and Socialists were unionising North Africans who became involved in a series of bitter strikes for improved pay and conditions.

During this period Octave Depont became the leading colonial propagandist on the dangers presented by migration and the transmission of the virus of Communism into rural Algeria. During his period in Algeria as a senior officer in the *Affaires Indigènes* and Inspector General of the native communes, Depont had become the leading authority on tribal rebellions which he ascribed to the conspiratorial activities of the Muslim confraternities and Pan-Islamism.[29] After 1922 his fears for the long-term political security of North Africa deepened: an almost global ferment of events, the advent of a Republic in Turkey, the Rif War in Morocco, nationalist and independence movements in Tunisia, Egypt, India and elsewhere, represented 'the revolt of oriental anarchy against the moral, industrial and scientific work of European civilisation'.[30] An uncontrolled migration had allowed every kind of degenerate to enter France and, 'this scum, more or less Berber tramps, has continued for far too long to insult our civilisation through means of its alcoholism and debauchery'. This rootless dross was proving an easy and impressionable target for Communist agitators like Captain Khaled who came to Paris, 'to inflame with nationalism, in turbulent meetings, a Berber pleb made up of the ambitious, deserters, rebels and filthy hooligans (*apaches*)'.[31]

Depont was in no doubt about the extent to which Communist agitation among the immigrants presented a far greater danger to Algeria than it did to metropolitan France. He called for, 'indispensable steps to contain the violent effects of the Bolshevik poison that has been poured in full measure for our North Africans', steps which would include a stringent pre-selection and policing of all migrants. From at least 1923 onwards Depont was able to find a ready audience for his ideas in Paris, particularly through the *Comité de l'Afrique française*. The *Comité*, founded in 1890, constituted the single most powerful colonial lobby group, was closely associated with the imperialist drive in North Africa and provided a forum which virtually determined government policy.[32] By 1927–8 the *Comité* was firmly won over to Depont's position and issued a call to arms against Bolshevik plans for the destruction of colonial Algeria.[33]

THE SETTLER LOBBY

The pressure exerted by the colonial administration for an end to free migration was reinforced by a rather different interest group, the settler lobby. From the earliest days of migration colonial employers, particularly in the farming sector, were concerned that the departure of Algerians would create a serious labour shortage and also drive up wage levels. As early as 1911 a member of the *Délégations Financières*, noting the emigration of thousands of men, stated that France after making so many heavy sacrifices to colonise Algeria should use, 'all her power to preserve the labour force which we require'. Another writer, Mallebay, claimed in 1914, without any ambiguity, that the *colons* 'should have the monopoly' of Algerian labour since it was 'absolutely and fundamentally indispensable to us'.[34] This was at a time when employers were shifting from dependence on Spanish immigrants to Algerian labour. The *colons* were also concerned that remittance money was being used to buy back land from Europeans on such a scale as to threaten the whole colonial order. According to Depont, this was part of a deliberate strategy, 'a veritable hunt against the European *colons* to retake their former lands'.[35] In reality such acquisitions made hardly a dent in colonial land ownership and settler anxiety was a reflection of increasing insecurity in the face of a rapidly growing Algerian population.

During the course of the First World War settler opposition to the huge drain on Algerian manpower was muted, in recognition of the need to make a sacrifice for the *patrie*, and because the outflow was seen as a short-term emergency measure. However, this did not stop all protest: the *colons* of Miliana, for example, demanded that the government requisition Algerians, 'and place them at the disposition of the *colons* rather than sending them to the metropole', that it impose a fixed wage, and that mayors and administrators, 'be given the power to force natives to work in order to overcome their unwillingness and idleness'.[36] At the end of the war in December 1918 the settlers asked for a complete halt to emigration and the rapid repatriation of 'our labourers'.[37]

The dramatic increase in post-war migration, especially during 1922–4, led to a concerted opposition by powerful settler organisations, especially the *Fédération des Municipalités Algériennes*, the *Confédérations des agriculteurs*, and the *Délégations Financières*. The Algerian deputy and landowner Gabriel Abbo co-ordinated a campaign in June 1923 by circulating a model resolution to all municipalities by which they called on, 'the higher Algerian administration, the parliamentary representatives of the colony, the Federation of Mayors and the Governor General' to introduce rigorous controls.[38] This opportunist petition emphasised in detail the dangers of migration to metropolitan France – high levels of unemployment, the spread of disease, the costs of hospital treatment and repatriation, and growing criminality – before concluding with the real objective which was, 'at the same time to reserve for Algerian agriculture, the production of which is so necessary to the food supply of the metropole, a labour supply which can only be utilised in Algeria'.[39] At the same time strong pressures were building up among the administrators of the *communes mixtes* who complained about local shortages of labour and native defiance of their orders, which were strictly illegal, not to emigrate.[40]

The *Gouvernement Générale* regularly transmitted these *colons* anxieties to the *Direction des Affaires Algériens* in the Ministry of the Interior in Paris which responded by initiating a detailed investigation of the global impact of migration. In Algeria native administrators were ordered by a circular to take a census of all Algerians absent from their commune in France.[41] On 16 July the *Direction* sent a further circular to French Prefects requesting them to collect all available data on Algerian criminality from court and police records and to give their personal comments.[42] The returns from the two surveys were integrated into an official 'Report on Native Emigration' which served as a background paper for government policy.[43] The Report, rather surprisingly, concluded in favour of continuing migration. It pointed out that the majority of French Prefects returns were 'favourable', and that most offences committed by Algerians were trivial misdemeanors (*délits*). It could not be concluded that Algerians in France constituted 'a particular risk to security'. Migration may have caused some difficulties for the *colons* but, it was implied, this was because colonial wages were far too low. Overall it would be wrong to claim that, 'emigration could constitute any kind of threat to French power in this country'. There is some evidence to suggest that the authors, one of whom was an Algerian, were sympathetic to the francophile Algerian élites who favoured retaining freedom of movement which they saw as a key political symbol of French assimilation policy.

The report was, however, rapidly overtaken by events and left to gather dust due to an event which was to have a crucial impact on policy, the Rue Fondary murders of 7 November 1923.[44] The killings could not have come at a more opportune moment for the colonial lobby, which seized the chance to push home the message of Algerian criminality in France. The deranged Kabyle had, it was claimed, pestered a shop-keeper for sexual favours, and when he was rebuffed he had cut her throat with a knife. For the press, which gave the event major coverage, the murders provided dramatic evidence for the image of the 'Sidi' as a sexually violent primitive who was prone to uncontrollable savagery and acts of revolting cruelty.

The scale of the ensuing moral panic, which was whipped up by the colonial and right-wing press, was swiftly used by the settler lobby to press home the need for controls on emigration. Within a week of the crime the General Secretary of the *Comité Franco-Musulman de l'Afrique du Nord* had written to the Governor General to express the widespread public shock and the dangers of leaving migrants 'unprotected' and exposed to 'the numerous temptations' of the city.[45] A week later a special meeting of the *commissaires de la police judiciaire* was called to discuss Algerian criminality and following this, on 22 November, the Director of the Algerian *Sûreté générale* wrote to the Governor General, attacked the 1914 law on free movement, and suggested various new controls.[46] Four days later (26–7

November) the *Confédération des Agriculteurs d'Alger* met in an emergency session to consider measures to halt emigration and noted the increase in 'the army of crime'. They sent a resolution to the Governor General with requests to establish an *Office de Contrôle* which would filter out undesirable men with a criminal record and also require emigrants to obtain a French work contract before departure.[47]

Under this strong pressure the Minister of the Interior referred the question of controls to an important inter-departmental body, the *Commission Interministérielle de la Main d'Oeuvre* (CIMO), which decided on policy relating to all immigrant labour.[48] After sessions held in Paris on 10 June, 10 April and 28 July 1924 the Commission recommended new restrictions on movement. These were promulgated by the Minister of the Interior, Chautemps, through administrative circulars on 8 August, 11 August and 12 September. The new measures sabotaged the law of 15 July 1914 on free movement: every future migrant would be required to obtain a French work-contract, verified by the Ministry of Labour, before departure; had to undergo a medical inspection by a government doctor for tuberculosis and other contagious diseases; and had to obtain an identity card with, for the first time, a photograph.[49]

The measures, which the government hypocritically announced as in 'the natives own interest',[50] may seem from a contemporary perspective to be unexceptional, but in practice for illiterate and impoverished peasants located in the interior many miles from towns or administrative centres the bureaucratic requirements presented formidable hurdles. The Prefect of Constantine noted that for natives, 'far from any European centre', access to a photographer was, 'a physical impossibility which was for them equivalent to a total ban on movement to France'.[51] Mayors and local administrators who were opposed to emigration and the loss of cheap labour made it difficult to obtain the necessary certificates or, in other cases, they used the opportunity to extort fees or bribes.

The impact of the new measures on the rate of emigration was instant and dramatic. Even regular workers for *Michelin*, on vacation in Kabylia, found themselves blocked in Algeria.[52] Registered departures from Algerian ports collapsed in October 1924 compared to the previous year:

	1923	1924
August	8057	8422
September	3052	7640
October	3952	331
November	4908	384
December	3082	603[53]

Hundreds, if not thousands, of men resorted to clandestine methods to get to France. They purchased forged work contracts or medical certificates and stowed away on ships. Every kind of ruse was used to get across to France: in October 1924 it was discovered that migrants were travelling to Marseilles in the expensive First or Second Class because passengers of higher social status, French and Algerian élites, were not subject to any control.[54]

The Paris government and the *Gouvernement Générale* were well aware that any moves to place an absolute block on the right to emigrate would arouse intense political opposition among Algerians, particularly the nascent nationalist movement of the *Jeunes-Algériens*. The granting of the right to unimpeded emigration by the law of 15 July 1914 was an important symbol of French *bona fides* and proclaimed committment to native assimilation (see Introduction). To renege on the right to free movement, especially after thousands of Algerians had just died fighting for French, was politically unacceptable to central government. After 1918 the French government had come under intense pressure, especially from settler interests and local administrators, to scrap the 1914 law. On numerous occasions the *Gouvernement Générale* wrote, in reply to administrators' requests for a block on emigration, that this was legally and politically impossible. The government had to be seen to uphold the letter of the 1914 law.[55]

The government was constantly worried that a too overt restriction would stir up nationalist unrest. On a typed report of 1927 a senior official wrote in ink that Communists were trying to incite native unrest on the issue of controls which, if too severe, would be 'disastrous for French influence and would work in the interests of Moscow'.[56] However, the objective of the Chautemps circulars was clearly to block migration by **administrative** measures, without openly challenging the 1914 law. The cynical opportunism underlying the controls was revealed in a session of the *Délégations Financières* in June 1924 when one delegate, Passerieu, stated that medical controls would be one way to halt, 'an exodus which is causing us great harm'. The *colon* delegate Pelissier argued, 'We always hear the objection that this is a hindrance to individual freedom. However the administration is not powerless, if not to halt emigration entirely, at least to restrict it by indirect methods.'[57] The colonial lobby's racist campaign to blacken the migrants as dangerous criminals and vectors of disease had paid off.

However, Chautemps' attempt to persuade Algerian opinion that his circulars were not intended to halt emigration but had been inspired, 'by the constant desire to safeguard the workers own interests', failed to impress.[58] The elected native members of the *Délégations Financières*, the *Conseil Général* of Oran and Algiers, and of the Algiers Municipal Council, organised a strong protest movement. They claimed that the new measures would have 'disastrous consequences', were vexatious to all Algerians, and would ruin, 'the prestige of France in Algeria'. But in particular they appealed against the illegality of the circulars to the *Conseil d'État*.[59] Eventually the *Conseil* adjudicated on 18 June 1926 that the Chautemps circulars were illegal. A minister could not take administrative measures that were in contradiction with a law that provided its regulatory framework.[60] However, this was a Pyrrhic victory: by ruling that such circulars would be legal if signed by the French President, the *Conseil* opened the way to a rapid reinstatement of controls and within a matter of weeks this was achieved through the Doumerque Decree (4 August).[61]

The incident throws light on the extent to which the whole field of Algerian migration was regulated throughout the inter-war period without any discussion in the French parliament. Gary Cross argues that immigration in general was largely irrelevant to party politics, hence the absence of any legislation during the four years of the Bloc National (1919–24).[62] A number of experts on immigration policy deplored the absence of a coherent, regulatory framework and pushed, without success, for the creation of a new ministry or single authority.[63] The absence of a strong and unified regulatory agency meant that immigration policy was fragmented and this was abandoned to government ministries, each working to its own agenda and particular interests.[64] This pattern, combined with a lack of parliamentary control, presented the danger of important aspects of immigration policy being influenced by special interest groups and implemented by administrative fiat. Nowhere were these dangers greater than in the case of Algerian migration. Under the so-called *régime des décrets* the Ministry of the Interior possessed extraordinary powers by which his administrative orders had the force of law in Algeria.[65] The circuit of influence between the settlers, the *Gouvernement Générale* and the Ministry of the Interior was tight and closed. Algerian immigration policy was elaborated in a piecemeal way, through an accumulation of circulars and instructions, that opened the door to highly arbitrary methods.

The colonial administration was perfectly aware of the fact that the actions of the Ministry of the Interior were illegal. The colonial lobby, not satisfied with the degree of control over migration achieved through the Doumerque decree of 4 August 1926, pushed for an even tougher policy. Eventually the Sarraut decree of 4 April 1928 added extra requirements to the existing list: a further health inspection at the point of embarkation, a deposit of 125 francs to pay for possible repatriation, and a further 150 francs as subsistence cash.[66] In the early 1930s Jean Mirante, *Directeur des Affaires indigènes*, in a confidential reply to a demand for even further restrictions, remarked that the Doumerque and Sarraut decrees were, 'in effect of questionable legality' since they contravened the law of 15 July 1914. It was better, he said, to let things lie as they were. 'These texts have passed into practice and fortunately are taken for granted. This is a major reason for not raising this delicate issue again and risking an appeal to the *Conseil d'état*, which would be likely to decide against the administration.'[67] But the Ministry of the Interior was quite prepared to secretly instruct native administrators to block emigration by bureaucratic inertia.[68]

THE HIERARCHY OF RACE

A final aspect of the élite racialisation of Algerians that needs to be considered is evidence that they were more consistently targeted by negative stereotypes than any other nationality, including other Arab people. Working-class or populist racism rarely differentiated between Algerians, Moroccans and Tunisians. At street level all three groups appeared to be physically identical and the popular terms used treated them as a whole: 'Sidi', 'Arab', 'bicots' and 'bougnoules'. The articles, essays and books written by colonial ideologues and specialists on Maghrebian immigration used a different, apparently non-racist terminology, moving between general terms like 'North African' and 'Musulmanes française', and more specific references to national (Algerian, Moroccan, Tunisian) and ethnic or regional identity (Kabyle, Chaouia, Soussi, etc). When two priests visited the shantytown of Les Grésillons in 1929 and asked a passing French worker for directions to the **Algerian** sector, he readily switched categories:

'Are there many Algerians here?'
'The "*bicots*"! But my dear sir, there's masses of them! Look! Go down to the Grésillons. In five minutes you'll be right in Arabia.'[69]

However, élite discourse – unlike populist statements – frequently not only demarcated 'Algerians' and 'Moroccans' but also contrasted the two so as to create a more negative and racialised stereotype of the Algerian.[70] Experts produced a racial hierarchy in which 'North Africans' were placed at the bottom, below other immigrant groups (Poles, Belgians, Italians etc.). But the Maghrebians were then further subdivided to produce the ultimate nadir, the lowest of the low, the Algerians.

This refinement of racial hierarchy can be most clearly seen at work in the debate on immigrant labour and productivity. As we have seen (Chapter 4) numerous commentators made general remarks like that of Gomar, 'They are all lazy, with an ancestral idleness, and are characterised also by an almost total lack of method, being very capricious and dreamers, capable of enormous effort for insignificant results.'[71] In the inter-war period 'scientific' Taylorist techniques of measuring work efficiency spread into French industry, especially in the most advanced sectors like car production.[72] Several studies, which assessed workers by nationality, consistently placed 'Arabs' at the bottom. In 1926 a major car manufacturer asked eight *chefs de service* in its Paris factories to grade the eleven foreign groups they employed, a total of 5074 men, on a number of criteria in which a maximum score of ten points was equal to a very good French workman (Table 8.1).[73] Although North

Table 8.1 Supervisor ranking of foreign workers in the Paris car industry, 1926

	Belgians	Italians	Spanish	Poles	Greeks	Arabs
Physical aspect	10	7.5	5.7	8.7	5.6	1.2
Time-keeping	8.1	7.5	7.5	6.8	5	4.3
Daily productivity	8.1	6.2	4.6	6.2	3.7	1.2
Piece-rate productivity	10	7.8	6.6	8.5	5.8	3.2
Mental discipline	6.8	5.3	5.7	6.5	6.4	2.8
Degree of satisfaction with workers	10	8.5	9.1	5	5.7	4.2
Comprehension of French	10	8.7	7.1	3.1	4.3	3.7
Total points	63	51.5	45.9	44.8	36.5	20.6
General average	9	7.3	6.5	6.4	5.2	2.9

A mark of ten represents a maximum positive score.
Adapted from: A. Pairault, *L'Immigration Organisée* (1926) p. 189.

Africans, illiterate men from rural societies and without any experience of industrial labour, undoubtedly took some time to learn new skills (just as did peasants from Brittany) it seems likely that gradings of 'appearance' or 'mental discipline' were less a reflection of scientific testing than employer prejudice. This table, I would argue, provides an accurate measure of the hierarchy of 'race' within French society generally.

One of the fundamental reasons for the employers consistent denigration of North Africans was in order to super-exploit them as a pool of low-paid labour.[74] This economistic argument cannot, however, readily explain a further refinement of racial stereotyping which placed the Algerians below the Moroccans. Gomar's comments are quite typical: 'The Moroccans are stronger, more abstemious, better workers and more conscientious than the Algerians. As a result the Moroccans are less affected by health problems than the Kabyles, are much preferred by employers, and hardly suffer from unemployment. Moroccan labour does not bring with it distressing problems like that of Algerian labour ...'[75] Joanny

Ray was so keen to support the superiority of Moroccan over Algerian workers that he argued, through a tortuous logic, that the category 'Arabs' in Pairault (see Table 8.1) referred uniquely to Algerians.[76]

The evidence would suggest that French and colonial élites racialised Algerians above all other immigrant groups, including the Moroccans, since they regarded them as particularly problematic or, to use Gomar's words, 'distressing'. There could be various reasons for this discrimination between the two Maghrebian groups. Possibly Moroccans, as a people who had only been conquered since 1912, were felt by employers to be less 'spoilt' or corrupted by contact with French ways and therefore more malleable, while Algerians had, during a century of domination, picked up 'bad habits' and showed resistance through go-slows, surliness, and workplace demands. Perhaps the Algerians were perceived and named as a threat simply because they made up the bulk of North African immigration.

However, the basic difference between the two national groups was primarily to do with contrasting colonial regimes and political status. Because Algeria was an extension of France and all Algerians had French citizenship or subject status it was, as we have seen, particularly difficult to control emigration. But this was not true of the protectorates of Morocco and Tunisia. Moroccan immigrants had basically the same status as foreigners and this made it particularly easy to regulate the flow of migrants. Departures were strictly controlled according to the level of demand in the French economy and forced repatriation was easy. 'Their surveillance', noted Gomar, 'their control and the definitive removal of those among them who are defective or undesirable presents far fewer problems than in the case of the Algerians.'[77] The logic of the colonial élite was to win over public opinion to the need for controls not on 'Arabs' per se, but **specifically on Algerians**, through a campaign that racialised them as a particular threat to public health and law and order.

By 1924 the colonial and administrative lobbies had succeeded in gaining the implementation of new controls. However, these were still seen as insufficient to contain the political dangers of emigration. The decision-making élites went on to try and extend a system of police surveillance over those who remained in France. This is the subject of the next chapter.

9 Policing and Surveillance in France

Although the colonial lobby was successful in its campaign for stringent immigration controls, the administrative hurdles were still insufficient to block the movement to France. The statistics of departures from Algerian ports, while showing a dramatic fall immediately following the Chautemps decrees, soon recovered and in 1926 reached nearly 50 000 men (see Table A1). Experienced migrants quickly learned how to cope with the administrative requirements, while there was a dramatic increase in clandestine migration. Whether they liked it or not the lobby was faced with the existence of a large and irreducible Algerian presence in France, a community which was increasingly recruited into the ranks of the Communist Party, trade unions and the nationalist/independence movements of the *Oulémas* and the *Étoile Nord-Africaine*. The colonial lobby therefore engaged in a campaign, complementary to that for immigration controls, to create a special policing and surveillance apparatus to contain these subversive dangers. The surveillance operation was established first in Paris in 1925 as the *Services de Surveillance, Protection et Assistance des Indigènes Nord-Africains* (SAINA) and was later extended to the rest of France in 1928. This represented an attempt to insert colonial methods of policing and 'native management' into metropolitan France on a scale that was unprecedented in Europe.[1]

The expansion in the range and complexity of the French state during the nineteenth century was in part linked to the elaboration of new techniques for the identification, tracking and counting of all individuals. This fundamental shift in the structure of the modern state related to interlocking issues of new statistical 'sciences', accurate civil registration, and other forms of identification for purposes of taxation systems, elections, military conscription, universal education and policing.[2] By the turn of the century, French bureaucratic structures and culture showed an obsessive concern with identification and location: nobody must be able to escape the all-seeing eye of the official. This drive towards identification and control

153

assumed a particularly overt form in colonial Algeria where millions of natives were without 'name', unregistered at birth or death, and as nomads escaped the web of civil authority. The long, drawn-out process of 'capturing' the Algerian population involved the sedentarisation of nomads, their permanent settlement on demarcated areas of land, the imposition of new names and civil registration (1885–94), the establishment of tax registers, the draconian regulations of the *Code de l'indigènate* (1881), and enforced military conscription (1912).[3] In 1882 settler interests stated, 'that it is vital that the natives are totally in the grasp of the administration'.[4]

The key enforcers of this system were the native administrators who, helped by a small team of native interpreters and officers, oversaw the enormous territories of the *communes mixtes* of the interior. The administrators of the early twentieth century, following in the steps of the *bureaux arabes*, were frequently inspired by a missionary zeal to introduce 'their' natives to the benefits of French civilisation – improved roads, western medicine, schools, efficient justice, irrigation, and scientific agriculture.[5] However, this paternalism was entirely consistent with levels of authoritarianism under the 'special regime' that would have been both unheard of and unacceptable in France. Under the *code* Algerians could, for example, even be punished for acts of 'disrespect, or offensive remarks' made towards any official, whether in or out of his function.[6] Even humane administrators justified such practices on the grounds that Algerians, as backward and ignorant people, could – no more than young children – know what was in their true interest. The firm but kindly hand of the French should guide the naïve and often recalcitrant natives until that time (perhaps centuries away) when they were sufficiently educated to assume the full political rights of an adult.

Octave Depont, Pierre Godin, Adolphe Gérolami and Julien Azario, the founders of the SAINA apparatus in Paris and Lyons, had all passed their formative years as native administrators. Moulded by their shared experience of training in the schools for colonial officers and by years in the *bled*, they brought to the 'problem' of immigration all the attitudes, both paternalist and authoritarian, of the colonial system. These ex-administrators, fluent in Arabic and Berber, had an unparalleled knowledge of Algerian rural society. It was precisely this expertise, a claim to understand the peculiarities of native psychology and culture, that gave the lobbyists a special authority with ministers, politicians and newspaper editors in Paris. They claimed to know what made the *indigène* migrant tick, the nuances of language and approach required to win his confidence, and the kinds of measure that would safely contain him. Gérolami, for example, in persuading a committee to appoint him as director of the Paris Muslim Hospital stated that the new incumbent would manage best, 'if he possessed an in-depth knowledge of the Berber and Arab languages and if, through a long experience of the Muslim world, he was knowledgeable of the customs and values of the natives of North Africa. In this respect, I believe that I can provide all the necessary guarantees through my long experience as an administrator in the Algerian *communes mixtes*.'[7]

A fundamental anxiety of the colonial lobbyists, and of the senior metropolitan police officers whom they advised, was the ability of the Algerian migrants to escape identification. By crossing the Mediterranean the migrants, while still technically within the same country, were able to avoid the powerful colonial apparatus of control for the 'free air' of the metropole. As the jurist Gomar remarked, 'In Algeria they are under the surveillance of an administration created specially for them. Nothing like this exists in France, where they have the same rights as everybody else and escape practically all authority'. This freedom, he added, included the right to buy revolvers.[8] The authorities were frustrated and worried by their inability to penetrate and gather intelligence on the secretive and closed-in society of the migrants. As has been seen (Chapter 5) the Algerians grouped in micro-ghettos or enclaves, linked in social networks based on kin and village ties and bound by their own language, customs and café culture, were segregated from French society.

The discourse of the colonial lobby emphasised the threatening nature of the 'encysted' Algerian presence. Gomar noted that no special policing apparatus existed before 1923, 'The Kabyles, disembarking one fine day in France, lose themselves in the anonymous crowd. Always difficult to identify, they lodge eight or ten in a single room and their surveillance by the police, lacking in special means, is an almost impossible task ... The police do not know how many there are nor what they

are up to. They form an impenetrable core . . .'[9] The Prefect
of the Gard reported in 1937 that the surveillance of North
Africans in the mining region was almost impossible since,
'the individuals we want to control do not mix with the indigenous population; they speak a foreign language most of the
time and they are secretly strongly united by their respect for
Koranic laws, all of which makes it extremely difficult to uncover what is going on in this milieu.'[10] Control was also made
difficult because of the very high levels of geographical mobility of Algerians as they moved frequently from one job to
another and between lodging-houses, a mobility which was
ascribed to their 'hereditary nomadism'.[11]

Algerian migrants quietly resisted control. For them contact
with French officialdom was not a new phenomena; for a century Algerians had experienced the colonial administrators as
the foreward agents of domination, of land appropriations,
new and heavy taxation, and the native code. After an initial
phase of armed rebellion which ended in the defeat of 1871
Algerians tried to protect themselves from the oppression of
settlers and colonial officials through forms of social and cultural resistance which included a strategy of ruse and silence,
a masking through which the colonial masters could not see.[12]
Jacques Berque noted that, while apparently adapting to the
French presence, 'The Muslim population maintains zones
which are absolutely inviolable. It pulls back into a protective
shell.'[13] Passive resistance could take many forms, including
the response of feigned ignorance or *manarf* ('I don't know')
in reply to the questions of colonial masters and officials.[14]

Algerians in France reproduced these forms of resistance
when confronted with officialdom which, for them, usually
spelt out trouble. Joanny Ray noted a similar pattern among
Moroccans in inter-war Paris, the 'phobia of the Soussi for
everything to do with the *maghzen* [zone of French control], as
opposed to the *siba* or zone of dissidence. In Paris some Moroccans claimed that, "every control is a form of spying, every
form of assistance a means of grassing (*mouchardage*)"'. North
African migrants employed a battery of ruses to avoid identification, including the alteration or the swopping of identity
cards.[15] In reply to the 1923 investigation of Algerian criminality the state prosecutor in St Omer reported that Algerians
rarely had a proper identity card and were constantly changing

their name.[16] Other local authorities reported that Algerians were 'liars', 'deceitful' or that 'they try to remain unnoticed ... avoid drawing attention to themselves'.[17]

Pierre Godin, former native administrator and senior colonial police officer, and a prominent member of the Paris city council, was the moving force behind the creation of the special police force that became known as the 'Rue Lecomte'. Seizing on the moment of moral panic that followed on the murders in the Rue Fondary on 7 November 1923 he, supported by two other Paris councillors, Besombes and Emile Massard, presented a first project for the SAINA to the council on 20 December.[18] Godin, drawing attention to the 'sensational crime' and the dangers of an uncontrolled North-African 'invasion', remarked that in Paris, 'the police are disorientated, overcome by a phenomenon which they are not trained to understand or to control'.[19] Effective surveillance had to be based on an apparatus which could locate and identify every individual migrant, forms of control that Godin clearly hoped would reproduce the policing techniques of Algeria. This would involve the creation of an 'infallible' *fichier* or system of indexing:

> The first service which we render to the immigrants is to identify them. A necessary if demanding and delicate task ... And how necessary! Imagine what would become of this confused anonymous mass if it was impossible to isolate and locate with certainty the units of which it is composed? What a sanctuary of criminality [*cour des miracles*]. And what a danger to everyday life in Paris! Once they are recorded in our files we will be able to follow and track down our protégé and easily investigate offences and crimes among this population that does not speak our language ... Thus, eventually, we shall have a rapid system of repression which corresponds to the traditions and mentality of our subjects and guarantees their security as well as our own.[20]

In order to crack the Algerian resistance and impose a 'minute and constant control', Godin would have to establish an unusual policing agency, what he called an 'elegant and precise machine'.[21]

Godin, in his campaign of 1923–4 to win over the municipality, received strong support and advice from the Ministry of the Interior.[22] Eventually the City Council voted through the project on 31 July 1924, although it took another year for the *Service* to begin its operations in a former school building in the Rue Lecomte. The SAINA, which had a complex and evolving structure, was divided into two main sub-sections, one concerned with surveillance operations by a specialist brigade, and the other with various forms of welfare (health care, employment, housing). The welfare section, although in principle quite separate from policing, was used to collect information for the individual files used by police intelligence. The first head of the unit was Adolphe Gérolami who, throughout his seven years in this role, was technically still a functionary of the *Gouvernement Général*.[23] From July 1932 he was succeeded by Pierre Godin's son, André Godin, who transferred from his post as personal secretary to the Prefect of Police.[24] The police section was administered by the Prefecture of Police, which also provided about 35 per cent of overall SAINA funding, while the welfare functions were co-ordinated by the Prefecture of the Seine. The remaining funding came from the Paris council (15 per cent) and from a special local business tax, the *patente* (30 per cent).

Why this unusual hybrid organisation was established in this way and not as a central government initiative is unclear. Initially the *Gouvernement Générale* was not too keen to support the project on the grounds of cost and because the *colons* disliked any form of welfare which would encourage further emigration of labour.[25] It seems probable that a proposal for a colonial police apparatus in the metropole would have met stiff opposition in parliament from the left and from civil rights groups. Public controversy would also have revealed the true purpose of the project, to counter Communism and the Algerian nationalists.[26] Chautemp's backing of Pierre Godin enabled the police unit to be established through the back door, via the City Council. The arrangement also gave Gérolami enormous freedom of movement and power which, as will be seen, he used in an arbitrary way to oppress the Algerian migrants.

Below we examine in turn the dual police and welfare functions of the SAINA.

POLICING AND SURVEILLANCE

The police brigade of the Rue Lecomte was made up of 25 (later 32) inspectors under four officers. These men had to undergo an oral examination in Arabic or Berber, a condition which largely restricted entry to men who had been born in Algeria or seen service there in the army and police.[27] Like the *harki* units introduced to France during the Algerian war to track the FLN they brought to their task a knowledge of the 'enemy' as well as the repressive attitudes of the colonial police force. Paris and its suburbs were divided up into eight sectors, each of which was patrolled by a team of four men who could, if necessary, call for support from regular police forces. Pierre Godin described their main functions as intervening wherever North Africans were involved in incidents (drunkeness, fighting) or criminal activity (gambling, procuring), and to track down wanted men.[28] A common form of action was to carry out raids on North African cafés and to check identity cards to locate deserters and clandestine immigrants.

However, Pierre Godin's detailed published account of the SAINA completely concealed the principal activity of the brigade which was to gather intelligence on Algerian political activity, the involvement in strikes, the Communist Party and the *Étoile-Nord-Africaine*. SAINA agents attended almost every public meeting of the ENA, of which there were hundreds, and placed spies in the ENA executive. André Godin, after 1932, collated all the reports which he received and sent a summary, via the Prefect of Police, to the key departments concerned with North African security, including the Ministry of the Interior, the Foreign Office, and the War Office.[29] André Godin was regarded as the leading expert on the *Étoile* and it was he who took the iniative in preparing the information which led to the imprisonment of Messali Hadj and the proscription of the ENA in 1934.[30] Another form of action by the brigade was to harrass and disrupt the activities of ENA militants. A common tactic was to throw a police cordon round large ENA meetings and to arrest and index all those without identity cards. Many of these men were then reported to employers who sacked them: as unemployed migrants they were then illegally 'repatriated' by SAINA to Algeria. The cafés which were the centre of political activity were also subjected to frequent raids, and the proprietors threatened with withdrawal of their licence.[31] In 1935 Azario, the head of the SAINA in Lyons, through continual harassment of café owners successfully drove a wedge between them and the ENA and forced them to make a humiliating 'apology' (*aman*).[32]

However, in many ways the most typically colonial form of control was achieved through the welfare services of the Rue Lecomte.

WELFARE, PATERNALISM AND SURVEILLANCE

Although Godin and his associates underlined the dangerous criminality of immigrants as a reason for special police controls, their public propaganda for the SAINA placed a much larger emphasis on its humane paternalist and civilising role. For these purposes the Algerian migrant was presented not as a cunning robber or rapist armed with a knife, but as a naive primitive, a 'big child', who required protection from the evils of industrial and urban society. Godin assumed the moral high ground: aid and protection, he claimed, was provided without any ulterior motive but simply because, ' "humanity" must not become a vain word' and immigrants, as subjects and 'adoptive sons' of the nation, had 'moral rights that we will not allow to lapse'. Through the SAINA the migrants would no longer be, 'anonymous in a flock without a shepherd and a sense of direction'.[33] To imagine that immigrants disliked strong leadership, 'would be to show ignorance of their ways and to forget that their most pressing need and desire is to feel protected, a sentiment that they can only fully appreciate under the guidance of the Administration . . . Our surveillance is not for them a form of subjection, but a protection – better still, a state of happiness.'[34] The model here was unambiguously that of the colonial administrator, the father of his people, to whom the natives came to resolve their problems and disputes.

Godin did, however, admit that SAINA fulfilled certain important political and imperial functions. The danger of uncontrolled migration was that hundreds of thousands of Algerians, inhabiting squalid slums, exploited, infected with disease, and physically broken and demoralised, would either fall prey to revolutionary agitators or transmit back into the tribes a highly negative image of France. The SAINA propagandists laid considerable emphasis on the imperial dimension of a coherent welfare policy. Through the welfare functions of SAINA migrants, who often arrived in France 'corrupted', would be educated, improved and return as 'a better trained labour force and improved human beings'. Through their daily contact with French civilisation and, 'through living like us, close to us, the natives will eventually come to see that they have evolved in our direction. They will become, not uprooted or classless people, but friends on their way to becoming equals and perhaps in time will be ready to enter the City.'[35] SAINA was thus legitimated by the classic colonial theory of assimilation according to which Algerians would assume full citizenship in some indeterminate future.[36]

Lastly, it was argued, a coherent welfare policy would have an enormous global impact by transmitting throughout the Empire and the Muslim world a positive image of France as an exemplar of humanity and civilisation. 'France has today become a great colonial power and a great Muslim power. North Africa is the keystone of her empire.' Migrants returning to Algeria would be emissaries of French enlightenment and thus, 'the grandiose problem presented in Algeria by the coexistence of the Orient and the Occident will perhaps find its first solution in Paris'.[37] Edouard Renard, Prefect of the Seine, who strongly supported SAINA, stated that its programme of hostel construction would make an impact, 'throughout the Islamic world, in which France enjoys an exceptional prestige and in which Paris has gained the reputation of a unique city, the capital of the civilised universe'. The competitive imperialistic dimensions of sound welfare policy was clear. 'The slums of Paris', he added, 'must not come to equal those of London nor, in the lower depths of our luminous city, develop into ghettos of a medieval nature.'[38]

However, what Godin's detailed report of 1933 failed to mention or even hint at was that SAINA's welfare policies were also part of another, less noble agenda. Firstly, the aim in creating a range of specialist institutions (hostels, infirmaries etc.) was to segregate Algerians from the dangerous influences of French working-class life. Secondly, the welfare network was a crucial part of the repressive policing apparatus, a means to gather intelligence or, through a carrot and stick approach, a means of rewarding or punishing migrants according to their degree of involvement with 'subversive' organisations. The Communist Party and the ENA were both aware of these functions and one of the central campaigning issues of the *Étoile* was the call for dissolution of the SAINA. As one militant stated in an ENA meeting, the Rue Lecomte, 'under the cover of philanthropy has organised a system of informers'.[39]

The complex welfare apparatus of SAINA was elaborated over a number of years by a *Comité d'assistance et protection des indigènes Nord-Africains* set up by the Paris City Council on 3 July 1925, in which Pierre Godin played a prominent role as President.[40] The welfare functions can be broken down into eight forms of aid or intervention.

i) Advisory Services

A bureau in the Rue Lecomte, manned by interpreters and secretaries, helped the immigrants – many of whom were illiterate – with a range of administrative problems.[41] It gave advice on the social security system, on unemployment benefits, and work-place accidents and insurance claims. It helped with claims for family benefits and how to transfer funds to relatives in North Africa. SAINA handled all matters to do with the issue or renewal of identity cards, birth-certificates, naturalisation procedures and other documentation. Its activities even extended to the location of migrants 'lost' to their relatives in Algeria, advice for pilgrims going to Mecca, and arrangements for the burial and the disposal of the property of those who died.[42]

These, and the other welfare functions listed below, were used to build up a systematic index of all those who used the SAINA's various services. Through this means the Rue Lecomte during the period 1927–30 established files on 28 897 Algerians, 11 235 Moroccans and 628 Tunisians.[43] By August 1935 the Lyons service had established files on about 4000 of the estimated 5750 North Africans in the Lyons region.[44] These individual dossiers were of key importance to the police brigade in its operations against the ENA.[45] This form of intelligence gathering which depended on the carrot of welfare to draw unidentified foreigners into the ambit of the police shows continuity with methods established during the nineteeth century.[46]

ii) Repatriation

The SAINA helped organise the return home of ill or unemployed Algerians. However, during the economic recession of the winter of 1926–7 Gérolami exceeded his powers and pressurised hundreds of men to return in large convoys. Between 1 December 1926 and February 1927 2884 Algerians were sent back in this way.[47] After 1926, in spite of all immigrants having to pay a deposit to cover the costs of repatriation, Gérolami felt he had the authority to send a standard form directly to administrators of the *communes mixtes* naming individuals repatriated by 'my service' and asking them to, 'refuse all papers which will allow him to return to France', an entirely arbitrary directive.[48] In Lyons the SAINA organised seven convoys of 60 to 180 men each between December 1926 and January 1927. In one of these 184 men were tricked into believing that they were being sent to jobs in Corsica, but the ship was diverted to Bône, where they were dumped.[49] Gomar, acknowledging in 1931 that forced repatriation of Algerian 'subjects' was illegal, noted that SAINA still had recourse to 'persuasion', a euphemism for a programme that was 'evidently delicate'.[50] Forceable repatriation thus continued in spite of the fact that its legality was challenged by the political left and by the League for Human Rights.[51]

iii) Job Location and Strike Breaking

One of the welfare functions of the SAINA was the location of work for North Africans through its *bureau de placement*. However, this apparently laudatory service rapidly evolved into a formidable weapon that was deployed against the French and Algerian trade union movement. Major firms like *Renault, Citroën* and the *G7 garage* were encouraged to refer the names of all would-be North African employees to the SAINA so they could be checked out on the police files.[52] Through such procedures employers gained access to the poorest and most docile migrants. The SAINA also offered to screen men already in employment against its files and persuaded them to sack those who were active in the ENA or PCF. In May 1935 Azario, head of the Lyons SAINA, noted that a 'control has enabled us to uncover a dozen infiltrators, communist agitators, particularly in the dye works' and that an inquiry was proceeding into 'certain suspect elements' in the arsenals.[53] The SAINA also organised North Africans to break strike movements of other Maghrebians, as with the bitter dispute involving over 1000 car-washers in Paris in March 1934.[54] In Lyons in August 1934 twenty Algerians were supplied by the SAINA, under police protection, to replace striking French workers locked out by the construction company *Versille Frères*. In a bloody confrontation between the two sides the Algerians wounded several strikers and killed another, Gabriel Besse, with revolvers that the trade union claimed were supplied by the *Service*.[55]

iv) Unemployment Benefits

During the economic recessions of the inter-war period thousands of Algerians were laid off and began to claim various forms of unemployment benefit which were usually paid out by the local municipality. The Rue Lecomte attempted to centralise this system in the Paris region since it recognised that this would greatly increase its powers of coercion. In February 1927 the Prefect of the Seine wrote to all mayors in the department noting that municipalities had been issuing North Africans with certificates which enabled them to receive benefits. Since, he claimed, town-halls lacked the interpreters or competence to verify if immigrants were legally entitled to benefits all future requests for unemployment money should pass via the Rue Lecomte. The SAINA then used its new powers to withold benefits from ENA supporters who, reduced to desperate poverty, were also forced into repatriation.[56] The Lyons SAINA also reinforced its power by establishing a centralised control of both unemployment benefits and soup tickets in 1935 at the height of the Depression. By November Algerian migrants could not even get into the night-shelter without recommendation by Azario's service.[57]

Some Communist-controlled municipalities, particularly St Denis under the mayoralty of Jacques Doriot, opposed the SAINA and fought to retain the right to register the unemployed as part of a broader campaign to spread the political influence of the PCF among the North Africans. Both colonial and anti-colonial movements thus fought to control the purse strings and access to welfare as part of a broader contest for the hearts and minds of the Algerians.

v) Immigrant Hostels

Immediately after the First World War two semi-official hostels were established, one to house Algerians passing through Marseilles and the other to accommodate the homeless in Paris. These were run by Colonel Chardenet, a former senior officer in the Algerian *Service des affaires indigènes*.[58] From 1923 onwards it was recognised that these were entirely inadequate to cope with the scale of immigration from North Africa.[59] In July 1926, following an investigation of slum conditions by Paris councillors on the *Comité d'Assistance*, the SAINA established a *Service des Foyers* and Octave Depont was appointed as the official inspector. A spartan hostel was opened in the Rue Lecomte itself and another, purpose-built in a 'Moorish' style, opened in 1930 in the Rue de l'Arbre-Sec in Gennevilliers. This four storey building could accommodate one hundred men and was well-equipped, with a large cafeteria, a prayer room, central heating, showers and baths.[60]

In December 1931 the Paris Council accepted a proposal, presented by the Prefect of the Seine, for a contract with a new *Régie des foyers ouvriers Nord-africains*, an organisation headed by M. Robert-Raynaud, General Secretary of the *Institut musulman*. The city provided a long-term loan of seventeen million francs and sites for the construction of up to twenty foyers. In all five hostels were opened in the suburbs with high concentrations of North Africans, at Boulogne-Billancourt, Asnières, Saint-Ouen, Charenton and Colombes.[61] By late 1936 all but one of these hostels was forced to close because of poor financial management and a boycott campaign led by the ENA. When Laroque visited the Billancourt hostel in late 1937 or early 1938 he found 210 men housed in a delapidated building, with the showers and baths out of order, a squalid and overpriced cafeteria, and signs of prostitution.[62]

The official hostels were attacked by the Communist Party and the ENA as an extension of the SAINA system of surveillance. In an ENA meeting on 13 January 1934 Messali Hadj described them as 'barracks under the surveillance of the Rue Lecomte police'.[63] The Communist newspaper *El Amel* also described them as, 'police outposts ... each hostel has an informer's bureau involved in the surveillance of men arriving and leaving, of the mail, and of visitors'. The *Étoile* recognised an attempt, as with the SOTC barracks of the First World War, to place immigrants under a para-military régime that would segregate them from 'all political movements, organisations and associations'.[64] In 1933–4, the ENA campaigned for support among North African café-hotel owners, led by Ahmed Mansouri, who felt that their business was being damaged by the hostels.[65]

vi) Health Care

After 1925 the SAINA established a number of specialised medical centres, equipped with x-ray machines, for the detection and treatment of disease among North Africans. The first clinic, located in the Rue Lecomte in 1925, centred on the diagnosis of venereal disease and tuberculosis, and this service was then extended to dispensaries at the Paris Mosque (1928), the Rue Tiphanie in the 15th *arrondissement* (1932) and worker hostels in the Rue Nationale and in the suburbs of Asnières and Boulogne-Billancourt.[66]

The most prestigious project, quite on a par with that of the Paris Mosque, was one for a Franco-Muslim Hospital which was eventually opened in March 1935 in Bobigny. This purpose-built 270 bed hospital, constructed in a Moorish style by the architect who designed the Paris Mosque, was modern and well-equipped.[67] The connections between the hospital and SAINA were close. Pierre Godin chaired the foundation committee set up in 1926, while detailed planning was in the hands of a smaller sub-committee which included Gérolami, Octave Depont and the doctors from the SAINA clinics. In July 1932 Gérolami surrendered his position as head of the Rue Lecomte to André Godin and was immediately appointed the director of the hospital. He also, along with Octave Depont, taught Arabic and Berber to trainees who applied to a special school of nursing.[68] Among those who worked there was a Dr Destouches, the writer Céline.

This elaborate medical provision was undoubtedly inspired

by a humane concern for the appalling level of illness suffered by malnourished and physically exhausted immigrants who moved daily between dangerous, polluted factories and damp, overcrowded slums.[69] However, once again there was a reverse side of the coin. In colonial North Africa the provision of scientific medical care (innoculation, surgery etc.) was regarded as a potent propaganda weapon in the campaign to win Muslims away from 'superstition' and traditional remedies by demonstrating the superiority of French civilisation and rationality. The SAINA introduced this colonialist strategy and discourse into France. Pierre Godin remarked that immigrants, who were only yesterday, 'the slaves of empiricism, magic charms and amulets', flocked to the medical consultations.[70] Octave Depont insisted, in praising the hospital project, that 'medical aid holds a place of honour among the best agents of our native policy ... medicine causes wonder among the clients of the quacks and magicians in the *bled*'.[71]

However, the most damaging criticism was that the hospital was, once again, an extension of the surveillance apparatus. In a debate in the City Council one councillor, Camille Renault, complained that the director of the hospital was a policeman, as were the majority of members on the organising committee, whereas a project of this kind should be controlled by doctors and citizens. 'What one is trying to do through this committee is primarily to track the North Africans who come to Paris. One wants to know what they are doing and where they are going. This is a social programme that is being diverted from its purpose ...' René Fodère also attacked the confusion of medical and policing functions, warned of the danger of alienating the Muslims, and regretted that 'the price of medicine should be informing'.[72] The 'capture' of the hospital as an instrument of SAINA policy was also reflected in Pierre Godin's drafting of the hospital statutes which changed the original spirit of the project, which had been intended for all Muslims in Paris, by restricting its use to North African immigrants.[73] The pro-Communist *Le Peuple* claimed that Gérolami maintained, 'a veritable atmosphere of distrust, terror and informing among the staff and the patients', and had threatened those employees who had joined the CGTU.[74] Finally both the Communist Party and the ENA nationalists attacked the hospital as part of a policy of racial segregation and demanded that North Africans be allowed to attend any hospital in the Paris region.[75] During the Popular Front the *Haut Comité Méditerranéan* recommended desegregation but it seems unlikely that this was implemented until after the Second World War.

vii) Educational Provision

The SAINA, in conjunction with the League for the Education of Illiterates, ran courses for immigrant workers and also utilised educational films (*cinéma éducateur*).[76] Rager claims that these failed because, 'the police inspectors of the North-African brigade were ordered to engage in propaganda. The result was the precise opposite of what was intended'.[77] However, the biggest intervention was in the special provision made for North African students, a future intellectual élite whom it was thought crucial to 'watch over' with care. The *Gouvernement Générale* was concerned about its loss of control over students who escaped the repressive atmosphere of Algeria and the Algiers faculties.[78] In December 1931 the Paris council accepted the recommendation of Godin's *Commission* to establish a student centre, the *Cercle intellectuel de la Méditerranée*, and this was eventually opened at 26 Rue Gay-Lussac in late 1933. Ironically this project was opposed by the *Commission Interministérielle des Affaires Musulmanes* on the grounds that there was insufficient surveillance and that it could become the centre of political agitation by Arab students from the Maghreb, Egypt, Syria, the Lebanon, and Iraq. Pierre Godin heatedly rejected such a system of 'spying', a type of 'secretly resuscitated *bureau arabe*'![79] However, the effective control of the *Cercle* was placed in the hands of the general secretary, André Godin, who had just become head of SAINA. In late 1933 the student union, the AEMA (*Association des Étudiants Musulmans Algériens en France*), which initially supported the creation of the *Cercle*, became rapidly politicised and formed contacts with the ENA. André Godin decided to use the *Cercle* as an instrument of surveillance. In early 1935 the new President of AEMA, Ahmed Boumendjel, accused Godin of hijacking the *Cercle* by packing the Management Committee, in order to make, 'a subsidiary organisation of the police service and, of our student milieu, a terrain favourable to the most shady police operations.'

Boumendjel even went so far as to encourage an ex-soldier, Captain Djeziri, to stand against Pierre Godin in the municipal elections and to campaign for the closure of the Rue Lecomte.[80]

viii) Arbitration

Perhaps the most remarkable instance of the transplantation of the structures and culture of the native administration into France can be found in the SAINA's recreation of the *chikaïa* and the *aman*. In the *commune mixte* one of the important functions of the native administrator was to sit, as a kind of Justice of the Peace, to arbitrate over the innumerable disputes that arose between the Algerians. The colonial authorities thought that the officer, through his role of conciliator and his wise and balanced judgements, would reinforce his authority as a kind of 'father' to 'his' people. The system of the *chikaïa*, the ultimate symbol of colonial paternalism, was re-invented in metropolitan France. In the SAINA at Saint-Etienne particular times were set each week to receive plaintiffs and, after agreement was reached and sworn on the Koran, 'his administration delivered a document which was equivalent to a sworn statement. In Paris some plaintiffs challenge each other to swear an oath on the Koran of the mosque and an inspector accompagnies them to the edifice . . . a reproduction of the expeditious and paternal justice of the *bled*'.[81] This system of arbitration was to be revived in Paris during the Algerian war by the psychological warfare unit, the SAT (*Service d'assistance technique*), established to undermine the support base of the FLN among the immigrant population.[82]

Finally the director of the Lyons SAINA, Julien Azario, who had been a functionary in Morocco, modelled his service on that of a native administration. This extended to the employment of an Algerian *mokkadem* or assistant, Bel Hadj Ben Maafi, a *marabout* and official of the Rahmania religious fraternity who was barely able to speak French. Azario reproduced the procedures of the French conquest of Algeria when defeated natives were compelled to sue for a pardon in the ceremony of *aman*. The SAINA could bring enormous pressures to bear on ENA militants by gaining their dismissal from work, removing benefit rights and other procedures. When some finally cracked under the strain, Azario would force them to beg for a pardon, the *aman*, in a bizarre ceremony during which the retraction was registered in a quasi-legal document.[83]

In conclusion it can be seen that SAINA built up a formidable battery of techniques for the identification, surveillance and manipulation of Algerian immigrants. But how successful was it in containing the political threat offered by Communism, the *Étoile* and trade unionism, and in segregating Algerian immigrants from the dangerous freedom and influences of life in the *quartiers populaires*?

One sign of success was that the government and immigration experts held up the Paris SAINA as a model agency. The Minister of the Interior, Albert Sarraut, extended the system to the rest of France in a decree of 27 October 1928. France was divided into five regions administered from offices in Paris, Saint-Etienne, Marseilles, Bordeaux, and Lille.[84] The decree stipulated that the directors had to be recruited from former administrators of the *communes mixtes*.[85] The main purpose of the provincial SAINA, as in Paris, was to police the activities of the ENA and the Communist Party. The Lyons service – about which most is known – was established in 1934 in response to constant pressure on the mayor and Prefect from the *Direction des Affaires algériennes* in the Ministry of the Interior. Shortly after, on 4 January 1935 Pierre Godin came on a tour of inspection and gave advice on the shape of the new organisation.[86] However, in spite of this initiative from Paris the provincial SAINA offices were constantly underfunded and short of personnel and by 1933 the Bordeaux and Marseilles services were moribund.[87] Only the Rue Lecomte, backed by dynamic campaigners like Pierre Godin and Octave Depont, and well funded by the police who were keen to track the leadership of the *Étoile* which was centred in Paris, operated on a large scale.

The Rue Lecomte brigade's tactic of harassment and disruption of ENA activities (banning meetings, café raids, prosecutions etc.) did on occasions demoralise militants and restricted the level of support from immigrants. André Godin's meticulous and detailed report of November 1934 concluded that the ENA membership was in decline and that the majority of the 50 000 immigrants in the Paris region had not been 'infected' and remained 'quiet'.[88] The report also shows that the Rue Lecomte possessed an enormous body of intelligence on the activities and structure of the ENA in both France and Algeria, intelligence which was almost daily passed on to police, military and security agencies in France and North Africa. Janet Zagoria, in addressing the question of why the Messalist nationalist movement remained weak and was eventually pushed aside by the FLN in 1954, gives as one major factor the 'hostile environment' created by French repression.[89] However, the process of politicisation of immigrant workers and students in France and the formation of ENA and Algerian-Communist militants was strongly encouraged by the arbitrary and 'colonial' activities of the SAINA. The Rue Lecomte, the 'Commune Mixte de Paris', became a major target of ENA propaganda which was able to expose the organic links between the repressive régime in Algeria and its agents in metropolitan France. The official Laroque Report of 1938 noted that the amalgamation of both police and welfare services in the Rue Lecomte had been disastrous and had alienated immigrants from the social services which they needed. It recommended a clear separation of the two functions, a policy that was never implemented since the Popular Front soon disintegrated.[90]

As the later development of the Algerian independence struggle was to show the administrative lobby was entirely correct in its analysis of the danger presented by emigration to the colonial order. But, in spite of the sophisticated apparatus of surveillance and control which they elaborated, this proved incapable of stemming the tide of nationalism.

10 Colonial Crisis and Emigration, 1930–54

As we have seen, until the Second World War the majority of emigrants came from the Kabyle region. It is now time to look at the contradiction which was mentioned in Chapter 2 between this geographical distribution and the general theory of emigration put forward by post-colonial historians which maintains that emigration was a direct consequence of colonial destruction and land dispossession. The map of emigration (1910–49) shows an **inverse** relationship: the zones of maximum colonisation and capitalist penetration were those from which there was a minimum of departures.[1] Some historians have noted the anomaly but have been unable to provide a satisfactory explanation. Larbi Talha, for example, argues that emigration was precipitated in those areas from which soldiers and workers were recruited during the First World War.[2] But since conscription was universal, affecting entire age-groups or cohorts, Talha's explanation should correlate with an even spatial distribution of post-war emigration. However, soldiers who returned to zones of heavy colonisation, like Sidi Bel Abbès, Oran and Miliana, far from triggering a more generalised emigration, remained an exception when they returned to France.[3] The evidence which Talha quotes from Rager to support his theory demonstrates the very opposite: former soldiers who later became emigrants are mentioned in the census of colonised regions precisely because they stood out as the exception and failed to inspire a generalised departure.[4] Talha's difficulty in squaring the general theory of colonial/capitalist destruction with the pattern of emigration can be found explicitly or implicitly in the work of most historians from Benachenhou, Hifi and Ben Fredj to Bennoune, Massard-Guilbaud and Stora.[5]

The apparent contradiction can be resolved through seeking to answer the question, what factors inhibited departure from zones of **low** emigration? Historians and sociologists of emigration have tended to concentrate their attention on zones of high emigration, like Kabylia, but this one-sided approach neglects half the equation.[6] As was shown in Chapter 2, the period from 1880 to 1930 saw the most dramatic expansion of capitalist production in Algeria, marked by commercialisation of agriculture (vines, grain), mining, and the building of a modern infrastructure (ports, railways, dams and roads). The increasing demand for indigenous labour in the colonised plains was in part resolved by the 'capture' of traditional Kabyle seasonal migration, but an equally important reserve was found in the local, sedentary population encamped on the edges of the big estates. Through *cantonnement*, the forceable removal of tribes from the richest, irrigated land of the plains, the indigenous people were pushed back into more hilly, infertile and arid lands bordering the colonial farms. Unable to survive, the native population was later drawn back to work on the colonial farms, first as sharecroppers and later as wage-labour, on the lands that had once been theirs.

In the peripheral labour reserves the Algerians were close enough to the settler farms to walk there daily. Settlers had on tap a localised and permanent supply of cheap labour which was complementary to the seasonal input of Kabyle and Moroccan long-distance migrants. 'If the *colon* is in need of labour', noted Van Vollenhoven in 1903, 'he sends one of his workers to the neighbouring *douar* to inform the inhabitants . . . next day they present themselves at the work place.'[7]

For example, tribes displaced from the Mitidja plains and confined in the Atlas of Blida underwent demographic growth between 1880 and 1930 and a subdivision of holdings into minute plots so that only one family in ten or fifteen had enough land for subsistence. A solution to the Malthusian crisis was found by men going to work daily on the rich farms of the Mitidja plain to the north.[8] Yacono has analysed the same process at work in the Chélif, where labourers descended every day by bicycle from the mountain *douars* to work on the *colons* farms.[9] This pattern suited the settlers since they avoided the security problem of a large native presence close to the farms and, more important, it enabled Algerian families to be partly self-supporting on microfundia, helping to keep wages depressed. As *colons* spokesmen made clear, native land plots should be too small to feed a family, forcing them into wage-labour, but sufficient to provide a supplement to low pay.[10]

The reason for low levels of emigration from these zones

before about 1930 was that Algerians were integrated into the colonial economy. In all regions of Algeria peasants preferred to gain off-farm income close to their villages, rather than to emigrate. Even when wages were very low, this had to be offset against the alternative, the trauma and risk of leaving the protective and sentimental environment of the family and village. Lizot, for example, has shown how a zinc mine, which employed men from the Beni Hendel, constituted 'a brake on emigration'.[11] In the mountainous regions like Kabylia local opportunities for off-farm employment were rare, while in the plains the dynamic growth in the colonial core economy offered new opportunities and acted as a magnet to local labour.[12]

However, low levels of emigration were not only a consequence of economic factors but were actively reinforced through the political-juridical power of the *colons*. In the zones of heavy colonisation, the *communes de plein exercise*, Europeans monopolised power in the municipality, and through the Native Code administered a repressive apparatus in which they functioned as police, judge and jury. Under the Third Republic the Code was used to block labour moving beyond the borders of the commune by witholding travel permits. The settlers were able to exert a virtual monopoly over local labour, drive down wages, extort *corvée* and bribes (*backchich*) and 'discipline' Algerians through a panoply of fines and imprisonment.[13] In principle the law of 15 July 1914 allowed freedom of movement, but in practice mayors and officials in the *communes de plein exercise* continued to block emigration until the Chautemps decrees of 1924 reinforced their hand. In contrast administrators and officials in Kabylia, a region in which there was a low *colons* presence and demand for labour, actively encouraged emigration since remittance money had become vital to the local economy and the well-being of hundreds of villages.[14]

The general distribution of emigration in Algeria can be linked to a basic economic and spatial dualism between a heavily colonised west (the department of Oran) and a much less developed east (the department of Constantine). 'In contrast to the modern West', noted the geographer Isnard, 'equipped, structured, the East remains traditional, clearly underdeveloped and overpopulated: a native reserve quite the opposite of the well-maintained European province.'[15] In 1921–31 the department of Oran had about 35 Europeans to every 100 Algerians, and only 1.6 per cent of total emigrants, while the department of Constantine had 8 Europeans to every hundred Algerians and about 56 per cent of all emigrants.[16]

As we have seen (Chapter 2), the economic dualism between east and west, better explained at the local level as one between mountain and plain, fits well with Meillassoux's theory of the 'domestic economy', according to which colonial capitalism was able to tap the reproductive capacity of traditional self-sustaining peasant economies. The problem for capitalism was its inability to maintain such a fine balance indefinitely. From the late 1920s the dualism began to break down as the colonial economy entered a phase of deepening crisis. This was marked by a spatial 'seepage' of the emigration phenomenon down from the mountains into the plains of the colonial sector, an event which was a harbinger of the mass emigration of the post-1945 period.

By 1920 the standard of living of the Algerian rural population was very low, but during the inter-war period conditions deteriorated even further. Detailed evidence of this deepening crisis and its links to a 'new wave' of emigration exists for the High Plains, a zone of prairie-like grain and livestock farming near Sétif. The spread of techniques of 'dry-farming' accelerated a process of land concentration, in which wealthy European and Algerian owners, many of whom were absentee landlords living in the towns, consolidated large estates. The great mass of Algerian poor lost any remaining land they owned to the rich farmers, and shifted from the status of sharecropper (*khammès*), paid in kind, to that of waged-labour. For example, in 1918 the 900 hectare estate of Abel Lochard at Tamentout, north-east of Sétif at Djemila, employed five property owning *khammès* and seasonal workers. By 1924–6 the *khammès* had all become wage-labourers and owned no parcels of land.[17] During these years the entire region was increasingly integrated into the national and global economy, and was badly hit by the Depression of the 1930s. Algerians, who as small producers engaged in auto-consumption had previously some protection against large fluctuations in market prices, were now fully exposed to the impact of increased food prices and declining wages. The rural population was reduced to an extremely precarious situation and in desperation resorted to loans of grain or cash at usurious rates, deepening the spiral of impoverishment. At the same time the Algerian population passed through the first phase of a dramatic demographic transition. The population growth rate doubled between 1921–5 and 1926–30 from 7.8 to 15.7 per thousand, increasing the pressure on resources.[18] In the *commune mixte* of Eulma, to the east of Sétif, the native population increased by 11.5 per cent between 1926 and 1936, and seventy-four per cent of families lived in extreme poverty on under 2000 francs per year.[19]

The opportunity for alternative sources of work and income in the rural areas was almost nil. Even traditional artisan production collapsed as the spread of roads enabled vans to bring European goods to the most isolated villages. The first response of the rural poor was to engage in **internal** migration, either of a seasonal or permanent kind, to the major urban centres like Sétif, Constantine, and Algiers. In Sétif a forty per cent increase in native population from 28 000 in 1936 to 40 000 in 1948 was almost entirely due to migration from the hinterland where rapid mechanisation with harvesters and tractors further displaced labour. As in Algiers, Oran, Relizane and other colonial centres the rural poor flocked into inner city slums and peri-urban shantytowns (*villages nègres*). In Sétif some migrants found work in agro-industries (milling, pasta works, abattoirs) and construction, but overall there was a lack of work and a 'surplus' population of about 15 000 survived through an economy of makeshifts (hawking, prostitution, charity, public works) and through the aid of kin and fellow villagers. Rural–urban migration continued despite the lack of employment since the chances of survival were greater than in the desperate and isolated context of the *bled*.[20]

The relationship between internal migration and emigration in the High Plains and elsewhere in Algeria is an extremely complex issue that has been neglected by historians and geographers. Certain villages scattered throughout Algeria engaged only in temporary internal migration to the towns where the men tended to specialise in particular kinds of work. If it was well-established, such a practice probably impeded emigration. It is also quite possible that internal migration was a preference of highly conservative societies which, for religious and cultural reasons, could not contemplate living in a non-Muslim country like France.[21] However, in other localities temporary internal migration prepared the ground for eventual emigration by providing men with some experience of work conditions and employment outside the traditional rural economy.[22]

In the High Plains area from about the mid-1920s increasing rural urban migration coincided with the first significant emigration to France as villagers sought every possible means to escape the desperate poverty of the rural areas.[23] By 1932, for example, some 250 men were departing annually from the *commune mixte* of Eulma.[24] The spread of emigration into this previously unaffected region can be picked up in the shocked response of the big landowners, both French and Algerian, to their loss of control over local labour. In spite of the introduction of the Chautemps circulars on emigration after September 1924 farmers in the region mounted a campaign in 1927–30 for further restrictions.[25] As Meuleman shows, the employers' hysteria at the 'crisis' in labour-supply did not reflect a real shortage of man-power but disquiet at the first breach in their ability to brow-beat locals and impose wages at or below subsistence level.[26]

The spread of emigration after the mid-1920s beyond the confines of Kabylia into the colonised regions represented the beginning of a new trend. Although the numbers departing from the High Plains was initially small, the emigration was quite different in structure from that of Kabylia and provided the first signs of a new type of movement that was to become massively predominant in the post-war period.[27] Kabyle migration was based on a traditional society of small peasant landowners from which the family group despatched single males to procure external resources which were reinvested in the farm/household. In the High Plains the process of colonial appropriation of lands had been carried much further and a landless proletariat was reduced to a desperate level of poverty. The disintegration of pre-colonial social structures was so advanced that even the cohesion of the extended family, the base of the social order, was weakened.[28] This new type of emigrant was much more likely than the Kabyle to make a rapid transition from temporary to permanent emigration; he had little to tie him to his village of origin, no stake in the land, in the quasi-religious obligation to maintain the lineage, and fewer ties or obligations to kin. Massard-Guilbaud has shown that migrants from the High-Plains in the Lyons region during the inter-war period had a much more dispersed settlement pattern than those from Kabylia reflecting a higher level of individualism and an absence of strong group bonds. Since they were less bound by the obligation to save every penny for the household group and had no land in Algeria the High-Plains men were willing to spend more on rent and to move outside the borders of the enclave with its cheap, shared lodgings. Most surprising of all is the evidence that Algerian wives were beginning to settle in France, a phenomenon that most sources had previously seen as a post-war event.[29] The arrival of women from Eulmas, Saint-Arnaud, Constantine and Aïn Smara in the High Plains can be linked to the profound impact of colonial and capitalist forces, the rupture of social and familial structures and the decision to emigrate permanently.[30]

In the period after 1930 all the conditions for both a massive increase in emigration as well as a shift in its structure towards family reunification were emerging. However, two events combined to block the pressures to emigrate that were building up within Algeria. Firstly, the impact of the world depression on the French economy and a leap in unemployment acted as a sharp brake on emigration. As the Laroque Report noted in the 1930s the rate of emigration varied little in relation to fluctuations in the colonial economy, years of famine or relative plenty, but was linked to, 'fluctuations in the metropolitan economy'.[31] During the Depression the normal pattern of circulation was arrested, fewer men departed from Algeria, while of those already in France, some returned while many – even the unemployed – sat tight waiting for conditions to improve.[32] French economic recovery had only just begun in 1937–8, stimulating an increase in departures, when the Second World began and after 1943 the Allied landings in North Africa cut all cross-Mediterranean traffic. These oscillations are clearly shown by the average annual number of departures from Algeria for each five-year period:

	Annual departures
1926–30	38 688
1931–5	15 682
1936–40	29 035
1941–5	3 371
1946–50	70 932

During the fifteen years of stagnant or totally blocked emigration between 1931 and 1945 the Algerian economy entered a phase of deepening crisis. The Muslim population increased by 37.4 per cent from 5 588 314 in 1931 to 7 679 078 in 1948, and *colons* complaints about a shortage of labour fizzled out after 1930. The growth of a huge reserve of underemployed and desperately impoverished natives meant that settlers were able to drive down wage rates to such a low level that the *Gouvernement Générale* was forced to intercede in 1936 and tried to impose, without success, a minimum wage.[33] Settler opinion went through a rapid U-turn: no longer did it try to block emigration but, on the contrary, emigration was approved as a safety-valve to relieve the dangerous Malthusian and political pressures presented by a hungry and threatening undermass.[34]

The outbreak of the Second World War marked an abrupt halt to 'free' emigration. In 1926, 1934 and 1938–9 various government instructions had laid the basis for any future, wartime recruitment of colonial labour by the *Service de main-d'oeuvre indigène, nord-africain et coloniale* (MOI).[35] In January 1940 the Ministry of Labour proceeded to lay plans for the recruitment of a first contingent of 3000 men. The conditions under which these men were recruited in Algeria, escorted by ex-officers and organised in brigades of 500 men who worked and lived under a para-military régime, were almost identical to those of the SOTC in the First World War. The military collapse of France in June 1940 temporarily halted all immigration and some 14 000 North African workers who fled south to Paris from the invasion zone were repatriated by the Rue Lecomte.[36]

Departures from Algeria remained low in 1941 (3082), but began to pick up again in 1942 as various recruitment agencies, particularly CENTRALAG, began to operate in Algeria. In September 1942 the Vichy government, under pressure from the German Todt organisation which wanted to use Algerian labour in the construction of the 'Atlantic wall', laid plans to accelerate recruitment to 10 000 men per month. However, the Allied landings in North Africa brough an abrupt halt to these plans and stopped all emigration between November 1942 and the end of 1945. The stranding of tens of thousands of Algerians in France led to a significant increase in mixed marriage or co-habitation and the number of births.[37]

The figures for the number of Algerians in France in November 1942, and who remained blocked there for the duration of the war, is uncertain, but was probably in the region of 120 000 men.[38] The termination of all remittance payments between France and Algeria had a drastic impact, especially in those regions like Kabylia where the local economy had become crucially dependent on labour migration.[39] Harold Macmillan noted in his wartime memoirs that lack of remittances, which he likened to Irishmen in the USA and Britain ceasing to send money home, was causing great hardship and, 'has caused us all a lot of worry'.[40] The crisis in Algerian agricultural production which began in 1930–5 deepened dramatically during the war. The poor harvest of 1940, after a slight recovery in 1941, entered a catastrophic cycle during 1942–5 due to drought and locust invasions. The 1945 harvest of 5 million quintals of grain, the lowest since 1856, was only sufficient for the next years seed. By 1946 some half a million landless families, 'an immense agrarian proletariat', lived a precarious existence, increasingly dependent on emergency distributions of grain and public works programmes.[41]

As soon as the end of the war restored freedom of movement by plane (1 May) and ferry (1 June 1946) a massive and accelerating emigration got under way.[42] Attempts by the French government to control this movement through the agency of the new *Office national d'immigration* (ONI), which attempted to recruit contract labour on behalf of employers, soon collapsed.[43] The pressures of an increasingly impoverished and desperate population that had been largely blocked from emigrating over a period of fifteen years finally burst through. As René Gallissot has pointed out, the degree of impoverishment of the Algerian peasantry in the first half of the twentieth century gave rise to a relatively feeble emigration, an emigration which was 'deferred' until 1950 by 'rural retention', a kind of entrapment or immobilisation within the colonial economy.[44]

Louis Chevalier, during his tour of investigation in Algeria in 1946, witnessed the frantic departure, 'It has to be seen how the ticket offices of the shipping lines are beseiged from daybreak by a crowd of people determined to leave at all costs. Often they have sold everything they possess.'[45] The stampede was encouraged by numerous French transport companies who engaged their own recruiters to go into the most distant villages.[46] There was a rapid growth in small airline companies which were highly competitive with each other and with the shipping companies and even opened ticket offices in the Kabyle villages.[47] Migrants were also encouraged to depart by their ability to defray their travel costs by selling in France their duty-free allowance in olive-oil, American cigarettes and coffee which obtained high blackmarket prices.[48]

The rapid growth in the scale of emigration during the nine years before the outbreak of the Algerian War (1 November 1954) still showed a considerable degree of rotation, but this disguised changes in the underlying structure of migration that were already underway before the war. Firstly, although the Kabyle region was still predominant, the process of emigration began to spread fast into new regions, particularly the heavily colonised zones of Oran and Constantine, the Saharan south, and the major towns.[49] Secondly, the fresh wave of migrants was made up of poor, proletarianised individuals who arrived in small groups of three or four men, from village societies that had no previous experience of emigration.[50] These small 'commando' work-groups were extremely mobile and were prepared to seek employment in those areas or occupations, such as the steel, mining and chemical industry of Lorraine, in which Kabyles had not achieved a monopoly.[51] The sheer scale of the influx of unskilled and illiterate peasants who had no previous experience of life and work in France produced a situation like that of 1920–4, with appalling housing conditions, ill-health and severe stress.

But the third and most distinctive feature of the post-war emigration was an unmistakable shift towards family reunification, the clearest indicator of a change from temporary migration to permanent settlement. Muracciole, during his investigations in Algeria and France during 1949–50, was one of the first to notice a new and, 'an extremely important stage in Algerian emigration', the departure of 'complete families with children and even old women'.[52] By August 1953 the new trend was unmistakeable: some 5000 women and 11 000 children were in France and families were continuing to arrive at the rate of one hundred per month.[53] Most of these families emigrated from the new zones of departure among the Arab-speaking people of Oran, Constantine and the Sahara.

A number of detailed enquiries carried out by local social services in 1950–4 throw a fascinating light on the social conditions and process of adaptation of these newly arrived families.[54] In one study of 101 families in Marseilles, it was found that about half the wives (48) followed their husbands to France after a period of one to four years, while the other half (46) had arrived together with their husbands, an indicator of a new type of definitive group departure. The couples, as might be expected, were relatively young (average age of men on arrival was 32 years, of women 26 years) and despite this they had large numbers of children, with an average of 3.61 per family.

Number of children	Number of families
0	5
1	10
2	19
3	16
4	19
5	15
6	8
7	6
8	0
9 and over	3
	101

The process of family emigration was encouraged by various forms of relatively generous and natalist inspired family allowances which were paid at a higher level in France than Algeria.[55]

These large Marseilles families faced even greater difficulties of accommodation than single males, and many tried to find a solution to lack of space by squatting ruined houses or building wooden huts on wasteland (*bidonvilles*). Several extended families from the Sahara lived in the underground levels of an abandoned German blockhouse in a single large but humid room without electricity or running water. Despite the atrocious conditions these new migrants tried hard to make the bunker as habitable as possible and to recreate some of the ambience of their home society:

The sun never penetrates here. The room, smokey and blackened by the wood fire or the paraffin lamp, is divided by a curtain into a dark bedroom and a living room where there are twelve people. An inventory of the furniture is quickly done: a bed without sheets for the parents and babies, a straw-filled mattress for two or three children, esparto mats rolled up during the day standing on a decrepit sewing machine, trunks and suitcases serving as storage space. Stools and boxes about 25 cm. high serve as a table and support the brass plate with the teapot and glasses to offer mint tea to visitors . . . These Saharan people continue to live according to their customs, sleeping dressed and even eating on the ground, sometimes from the same plate . . . The miserable living room which is very narrow has been arranged with taste. On the whitewashed walls, daubed with many-coloured arabesques, are pinned photographs of fashion models.

The women, none of whom could speak French, tried to avoid contact with local French society, undertaking shopping as quickly as possible in small groups. Pregnant women even preferred to give birth in their squalid accommodation rather than go to a hospital. Their dress remained unchanged from the Saharan region, long brightly printed cotton robes, heavy silver wrist and ankle bracelets, plaited hair worn under a turban and covered by a fringed shawl. But the cold climate compelled them to wear pullovers, thick stockings and old slippers. To break the monotonous and harsh life of caring for children in the *bidonvilles* the women would often gather during the day in a blockhouse to sing and dance.

A few families in the survey found it difficult to adapt to the harsh conditions in France and when asked about their future plans hoped to return soon to Algeria:

- A family hoping to save enough money to return to Algeria. Do not think of staying in France and do not want to adapt; the wife never goes out unless in a taxi and veiled.
- A family hoping to save enough money to buy date-palms and to return to live in Algeria. In spite of this they hope that the children, especially the boys, learn a trade.

However, a significantly larger group expressed a wish to settle in France permanently, and some had reached the critical point of no longer sending money to relatives in Algeria:

- Wish to settle in France and that the children learn a trade. Do not send money to Algeria. An adapting family
  . . .
- Wish to stay in France and teach the children, in the words of the father, to live 'à la mode française'.

The older pattern of emigration as a strategy to procure resources for the peasant household was shifting towards what Sayad has termed the 'second stage' of migration.[56] Family reunification, as village elders had always feared, would cut the emigrants' ties to home and redirect earnings from remittance savings towards consumption in France. The complex structure of many newly arrived families which, in addition to the couple and their children, often included grandparents, sisters-in-law, cousins and nephews suggests a 'total' regrouping in France so that close kin or dependent family members would not be abandoned in Algeria. The decision to terminate transfers of money to Algeria did mean that these families, in spite of the housing crisis, could begin to raise their standard of living in France.

EMIGRATION AND POST-WAR IDEOLOGY

The official or governmental response to post-war emigration showed some quite distinct differences from that of the interwar period. A first, striking feature of the period from 1945 to the outbreak of the Algerian War, was the extraordinary increase in studies of Algerian emigration. In the first five months of 1949 alone five different ministries undertook official surveys.[57] The important investigation of Louis Chevalier (1947) was soon followed by that of Rager (1950), Muracciole (1950), Robert Montagne (52–4), Bogart and Girard (1954), L. Henry et al. (1955) and Andrée Michel (56).[58] This flurry of activity in response to what Luc Muracciole called, 'the burning topicality of the subject' seems initially to have been a response less to the scale of emigration than its predicted future importance.

Chevalier, for example, predicted an enormous influx of one million North Africans during the next decade.[59]

A major characteristic of many of the new inquiries, compared to much of the pre-war literature, was the predominance of sophisticated demographic and sociological methodology. A whole series of reports (L. Chevalier, L. Henry, A. Girard) were commissioned and published by the newly founded *Institut National d'Études Démographiques* (INED) or in its house journal *Population*. The approach was broadly 'technocratic'; a vast quantity of statistical data was utilised to provide an avowedly 'scientific' analysis of migration which could then serve as a basis for planners to implement coherent and informed policies. This heavily statistical and demographic approach has to be seen within the broader context of state planning of postwar economic recovery and the Monnet Plan which, in 1947, proposed a future recruitment of 200 000 Algerians.[60] Although these technocratic reports consciously avoided making comments on the turbulent political situation in Algeria or the terminal crisis in the colonial system, and pretended to the neutrality of data collection and analysis, they still carried an ideological message.

This can be seen, for example, in the influential report by the demographic historian Louis Chevalier, which was undertaken to assess the implications of future labour recruitment in North Africa. Chevalier's conclusion was that Algeria was undergoing a classic Malthusian crisis in which a population explosion and stagnating agricultural production had 'ruptured' the balance between people and resources.[61] In this analysis crisis assumed the form of a certain mechanical 'inevitability', the conjuncture of natural forces (adverse climate, soil depletion), such that it owed little if anything to the negative impact of colonialism. The book is silent on the colonial domination and exploitation of Algeria as a root cause of emigration. Muracciole, an Algerian jurist, was more explicit and remarked that one could not 'accuse' colonisation of being the cause of emigration.[62] Muracciole, in line with inter-war colonial propagandists like Octave Depont, attributed Algerian demographic pressures to the **success** of French civilisation which established peace, prevented murderous factional conflicts (*çoffs*), spread the benefits of western medicine, reduced infant mortality and introduced modern agricul-

techniques.[63] The attempt to ignore the negative impact of colonialism is evident in the contradictions of Rager: viticulture, he noted, had generated good wages for Algerians but could no longer absorb 'the mass of unemployed', but the fact that 400 000 hectares of vines had displaced food crops for a product that was not consumed by Muslims went unmentioned.[64]

During the decade which preceded the beginning of the Algerian War the outpouring of 'technocratic' works on emigration was written from within a colonialist paradigm. However, these reports did all acknowledge – it would have been impossible not to – that Algerian society was confronting very serious problems of hunger. All commentators agreed that the official encouragement of labour migration to France was a necessary 'safety-valve' for the ominous demographic pressures building up in Algeria, although there was some disagreement' about the ultimate form of the movement.[65] Chevalier, taking an idiosyncratic position, argued that any emigration in order to be 'worthwhile' had to be definitive and involve the total assimilation of the minority. But he concluded with the highly ambiguous and pessimistic note that he could not see how such an objective could be reached because the enormous resistant power of Islam would not allow Algerian integration.[66]

However, the majority position of experts was that migration was or should be only a temporary phenomenon. Rager, Muracciole, and Montagne basically agreed with the position of the pre-war colonial lobbyists. The new, and rapidly growing unregulated migration was thought to present a range of problems – the transmission of disease, rising criminality and the abandonment of peasants to material hardship and moral degeneration. Migrants were also totally lacking in skills and unsuited to fill the needs of the post-war economy. The solution to this was to try and reformulate a 'rational' system of migration selection in Algeria in conjunction with a social welfare programme in France which would assure the provision of decent housing, education, health care and welfare support. Migrants should be offered special educational and training programmes so that they could either benefit the metropolitan economy or, on their return, help modernise the colonial economy.

Where this modernising programme differed from that of the inter-war ideologues like Depont and Godin, was that it was stripped away from any apparent wish to link it to surveillance and political control. In 1945 the policing functions of the Rue Lecomte had been closed down, partly as a consequence of its collaborationist functions during the war.[67] In the more progressive and reforming atmosphere of post-war France nobody wished to repeat the fatal mistake of combining police and welfare functions.

However, Rager, Montagne and others still showed signs of the old colonial paternalist strategy in their highly ambiguous attitude towards modernity. Firstly, they all agreed that migration to France was not something that was desirable in itself. Rather, given the depth of crisis in Algeria, it was a kind of stop-gap, a means of buying time until a fundamental reform and modernisation of the colonial economy could be achieved. Eventually, it was hoped, a programme of agricultural reform and industrialisation would generate sufficient employment and wealth to remove the root causes of emigration. It was tardily acknowledged that the long-term refusal of metropolitan capital to allow the growth of competitive industry in Algeria had dampened forms of economic growth that might have employed the millions now fleeing from the poverty of the *bled*. But this progressive, technocratic dream went hand-in-hand with a certain nostalgia for the 'good old days', a kind of pre-industrial Algeria in which a noble and exotic tribal society owed allegiance and gratitude to the benevolent soldier-administrator – an orientalist version of the conservative regret for the disappearing world of French landed gentry and their much loved servants.

This conservative anti-modernist regret can be traced in Montagne and Rager's hope that traditional 'tribal' structures might be preserved in the emigration. Rager was worried that Algerian migrants might become, 'in the technological city another wreck to inflate the crowd of collectivised and mechanised men, sated with vacuous ideas, shorn of old principles, without a framework, battered with socialism, deafened by nationalism, stupefied by the simplistic recipes and slogans thrown out in profusion by modern forms of indoctrination.' Rager's solution to this was to buttress Islamic institutions in France, to combat 'the dangers of corruption presented by the modern world', but also to reinforce, as far as possible, within the French context, the cohesion of 'tribal' groupings.[68]

The most consistent advocate of this latter position was the influential anthropologist Robert Montagne. In 1952 Montagne was commissioned by the Minister of the Interior, Charles Brune, to carry out an official inquiry into Algerian emigration.[69] Montagne's theory was that Berber social structure best lent itself to the strategies of temporary labour migration. The 'existence of a family property, more or less indivisible, to which is tied the small social group that constitutes the patriarchal family, more or less agnatic, is the solid institution that enables the departure of emigrants.'[70] The Montagne report showed an obsession with plotting the spatial distribution and structures of such village groupings in France. What clearly worried him about the post-war spread of emigration into the non-Berber zones was that Arab society was lacking in the family structures that could sustain group cohesion in France and preserve an identity for an eventual return and re-insertion into the colonial order. But Montagne's essentialist view of Berber cohesion as opposed to a highly negative idea of 'weak' Arab kin structures represented a sophisticated re-working of the old 'Kabyle Myth'.[71] What it obscured was the extent to which the 'new' emigration from the plains carried not the mark of inherent Arab inadequacies but the imprint of destructive colonialism in the form of extreme poverty, landlessness and family/social dislocation.[72]

Robert Montagne, born in 1893, represented very much the old guard. He was in the mountains of Kabylia investigating emigration when the uprising of 1 November marked the opening shots of the War of Independence. Montagne was taken ill there and died on 26 November, the same day that a huge French military counter-insurgency operation began, supported by artillery and aviation, under the eyes of the Minister of the Interior, François Mitterrand.[73] One of the tragedies of colonial Algeria was that the French had just begun to acknowledge the links between emigration, a deepening socioeconomic crisis, and the need for radical reform, when they were overtaken by events.

11 Emigration and the Algerian War, 1954–62

The Algerian War of 1954–62, one of the longest and bloodiest wars of decolonisation, was to mark a watershed, a dramatic increase in the rate of emigration to France. During this period of strife the number of Algerians in France grew from 211 000 to 350 000. One paradox of the crisis was that it almost doubled the number of immigrants in the metropolitan heartland of the colonial power with whom Algerians were at war. As airplanes departed incessantly with young national servicemen destined for anti-guerrilla service in the *bled*, others landed with Algerian workers. The growth in emigration was in part caused by the terrible conditions of warfare, especially in the rural areas where villages were bombed or torched and entire populations displaced into military camps. But even the coming of independence in 1962 did not bring what Algerian nationalists had long hoped for or expected, a slow-down in departures and even a return home of 'exiles' to help reconstruct a new society. The newly independent Algerian government was unable to halt, as it intended, the emigration which was a mark of colonial exploitation as it had inherited a catastrophic economic situation. This was a combination of wartime destruction, French departure and economic sabotage, and the accumulated underdevelopment of industry and agriculture. Emigration continued to be a necessary safety-valve and source of foreign exchange earnings for the infant Republic, as it was to be for many other post-colonial states. Emigration thus continued to rocket during the post-war period and the 350 000 Algerians in France in 1962 had grown to 530 000 by 1968 and 800 000 in 1972.[1] At the same time independence had finally removed for the French government the embarrassing impediment to full and unambiguous immigration controls that it had faced between 1914 and 1962, the fact that Algeria was legally an overseas extension of French soil. Independence provided both French and Algerian states with the means to unilaterally (or bilaterally) halt all emigration if they

189

so wished, an option that was to come into play with particular force in 1973–4.

This chapter looks at the position of the Algerian émigrés in France just before and during the war of independence. The purpose is not to provide a detailed political history of these crisis years, something that has already received enormous attention, but to look at the conditions of everyday life for the ordinary Algerian workers and their families as they organised themselves to survive in an increasingly hostile and xenophobic environment. The period witnessed deepening segregation and social distancing between the two communities, rather than the 'normal' pattern of gradual integration.

The rapid increase in Algerian immigration between 1945 and 1954 appears, in spite of the terrible housing shortage, to have led to relatively little initial popular racism. This can be attributed in part to the experience of the occupation, of resistance and the more politically progressive and optimistic tenor of post-war society. The arrival of Algerian women and children among the previously all-male immigrants was accepted sympathetically by the French working class among whom they lived. A study of 101 families in Marseilles found that relations with European neighbours were good, with only three cases of tension, in spite of some difficulties of communication in French. Men frequently, 'only know the rudiments of French peppered with dialect terms, a result of picking up language in the workplace', but their wives had even less opportunity to learn a smattering of French. Despite these difficulties, social workers involved with immigrant families noticed Algerian men playing *pétanque* with French neighbours or playing cards together in local bars. Another Marseilles group of Saharan immigrants, 'have gradually learned to get on with their metropolitan comrades who kept them at arms-length in the beginning'. French mothers who were initially worried that ragged Algerian children would behave violently towards their own offspring came to see this was not the case and even provided second-hand clothing.[2] The oral evidence of Zoulika M., raised in a micro-*bidonvilles* in the Rhône, confirms this pattern: 'The French people who lived round about liked us a lot, especially us children.'[3] The sociologist Andrée Michel, who had a close first-hand knowledge of the immigrant environment in 1956, concluded that antipathy was lowest among those Europeans who shared the same socio-economic conditions and that where initial suspicion and hostility existed this often evaporated through the experience of everyday contact in the *quartiers populaires*.[4]

However, the process of gradual integration which might have been expected with family reunification was arrested by several factors which will be examined in turn. These were: i) a virulent police and press racism that sharpened in about 1948 and then deepened during the war, ii) a process of segregation and discrimination in housing which continued to isolate Algerians socially and spatially, iii) the further reinforcement of this by the FLN which, in constructing a base in the émigré community, sought to build a 'fortress' that would keep Algerians apart from French society and the counter-intelligence operations of the police and iv) the growth of a hostile public opinion, especially as the FLN extended the war to metropolitan France. However, countering these negative factors in part was a much stronger political support than had ever existed before the Second World War from a minority of far-left and Christian groups who were opposed to colonialism and ready to aid the emigrants and the FLN.

The rapid increase in post-war immigration from Algeria after 1946 led to an almost identical racist reaction by the right-wing press and the police to that of 1923–4 and 1936–7. During 1947–8 the Paris Prefect of Police repeatedly denounced North Africans for high levels of criminality and claimed that they were responsible for forty per cent of 'nighttime assaults' in the capital. Such public statements by the senior police officer encouraged the press to revive the sensationalist and racist criminalisation of North Africans that had existed before 1939. The right-wing newspaper *L'Aurore* carried headlines like that of 5 November 1948, 'In some quarters of Paris, the Arab is king of the night'. Even the liberal *Le Monde*, on 16 September 1949, carried a three-column headline, 'North African criminality has become a national problem.'[5] Such alarmist reports persuaded the *Conseil Général de la Seine* to carry out a detailed inquiry into Algerian crime rates in 1949 which found that the Prefect of Police's claims were unfounded.[6] But the damage had been done and the old stereotype of the Algerian as a criminal, especially as the rapist and child-molester, persisted. Typical was an incident in December 1955 when a young girl,

Martine Skoura, disappeared in the suburb of Bagnolet. An evening newspaper, without any evidence, carried the headline, 'Little Martine abducted by a North African', but next day simply noted, without any reference to its previous report, that the child had been 'taken' by her mother who had separated from her husband.[7] This type of press sensationalism and distortion had become so regular by the 1950s, that it had created a widespread public fear of Algerians. So frequently and automatically were Algerians scapegoated by the press that it had become banal.[8]

Within the Paris police force anti-Algerian and racist attitudes had become endemic and institutionalised well before the Algerian war commenced. In spite of the disbandment of the Rue Lecomte brigade in 1945 for collaborationism, large-scale operations against North Africans continued unabated by a replacement unit, the *Brigade des agressions et violences* (BAV).[9] In 1947 they carried out regular sweeping operations through the Algerian enclaves and arrested hundreds of men in Montmartre, Pigalle, and elsewhere.[10] Although the police claimed that its actions were aimed at criminal behaviour this was increasingly used as a cover for the political harassment and intimidation of the Algerian community.[11] This was made particularly evident by a combined police operation on 30 July 1955 which involved throwing a cordon around and sweeping the famous 'Arab ghetto' of La Goutte d'Or. According to the Minister of the Interior the aim was to 'cleanse' the 'medina' by arresting the hundreds of thieves, gamblers, pimps, pickpockets, receivers, and muggers which, he claimed, lurked in the sector centred on the Rue de la Charbonnière. The huge operation only netted one Algerian, Mohamed Maadi, charged with stealing a shirt, a charge for which he was later cleared in court. Despite this overkill, which provoked a full-scale riot in which some 2000 North Africans battled with the police, the press supported the need to, 'cleanse the quarter of its undesirable elements'. The media made no reference to the true political motivation of the operation, in spite of the Minister of the Interior's statement that La Goutte d'Or also happened to be a, 'an ideal terrain for subversive propaganda'.[12]

The sweeps which became ever larger in scale and more frequent – 6 September 1955 (30 000 'controls' and 300 arrests), 9 to 12 March 1956, 30 to 31 March, 1 to 4 April, 1 May

1956 – undoubtedly drove a wedge between the Algerians and local Europeans. The Goutte d'Or operation of 30 July 1955 led to a deterioration in relations and an increase in French hostility.[13] Local French inhabitants, witnessing constant police stop-and-search operations, began to view Algerians as a dangerous and illegal presence. Faced with such hostility the Algerian immigrants were increasingly driven back into the confines of their own enclaves, the 'Arab' quarters of the inner city and the suburban *bidonvilles*, enclaves which were to become the territorial basis of nationalist resistance.

SPATIAL SEGREGATION AND HOUSING

During the war Algerians became spatially segregated from French society through a combined process of external pressure and discrimination and the auto-defensive organisation of the immigrant community. The *bidonvilles* which mushroomed on the outskirts of Paris and Marseilles were a typical site of these developments. Conditions in the squatter camps were similar to those in 'Third-world' shantytowns: huts were constructed of wood, corrugated-iron, tarred felt, and breeze-blocks, and had no basic services like running water, electricity or sewerage. Water had to be carried, often considerable distances, from stand-pipes and through unpaved lanes that were a sea of mud in winter. The greatest risk to the inhabitants, a source of continuous anxiety, was from fire and asphyxiation due to primitive stoves.[14] In the suburb of Nanterre by 1955 some 4300 Algerians, half of the total in the commune, lived in these shacks, a figure that had increased to 6600 just after the end of the war.[15]

The *bidonvilles* were in locations that placed them socially and spatially on the margins of French society. They developed primarily in industrial suburbs on the periphery of the city, but even within these dreary fringe communes they were further marginalised by their location on wasteland where nobody else would live and often cut off from French peri-urban centres by railway tracks, factories, quarries and electricity pylons. Few French people, apart from some dedicated social workers and policemen, had any call – or indeed the courage – to penetrate the maze of these 'no-go zones'. Dr Suzanne

Urverg, one of the very few who would enter the shantytowns to tend the ill, remarked that some local GPs had separate waiting rooms for Algerians and French in their surgeries.[16] The North Africans, especially the women, also had very restricted contacts outside the *bidonvilles*. The growth of small shops (butchers, cafés, grocers) which traded in North African produce like couscous, spices and mint tea, enabled the inhabitants of the squatter zones to lead, 'a quasi-autarchic economic life'.[17]

From the late 50s, as a programme for the construction of state housing or *Habitation à Loyer modéree* (HLM) got under way, a small number of Algerian families were rehoused.[18] However, for most access to the HLM was blocked by high rents, the small size of standard flats which could not accommodate the large Algerian families, and by administrative policy. Senior housing administrators and social workers thought that Algerians would need to undergo a period of training into western styles of living, the correct use of appliances like gas cookers, bathrooms, and hygiene before they could be admitted to modern flats.[19] This transition was to be effected by removal from *bidonvilles* into the *cités de transit*, prefabricated camps, which came under the quasi-military control of the Prefecture.[20]

The provision of social housing was undertaken as part of a political strategy to remove Algerians from the FLN dominated bastions of the *bidonvilles*. This policy was implemented by SONACOTRA (*Société Nationale de Construction de logements pour les Travailleurs Algériens*), a government-financed agency founded at the height of the Algerian war in 1956 and which specialised in the construction of hostels and *cités de transit* for North African workers. SONACOTRA hostels, managed by former policemen, army officers or native administrators from North Africa, were part of a wider system of political surveillance. One of the aims of SONACOTRA in its early years was to 'absorb' the Nanterre *bidonvilles*, 'considered as a key base for the FLN Fédération de France'.[21] Overall, however, government interventionist programmes to rehouse Algerians from *bidonvilles* had very little impact before the 'Debré Law' of December 1964 initiated a programme of slum clearance and rehousing. 'Ghetto' zones actually increased in number and population during the war and remained centres of FLN activity.

The segregation of Algerians was also in part a consequence of an entirely new phenomenon of considerable moment, French departure or 'flight' from immigrant areas. As early as 1955 the *Police judiciaire* reported, 'In the sectors of heavy North African implantation the metropolitans tend to desert the quarters or blocks of housing where the North Africans are installed.' European parents began to move their children from schools where North African children were present. Municipalities, like that of Puteaux and Corbevoie, also began to refuse permission to construct hostels or other forms of social housing intended for North Africans.[22] These processes of public and official rejection of North Africans, which first began to appear during the Algerian War, were in the long term to lead to one of the major social problems in contemporary France, the segregation of Maghrebians and their descendents in the huge 'problem' estates of the *banlieue*.[23]

THE FLN ENCLAVE

As the war deepened the Algerian community retreated further into the protective shell of the enclave. The newly emergent FLN, which was virtually unknown to both French and Algerians when it organised the rebellion of 1 November 1954, became rapidly embroiled in France in a war on two fronts, against the MNA and the French security forces. In 1955 a deep split developed between the *Mouvement national algérien* (MNA), the older independence movement of Messali Hadj, and the new FLN, and by 1956 this had deteriorated into an exceedingly violent and murderous battle for control over the emigré community in France. Trained assassination squads from both camps tracked down and murdered opponents in cafés, lodgings and the street: by 1962 some 4000 were dead and 10 000 wounded.[24] The internecine murders reinforced moves to establish control over their own ghettos which became defensive 'safe-zones' to prevent infiltration or murderous commando raids.

By 1958 the FLN had gained dominance in France and put in place a highly sophisticated structure. One central objective of the network was to establish, through persuasion and force, a total control over the social and political life of Algerian immigrants. The grass-roots base of the FLN organisation was local cell leaders and owners of lodgings who were responsible for making monthly collections of funds from every individual in their sector or building. Through this means the FLN raised, during the eight years of war, some four hundred million new francs to finance the Algerian Liberation Army.[25] FLN 'containment' extended to an almost absolute control over all aspects of the daily lives of the militants and supporters. In part this was to do with security and the policing of external contacts: permission was required to leave a *quartier*, to change jobs, to go to the cinema, to enter into a relationship, and to receive visitors. But its purpose was also to mould a new Islamic-Socialist society, with all the puritanism and self-denial common to populist revolutionary and millenarian movements. Local *Comités de justice* imposed Islamic law (*sharia*), regulated disputes, marriage and divorce, and imposed fines while *Comité d'hygiéne et d'aide sociale* inspected unhealthy lodgings and *bidonvilles*, regulated building repairs and rubbish disposal, and gave advise on welfare rights. Through this 'counter-society' the FLN sought to weld the Algerian enclaves into self-contained societies that would, in its own words, 'isolate Algerian Muslims from French society', and prove impenetrable to the operations of the police.[26]

The French police, faced with a problem that was almost identical to that of the inter-war period, of how to penetrate and counter the political base of Algerian nationalism in the bastion of the enclave, revived the 'colonialist' techniques of the former Rue Lecomte. Since the FLN, in the classic Maoist image of the guerrilla, operated like fish in water, an obvious strategy was to drain the pool – to destroy the support base among the wider immigrant community. In March 1958 Maurice Papon was appointed Paris Prefect of Police after two years as Prefect of Constantine where he had gained a reputation for his ruthless methods in the battle with the FLN.[27] Under Papon's direction three army officers of the *Section Administrative Spécialisée* (SAS), the corps which worked in the rural areas to win over the population, were secretly flown in to advise on ways to undermine the FLN. All three officers had been trained as native administrators in the school for *Affaires Indigènes* at Rabat in Morocco, had been influenced by Robert Montagne, and were knowledgeable about the structure and activities of the *Brigade nord-africaine* of the Rue Lecomte which had been dissolved in 1945.

The officers established the *Service d'assistance technique aux français musulmans d'Algérie* (SAT) which, under the guise of providing assistance on housing, welfare, employment and administrative problems, collected intelligence. Paris was divided into four (later six) areas each of which had its own advice centre, a *Bureau de Renseignements Spécialisée*.[28] Within the bureaux Commander Cunibile tried to establish lines of trust between each Algerian client and the SAT officers, a paternalist relationship which mirrored that of the native administrator as dispensor of justice (*chikaïa*). In time, argued Cunibile, the officers would receive 'confessions ... inspired by the confidence and trust placed in their authority', as to FLN activities. However, under the cosy façade, the SAT was systematically establishing files on all those who used its services and by late 1960 had information on 70 000 individuals, about fifty per cent of the population in the Paris region.[29] SAT officers also headed 'commando' teams of five men, among them an agent from the *Service des Garnis et de l'Hygiène*, which, under the pretext of inspecting health conditions and rents, went into the Algerian slum enclaves to collect intelligence. By March 1961 they had collected information on another 30 000 individuals and located 536 'suspect places' or FLN centres of activity.[30] All information was passed on to the central police agency which co-ordinated operations against the FLN, the *Service de Co-ordination des Affaires Algériennes* (SCAA).

Finally, the SAT officers, like those of the Rue Lecomte, recognised the importance of deploying a native police force which spoke Berber or Arabic in order to counter Algerian nationalists. In July 1959 they persuaded the government to fly in Algerians to form the *Force de Police Auxiliaire* (FPA), the special units known as the *harkis*. The FPA units soon achieved notoriety for their ruthless methods, including the use of torture, and their success in taking the battle into the FLN bastions like the Goutte d'Or.[31]

The Algerian War, as with the SAINA operations of the interwar period, was thus to see the introduction into metropolitan France of colonial personnel and techniques to penetrate and control what Cunibile termed the 'cyst of auto-segregation' of the immigrant community.

PUBLIC OPINION

The extent to which the Algerian War deepened French hostility and racist attitudes towards the Algerian immigrants during 1954–62 is hard to assess. Historians have paid considerable attention to the reactions of the French élites, especially intellectuals like Jean-Paul Sartre and Camus, but popular opinion has been relatively neglected.[32] C.-R. Ageron has examined changing public opinion through the use of opinion polls. This showed a relative indifference towards the colonial empire, towards the fate of the Europeans of Algeria (*pieds noirs*) and the early stages of the 'events' or the war 'without a name'.[33] Many French were also indifferent towards the Algerian immigrant population which was segregated in restricted areas of the suburbs or inner-city enclaves and with whom they had little if any contact. However, a number of key events were to change all this. Firstly, the introduction of conscription (11 April 1956) saw an increase in the size of the army in Algeria from 60 000 to over 400 000 men. Conscript responses to the harsh conditions and violence in Algeria were complex; some developed a contempt for settler egoism and wealth and became sympathetic towards the locals who lived in utter poverty in the arid and rocky interior. But in general the macho ésprit de corps of the platoon had little space for tolerance towards the enemy: according to Armand Frémont, an ex-soldier, 'racism was the rule. A whole generation underwent its apprenticeship'.[34] Returning soldiers injected the forms and language of colonial racism (*bougnoules, bicots, ratons . . .*) into the body of metropolitan society, while the relatives of soldiers killed or wounded in action often nursed bitter feelings towards the 'enemy' present on French soil.

Secondly, the bloody and inexplicable civil war between the MNA and FLN in which over 4000 people were killed allowed the media to reinforce the old stereotype of 'Arab criminality' and savagery. Newspaper headlines were explicit: 'A Muslim has his throat cut at Issy-les-Moulineaux' (*Le Monde*); 'Two Muslims killed at the Buttes-Chaumont a bullet in the neck' (*L'Aurore*); 'Massacre at Bondy. Six North Africans murdered in their dormitory' (*France-Soir*) . . . Ageron argues that the French lower classes, far from remaining indifferent to this internecine slaughter, showed fear and anger: bloodshed 'helped to reinforce the racist stereotype of the Algerian as aggressive and violent, vindictive and heartless'.[35]

A third factor in reinforcing French hostility towards Algerian immigrants was the decision of the FLN to open a 'second front' in the metropole so that armed forces would be tied down and relieve pressure on the ALN in Algeria. On the night of 25 August 1958 specially trained Algerian commandos simultaneously attacked police patrols and sabotaged strategic targets across France. At Mourepane the biggest stock of petrol in southern France burned for ten days. Between 21 August and 27 September 1958 raids were mounted on 181 targets.[36] Although FLN policy was not to alienate French public opinion and to refrain from actions that would endanger civilian lives, acts of sabotage and the assassination of police officers inevitably produced a strong reaction. A confidential FLN report of 30 August noted, 'The civilian population is getting involved (attacks on Algerian cafés and single Algerians by gangs of youths). Yesterday an Algerian killed, another wounded at Villeurbanne.'[37] But the strongest and most virulent response was to come from the police.

THE OCTOBER MASSACRE

An insight into the position of Algerian immigrants within French society towards the end of the war, their degree of isolation and the depth of racism, is provided by the events of 17 October 1961. On 6 October the chief of police, Maurice Papon, ordered the closure of all Algerian cafés from five in the evening and imposed a curfew that banned Algerians from the streets of Paris and its suburbs between 8.30 pm and 5.30 am. The ban came at a critical moment in the negotiations that were already under way at Evian between representatives of the French government and the FLN. The leaders of the FLN *Fédération de France* decided to organise, in the greatest secrecy, a peaceful mass demonstration of Algerians in the centre of Paris the aim of which was to show Algerian solidarity to the French public and to reinforce the hand of the Evian negotiators. In the *bidonvilles* and lodging-houses of Nanterre, Gennevilliers, Puteaux, Courbevoie, St Denis and other outer suburbs, FLN militants organised and instructed men, women and children as to their duties. On the evening of 17 October several large columns, about 40 000 people in all, began the march on central Paris, while other groups arrived by Metro. For some Algerian women, marginalised in the shantytowns, this was their first visit to centre of the capital. The immigrants, until that moment relegated quite literally to the margins of urban society, were proudly making their presence felt. Parisian bystanders were astonished by the 'invasion', hundreds upon hundreds of Algerians marching through the dark and rain of the Grands Boulevards shouting slogans, 'Algeria for the Algerians', 'Power to the FLN', or, in the case of the women, uttering the shrill 'You You' of North Africa.[38]

The demonstrators, still grouped in columns in various locations, then ran into a violent and murderous police assault. At the Pont de Neuilly, in the Boulevard Bonne-Nouvelle, the Boulevard Saint-Michel and other locations demonstrators were clubbed, shot and beaten to death. Dozen upon dozens of Algerians were knocked unconscious and then thrown, often with hands and legs tied, into the Seine. About fifty Algerians held in the courtyard of the Prefecture of Police, where Papon was at the time commanding operations, were killed in this way. In all some two hundred Algerians were murdered by the police, while another 11 500, in an operation reminiscent of the round up of the Jews in the Vélodrome d'Hiver in 1942, were arrested and held in the Stadium of Courbevoie and the Palais de Sport. The extreme level of violence has been attributed to the fact that the police had been infiltrated by a pro-OAS organisation, the Dides network, but more crucial is evidence that senior police officers, including Papon himself, had given assurances to rank-and-file officers that they were 'covered' for their actions. For a period of about six weeks, from 1 September to 18 October, police squads were given carte blanche to engage in killings with relative impunity, as long as they covered their tracks.[39]

The massacre reveals much about French reactions to Algerian immigrants in the dying phases of the war. Firstly, and most obviously, it showed how far the police and government had become penetrated by what Claudius-Petit denounced in parliament as, 'the hideous beast of racism'.[40] Secondly, public reaction to the event revealed a rift in opinion that was typical of the war period as a whole. Attempts to expose the scale of the massacre was made by a minority of intellectuals, professors, writers, students, journalists and *'Porteurs de Valises'*, many of them on the far left.[41] Where these individuals differed from the inter-war left in their relationship to Algerians in France was that they were much more radical in their opposition to colonialism and prepared to actively support their battle for independence.

During the Algerian demonstrations there were two kinds of response. A small number of individuals, often with great courage, intervened to help wounded men into taxis, or remonstrated with the police. The majority, however, showed the same indifference as they had to what had already become a common sight in Paris, armed police rounding up Algerians, hands on head, and subjecting them to violent blows with rifle-butts and truncheons. On the night of 17 October some onlookers urged the police on or even gave a direct hand. The outstanding feature, however, of the October events was the relative ease with which the government was able to block calls for an investigation. This it was able to do since the great mass of the working class, the trade unions and the Socialist and Communist parties, were prepared to turn a blind eye.[42] The lack of action also meant that racists were able to remain in their positions, lodged for decades in the core of the police force or in higher levels of the state. Papon, for example, remained Prefect of Police until January 1967, and later became deputy for the Cher and national treasurer to the UDR.

A few months after the massacre of Algerians on 8 February 1962 a police charge on an anti-OAS demonstration led to the death of eight French people at the Charonne Metro. This evoked a powerful response from the main unions and the Communist and Socialist Parties and half a million people turned out for a spectacular funeral procession. This response was in marked contrast to the silence of the mainstream left in October. Charonne remained alive for decades in the collective memory of French society, and in doing so helped to overlay and to erase any surviving traces of October 1961. The collective amnesia of the French, the auto-censorship of those who witnessed but failed to 'see' or register police smashing Algerian heads with rifle-butts, was one symptom of a deeper malaise.[43]

POSTSCRIPT: EMIGRATION AFTER INDEPENDENCE
(1962–73)

With the coming of independence it was to be expected that
the new Islamic Republic would terminate the emigration which
nationalists had always regarded as a shameful mark of colonial dependency. Many of the militants of the ENA (1926–37)
and later independence movements (PPA, MTLD, FLN) had a
first-hand and often bitter knowledge of emigration and of the
harsh and often humiliating conditions of work and housing
in France. The Messalists, however, recognised the economic
necessity of emigration to the sending regions. During the
inter-war period the ENA campaigned to remove the impediments to free movement and sought to improve the overall
rights and conditions of immigrants, from wages to family
benefits and health insurance. But significantly the ENA did
not bring pressure to facilitate family reunification in France
but instead asked the authorities to improve the ability of
workers to return home to visit their families by extending the
length of paid leave.[44] The general assumption of the nationalist movement, although it was rarely spelt out in any detailed
programme, was that independence would terminate emigration, which was a product and symbol of colonial dependency.
Once the French had gone, the dynamic expansion of the
Algerian economy would enable all men to find employment
and a fulfilled life in their own land. The idea of eventual
return to a newly independent Algeria helped sustained the
nationalist militants during their long exile in France.

However, the situation at independence in 1962 was totally
adverse to the ending of emigration. Firstly, the Algerian
economy was in disarray; not only had the departure of almost
the entire *pied-noir* community removed the most educated
and experienced engineers, technicians and administrators,
the essential professions from which Algerians had been largely
excluded, but the OAS engaged in a systematic destruction of
capital equipment, public buildings, schools, and oil depots.[45]
The eight-year war had a particularly destructive impact on
rural areas, historically the major source of emigration to
France. The forced military displacement or *regroupement* of 2
350 000 villagers into camps, combined with other movements
to urban centres, meant that 3 525 000 people or about half

of the total rural population abandoned their homes and, in many instances, their fields and livestock.

This traumatic rupturing of the fragile structure of the traditional agrarian system, which was already under severe strain before the war, accelerated permanent flight from the land.[46] Many hundreds of thousands of peasants, instead of returning on independence to their fields infested by scrub and weeds, headed for the towns or the ferry ports.[47] The newly independent government was unable to expand job opportunities in the urban/industrial sector of the economy fast enough to soak up the huge pool of unemployed, a pool that was primed by an exceptionally high birth-rate. Emigration continued to function as a safety-valve as it had under colonialism and the number of Algerians in France continued to rocket from 350 000 at independence in 1962 to 845 000 in December 1973.

After independence some socialist ideologues argued that emigration should be halted immediately. Mohamed Harbi, for example, argued that the 'emigration of our brothers' was not 'an acceptable solution to our problems', but helped to 'furnish our enemies with a way of applying pressure on us' and he called for 'an immediate halt'.[48] The more pragmatic position of the government of Ben Bella was that, although not desirable in the long term, emigration would have to continue for the foreseeable future. Until the Algerian economy could be developed emigration was a necessary evil. The official newspaper *El Moudjahid* stated the government position: 'the departure of our brothers for France remains a necessity and serves the reciprocal interests of our two countries'.[49] It has also been suggested that Ben Bella was reluctant to see the return of FLN militants of the *Fédération de France* which had been opposed to his coming to power.

But why did France, which had just been defeated after an extremely bloody war, not exact some kind of revenge by slamming its doors shut on Algerian immigration? Two clauses in the Evian accords guaranteed that all Algerians with an identity card were, 'free to circulate between Algeria and France' and while resident in France they were guaranteed, 'the same rights as French nationals with the exception of political rights'. The underlying reason for this remarkably liberal provision was that France hoped to negotiate a package that would retain her monopoly over the exploration, production and marketing of Saharan oil and reinforce trade, technical and cultural links generally. France hoped to build a special relationship which would ensure her post-colonial economic domination. France also guaranteed emigration as a quid pro quo for clauses that would protect the property and rights of Europeans in Algeria. However, this last 'trade-off' condition of Evian quickly proved hollow for France as the panic-stricken mass exodus of the *pieds noirs* in the summer of 1962 removed one cause for reciprocity.

Throughout the 1960s Algeria remained almost totally dependent on France, for loans to ward off bankruptcy, for economic and technical assistance and other forms of aid. This 'neo-colonial' situation meant that France retained considerable power to dominate or dictate to the fledgling Republic. This became rapidly evident in the sphere of emigration when in the Nekkache-Grandval accord of 10 April 1964 France was able to impose humiliating terms which radically undermined the Evian agreement, enabled France to set unilaterally a quota restriction (soon after set at 12 000 immigrants per year) and enforced medical inspections by French doctors.[50] Algerian politicians interpreted this as a deliberate French ploy to use emigration restrictions as a means of placing pressure on the Algerian government which was moving in an increasingly socialist direction. Migrants, as in so many other post-colonial situations, were becoming a pawn in a larger power struggle.[51] France was, at the same time, encouraging immigration from other destinations like Portugal, Morocco and Tunisia, a form of diversification that gradually reduced the enormous reliance of France on Algerian labour.

Gradually, but firmly, Algeria was moving towards a position of economic recovery and a degree of independence from France that would enable her to achieve the preferred goal of ending all labour migration, one of the last vestiges of colonialism. The process of disengagement from French economic domination is shown by the decline of Algerian exports to France from 77 per cent of all exports in 1962 to 20 per cent in 1973.[52] The most dramatic and crucial turning point in Algeria's bid for economic independence came with the nationalisation of French oil and gas companies in February 1971. The new-found oil revenues meant that Algeria was less dependent on remittance payments received from France. The decision of the Boumedienne government to go for an ambitious industrialisation programme (oil-related industry, cement, steel . . .) was crucially dependent on overcoming the desperate shortage of skilled labour. The government began to restrict the departure of skilled workers to France and, from 1971 onwards, launched a programme to persuade skilled emigrants to return.[53] Simultaneously, the success of the *Révolution Agraire*, launched in November 1971, the nationalisation of land and its redistribution to peasant collectives, was dependent on arresting the departure of peasants from the rural areas towards the cities and France.

By 1973 neither France nor Algeria had any strong incentive to maintain emigration. Nationalisation of oil and the end of the 'special relationship' meant that France no longer had a strong motive to keep Algeria 'sweet' through any preferential treatment of her emigrants. France now became preoccupied with the high social costs of Algerian immigration, especially in rehousing the inhabitants of the *bidonvilles*, and in stopping the tens of thousands of clandestine workers who found entry as 'tourists'. The Algerian government, although faced with an enormous demand to emigrate, now felt it had the means to assert a firm grip over its citizens and to tie their education, training and employment to the construction of the new socialist economic and social order.

The opportunity for Algeria to finally cut all labour emigration, seventy years after its inception, came with an outburst of racist violence in France during August 1973. Following on the wave of killings of Algerians, particularly in the Marseilles area, the Boumedienne government unilaterally halted all further emigration on 19 September. This was to mark the definitive end to primary, labour migration, although family reunification was to continue for many years. A number of researchers have argued that racist violence was a pretext to halt the movement, a measure which was really imposed because the new state had gained sufficient economic independence to cut its ties to France. However, as Adler points out, emigration still remained, 'the last important link with the colonial past, and the last tangible reminder of Algeria's former status'. For the confident and assertive Boumedienne government, an inability to protect its own citizens against the racism that all Algerians had faced under colonialism was a source of shame and humiliation. This was felt with particular keenness as Algeria was beginning to project itself as a global leader of 'Third World' nations and the Marseilles killings began just one week before Algeria was host to a summit conference of non-aligned nations.[54]

Conclusion

Mais pourquoi les Algériens sont les plus détéstées? Qu'est-ce qu'ils ont?

(Saïd, Algerian immigrant)[1]

In France in recent years there has been a growing debate among politicians, journalists and academics about what has been termed 'exclusion', the deepening social, economic and political marginalisation of the poor, of unemployed youth, and of ethnic minorities. Attention has focused in particular on the '*banlieue*' [suburb], a key-word that has come to signify the enormous, high-rise estates of public housing located on the fringes of the major cities, 'ghettoised' zones associated with rebellious minority youth, educational failure, the 'breakdown' of the family, criminality, rising drug abuse, and rioting.[2] There is a widespread fear that alienation, particularly of youth of Maghrebian descent (*Beurs*), is creating the conditions under which Islamic fundamentalism can find a growing support base. The police hunt and shooting of Khaled Kelkal, a disaffected youth from the *banlieue* of Vaulx-en-Velin, who was recruited by fundamentalists to carry out bombings, appeared to confirm these anxieties. The considerable impact of Kassovitz's film *La Haine*, which gives a powerful picture of anomie, frustration, rebellious minority youth and police violence in the *banlieue*, was also symptomatic of widespread public interest and concern.

The crisis and loss of confidence that the French are feeling in relation to their own national identity – an anxiety fuelled by the perceived loss of great power status, the erosion of French culture by American consumerism, the inroads of Anglo-Saxon terminology and related processes of globalisation – is focused in particular on the concern that the unifying and universalist traditions of Jacobinism are in jeopardy.[3] The dominant Republican ideology shared by the political left and right is that ethnic minorities should and must be eventually absorbed (assimilated) into France 'one and indivisible'. For many French the future nightmare scenario is represented by the United States, perceived as a society torn apart by deepening

207

conflict and political struggle based on national/ethnic enclaves and organisations (Italian, Porto-Rican, Jewish, Polish . . .).[4]

A major debate is now under way among French sociologists, demographers and political scientists on transformations in minority identity, and prognostications are continually being made as to the extent to which ethnic groups are becoming incorporated and eventually assimilated or are maintaining a strong socio-cultural cohesion, forms of 'resistance' and separatist tendencies. Michel Rocard's establishment of the *Haut Conseil à l'Intégration* was a measure of the official concern that an Anglo-Saxon model of multiculturalism might lead to a 'balkanization' of French society.

Much of the debate has centred on the position of North African immigrants and their second and third generation descendants, since they appear to be the most 'problematic' group, the most excluded, and the most weakly integrated into French society. Most investigations of Maghrebian marginalisation have explored the complex of factors that have operated during the past thirty years, the impact of severe economic recession, spatial concentration in de-industrialised zones, educational disadvantage, discrimination in employment and so on.[5] However, the present position of Maghrebians, and particularly of Algerians, cannot be adequately explained unless account is taken of colonialism, how it initiated processes of domination and exclusion and how these became embedded in institutions, ways of thinking, 'common sense' racism and other forms that have continued to be reproduced within contemporary, post-colonial society.

In the current debate on the 'crisis' of integration, Italian immigration has frequently been referred to as the 'classic' model of successful assimilation into French society.[6] Italians represented the earliest and most numerous 'first-wave' of labour migration in modern times and passed through three phases: one of initial conflict with xenophobic French, followed by a transition stage of growing contact with French society and a degree of toleration, and a final stage of assimilation marked by upward social mobility, naturalisation, intermarriage and adoption of French culture. This 'melting-pot' theory assumes that eventually all immigrant minorities will be assimilated, and that it is only a question of time before more recent arrivals will follow the same pathways as the Italians.

However, this model does not fit the pattern of Algerian immigration. Firstly, Algerians have one of the longest histories of immigration and should, therefore, have readily passed on to the second or third phase of integration. Algerians were long established in France before the Portuguese, yet the latter who arrived much more recently and constituted the single largest group in France by 1982 (859 520 Portuguese nationals compared to 795 920 Algerians) have remained relatively 'invisible', faced little xenophobia and have integrated rapidly and smoothly. Noiriel and others have argued that the main waves of French xenophobia can be linked to periods of economic recession and job insecurity, the 1880s, the 1930s, and the period after 1974. At a general level this is the case, but what an economistic model cannot readily explain is why during the current economic downturn some migrant groups, most notably the Algerians, have been more disliked than others (the Portuguese).

What the 'melting-pot' model overlooks is the profound impact of colonialism in differentiating 'Third World' immigrants from those of European origin. I shall conclude by examining some of the ways in which colonialism has continued to impact on Algerian exclusion in contemporary France. The claim is not, of course, that colonialism was the unique or sole source of modern racism and discrimination but that historically it provided an enormous dynamic and particular shape to anti-Algerian perceptions and institutions, an impetus that has continued to reproduce itself at every level within post-colonial French society. Two interrelated features of Algerian exclusion are examined: first those factors which continued to make them the major target of racism, and secondly those factors which operated to impede their integration into French society.

POST-COLONIAL RACISM

To trace all the processes and routeways through which the legacy of colonialism has been transmitted and sustained as an integral part of contemporary, post-colonial French society, what Grillo terms the 'continuing presence of the past in the present', would require a further study. A comprehensive investigation would need to look at a complex of factors, from images in advertising, newspaper texts, school books, and the cinema, to comics, popular jokes and television.[7] However, I would emphasise three channels in the reproduction of anti-Algerian racism.

i) Stereotyping and Racial Hierarchy

Once racial stereotypes have been constituted and established they appear to assume an extraordinary fixity and can be transmitted and perpetuated within popular culture, quite unchanged, over long periods of time. Thomas Holt has argued convincingly that racism is embedded and reproduced within the 'everyday', through the micro-level expressions that **mark** the racial Other and 'that racist ideas and practices are naturalized, made self-evident, and thus seemingly beyond audible challenge. It is at this level that race is reproduced long after its original historical stimulus . . . has faded.'[8] This 'common sense' racism attributes specific negative qualities to different racialised categories ('Arabs', 'Blacks', 'Chinese' . . .) but also arranges them into a hierarchy. F. Batier organised training programmes on inter-ethnic relations for eight hundred supervisors at *Renault* between 1973 and 1980. He found that irrational phantasies and stereotypes were profoundly anchored and constituted, 'a kind of ladder of civilisation which also constituted a scale of preference with, at its lowest level, a world of savages, and at its summit, our western world.' In between came a range of 'types' (Black, Jew, 'Chinese') and for 'the Arab', 'who constitutes in a way the archetype of the immigrant, an emphasis is always placed on his dangerousness, with strong sexual connotations, and on his dirtiness.'[9]

The 'banalisation' of racial stereotypes takes on a life, a dynamic of its own in which the psychological need to target prejudice on the most negative Other, the most detested and feared, always has recourse to a ready made set of images, like Epinal types, among which the 'Arab' figures as the automatic choice as culprit and victim. Throughout the 1970s and 1980s French journalists investigating racism in the popular *quartiers* of Marseilles, Paris, Lyons and elsewhere recorded, year in year out, endless permutations of an anti-Arab message the core topics of which were danger, libidinous violence, and disease. 'And when they [North Africans] instal themselves in a locality people no longer want to stay there. They are afraid and there's no more safety. They [Arabs] impose their way of life ... Yes, they take up the street, they say things to the women' (Maurice Arreckx, Mayor of Toulon).[10] 'Send your daughter to the Porte d'Aix, she will be touched up or raped; go there yourself and they'll steal your wallet' (Marseilles worker).[11] 'Enough of the Algerian thieves, Algerian rioters, Algerian braggarts, Algerian pimps, Algerian syphilitics ...' (G. Domenech, editor of the *Méridional*).[12] Such noxious banalities could be multiplied ad infinitum.

This armoury of simplistic but none the less potent stereotypes has existed in a continuous form since the inter-war period. It first assumed a permanent and recognisable shape at a particular moment, during 1919–24. The appearance at this time was not a chance or random occurence, but can be traced to the deliberate injection of colonial prejudices into metropolitan society, linked to a strategy to criminalise Algerians (legitimating the need for controls on immigration and for a special North African police unit), to present them as a moral-health threat (to justify sanitary inspections, especially for syphilis and TB), and to throw a *cordon sanitaire* around the native and to segregate them from French women, from Communism and other subversive influences.

ii)   The *Pieds noirs*, the Army and the Extreme Right

The eventual loss of Algeria, the 'jewel in the crown' of the French empire, after a long and bloody war left a profound mark on French society. This, more than the Suez fiasco and the independence of Cambodia, Vietnam, Morocco, and Tunisia, was felt as a deep humiliation, a symbol not only of decolonisation but of France's decline as a great power. All the feelings of battered national pride, bitterness and disillusionment that remained after 1962 became centred on the Algerians in France. During the colonial period Algerian migrants were disliked since they represented an incursion of primitives and barbarism into the territorial heartland of civilisation. But resentment was in part contained by the feeling that the Algerian worker was a 'pauvre type', who tried to keep himself to

himself, segregated in ghettos, and certainly not a kind to
assert himself with confidence or to display 'arrogance' vis-à-
vis the French. But after 1962 the Algerian immigrant was
transformed overnight into the 'victor' and his physical presence was a cause of revulsion, a constant painful reminder of
a national humiliation that most French people preferred to
suppress and forget.[13]

The first large-scale manifestation of anti-Arab racism after
Algerian independence came with a wave of violence and killings which swept through the south of France between June
and December 1973.[14] It is noteworthy that this racism was in
part inspired by French perceptions of Algerians displaying
arrogance, an assertiveness that took the symbolic form of the
immigrants 'invading' the public spaces of the central city which
had been the preserve of the French. The Algerians, it was
felt, were now refusing to remain 'hidden' in the segregated
slums and HLM estates. In June the Mayor of Grasse violently
broke up a peaceful demonstration of Algerian immigrant
workers as they approached the town hall. 'The Arabs', he
claimed, 'behave in the old town as if in a conquered territory
... it's very painful to be invaded by them.'[15] During June to
August gang attacks (*ratonnades*) in Grasse, Toulon and Marseilles others complained, 'they hog the street', 'they rule the
roost', 'they invade the café terraces', 'the immigrants end up
believing they are at home here' ...[16]

Such resentment assumed a particularly bitter and lasting
form among sections of the army and the *pied noir* community. During the Algerian war all those young men born between 1932 and 1943 were called up and 2.3 million crossed
the Mediterranean – 4.3 per cent of the French population
compared to the 1.2 per cent of Americans that served in
Vietnam.[17] A large number of these men returned from Algeria conditioned by brutal actions against the civilian population, by the coarse barrack-room 'humour' and racism of the
platoon, and by the values and practices of colonial society.
But it was among the million *pieds noirs* refugees that were to
be found the largest numbers who injected into French society
both colonial attitudes towards Algerians and the most virulent hatred. The *pieds noirs* settled mainly in the south of France:
in Marseilles they numbered over 100 000, constituting about
one-eighth of the total population.[18]

At the core of extreme-right politics in France from 1962 onwards, were numerous former members of the OAS (Roger Holeindre, Pierre Lagaillarde, Pierre Sergent, J.-J. Susini, Jean Gardes . . .) or *pieds noirs* activists like Germaine Burgaz, General Edmond Jouhaüd, Marcel Ronda and Joseph Ortiz, many of whom found an eventual home in the *Front National* founded in 1972. A complex network of *pieds noirs* and ex-soldier organisations proliferated in the south of France, the *Unités rapatriés*, the *Comité nationaliste des rapatriés*, the *Association des Français d'outre-mer, Jeune Pied Noir*, the *Union nationale des anciens combattants d'Afrique du Nord* . . .[19] The wave of anti-Arab violence which swept through the south in late 1973 was orchestrated by the newly formed *Front National*, by the fascist *Ordre Nouveau*, and various *pieds noirs* and ex-soldier organisations. A communiqué issued after the bombing of the Algerian consulate on 14 December 1973 stated, 'There are more Arabs in France than there are Pieds Noirs in Algeria. They expelled us with violence, we shall expel them with violence.'[20]

It is in the Midi that the *Front National*, with strong *pieds noirs* backing, has gained its biggest electoral successes and obtained a strong presence in regional and municipal government. In the first round of the 1995 Presidential elections Le Pen scored 23.5 per cent in Greater Marseilles.[21] In appealing to the electorate Le Pen has been able to deploy a racist discourse that draws upon and amplifies the anti-Arab stereotypes that became so entrenched in popular culture from 1920 onwards. At a Front National rally in Avignon in November 1989 Le Pen centred his speech on the recent attempted rape and murder of a local woman by an Algerian. 'She died to defend her honour as a woman and as a French person . . . a martyr to uncontrolled immigration.' He called on 'all French people, faced with the formidable danger represented by those who invade us, to engage in a national resistance'.[22] The populist-racist and former Algerian paratrooper Le Pen has an almost instinctive feel for the 'common-sense' racial prejudices sedimented within French society. His attacks on the 'immigré', meaning the 'Arab' and, in particular the Algerian minority, are constantly larded with references to attacks on women and children, images of defilement, and the need to establish 'sidatorium' to contain the 'invasion' of AIDS carriers, thus reinvigorating the old colonial stereotypes.

iii) Colonial Institutional Survivals

One crucial way in which colonial influences and institutional racism continued to function long after 1962 was through the role of the thousands of '*Africains*', Algerian army officers, administrators, lawyers, doctors, engineers and other professionals who went on to fill a range of related functions in metropolitan France. It is difficult to quantify the numbers of those among the decision making élites of metropolitan France who had been raised in Algeria or been posted there during their career. As has been seen in the case of Octave Depont, Adolphe Gérolami and Pierre Godin it was a widespread practice in French government that senior career functionaries should be constantly circulated between France and the colony.

The number of ex-colonial state functionaries was not only large but they were also concentrated in certain sectors of government which played a key role in forming and implementing policy towards immigrants **after** Algerian independence – the Ministry of the Interior, the police forces, the national health service, housing and urban planning, education and local government. Maurice Papon, for example, former Prefect of Constantine, and responsible for operations on the night of the Paris massacre of 16 October 1961, continued to serve as Prefect of Police until 1967. Later he became the director (PDG) of the aircraft corporation *Sud-Aviation*, national treasurer and deputy in the Gaullist UDR, and in April 1978 Minister for the Budget under Raymond Barre.[23] Patterns of colonial authoritarianism, paternalism and discrimination survived in an institutional form within numerous agencies that were formed in the imperial age but which continued to function – frequently unreformed – long after Algerian independence. For example, SAT, the special welfare and surveillance organisation set up to counter the FLN, was still functioning in 1965, maintaining secret contacts with 700 major employers to advise on, 'the elimination of the incapable, the unadaptable, and troublemaker elements'.[24] Numerous government hostels for North Africans were run by ex-soldiers or administrators from Algeria or Morocco who imposed strict discipline and regulations that reproduced colonialist master/native relations.[25] A similar pattern existed in large companies when appointing supervisors to control North African workers.[26] Agencies like SONACOTRA and FAS, concerned with the construction and allocation of immigrant housing, relegated thousands of Algerian families to tawdry *cités de transit*, a policy based on perceptions of North Africans as primitives who needed to be trained by social workers and 'civilised' before gaining access to HLM flats. An almost universal story among housing officials and social workers was that of the 'sheep in the bath', the ritual slaughter during Aid-el-kebir, a myth that through the image of blood-letting in the ceramic clean zone of the bathroom provided the sharpest contrast between barbarism and modernity and the violent transgression of the correct rules of domesticity.[27] It was this discriminatory ethos among housing officials and local politicians that initiated the processes of housing allocation through which Algerians eventually became segregated in the huge estates of the *banlieue*.

ALGERIANS: A DIFFICULT INTEGRATION

Finally, I want to outline some of the implications of my findings for the current debate on the integration/assimilation of ethnic minorities. Recently, French historians and sociologists have emphasised that the destiny of immigrants, massively concentrated in unskilled industrial employment, was inexorably tied to that of the French working class. As Tripier notes, 'It is crucial that we understand that their conditions of employment, their way of life, their daily social intercourse, their strategies of integration, the dynamic choices affecting their identity, were essentially played out in the factories, the schools, the lodgings of the popular neighbourhoods, in contact with other strata of the working class.'[28] Italian, Polish, Spanish and other migrants found a bridge into French society through their contact and involvement with the key institutions of the working class, the trade unions, the Communist Party, the Catholic Church, the local café, sports clubs and other associations. How did Algerians interact with the French proletariat within the work place and, outside the factory, in the working class *quartier*?

i) Work-place Relations

Most minorities on their first arrival in France faced problems, of language and culture, in establishing good working relations with the indigenous work-force. For Algerians the process of acculturation into the mores of the working class appears to have been more difficult than for any other group. This was partly due to segregationist practices within the factory, since Algerians were either concentrated in the sectors in which the worst physical conditions and lowest wages predominated or because employers preferred to organise teams of immigrant workers on an ethnic basis. In such situations contact with French workers was often restricted to supervisors who as controllers maintained the distance of authority. During the inter-war period French workers often demanded that North Africans be provided with separate canteen facilities and refused to work alongside them in teams on the grounds that their level of productivity was much lower.

The single most crucial factor which impeded Algerian integration into the working class was the predominance of the pattern of short-term migration and rotation until the early 1970s. The Algerian workers were always in an unstable and temporary position, peasant-labourers whose central preoccupation was to maximise savings as rapidly as possible for an eventual return to North Africa. This created a division in the working class: for the autochthons the Algerians were perceived as 'birds of passage' who had an instrumental relationship to work, a short-term interest, that was quite different from their own.[29] Algerian rotation survived over an unusually long period of time, some seventy years, whereas for most other immigrant groups patterns of permanent settlement appeared much earlier. The geographical proximity of North Africa, the closest 'Third-World' and colonial source of labour to the European heartland, also facilitated relatively cheap and easy communication that enabled the Algerian to constantly renew his roots in the values, traditions and preoccupations of his village society. The migration flow was constantly being replenished, as in the period after 1948, by men arriving from locations in Algeria previously unaffected by emigration. Such new arrivals had to go through the same processes of slow adjustment and acculturation to western life that Kabyles had faced forty years earlier.

Lastly, work-place integration through affiliation and involvement with the trade unions and associated political organisations, especially the CGTU and the Communist Party, was feeble. This was not because Algerians were reluctant to participate in industrial action; indeed during the 1930s they showed a very high level of militancy and were involved in numerous strike movements. However, when the PCF/CGTU made central decisions to extend their organisation and influence among the North Africans this was implemented in a half-hearted way, while the regional and local cadres, who shared the colonialist perception of their innate superiority over 'natives', simply ignored directives. When Algerians did come out on strike, they all too frequently found little if any support from their French 'comrades'. In time these divisions may have been overcome but for the fact that the *Étoile-Nord-Africaine* split away from the Communist Party and eventually entered into bitter opposition to the Communists who remained opposed to Algerian independence.[30] The Messalist movement rapidly became the most influential organisation among the Algerian émigrée community, but since its central concern was national independence it powerfully reinforced the migrant's perception that his future lay tied to the homeland.

Although it is difficult to establish longitudinal statistics on the income of Algerians all the evidence points to the fact that over the half century 1920–70 there was very little promotion and upward social mobility. Trapped by discrimination in the lowest echelons of the unskilled labour market, the Algerians failed to achieve the levels of income that would have facilitated integration by access to better housing, to educational opportunity and to a standard of living that would have improved their status in the eyes of the French.

ii)   Integration in the Working-class *Quartier*

Once the Algerians left the factory gates they found themselves in a closed circuit of housing and leisure activities that isolated them from the French working class and other immigrant groups. There were no French ghettos, in the American sense of entire urban sectors inhabited solely by black people, and Algerians lived in the same localities as French, Italian, Belgian, Spanish and Polish workers. However, Algerians were

usually concentrated in particular streets in which they inhabited overcrowded lodgings or patronised cafés that were the
unique preserve of their compatriots.

Such segregation at the micro-urban level was due to a combination of both French discrimination and Algerian cultural
and political auto-defence. Robert Montagne and other colonial sociologists explained the resistance of Algerians to integration in France by the powerful kin solidarities of Berber
migrants. This line of approach has been recently revived by
Emmanuel Todd by the argument that Maghrebian family structures were inherently incompatible with those of France.[31]
However, such a structuralist approach implies that the onus
for the failure of Algerians to integrate in contemporary France
lies with them. This is just a more sophisticated version of the
French common-sense assumption that immigrants constitute'
a 'problem' largely because they refuse to become 'like us'.

Firstly, it can be noted that inter-group aid and support
networks, accompanied by a degree of residential segregation,
has been an almost universal feature of early migrations –
from Bretons in Paris to Italians in New York. What distin-
guished the Algerians from other minority groups was the
extent to which they continued, after fifty or sixty years, to
remain marginalised and cut off from the mainstream of French
society. The reasons for this are political rather than to do with
family structure or the atavistic 'tribalism' of Algerian migrants.
The deeply entrenched and long-term nature of anti-Algerian
racism forced the immigrants back onto their own resources,
into a defensive enclave. But this pattern was also strongly
reinforced by the policies of the *Service des Affaires Indigènes*
(SAINA) which attempted to segregate Algerians from French
society through the provision of special institutions (the Rue
Lecomte, North African hostels, the Franco-Muslim hospital)
and a neo-colonial police brigade. Parallel with this went the
moves of the colonial lobby and right-wing interests to alienate
the French working class from the Algerians through a relent-
less campaign of denigration and criminalisation.

However, the weak integration of Algerians was also rooted
in a tradition of cultural and political resistance. From the
moment of the French conquest of Algeria in 1830 the indigenous society, in spite of enormous land expropriations and
violent repression, sought to defend its core identity through

a complex range of cultural resistances. These forms of auto-defence, the crux of which lay in Muslim identity, were carried by the migrants into the metropolitan context. The ruse of Depont, Gérolami, Godin and others to reinvent colonial mechanisms of control in the metropole found an equal match in the migrants' deeply rooted knowledge of techniques of resistance to colonial domination. Basically the historic refusal to be 'assimilated' into colonial society, meaning a rejection of domination and absorption into French 'civilisation', shaped Algerian society so powerfully that it carried over into a refusal to be 'integrated' into contemporary metropolitan society.

A key measure of this resistance was the low level of natural-isations. In colonial Algeria the indigenous people, with the exception of the Jews, could only achieve French citizenship by renouncing their Muslim identity, the *statut personnel*. The extraordinary resistance of Algerians to 'frenchification', in spite of the considerable advantages attached to citizenship, is shown by the minute numbers who became naturalised, about 26 per year throughout the period from 1865 to 1934.[32] The statistics of naturalisation in post-colonial France has been used by sociologists as a key index of the degree to which different minorities have opted for full integration into French society. The proportion of Algerian immigrants who had acquired French nationality by 1990 was still very low at 12.7 per cent compared to the Italians (57.4 per cent), Poles (68.3) Indo-Chinese (42) and Tunisians (25.8).[33]

The impressive power of the 'myth of return', the Algerian emigrants' inability to accept that their future might be one of permanent settlement in France, was also sustained by the ENA-PPA and the FLN which were committed to a programme aimed at independence and eventual return. The entire psychological orientation of the militant was one which projected the future in terms of a post-colonial Algerian society. The nationalist movement saw one of its functions as the mainten-ance, within the French context, of a specifically Algerian-Muslim identity with a view to eventual return. To this end it discouraged practices, especially family reunification, which might begin to sever the links to the home society and culture. Even after independence in 1962 the Algerian government laid claim to sovereignty over the immigrants in France, attempted to control them socially, politically and culturally through the *Amicale des Algériens en Europe*, and impeded family emigration as much as possible. Post-1945 French governments were also opposed to Algerian family migration since they preferred to seek a solution to the low French birth rate through settlement of European people of compatible 'racial' stock. Hence one of the key indicators of integration, the transition from single-male rotation to permanent family settlement, was also impeded and long delayed by a kind of collusion between sending and receiving states.

The long historic delay in Algerian family reunification was a crucial factor in retarding integration. Janine Ponty has shown that Polish immigrants, who began to arrive in France at the same time as the Algerians, faced problems of weak integration and isolation from French society not unlike that of the North Africans. This was because the Poles established a complex of Catholic, welfare, commercial and sporting associations in the northern mining regions that segregated them from French working-class life. The mining companies encouraged the ethno-community so as to isolate it from the malign influence of the unions and left-wing politics.[34] However, a crucial difference with the Algerians was that the Poles, with the encouragement of the employers and the French government, emigrated with wives and children from the very beginning. By 1925 in the Pas-de-Calais the immigrant community was made up of 43.4 per cent men, 17.8 per cent women, and 38.9 per cent children. Because of family migration Polish immigrants very rarely made the long journey home on vacation.[35] In spite of the cultural and social autonomy of the Polish community and very low levels of intermarriage with the French, integration inevitably accelerated as the 'second generation', schooled in France, reached maturity by the end of the Second World War.

The definitive moment in the permanent settlement of the Algerians came with the complete halt of primary emigration in 1973/4. It was this blockage which put a rapid end to the old pattern of circulation, and migrants opted to stay in France rather than risk being denied re-entry if they should go back to Algeria on leave. The process by which Algerians therefore abandoned the 'myth of return' and came to terms with the reality of the fact that they were in France for good came at a very late stage in the history of North African emigration.

The moment at which the first generation of migrants began to face up to the necessity for integration, to invest in housing in France rather than in Kabylia, that their children needed to succeed in the French educational system, and so forth took place against a background of economic recession, rising unemployment and deepening crisis in the sectors of industry in which Algerians were most heavily concentrated. Algerian attempts to break out of the 'ghetto', to overcome the hurdles of discrimination, racism and social and political exclusion could hardly have come at a more difficult moment. The powerful surge of the *Front National* onto the political stage from 1983–4, once again reviving the entrenched anti-Arab stereotypes of the colonial past, ensured that the Algerians remained the prime target of racist violence.

However, in recent years a number of researchers have begun to argue that the second and third generation *Beurs* are quietly being incorporated into French society, largely unnoticed by the general public.[36] A variety of sociological and statistical indicators can be used to measure the process of adaptation and insertion. Investigators have, for example, studied the data on naturalisation, and the rate of minority 'convergence' with the French in educational achievement, levels of employment, socio-economic status, and demographic structures. For example, the percentage of females among the Algerian immigrants has changed from 2.3 per cent in 1946 to 41.3 per cent in 1990, slowly approaching a French 'norm'. Perhaps the most sensitive indicator of Algerian incorporation is the level of intermarriage and co-habitation. Traditionally, Algerians practised an extremely high level of endogamy, for religious and cultural reasons, and were particularly opposed to marriages between Muslim women and European males.[37] The research of Michèle Tribalat shows a continuing high level of female endogamy, but of people born in France from two Algerian parents, 50 per cent of the men married French natives compared with 24 per cent of the women, figures that would suggest an accelerating fusion with the majority society.[38]

Today first generation Algerians and their descendants, most of whom have been born in France, are definitively rooted in French society. The totality of the Maghrebian 'third generation', children born in France of parents who were themselves born in France, will automatically become French citizens under

Article 23 of the nationality law. However, there continues to be a large **gap** between the de facto level of Algerian integration and French perceptions of Algerians as an unassimilable and threatening minority. In a 1993 survey seven out of ten young Maghrebians said they identified more closely with the lifestyle and culture of France than with their parents' values. Yet French perceptions were diametrically opposed and eight out of ten thought it would be difficult to integrate young Maghrebians born in France.[39] The 'melting-pot' model suggests that Algerian integration should lead to a growing acceptance and toleration by the French. But this is not happening and as Algerians and their descendants become more and more like the French they continue to be the prime target of virulent racism.

How can this be explained? Contemporary French racism which continues to target Arabs and especially Algerians above all other minorities is not sustained primarily by economic, but by political factors. It was colonialism which first targeted the Algerians. Once anti-Algerian racism had been established and consolidated it, like anti-semitism, was able to take on a 'life of its own', a kind of autonomy, and to reproduce itself through time regardless of changes within the economy and regardless of the degree of Algerian incorporation/integration into French society. It is the generation of Le Pen, of Chirac, Giscard d'Estaing and Pasqua which entered politics before and during the last and bloodiest of the wars of decolonisation which has continued to sustain an anti-immigrant politics focused on the 'Arab'. The Iranian revolution, the Gulf War, the Rushdie affair, the civil war in Algeria and the fear of fundamentalism establishing a beach-head within French society has provided a context within which the old, deeply entrenched prejudices can be dusted down and given a new élan. The moral panic that has arisen in response to the Muslim presence is not a unique post-Communist and fin-de-siècle phenomenon, but one that has deep roots in the colonial past.

Appendix

Table A1 Statistics of port registered movement between Algeria and France

Date	Departures from Algeria	Returns to Algeria	Annual Balance	Cumulative total in France
1914	7 444	6 000	+ 1 444	14 444*
1915	20 092	4 970	+ 15 122	29 566
1916	30 755	9 044	+ 21 711	51 277
1917	34 985	18 849	+ 16 136	67 413
1918	23 340	20 489	+ 2 851	70 264
1919	5 568	17 497	− 11 929	58 335
1920	21 684	17 380	+ 3 404	61 739
1921	17 259	17 538	− 279	61 460
1922	44 466	26 289	+ 18 197	79 657
1923	58 586	36 990	+ 21 596	91 253
1924	71 028	57 467	+ 13 561	114 814
1925	24 753	36 328	− 11 575	103 239
1926	48 677	35 102	+ 13 575	116 814
1927	21 472	36 073	− 14 601	102 213
1928	39 726	25 008	+ 14 718	116 931
1929	42 948	42 227	+ 721	117 652
1930	40 630	43 877	− 3 247	114 405
1931	20 847	32 950	− 12 103	102 302
1932	14 950	14 485	+ 465	102 767
1933	16 684	15 083	+ 1 601	104 368
1934	12 013	15 354	− 3 341	101 027
1935	13 915	12 195	+ 1 720	102 747
1936	27 200	11 222	+ 15 978	118 725
1937	45 562	25 622	+ 20 940	139 665
1938	34 019	36 063	− 2 044	137 621
1939	24 419	32 674	− 8 255	129 366
1940	13 974	27 824	− 13 850	115 516
1941	3 082	3 517	− 435	115 081
1942	13 773	2 524	+ 11 249	126 330
1943				
1944				
1945	577			
1946	34 929			
1947	66 234	22 251	+ 43 983	
1948	80 714	54 209	+ 26 505	
1949	83 377	75 257	+ 8 120	194 800**

Table A1 (Cont.)

Date	Departures from Algeria	Returns to Algeria	Annual Balance	Cumulative total in France
1950	89 405	65 175	+ 24 230	
1951	142 671	88 084	+ 54 587	
1952	148 912	134 083	+ 14 829	
1953	134 133	122 560	+ 11 573	
1954	159 786	133 517	+ 26 269	
1955	193 862	169 872	+ 23 990	
1956	78 976	78 176	+ 800	330 000***
1957	69 355	54 768	+ 14 587	
1958	42 379	56 238	− 13 859	
1959				
1960				
1961	132 210	126 755	+ 5 455	
1962	180 167	155 018	+ 25 149	
1963	262 075	211 532	+ 50 543	350 484 (Census)

* Includes 13 000 Algerians resident in France prior to 1914.
** Ministry of the Interior Census (April to May 1949). *Source*: L. Muracciole, *L'Émigration Algérienne*, p. 30. If to the number of Algerians blocked in France during the war (120 000) is added the balance of migration in 1947–9, a comparable figure of 191 938 is reached.
*** *Source*: J.-J. Rager, *L'Émigration en France*, pp. 60, 100–1.

Note on sources
The figures for the period from 1914 to 1949 are taken from L. Muracciole, *L'Émigration Algérienne*, p. 31 who collated them from data provided by the *Services de la Sécurité Générale* (1914–41) and the *Services de Santé* (1942–9). The figures for 1950 to 1963 are taken from A. Gillette and A. Sayad, *L'Immigration Algérienne*, p. 258.

The statistics must be treated with caution. The figures include those Algerian élites who went to France as tourists or on official business, although they were very small in number. Since many individual workers crossed between Algeria and France on two or more occasions, the same person could be counted as several passengers. However, since few workers made a return trip more than once in any year the figures for the annual net balance are reasonably accurate.

To the cumulative total (last column) after 1914 I have added the 13 000 workers which G. Meynier, *L'Algérie révélée*, p. 77 estimates were already in France on the eve of the war. The figures for the war period are only for civilians and exclude the 173 000 soldiers who crossed to France. For the period from about 1928 to 1930 the total of those remaining in France in any one year (last column) probably underestimates the true figures. For example, most experts on immigration writing during the period estimated the total resident in France from the end of the 1920s as 130 000. The figures for 1937–9 are, on the contrary, probably too high and most experts estimate, that in spite of the brake on migration during the Depression, about 130 000 workers were in France on the eve of the Second World War.

For the post-war period I have not calculated an accumulative balance and, because of the greater freedom of movement from 1947, the figures may be more inaccurate than those for the period after 1924. To the balance of movements post 1946 would have to be added those Algerians who remained in France during the war, a number variously estimated at 60 000 to 120 000.

Despite the approximate nature of the statistics they do provide a useful indication of the general trends in migration. In particular, the annual oscillations provide a good indicator of the sensitivity of emigration to economic and political conjunctures.

Notes

Introduction

1. SOFRES, *L'État de l'opinion 1991* (Seuil, 1991) quoted in B. Stora, *La gangrène et l'oubli. La mémoire de la guerre d'Algérie* (La Découverte, 1991) p. 285.
2. There exists an enormous literature on the contemporary politics of immigration, integration and racism. Excellent surveys are C. Wihtol de Wenden, *Les Immigrés et la politique* (Presses de la FNSP, 1988); J. Costa-Lascoux, *De l'Immigration au Citoyen* (La Documentation Française, 1989); F. Dubet, *Immigrations: qu'en savons-nous?* (La Documentation Française, 1989); P. Weil, *La France et ses Étrangers* (Calmann-Lévy, 1991); D. Schnapper, *La France de l'intégration* (Gallimard, 1991); P.-A. Taguieff (ed.), *Face au racisme*, 2 Vols (La Découverte, 1991).
3. See the statistics of racist incidents registered by the Ministry of the Interior for 1990–1991 in Commission Nationale Consultative des Droits de l'Homme, *1991. La Lutte Contre le Racisme et la Xénophobie* (La Documentation Française, 1992) pp. 17–28.
4. A. Perotti and F. Thépaut, 'L'Affaire du Foulard Islamique', in *Migrations Société*, Vol. 2. No. 7 (Jan.–Feb. 1990) 61–82; A. Perotti and P. Toulat, 'Immigration et média: Le foulard surmédiatisé', *Ibid*, Vol. 2, No. 12 (Nov.–Dec. 1990) 9–45.
5. In 1984–5 the French press revealed details of Le Pen's involvement with torture while serving as a lieutenant in Algeria. See B. Stora, *La gangrène et l'oubli*, p. 290; E. Plenel and A. Rollat, *L'effet Le Pen* (La Découverte, 1984) pp. 225–6.
6. Germany, which failed to build up a significant colonial empire and which was dispossessed after 1918 of her African territories, did not recruit colonial labour. During the first half of the twentieth century she relied on labour from eastern Europe (mainly Poles) and after the Second World War resorted to a very different system of guest-worker recruitment through inter-governmental agreements with Turkey and other states. It may be that other ex-colonial powers like Portugal, Belgium and the Netherlands also have a 'hidden' history of pre-1939 non-European immigration that has yet to be investigated.
7. See for example the work of P. Rich, *Race and Empire in British Politics* (Cambridge: CUP, 1986); P. Fryer, *Staying Power: The History of Black People in Britain* (London: Pluto, 1984); J. Walvin, *Black and White: The Negro in English Society, 1555–1945* (London: Allen Lane, 1973); F. Halliday, *Arabs in Exile. Yemeni Migrants in Urban Britain* (London: I.B. Tauris, 1992); Laura Tabili, 'The Construction of Racial Difference in Twentieth-Century Britain: The Special Restriction (Coloured Alien Seamen) Order, 1925', *Journal of British Studies*, No. 33 (January, 1994) 54–98; M. Sherwood, 'Race, nationality and employment among Lascar seamen, 1660 to 1945', *New Community* Vol. 17 (Jan. 1991) 229–44.

Several BBC programmes, such as *Timewatch. A War Far from Home* and *Black Britain* (1990) have shown through old film and interviews the experiences of colonial soldiers in the European theatre during the First World War, and the anti-black riots of 1919 in Cardiff and Liverpool.

8. In October 1925 there were 7408 coloured alien seamen in British ports (excluding London); see L. Tabili, 'The Construction of Racial Difference', 85. This census included all non-European groups from the West Indies, West Africa, Aden, North Africa and elsewhere. The majority of these men would have been waiting in port between ships. An informed guess of the total colonial minority presence would be of the order 10 000 to 15 000 or about one tenth of the Algerian numbers in France.

9. See the pioneering study of Cardiff by K.S. Little, *Negroes in Britain* (London: Kegan Paul, 1947).

10. C. Dyer, *Population and Society in Twentieth Century France* (London: Hodder and Stoughton, 1978).

11. G. Noiriel, *Le Creuset Français. Histoire de l'immigration XIXe–XXe siècles* (Seuil, 1988) p. 21. On the system of foreign labour recruitment see also G.S. Cross, *Immigrant Workers in Industrial France. The Making of a New Laboring Class* (Philadelphia: Temple University Press, 1983); G. Mauco, *Les Étrangers en France* (A. Colin, 1932).

12. R. Schor, *L'Opinion Française et les Étrangers en France 1919–1939* (Publication de la Sorbonne, 1985) pp. 34–9. The census figures for North Africans (Algerians, Moroccans, Tunisians) underestimates the real numbers as will be shown later.

13. There is a considerable literature on European discourse and the construction of the 'Other', see especially the influential work of Edward Said, *Orientalism* (London: Penguin, 1987 reprint); II.L.G. Gates (ed.), *'Race', Writing and Difference* (Chicago: University of Chicago Press, 1986); D.J. Winthrop, *White Over Black: American Attitudes Towards the Negro, 1550–1812* (Chapel Hill: University of North Carolina Press, 1968); J.M. MacKenzie, *Propaganda and Empire* (Manchester: Manchester University Press, 1984); W.B. Cohen, *The French Encounter with Africans. White Response to Blacks, 1530–1880* (Bloomington: Indiana University Press, 1980); W.H. Schneider, *An Empire for the Masses. The French Popular Image of Africa, 1870–1900* (Westport: Greenwood Press, 1982); J. Nederveen Pieterse, *White on Black. Images of Africa and Blacks in Western Popular Culture* (New Haven: Yale University Press, 1992).

14. P. Catrice and Buchet, G., 'Les Musulmans en France. Enquête', *En Terre d'Islam* (1929) 336–48; *Ibid.* (1930), 22–7.

15. N. Gomar, *L'Émigration Algérienne en France* (Les Presses Modernes, 1931) p. 39; O. Carlier, 'Pour une histoire quantitative de l'émigration algérienne en France dans la période de l'entre-deux-guerres', in J. Costa-Lacoux and E. Temime (eds), *Les Algériens en France* (Publisud, 1985) p. 181.

16. On the complex and changing meanings of 'assimilation', see M.D. Lewis, 'One Hundred Million Frenchmen: The "Assimilation" Theory in French Colonial Policy', *Comparative Studies in Society and History*,

Vol. 4 (1961) 129–53; R.F. Betts, *Assimilation and Association in French Colonial Theory and Practice* (New York: Columbia University Press, 1961); G. Meynier, *L'Algérie révélée* (Geneva: Droz, 1981) pp. 30–5.

17.   C. Collot, *Les Institutions de l'Algérie durant la période coloniale (1830–1962)* (CNRS, 1987) p. 265.

18.   For a recent statement of this position see S. Palidda, 'Eurocentrisme et réalité effective des migrations', *Migrations Société*, Vol. 4, No. 24 (1992) 7–23.

19.   There are some notable exceptions, mainly the work of those who have brought an anthropological perspective to international migration: see for example J.L. Watson (ed.), *Between Two Cultures. Migrants and Minorities in Britain* (Oxford: Blackwell, 1977); S.B. Philpott, *West Indian Migration: the Montserrat Case* (London: 1973); A. Shaw, *A Pakistani Community in Britain* (Oxford: Blackwell, 1988); U.-B. Engelbrektson, *The Force of Tradition. Turkish Migrants at Home and Abroad* (Gotenborg: Acta Universitatis Gothoburgensis, 1978).

20.   Abdelmalek Sayad and others have used the term *noria* after the arab water wheel in which a chain of buckets constantly rotates.

21.   S. Castles, *Here For Good* (London: Pluto, 1984); W.R. Böhning, 'The Self-Feeding Process of Economic Migration', in P. Braham *et al.* (eds), *Discrimination and Disadvantage in Employment* (London: 1981) pp. 28–41; and especially the influential essay by A. Sayad, 'Les trois "âges" de l'émigration algérienne', *Actes de la Recherche en Sciences Sociales*, XV (1977) 59–79.

22.   For Algerian migration see for example the studies of A. Ben Younes, *Émigration et société: un village de Kabylie*, Dissertation for the diploma in Études Supérieures de Sciences Politiques, University of Algiers, June 1977; C. Lacoste-Dujardin, *Un village algérien: structures et évolution récente* (Algiers: SNED, 1976); M. Miyaji, *L'Émigration et le changement socio-culturel d'un village Kabyle*, Studia Culturae Islamica No. 6 (Tokyo: 1976).

23.   On this problem see J. Connell *et al.*, *Migration from Rural Areas. The Evidence from Village Studies* (Delhi: OUP, 1976) pp. 7, 218.

24.   Quoted in B. Parry, 'Problems in Current Theories of Colonial Discourse', *Oxford Literary Review*, Vol. 9 (1987) 34–5. On the debate on colonial discourse see: E. Said, 'Representing the Colonized: Anthropology's Interlocutors', *Critical Inquiry* (1989) 205–25; G.C. Spivak, 'Can the Subaltern Speak?', in C. Nelson, L. Grossberg (eds), *Marxism and the Interpretation of Culture* (Urbana: University of Illinois Press, 1988); H.L.G. Gates (ed.), *"Race", Writing and Difference*; P. Williams and L. Chrisman (eds), *Colonial Discourse and Post-Colonial Theory. A Reader* (London: Harvester Wheatsheaf, 1993). The contemporary debate on colonial discourse has its roots in the work of Franz Fanon, most of which was elaborated in the Algerian colonial context.

25.   A very rich deposit of these reports is located in the library of the Centre des Hautes Études sur l'Afrique et l'Asie Modernes, Paris (henceforth CHEAM) and in the Archives d'Outre-Mer, Aix-en-Provence (henceforth AOM) in the series 8X and 9X. See the end bibliography.

26.   G. Meynier, *L'Algérie révélée.*

27.   See A. Sayad, *L'immigration ou les paradoxes de l'altérité* (Brussels: De

Boeck-Wesmael, 1991). A research project is urgently required on the oral evidence of early Algerian migrants.

28. J.C. Scott, *Domination and the Arts of Resistance. Hidden Transcripts* (New Haven: Yale University Press, 1990).

29. AOM. 762. R. Montagne, *Étude sociologique de la Migration des Travailleurs Musulmans d' Algérie en Métropole.* Cahier No. 1, p. 2.

30. B. Stora, *Ils Venaient d'Algérie. L'immigration algérienne en France 1912–1992* (Fayard, 1992) p. 398.

31. L. Talha, *Le Salariat Immigré dans la Crise. La Main d'Oeuvre Maghrébine en France (1921–1987)* (Éditions CNRS, 1989). Omar Carlier argues that there has been a relative 'over-investigation' of migration from Algeria compared to Morocco and Tunisia and that this distortion is a reflection of the powerful image that Algeria held in French ideology (the colony par excellence, the most traumatic process of decolonisation). See O. Carlier, 'Aspects des rapports entre mouvements ouvrier émigré et migration Maghrébine en France dans l'Entre-Deux-Guerres', *Annuaire de l' Afrique du Nord*, XXI (1982) 50–67.

32. A. Sayad, 'L'Immigration Algérienne en France, une Immigration "Exemplaire"', in J. Costa-Lascoux and E. Temime (eds), *Les Algériens en France* (Publisud, 1985) pp. 19–49.

33. L. Muracciole, *L'Émigration Algérienne. Aspects économiques, sociaux et juridiques* (Algiers: Ferraris, 1950) p. 29.

34. G. Mauco, *Les Étrangers en France. Leur rôle dans l'activité économique* (A. Colin, 1932) p. 133, fn.1.

35. Tables of annual departures and returns have been utilised by most of the historians of Algerian migration and can be found in L. Muracciole, *Émigration Algérienne*, p. 31; L. Talha, *Le Salariat Immigré*, p. 81; A. Gillette and A. Sayad, *L'Immigration Algérienne en France*, 2nd ed. (Entente, 1984) pp. 257–9. The most exhaustive and meticulous work on the statistics of migration is O. Carlier, 'Pour une histoire quantitative de l' émigration en France dans la periode de l'entre-deux-guerres' in J. Costa-Lascoux and E. Temime (eds), *Algériens en France*, pp. 153–82.

36. On the length of stay in France see L. Talha, *Le Salariat Immigré*, p. 116; L. Muracciole, *Émigration Algérienne*, pp. 32–43; Gomar, *Émigration Algérienne*, pp. 34–9; J.-J. Rager, *Les musulmans algériens en France et dans les pays islamiques* (Les Belles Lettres, 1950) pp. 125–9.

37. In Britain, by contrast, the distance of colonies in the Caribbean, Africa and Asia restricted immigration until after the 1948, with the exception of war-time mobilisation and the movement of workers employed by shipping companies.

38. J. Ray, *Les Marocains en France* (Syrey, 1938) estimates that the number of North Africans who never returned home through mortality was as high as ten per cent of total immigration.

39. O. Depont, *Les Kabyles en France. Rapport de la Commission chargée d'étudier les conditions du travail des indigènes Algériens dans la Métropole* (Beaugency: 1914).

40. L. Talha, *Le Salariat Immigré*, p. 70.

41. G.S. Cross, *Immigrant Workers*, p. 124. Ceri Peach has provided an excellent case-study and model of the linkage between fluctuations in

the metropolitan economy and cycles in international migration.
C. Peach, *West Indian Migration to Britain. A Social Geography* (London:
Oxford University Press, 1968).

42. J.-J. Rager, *Les Musulmans Algériens en France,* pp. 72–8.
43. Estimations of the number of Algerians who were stranded in France
until the Liberation vary considerably. L. Muracciole, *Émigration
Algérienne,* p. 45 gives a high figure of 120 000 compared to the official
estimate of 55 000 at 31 December 1945. To this variable base can
then be added the balance between departures and returns going
through the ports.
44. *Ibid.,* p. 22.
45. O. Carlier, 'Pour une histoire quantitative', p. 176.
46. J.-J. Rager, *L'Émigration en France des Musulmans d'Algérie,* Documents
Algériens No. 49 (July 1956) pp. 60, 100–1.

1 Colonial Destruction of Algerian Society

1. There exists an enormous literature on the colonial origins of these
different migration flows, but for a useful summary see R. Cohen, *The
New Helots. Migrants in the International Division of Labour* (Aldershot:
Gower, 1987); Lydia Potter, *The World Labour Market. A History of Migration* (London: Zed Books, 1990).
2. M. Côte, *L'Algérie ou l'Espace Retourné* (Flammarion, 1988) p. 7; L. Talha,
Le Salariat Immigré, pp. 36–7, estimates that colonial land appropriations represented 40 per cent of the total in Algeria, 11 per cent in
Tunisia and 10 per cent in Morocco.
3. On the population, see X. Yacono, 'Peut-on évaluer la population de
l'Algérie vers 1830?', *Revue Africaine,* Tom. 98 (1954) 277–307. A good
background to pre-colonial Algeria is provided by L. Valensi, *On the
Eve of Colonialism: North Africa Before the French Conquest* (New York:
Africana Pub. Co., 1977); M. Côte, *L'Algérie ou l'Espace Retourné* (Flammarion, 1988); M. Bennoune, *The making of contemporary Algeria, 1830–
1987* (Cambridge: CUP, 1988); J. Ruedy, *Modern Algeria. The Origins
and Development of a Nation* (Bloomington: Indiana University Press,
1992); R. Tlemcani, *State and Revolution in Algeria* (London: Zed Books,
1986), Chapters 2–3.
4. On the complexities of this issue see C.-R. Ageron, *Les Algériens
Musulmans et la France,* Vol. 1 (Presses Universitaires de France, 1968)
pp. 66–78; A. Nouschi, *Enquête sur le niveau de vie des populations rurales
constantinoises de la conquête jusqu'en 1919* (PUF, 1961) pp. 85–94; T.K.
Park, 'Rural north-east Algeria, 1919–1938', *Peasant Studies,* Vol. 15
(Winter, 1988) 118.
5. M. Côte, *L'Algérie,* pp. 17, 60–1; L. Valensi, *Eve of Colonialism,* pp. 31–
4; C.-R. Ageron, *Algériens Musulmans,* Vol. 1, pp. 367–8.
6. A. Nouschi, *Niveau de vie,* p. 62. Letter of Lestiboudois to Prince
Napoleon, 25 February, 1859.
7. On tribal and social structures see J. Berque, 'Qu'est-ce qu'une tribu
nord-africaine?' in *Eventail de l'histoire vivante: hommage à Lucien Fèbre,*
Vol. 1 (A. Colin, 1953), pp. 261–71; P. Bourdieu, *The Algerians* (Boston:

Beacon Press, 1962); M. Côte, *L'Algérie*, pp. 71–8; Bennoune, *Contemporary Algeria*, pp. 17–22; D. Prochaska, *Making Algeria French. Colonialism in Bône, 1870–1920* (Cambridge: CUP, 1990) pp. 54–6. For a more detailed analysis of the complexities of Algerian society, the differing communal forms imposed by geography and the feudal-like hierarchies internal to these communities, see R. Gallissot, 'Precolonial Algeria', *Economy and Society*, Vol. 4, No. 4 (1975) 418–45.

8. Historians have used different periodisations, but most agree that a crucial divide began in the early 1870s. See M. Bennoune, *Contemporary Algeria*, p. 38; R. Tlemcani, *State and Revolution*, p. 33.

9. C.-A. Julien, *Histoire de l'Algérie Contemporaine (1827–1871)*, Tom. 1 (PUF, 1964); P. Leroy-Beaulieu, *L'Algérie et la Tunisie* (Guillaumin, 1887), pp. 3–18; D. Prochaska, *Making Algeria French*, pp. 65–71; M.J. Heffernan, 'The Parisian Poor and the colonization of Algeria during the Second Republic', *French History*, Vol. 3, No. 4 (1989) 377–403.

10. A. Nouschi, *Niveau de vie*, pp. 274–9. On *cantonnement* and dismantling of tribal structures see also D. Sari, *La dépossession des fellahs (1830–1962)* (Algiers: SNED, 1975), pp. 19–21; J. Van Vollenhoven, *Essai sur le Fellah Algérien* (A. Rousseau, 1903) pp. 61–7; X. Yacono, *La colonisation des plaines du Chélif*, 2 Vols (Algiers: E. Imbert, 1955–6), pp. 285–7. There is an excellent summary of Yacono, and other works on expropriation, in Eric R. Wolf, *Peasant Wars of the Twentieth Century* (London: Faber, 1973) pp. 211–22.

11. C.-R. Ageron, *Algériens Musulmans*, pp. 39–40; A. Nouschi, *Niveau de vie*, pp. 248, 282–3. The colonial ideologue Paul Leroy-Beaulicu in *L'Algérie et La Tunisie*, pp. 120–1, noted, 'If in fifty years' time the Algerians have under half their present area, they can nevertheless be very much richer.'

12. A. Nouschi, *Niveau de vie*, pp. 352–71.

13. C.-R. Ageron, *Algériens Musulmans*, p. 32; A. Nouschi, *Niveau de vie*, pp. 447–9.

14. A. Nouschi, *Niveau de vie*, p. 414. Letter of De Gueydon, June 1871.

15. *Ibid.*, pp. 483–6.

16. D. Sari, *Dépossession des fellahs*, pp. 73–6; C.-R. Ageron, *Algériens Musulmans*, pp. 103–28, 489–93, 776–91; J. Van Vollenhoven, *Essai sur le Fellah*, pp. 112–19; F. Gourgeot, *Les Sept Plaies d'Algérie* (Algiers: P. Fontana, 1891) pp. 181–241.

17. Quoted in A. Gillette and A. Sayad, *Immigration Algérienne*, p. 24 from Captain Vaissière, *Les Ouled Rechaïch* (Algiers, 1863) p. 90.

18. A. Nouschi, *Niveau de vie*, pp. 293–5, 469–76; F. Gourgeot, *Sept Plaies d'Algérie*, pp. 43–86.

19. A. Nouschi, *Niveau de vie*, pp. 298–9.

20. On usury and peasant debt see F. Gourgeot, *Sept Plaies d'Algérie*, pp. 135–79; J. Van Vollenhoven, *Essai sur le Fellah*, pp. 282–94; L. Talha, *Le Salariat Immigré*, pp. 43–4; C.-R. Ageron, *Algériens Musulmans*, pp. 370–2.

21. C.-R. Ageron, *Algériens Musulmans*, pp. 98–101.

22. J. Van Vollenhoven, *Essai sur le Fellah*, pp. 206–7.

23. C.-R. Ageron, *Algériens Musulmans*, p. 2 notes that the period after 1871 was one which forged, 'the essential features of French Algeria'.

Both D. Sari, *Dépossession des fellahs*, p. 51 and S. Amin, *The Maghreb in the Modern World* (Harmondsworth: Penguin, 1970) p. 7, see the period from 1880 onwards as crucial to the consolidation of French colonial capitalism.

24. A. Nouschi, *Niveau de vie*, p. 658; see also C.-R. Ageron, *Algériens Musulmans*, p. 831. J. Van Vollenhoven, *Essai sur le Fellah*, pp. 210, 231, estimates that in the area of Sidi-bel-Abbès a family of five would require fifteen hectares which, making allowance for a bi-annual system of fallow rotation, meant effectively thirty hectares. But in 1885 Algerian peasants held an average of two hectares ten ares, a figure that had declined to one hectare seventy ares by 1900.

25. C.-R. Ageron, *Algériens Musulmans*, pp. 826, 838–40.

26. C.-R. Ageron, *Algériens Musulmans*, p. 845.

27. A. Gillette and A. Sayad, *Immigration Algérienne*, p. 28. There is considerable data on the decline in agricultural production and the nutritional base in Algerian society; see J. Van Vollenhoven, *Essai sur le Fellah*, pp. 207–22; D. Sari, *Dépossession des fellahs*, pp. 102–8; C.-R. Ageron, *Algériens Musulmans*, pp. 376–90, 562–5, 792–815; A. Nouschi, *Niveau de vie*, pp. 542–56, 698–737.

28. C.-R. Ageron, *Algériens Musulmans*, p. 805; A. Nouschi, *Niveau de vie*, p. 609; X. Yacono, Vol. 2, *Colonisation du Chélif*, p. 177.

29. A. Nouschi, *Niveau de vie*, pp. 442–6; C.-R. Ageron, *Algériens Musulmans*, p. 33, notes the case of the *douars* expropriated after the 1871 revolt to make way for the new colonial centres of Djidjelli and Strasbourg. Relocated on rocky soils on the periphery of the commune of Fedz Mzala, they returned several years later to work as *khammes* on their former lands. Among them was the father of the future nationalist leader Ferhat Abbas.

2 Kabylia and the Migrant Tradition

1. The Berber people were the original inhabitants of North Africa who, in the face of successive invasions (Roman, Arab), retreated into the mainly mountainous interior where they continued to retain their own language and distinctive culture. Today they constitute some twenty per cent of Algerian and forty per cent of Moroccan population, in addition to smaller pockets in Tunisia (Djerba), Mauritania, Egypt and Libya. The Kabyles of Algeria constitute one important regional grouping of the wider Berber ethnic group. See S. Chaker, *Berbères Aujoud'hui* (Harmattan, 1989) pp. 9–10. There was some Algerian emigration to France from Berber groups located outside Kabylia, particularly in the Aurès mountains, and in small pockets close to the Moroccan border to the west of Tlemcen (both show up on Map 1). I shall not look in any detail at these regions but the social and familial structures of these sedentary peasant zones were not unlike those of Kabylia and also leant themselves to emigration.

2. O. Depont, *Les Kabyles en France*; G. Meynier, *L'Algérie révélée*, p. 483.

3. In 1900 there were about 700 000 Kabyles and 3.3 million Arabs, the former thus constituting 21.2 per cent of total population. This agrees closely with a separate calculation which estimated Berber speakers as

22.8 per cent of total population in 1911. See C.-R. Ageron, *Algériens Musulmans*, pp. 874, 882–3.

4. The map has been adapted from J.-J. Rager, *Les Musulmans Algériens en France*, who based it on data from an official survey carried out by the *Gouvernement Générale* in June 1949. All mayors and administrators were requested to make a return of the number of Algerians from their commune who were resident in France. The data certainly underestimated the actual levels, particularly of those who had been absent for many years: see L. Henry *et al., Les Algériens en France. Étude démographique et sociale*, Travaux et Documents de l'INED, Cahier No. 24 (Presses Universitaires de France, 1955), p. 42. However, the distribution shown on the map gives a reasonably accurate picture of the zones of emigration.

5. On Robert Montagne see Chapter 10 below and my chapter, 'Patterns of Emigration, 1905–1954: "Kabyles" and "Arabs"', in A.G. Hargreaves and M.J. Heffernan (eds), *French and Algerian Identities from Colonial Times to the Present* (Lampeter: E. Mellen Press, 1993) pp. 25–6.

6. This study was never completed or published but its detailed findings, including numerous maps, are at Aix-en-Provence (AOM. 762), *Étude de la Migration des Travailleurs Musulmans d'Algérie en Métropole* (eleven volumes). The volumes are preceded by Montagne's '*Rapport Provisoire sur l'Émigration des Musulmans d'Algérie en France*, dated 1 August 1954, which has been much used by later researchers like Andrée Michel, *Les Travailleurs Algériens en France* (CNRS, 1956) pp. 167–76. Montagne's ideas on emigration can be most readily found in an essay, 'L'émigration nord-africaine en France: son caractère familial et villageois', in *Eventail de l'histoire vivante: hommage à Lucien Febre*, Vol. 1 (A. Colin, 1953) pp. 365–71.

7. M. Bennoune, *Contemporary Algeria*, p. 76. This generalised approach can be found for example in L. Talha, *Le Salariat Immigré dans la Crise*; D. Benamrane, *L'Émigration Algérienne en France* (Algiers: SNED, 1983); A. Benachenhou, *Formation du Sous-Développement en Algérie* (Algiers: Imprimerie Commerciale, 1978); B. Hifi, *L'Immigration Algérienne en France* (Harmattan, 1985); C. Ben Fredj, *Aux origines de l'émigration nord-africaine en France*, Doctoral thesis, University of Paris VII (1990). It is somewhat ironic that the neo-Marxist economistic model here meets up with neo-classical theory that it was the poor and landless who 'naturally' flowed from low-wage to high-wage areas, according to the dictates of the market.

8. Some specialists have acknowledged the importance of emigration from Kabylia but have failed to recognise that this presents a contradiction for the dominant economistic model which they share. P. Bourdieu and A. Sayad, *Le déracinement. La crise de l'agriculture traditionnelle en Algérie* (Minuit, 1964) p. 32 in a footnote come closest to a recognition of the inverse relationship: 'The zones of major emigration to France are precisely the mountain regions feebly affected by colonisation . . .' More recently A. Sayad has elaborated on this pattern in 'Aux origines de l'émigration Kabyle ou montagnarde', *Homme et Migrations*, No. 1 179 (September, 1994) 6–11.

9. During the last two decades there has been growing recognition of the

fact that indigenous peoples were not simply the passive receivers of colonial/capitalist domination. Local variations in the structure of pre-colonial societies could greatly affect how they reacted, through resistance or adaptation, to the European presence. See T. Ranger, 'Growing from the Roots: Reflections on Peasant Research in Central and Southern Africa', *Journal of Southern African Studies*, Vol. 5 (1978) 99–133; C. Bundy, *The Rise and Fall of the South African Peasantry* (London: Heinemann, 1979).

10.　R. Skelton, *Population Mobility in Developing Countries: A Reinterpretation* (London: Belhaven, 1990) p. 135, has argued that the ability of colonial regimes to recruit and mobilise indigenous labour was partly determined by pre-contact systems of migration. M. Chapman and R. Mansell Prothero, *Circulation in population movement. Substance and concepts from the Melanesian case* (London: Routledge, 1985) pp. 8–11 also note that 'externally-generated changes have reinforced customary circuits of mobility and added new ones . . .'

11.　F. Braudel, *The Mediterranean and the Mediterranean World in the Age of Philip II* (London: Fontana edition, 1975) p. 52.

12.　On the Kabyle climate, agriculture and socio-economic conditions see the classic study of A. Hanoteau and A. Letourneux, *La Kabylie et les Coutumes Kabyles*, 3 Vols (Imprimerie Nationale, 1872–3); J. Morizot, *L'Algérie Kabylisée* (J. Peyronnet, 1962); J. Morizot, *Les Kabyles: propos d'un témoin* (CHEAM, 1985); A. Nouschi, *Niveau de vie*, pp. 2–15; M. Côte, *L'Algérie*, pp. 47–9; M. Khellil, *L'Exil Kabyle* (Harmattan, 1979), Chapter 1; H. Roberts, *Algerian Socialism and the Kabyle Question* (Norwich: University of East Anglia, Monograph in Development Studies No. 8, 1981).

13.　J. Morizot, *Les Kabyles*, pp. 122–3.

14.　L. Muracciole, *Émigration Algérienne*, pp. 68–77, noted in 1950 that demographic explanations of emigration were '*à la mode*' in a flood of brochures, reports and newspaper articles. He explained Algerian population increase as in part a consequence of 'la paix française' which had put a stop to, 'the demographic brake which was constituted by frequent and bloody battles between villages or the *çoff* [tribal leagues]; and aided by the developments in public health and the decline in epidemics . . .'

15.　F. Braudel, *The Mediterranean World*, pp. 44–51; O.H. Hufton, *The Poor of Eighteenth-Century France* (Oxford: OUP, 1979), Chapter 3; A. Poitrineau, *Remues d'hommes. Les migrations montagnards en France 17e–18e siècles* (Aubier-Montaigne, 1983).

16.　Mountain and 'peripheral' zones, from Scotland to Ireland and Switzerland, provided reservoirs of manpower from which European states recruited mercenaries. F. Braudel, *Mediterranean World*, pp. 47–51; V.G. Kiernan, 'Foreign mercenaries and absolute monarchy' in T. Aston (ed.), *Crisis in Europe 1560–1160* (London: Routledge, 1966) pp. 117–40.

17.　J. Morizot, *Les Kabyles*, p. 63; J.-J. Rager, *Musulmans Algériens en France*, p. 63; C.-R. Ageron, *Algériens Musulmans*, pp. 522, 1071; L. Talha, *Le Salariat Immigré*, pp. 58–9.

18.　See for example the recruitment of Punjabi Sikhs, Kashmiris and

Sylhettis (*lascars*) from the mid-nineteenth century onwards, all of which gave rise to later emigration to Britain. R. Ballard and C. Ballard, 'The Sikhs: The Development of South Asian Settlements in Britain' in J.L. Watson (ed.), *Between Two Cultures. Migrants and Minorities in Britain* (Oxford: Blackwell, 1984) pp. 24–5; V. Saifullah Khan, 'The Pakistanis: Mirpuri Villagers at Home and in Bradford', *Ibid.*, pp. 64–5; C. Adams, *Across Seven Seas and Thirteen Rivers. Life Stories of Pioneer Sylhetti Settlers in Britain* (London: THAP Books, 1987) pp. 12–30. A similar transition from military to labour recruitment occurred in French Senegal.

19. A Kabyle dictum, recorded in the 1860s, stated, 'A good peddler should not, during his travels, spend anything on food; this economy is his first profit.' A. Hanoteau, *La Kabylie*, Vol. 1, p. 571.

20. A. Hanoteau, *La Kabylie*, Vol. 1, p. 569.

21. Quoted in J. Morizot, *Les Kabyles*, p. 76. Masqeray wrote a famous study of the Berbers, *Formation des cités chez les populations sédentaires de l'Algérie*, first published in 1886, but reprinted with an Introduction by Fanny Colonna (Aix-en-Provence: EDISUD, 1983).

22. J. Morizot, *Les Kabyles*, p. 78, 115; A. Nouschi, *Niveau de vie*, p. 259; C.-R. Ageron, *Algériens Musulmans*, p. 373.

23. J. Van Vollenhoven, *Essai sur le Fellah*, pp. 249–50.

24. The annual flow of Spanish seasonal migrants arriving by steamer in Oran fell rapidly from a peak of 144 530 in 1886 to 12 500 in 1907. Sixty-two per cent of the wage bill for the vineyard of Clos Combier at Aïn Bessem for 1892–3 (just prior to the first wine crisis) went to European workers and thirty-eight per cent to Algerians. In 1897–8 the situation was reversed with Europeans receiving thirty-six and Algerians sixty-four per cent. H. Isnard, *La Vigne en Algérie* (Gap: 1951–4), Vol. 2, pp. 220–1.

25. M. Larnaude, 'Déplacements des travailleurs indigènes en Algérie', *Revue Africaine*, Nos 360–4 (1936) 207–15. See also G. Mutin, *La Mitidja: décolonisation et espace géographique* (CNRS, 1977) pp. 428–9. It would be interesting to compare Kabylia with the Rif mountains of northern Morocco where high population densities also gave rise to large-scale seasonal migration, particularly towards the vineyards of the province of Oran, and eventually to emigration. See D. Seddon, *Moroccan Peasants: a century of change in the eastern Rif, 1870–1970* (Folkestone: W. Dawson, 1981); N. MacMaster, 'Labour Migration in French North Africa', in R. Cohen (ed.), *The Cambridge Survey of World Migration* (Cambridge: Cambridge University Press, 1995) pp. 190–5.

26. H. Isnard, *La Vigne en Algérie*, p. 222. On the traditional 'pre-industrial' attitudes to time and work see P. Bourdieu, 'The attitude of the Algerian peasant toward time', in J. Pitt-Rivers, *Mediterranean Countrymen. Essays in the Social Anthropology of the Mediterranean* (Mouton, 1963) pp. 55–72.

27. C. Meillassoux, *Maidens, Meal and Money. Capitalism and the Domestic Community* (Cambridge: CUP, 1991) pp. 3, 127.

28. For some discussion of these issues for Southern Africa see R. Cohen, *The New Helots*, Chapter 3 'The reproduction of labour power: southern

Africa'; H. Wolpe, 'Capitalism and cheap labour-power in South Africa', *Economy and Society*, Vol. 1, No. 4 (1972) 425–56; C. Murray, *Families divided: the impact of migrant labour in Lesotho* (Cambridge: CUP, 1981).

29. C.-R. Ageron, *Algériens Musulmans*, p. 838.
30. A. Hanoteau, *La Kabylie*, Vol. 1 Introduction; C.-R. Ageron, *Algériens Musulmans*, Chapter 1.
31. J. Van Vollenhoven, *Essai sur le Fellah*, p. 204.
32. F. Colonna, *Instituers algériens, 1883–1939* (Presses de la Fondation Nationales des Sciences Politiques, 1975) p. 112.
33. A. Sayad, 'Les trois "âges"', 75. The solidarity of the peasant household as a basis of migration strategies can be noted in many other instances. Corbin notes of the Limousin peasant who migrated seasonally to Paris during the eighteenth and nineteenth centuries, 'the goal which he pursued in coming to work in Paris was not rooted in an individual destiny; for him migration was integral to an all encompassing family strategy'. A. Corbin, 'Les paysans de Paris. Histoire des Limousins du bâtiment au XIXe siècle', *Ethnologie française*, Vol. 10 (1980) 171. See also L. Fontaine, 'Solidarités familiales et logiques migratoires en pays de montagne à l'époque moderne', *Annales. ESC* No. 6 (Nov.–Dec. 1990) 1433–50.
34. On the 'Kabyle Myth' see P.E. Lorcin, *Imperial Identities. Stereotyping, Prejudice and Race in Colonial Algeria* (London: I.B. Tauris, 1995); C.-R. Ageron, *Algériens Musulmans*, pp. 267–92, 873–90; C.-R. Ageron, 'La France a-t-elle eu un politique Kabyle?', *Revue Historique*, April 1960, 311–52; C.-R. Ageron, 'La politique berbère sous le second Empire' in *L'Algérie algérienne de Napoléon III à de Gaulle* (Sindbad, 1980) pp. 37–71.
35. J. Van Vollenhoven, *Essai sur le Fellah*, pp. 169, 195.
36. Morizot, *Les Kabyles*, p. 147.
37. F. Colonna, *Instituteurs algériens*, p. 46; C.-R. Ageron, *Algériens Musulmans*, p. 340.
38. J. Ray, *Les Marocains en France*, pp. 315–16 noted the same phenomenon in Morocco.
39. C. Lacoste-Dujardin, *Un village algérien*, pp. 32–5.
40. A teacher interviewed by Colonna remarked, 'In 1900 there were already twenty teachers in the Beni Yenni. My mother said to us: "You will not leave school until you are teachers."' F. Colonna, *Instituteurs algériens*, p. 111.
41. F. Colonna, *Instituteurs algériens*, pp. 90, 108–9.
42. It seems likely that the distinction that I have made between the 'open' and 'closed' village corresponds to the two types of Kabyle settlement, the *thaddarth* (nucleated settlement) and *tufiq* (association of dispersed hamlets). See H. Roberts, 'Notes on Relations of Production, Forms of Property and Political Structure in a Dissident Region of Algeria: Pre-Colonial Kabylia', University of East Anglia, Development Studies Discussion Paper No. 38 (Dec. 1978). In another essay, 'The Conversion of the Mrabtin in Kabylia' in E. Gellner *et al.* (eds), *Islam et Politique au Maghreb* (CNRS, 1981) 101–25, Hugh Roberts argues that the conservative *marabouts* retained their social and political power to

a much later stage in the dispersed villages (*tufiq*), which, in my view, were probably also the hamlets in which emigration was slow to develop.

43. Y. Turin, *Affrontements culturels dans l'Algérie coloniale. Écoles, médicine, religion, 1830–1880* (Paris: Maspero, 1970).

44. F. Colonna, *Instituteurs algériens*, p. 109.

45. *Ibid.*, p. 111.

46. C.-R. Ageron, *Les Algériens Musulmans*, Chapters 38 and 39.

47. A 1916 report on the difficulties of military recruitment near Miliana noted, 'One has to understand that the natives are raised by women who continue to live in a world completely closed from all outside ideas, all social change and all progress. Many of them profess hatred for the Christian and there are tribes in which soldiers on leave have to enter their villages at night and dressed in a *burnous* so as not to be exposed to the public ridicule and contempt of their coreligionists.' Quoted in G. Meynier, *L'Algérie révélée*, Doctoral thesis, University of Nice (1979), Appendix, p. CXLVI.

48. G. Meynier, *L'Algérie révélée*, p. 91.

49. *Ibid.*, p. 98.

50. A. Merad, *Le Réformisme Musulman en Algérie de 1925 à 1940* (Mouton, 1967) pp. 192–6 has data and a map of the implantation of Islamic Reformism in 1935 which shows a close correlation with the zones of emigration in Kabylia, the Constantine region and Tlemcen. Conversely, where Reformism made little impact, because of the strong hold of conservative *marabouts* traditions, there was little emigration.

51. The Mozabites were renowned traders within the confines of North Africa but were also particularly strong in their opposition to military service, see G. Meynier, *L'Algérie révélée*, pp. 99–100.

52. See J. Ray, *Les Marocains en France*, pp. 315–16.

53. F. Colonna, *Instituteurs algériens*, p. 41.

54. H. Isnard, *La Vigne en Algérie*, Vol. 2, p. 218.

55. C.-R. Ageron, *Algériens Musulmans*, pp. 952–3.

56. AOM. 9 H 112. During the First World War some employers even referred to 'Kabyle' workers as inferior to 'Arabs'. General Dervaux, technical inspector for the army engineers, thought, 'the mountain Kabyles were of rather limited intelligence'. G. Meynier, *L'Algérie révélée*, pp. 429, 479.

57. For such a system see B.G. Cohen and P.J. Jenner, 'The Employment of Immigrants: A case study within the Wool Industry', in P. Braham et al. (eds), *Discrimination and Disadvantage in Employment* (London: Harper, 1981) pp. 109–25.

3 Emigration: The Early Years, 1905–1918

1. For a critique of the *laissez-faire* model see R. Cohen, *The New Helots*, pp. 33–42. Cohen remarks that individual migrants do not,'operate with a rational, decision-making model of the world, with which they weigh options and possibilities within the constraints of the opportunities on offer'. Rather opportunities are tightly constrained by a complex

of factors, including transport costs, international law, immigration policies, work contracts and the need for passports, visas and other documents.

2. C.-R. Ageron, *Algériens Musulmans*, pp. 171, 652; L. Talha, *Le Salariat Immigré*, p. 33.

3. C.-R. Ageron, *Algériens Musulmans*, pp. 505, 628, 653.

4. *L'Akhbar*, 29 February 1928; C.-R. Ageron, *Histoire de l'Algérie Contemporaine* Vol. 2 (PUF, 1979) pp. 188–90.

5. The order of 28 January 1905 removed the need for a special authorisation from the Governor and for a financial deposit. O. Depont, *Les Kabyles en France*, p. 9.

6. *L'Akhbar*, 28 February 1928; C.-R. Ageron, *Algériens Musulmans*, pp. 854–5.

7. G. Mauco, *Les Étrangers en France*, pp. 36–51.

8. See G. Cross, *Immigrant Workers*, pp. 25–7; G. Mauco, *Les Étrangers en France*, pp. 61–5.

9. A Prefectoral survey of 1912 found them present in 25 of 51 departments. O. Depont, *Les Kabyles en France*, Annex 1.

10. G. Meynier, *L'Algérie révélée*, pp. 74, 77.

11. AOM. 9 H 113, *Rapport sur l'émigration des indigènes* (1923), p. 5; O. Depont, *Les Kabyles en France*, p. 28.

12. R. Lopez and E. Temime, *Migrance: Histoire des Migrations à Marseille*, Vol. 2 (Aix-en-Provence: Edisud, 1990) pp. 152–5.

13. G. Meynier, *L'Algérie Révélée*. Doctoral thesis, pp. 191–2.

14. G. Meynier, *L'Algérie révélée*, p. 73.

15. G. Meynier, *L'Algérie révélée*, pp. 73–4.

16. O. Depont, *Les Kabyles en France*, Annex 1.

17. L. Talha, *Le Salariat Immigré*, p. 55.

18. G. Meynier, *L'Algérie révélée*, 67–8.

19. L. Talha, *Le Salariat Immigrée*, p. 55. On the migration of Algerian, particularly Kabyle, labour within the Maghreb before 1914, especially into the mining operations in Tunisia, see J.-J. Rager, *Musulmans Algériens en France*, pp. 9–56; L. Chevalier, *Le Problème Démographique Nord-Africain*, Institut National d'Études Démographiques, Travaux et Documents, Cahier No. 6 (Presses Universitaires de France, 1947), p. 55; C. Sammut, 'La situation du prolétariat dans une entreprise coloniale française en Tunisie: La Compagnies des Chemins de Fer et Phosphate de Gasfa,' *Revue d'Histoire Maghrebine* (July, 1977), 350–9.

20. C.-R. Ageron, *Algériens Musulmans*, p. 855; *Journal Officiel – Débats Parlementaires*, 17 December 1913, p. 3858.

21. O. Depont, *Les Kabyles en France*, p. 13.

22. O. Depont, *Les Kabyles en France*, p. 28.

23. O. Depont, *Les Kabyles en France*, p. 8; N. Gomar, *Émigration Algérienne*, p. 13.

24. O. Depont, *Les Kabyles en France*, Annex 1, pp. 43–6.

25. Henri Doizy, a member of the *Socialistes Unifiés*, was a doctor and member of the central committee of the *Ligue des Droits de l'Homme*. He campaigned tirelessly between 1912 and 1917 on behalf of Algerians and for the extension of the vote. See C.-R. Ageron, *Algériens Musulmans*, pp. 668, 1110, 1195–7.

26.   *Journal Officiel*, 17 December 1913, pp. 3858–9.
27.   After serving as *khodja* with the sous-préfecture of Tizi-Ouzou, he was elected from Michelet to the *Délégations financières* from 1899 to 1913. In 1912 he supported the extension of conscription to Algerians, a policy which led to widespread revolt and mass emigration into Morocco and Tunisia. He was detested as a stooge of the French by the reformist movement of the *'Jeunes Algériens'*, which dubbed him the 'Démosthène des Beni-Oui-Oui', and he was eventually assassinated, probably by anti-French interests. See C.-R. Ageron, *Algériens Musulmans*, pp. 391, 877, 1041, 1075, 1129; O. Depont, *L'Algérie du Centenaire* (Bordeaux: Cadoret, 1928) p. 126.
28.   O. Depont, *L'Algérie du Centenaire*, p. 125. I have been unable to trace the original of Aït Mehdi's pamphlet.
29.   On Depont see *Dictionnaire de Biographie Francaise* (1965), Tom. 10; C.-R. Ageron, *Algériens Musulmans*, pp. 514–15, 620, 785, 1082, 1089. He wrote with X. Coppolini, *Les confréries religieuses musulmanes* (Algiers, 1897) and a confidential report on the insurrection of 1917, *Rapport sur les troubles de l'Aurès* (1917).
30.   Emile Masqueray had advanced the same idea as early as 1884: 'If there should be a surplus population then thousands of Kabyle and Chaouia workers can go and offer their labour in France and replace the Italians and Spaniards.' Quoted in C.-R. Ageron, *Algériens Musulmans*, p. 290.
31.   O. Depont, *Les Kabyles en France*, pp. 34–6.
32.   G. Cross, *Immigrant Workers*, Introduction; G. Mauco, *Les Étrangers en France*, pp. 61–5.
33.   O. Depont, *Les Kabyles en France*, p. 40.
34.   On the early military recruitment of Kabyles see Chapter 2. On labour mobilisation within the British Empire see H. Tinker, *A New System of Slavery: the Export of Indian Labour Overseas, 1830–1920* (London: 1974); on global movements see L. Potter, *The World Labour Market*.
35.   The number of 'colonial' workers was 78 566 Algerians, 48 955 Indo-Chinese, 36 941 Chinese, 35 506 Moroccans, 18 249 Tunisians and 4546 Madagascans: see B. Nogaro and L. Weil, *La Main-d'Oeuvre Étrangère et Coloniale Pendant la Guerre* (Presses Universitaires de France, 1926) p. 25; for numbers of soldiers see Lieutenant-Colonel Clément-Grandcourt, *Nos Indigènes Nord-Africains dans l'Armée Nouvelle* (Berger-Levrault, 1926) p. 1.
36.   For a concise analysis of the First World War as a turning point in Algerian emigration see R. Gallissot, 'Émigration Coloniale, Immigration Post-Coloniale', in L. Talha (ed.), *Maghrébins en France*, 34–9; R. Gallissot, 'Aux origines de l'immigration algérienne', in J. Costa-Lascoux and E. Temime (eds), *Les Algériens en France*, 210–15.
37.   This debate is examined by Clément-Grandcourt, *Nos Indigènes Nord-Africains*; C.-R. Ageron, *Algériens Musulmans*, Chapter 38, 'La Conscription des Musulmans Algériens (1907–1914)'; G. Meynier, *L'Algérie révélée*, pp. 88–104. The Governor General Jonnart stated before a Senatorial Commission on the Army in late 1904: 'there is on the other side of the Mediterranean an admirable reservoir which it would be a mistake not to draw on more readily; you can recruit from the native population thousands of volunteers as the need arises'.

38. Quoted in C.-R. Ageron, *Algériens Musulmans*, p. 1061.
39. G. Meynier, *L'Algérie révélée*, pp. 569–98.
40. The figures are from A. Bernard, *L'Afrique du Nord Pendant la Guerre* (Presses Universitaires de France, 1926) p. 5.
41. G. Meynier, *L'Algérie révélée*, pp. 415–19.
42. Quite similar segregationist measures were taken in relation to Black GIs serving in Britain during the Second World War. See G. Smith, 'Jim Crow on the home front (1942–1945)', *New Community* Vol. 8, No. 3 (Winter 1980) 317–28.
43. G. Meynier, *L'Algérie révélée*, p. 436. For an example of the liberating impact of the French experience on a future nationalist leader see B. Stora, *Messali Hadj (1974–1989)* (Harmattan, 1986) pp. 29–32.
44. G. Meynier, *L'Algérie révélée*, p. 441.
45. *Ibid.*, p. 450.
46. On the SOTC see B. Nogaro and L. Weil, *La main-d'Oeuvre Étrangère et Coloniale*, pp. 5–28; G. Meynier, *L'Algérie révélée*, pp. 459–84; J. Horne, 'Immigrant Workers in France during World War I', *French Historical Studies*, Vol. 14, No. 1 (1985) 57–88; T. Stovall, 'Colour-blind France? Colonial workers during the First World War', *Race and Class*, Vol. 35, No. 2 (1993) 35–55.
47. For a graphic account of the squalid, militarised conditions in the Marseilles camp see L. Talha, *Le Salariat Immigré*, pp. 66–7.
48. G. Meynier, *L'Algérie révélée*, pp. 463–4. J. Horne, 'Immigrant Workers', pp. 86–7 provides a detailed account of the '*encadrement*' of North African workers in Le Havre.
49. G. Meynier, *L'Algérie révélée*, pp. 459–60; B. Nogaro and L. Weil, *La Main-d'Oeuvre Étrangère*, pp. 19–24; J. Horne, 'Immigrant Workers', pp. 75–6.
50. T. Stovall, 'Colour-blind France?', 42–3.
51. A. Bernard, *L'Afrique du Nord Pendant la Guerre*, p. 11, estimates that during the war period there were 30 000 free and 89 000 contract workers in France.
52. I use the term 'enclave' in preference to the word 'ghetto', which has strong negative connotations, to refer to patterns of dense ethnic settlement. For a useful analysis of the concept see F.W. Boal, 'Ethnic Residential Segregation' in D.T. Herbert and R.J. Johnston (eds), *Social Areas in Cities. Vol. 1. Spatial Processes and Form* (London: J. Wiley, 1976) pp. 41–79.
53. G. Meynier, *L'Algérie révélée*, pp. 459–60, 476. Archives of the Paris Préfecture de Police (henceforth APP). BA. 67, 'État concernant les Kabyles'.
54. O. Depont, *Les Kabyles en France*, p. 27.
55. APP. BA. 67. Report of Prefecture de Police. Services des Renseignements Généraux, 6 April 1918.
56. O. Depont, *Les Kabyles en France*, p. 30.
57. G. Meynier, *L'Algérie révélée*, p. 475.
58. M.-R. Santucci, 'La Main-d'Oeuvre Étrangère dans les Mines de la Grand-Combe jusqu'en 1940', *Mines et Mineurs en Languedoc-Rouissillon et régions voisines de l'Antiquité à nos jours* (Montpellier, 1977) pp. 292–6.

59. Talha, *Le Salariat Immigré*, p. 69; H. Baroin, *La Main-d'Oeuvre Étrangère dans la Région Lyonnaise* (Lyons: Bosc Frères, 1935) pp. 38–9, 123–40; R.D. Grillo, *Ideologies and Institutions in Urban France: the Representation of Immigrants* (Cambridge: Cambridge University Press, 1985).
60. L. Talha, *Le Salariat Immigré*, pp. 72–8.
61. C.-R. Ageron, *Algériens Musulmans*, pp. 1145–6.
62. G. Meynier, *L'Algérie révélée*, pp. 466–7.
63. G. Meynier, *L'Algérie révélée*, pp. 467–8.
64. *Ibid.*, pp. 472–3.
65. C.-R. Ageron, *Algériens Musulmans*, pp. 1169–70.
66. J. Horne, 'Immigrant Workers', p. 60 points out that the war marked a sharp change in the ethnic or national composition of French immigration, the most noticeable difference being the increase in the proportion of Spanish and North African workers.
67. L. Talha, *Le Salariat Immigré*, p. 94 notes that the major zones of emigration were not those suffering from the greatest over-population or poverty, but where 'le recrutement militaire des travailleurs coloniaux a été le plus intense'. But he fails to explain why universal conscription did not create an even geographical spread of later emigration. See below Chapter 10.

4 Departure and Employment

1. For example, until the inter-war period Asturian peasants travelled daily to work in steel-mills and coalmines: see D. Ruiz, *El Movimiento Obrero en Asturias* (Madrid: Jucar, 1979). Ruiz uses the term *obrero-mixto* for this hybrid type.
2. Liauzu quoted in C. Ben Fredj, *Aux origines de l'émigration*, p. 760. The term 'peasant-worker' is also used by Janet D. Zagoria, *The Rise and Fall of the Movement of Messali Hadj in Algeria, 1924–1954*, PhD Thesis, Columbia University, 1973.
3. APP – BA 67. N. Gomar, *op.cit.* p. 21, estimates that only 5 to 6000 workers escaped the repatriation.
4. G. Massard-Guilbaud, *Des Algériens à Lyon, de la Grande Guerre au Front Populaire*, Doctoral thesis, University of Lyons II (1988) p. 59; J. Ray, *Les Marocains en France*, p. 58.
5. J. Cesari, 'Les stratégies identitaires des musulmans à Marseille', *Migrations Société*, Vol. 1, Nos 5–6 (1989) 59; G. Cross, *Immigrant Workers*, pp. 123–4.
6. Professor Gautier in *Revue de Paris*, 1 June 1921, quoted by G. Meynier, *L'Algérie révélée*, p. 700. On the famine of 1920–1 see M.L. Richardson, *French Algeria Between the Wars: Nationalism and Colonial Reform, 1919–1939*, Doctoral Thesis, Duke University (1975) pp. 58–61.
7. *L'Humanité*, 29 August 1926, quoted in C. Ben Fredj, *Aux origines de l'émigration*, p. 13.
8. AOM. B3. 167 Constantine. Letter from the Prefect of Saône-et-Loire to Prefect of Constantine, 19 March 1929. On the activities of recruiting agents (*rabatteurs*) see G. Meynier, *L'Algérie révélée*, p. 406; J. Ray, *Les Marocains en France*, pp. 44, 61.

9. M. Marty, *Un sidi ou la vie est belle* (Albin Michel, 1938), quoted in C. Ben Fredj, *Aux origines de l'émigration*, p. 32. Unscrupulous *rabatteurs* operating on behalf of shipping companies and, after 1945, of airlines, travelled through villages spreading propaganda as to conditions in France. See L. Muracciole, *Émigration Algérienne*, p. 98 and J.-J. Rager, *Musulmans Algériens en France*, p. 137.

10. N. Gomar, *Émigration Algérienne*, p. 24.

11. AOM. B3. 167, Constantine.

12. M. Bennoune, *Impact of Colonialism and Migration on an Algerian Peasant Community: a study in socio-economic change*, Doctoral thesis, University of Michigan (1976) p. 151.

13. A. Sayad, '*El ghorba: le mécanisme de reproduction de l'émigration*' (1975) reprinted in A. Sayad, *L'immigration or les paradoxes de l'altérité* (Brussels: De Boeck-Wesmael, 1991) pp. 38–9.

14. J. Ray, *Les Marocains en France*, p. 131, notes that emigration was less affected by levels of poverty in Morocco than by, 'French prosperity the phases of which it follows with flexibility and precision.' The comments in L. Henry *et al.*, *Les Algériens en France*, p. 87 holds good for the 1920s, 'A network of tight threads, strong but invisible, stretch between Algeria and France, linking a certain *douar* to a particular quarter of a French town, a specific factory or work-site. Rapid communications are established which help to explain the sensitivity of Algerian labour to the conjunctural situation in France'.

15. O. Depont, *Les Kabyles en France*, p. 13.

16. J. Ray, *Les Marocains en France*, p. 313, estimated that a clandestine migrant would require in 1937 some 3000 francs for the round trip, or the equivalent of six to eight months regular work.

17. In El Akbia 56 per cent of emigrants borrowed to pay their ticket, often by mortgaging land which fell into the hands of usurers; M. Bennoune, *Impact of Colonialism*, pp. 225–7.

18. A Kabyle worker wrote while on vacation in Fort-National, 15 October 1926, to the Communist newspaper *Al Lioua-Al-Ahmar* No. 2. November 1926, a bi-lingual paper for immigrants, to complain of the corruption among the Arab assistants (*chaouchs*) to the local administrator. 'In order to ask for advice or an identity card you have to have a note (bribe) ready in your hand. If you don't anger them you can wait weeks or months. If you complain you end up in gaol.' To pay his return he had also been forced to borrow money at 40 or 50 per cent. See K. Bouguessa, *Émigration et Politique. Essai sur la formation et la politique de la communauté Algérienne en France à l'entre-deux-guerres mondiales*, Doctoral Thesis, University of Paris V (1979), Appendix, Document 16.

19. C. Lacoste-Dujardin, *Un village algérien*, pp. 149–51. J. Ray, *Les Marocains en France*, pp. 128–30, found that in southern Morocco in the 1930s, '. . . in many cases the emigrant belongs to a relatively well-off family'. Poor households had neither the money or group resources to send a migrant to France and Ray concluded, 'poverty is not the direct cause of the exodus'.

20. R. Montagne, 'L'émigration nord-africaine en France'; A. Sayad, 'Les

trois "âges"'; P. Bourdieu, *The Algerians* (Boston: Beacon Press, 1962).

21.   Evidence of the links between first phase migration and extended families with relatively high incomes has been noted for other countries. See for example P.-R. Baduel, *Société et Émigration Temporaire au Nefzaoua (Sud-Tunisien)* (CNRS, 1980). Part 8, 'L'Émigration et la structure familiale tradionnelle', pp. 75–86; A.M. Abou-Zeid, 'Migrant labour and social structure in Kharga Oasis', in J. Pitt-Rivers (ed.), *Mediterranean Countrymen* (Mouton, 1963) pp. 41–53. South Asian migration to Britain which, like that of Kabylia started early in the twentieth century, was from prosperous farming or trading regions like Azad Kashmire, the Punjab, Baroda, Surat, Sylhet and elsewhere in which a tradition of emigration was founded on the extended family. See P. Lewis, *Islamic Britain. Religion, Politics and Identity among British Muslims* (London: I.B. Tauris, 1994) p. 16.

22.   C. Lacoste-Dujardin, *Un village algérien*, p. 79.

23.   A. Ben Younes, *Émigration et Société*, pp. 42–3. On the system of *remplacement* or job-sharing see J. Ray, *Les Marocains en France*, p. 134.

24.   Deviants who settled in France, cut family links and failed to send remittances were called *imjahen*, meaning someone who was 'perverted, debauched, lost': see C. Lacoste-Dujardin, *Un village algérien*, p. 91; A. Sayad, 'Les trois "âges"', p. 64.

25.   A. Sayad, 'Les trois "âges"', pp. 61–2. G. Massard-Guilbaud, *Algériens à Lyon*, p. 265 found that in 1921 most migrants were aged 25 to 34 years, although there were a few as young as 15 to 19 years.

26.   L. Muracciole, *Émigration Algérienne*, p. 145.

27.   J. Morizot, *L'Algérie Kabylisée*, pp. 57, 122.

28.   L. Muracciole, *Émigration Algérienne*, pp. 56–7; L. Henry *et al.*, *Les Algériens en France*, pp. 50–6.

29.   A. Sayad, 'Les trois "âges"', p. 64.

30.   See J.-J. Rager, *Musulmans Algériens en France*, pp. 109–10, 136 which quotes verses from Malek Ouary, *Chants d'Éxil* (1946).

31.   M. Khellil, *L'Éxil Kabyle*, p. 8.

32.   L. Muracciole, *Émigration Algérienne*, p. 9. There is a photograph of such a scene on the cover of B. Stora, *Ils Venaient d'Algérie*. Ironically, some clandestine migrants employed the ruse of travelling in the second class, dressed 'very correctly like Europeans', since immigration officials did not subject Algerian élites to controls: see AOM. 9 H 112, circular from *Gouvernement Générale* to Algerian Prefects, 28 November 1924. Exactly the same method was used by European migrants to avoid the controls introduced in Britain under the 1905 Aliens Act: see B. Gainer, *The Alien Invasion. The Origins of the Alien's Act of 1905* (London: Heinemann, 1972) p. 199.

33.   J. Ray, *Les Marocains en France*, pp. 67–8; C. Ben Fredj, *Aux origines de l'émigration*, pp. 67–90.

34.   Letter in *Al Lioud-al-Ahmar*, No. 2 November 1926, quoted in K. Bouguessa, *Émigration et Politique*, Appendix, Document 16.

35.   On the *Comité d'Assistance*, see AOM. 9 H 113, *Rapport sur l'émigration des indigénes* (1923), p. 27. A journalist in *Le quotidien*, 27 October 1928, described his visit to the camp – under the command of Colonel

Lolle de Chastaignier – and the squalid conditions in the former barracks. See C. Ben Fredj, *Aux origines de l'émigration*, p. 147.

36. AOM. 9 H 112, Report of Prefect of Vaucluse, 15 October 1923. The Mayor of Bourguin in the Isère wrote to the Sous-Prefect of La Tour Du Pin, 11 December 1924, that hardly a day went by without Algerians, recently disembarked at Marseilles, coming, 'to the townhall of our village, almost naked, without money, requesting food or work'.

37. AOM. 9 H 112, Report of M. Chardenet to the President of the *Comité d'Assistance aux Indigènes algériens*, April 1923.

38. A. Sayad, 'Elghorba', pp. 36–8.

39. J. Ray, *Les Marocains en France*, pp. 93–4; J.-J. Rager, *Musulmans Algériens*, pp. 201–13; N. Gomar, *Émigration Algérienne*, p. 65; AOM. 8 H 62, 'Rapport de MM. Laroque et Ollive . . . sur la main-d'oeuvre Nord Africaine' (1938), pp. 142–7. [hereafter *Laroque Report*].

40. The map has been adapted from A. Michel, *Les Travailleurs Algériens en France* (CNRS, 1956), Map 2.

41. Maps of the location of Algerians in France are to be found in several studies. For the distribution in 1926 see G. Mauco, *Les Étrangers en France*, p. 170; for 1931, 1936, 1946 and 1975 see J. Singer-Kerel, 'Les Actifs Maghrébins', 96–7; and for 1937 and 1955 see A. Michel, *Les Travailleurs Algériens*, pp. 14–16.

42. G. Cross, *Immigrant Workers*, pp. 160–3 gives data for 1906–31 which shows those sectors, particularly mining, construction and metallurgy, in which French workers were displaced by immigrant labour.

43. The best treatment of employment statistics from 1926 to 1975 is provided by the tables in J. Singer-Kerel, 'Les Actifs Maghrébins dans les Recensements Français', in L. Talha (ed.), *Maghrébins en France*, 87–9.

44. G. Mauco, *Les Étrangers en France*, pp. 196–7, Table 6.

45. For details of industrial accidents and disease see A. Michel, *Les Travailleurs Algériens*, pp. 36–47.

46. C. Ben Fredj, *Aux origines de l'émigration*, p. 487; K. Bouguessa, *Émigration et Politique*, Appendix, Document 19.

47. G. Mauco, *Les Étrangers en France*, p. 310.

48. *Laroque Report*, p. 31.

49. *Ibid.*, p. 40.

50. *L'Humanité*, 17 October 1930, quoted in C. Ben Fredj, *Aux origines de l'émigration*, p. 516.

51. O. Depont, *Les Kabyles en France*, pp. 11–12, 24–7; AOM. 9 H 113, *Rapport sur l'émigration des indigènes* (1923), pp. 15–17.

52. C. Ben Fredj, *Aux origines de l'émigration*, pp. 478–82; M. Bennoune, *Impact of Colonialism*, p. 238.

53. J. Ray, *Les Marocains en France*, p. 144.

54. An excellent analysis of such a system at work is in D. Brooks and K. Singh, 'Asian brokers in British foundries' in S. Wallman (ed.), *Ethnicity at Work* (1979) pp. 92–112.

55. *Laroque Report*, p. 37; J.-J. Rager, *Musulmans Algériens en France*, pp. 196–7, 206.

56. G. Cross, *Immigrant Workers*, p. 140.

57. *Laroque Report*, pp. 36–7. However, H. Baroin, *La Main-d'Oeuvre Étrangère*, p. 137 saw a danger to efficiency in village groupings which could fall under the control of native leaders.

58. There exists an enormous body of work on the economic factors underlying labour immigration into post-war Europe: for a useful introduction see S. Castles, *Here For Good*; R. Cohen, *New Helots*, Chapter 4 'The function of migrant labour in Europe'.

59. J. Singer-Kerel, 'Les Actifs Maghrébins dans les Recensements Français', pp. 81–100.

60. An employer told G. Mauco, *Les Étrangers en France*, p. 239, regarding the destroyed health of North African workers, 'that one "remedied this inconvenience" by sending back the most ill before their productivity was too lowered or before their condition gave rise to the worry of a fatal outcome and compensation payments'.

61. M. Ath-Messaoud and A. Gillette, *L'immigration Algérienne en France* (Editions Entente, 1976) p. 112.

62. For the debate on low productivity see N. Gomar, *Émigration Algérienne*, pp. 59–63; *Laroque Report*, pp. 33–41; J.-J. Rager, *Musulmans Algériens en France*, pp. 214–16.

63. L. Henry *et al.*, *Les Algériens en France*, p. 83. For an exhaustive analysis of the factors underlying the long-term relegation of Algerians to low-skilled labour see M. Trebous, *Migration and Development*.

64. *Laroque Report*, p. 26; N. Gomar, *Émigration Algérienne*, p. 43.

65. *Laroque Report*, pp. 139, 274; H. Baroin, *La Main-d'Oeuvre Étrangère*, pp. 92–101, 230–1.

66. H. Baroin, *La Main-d'Oeuvre Étrangère*, p. 239. G. Cross, *Immigrant Workers*, pp. 119–21 notes that the great advantage that France held over Italy, Poland and Spain as labour supplying nations had been significantly eroded by 1928. French employers then began to look further afield for recruits, including to North Africa.

67. *Laroque Report*, pp. 37–8.

68. J. Ray, *Les Marocains en France*, pp. 79, 115.

69. J.-J. Rager, *Musulmans Algériens en France*, pp. 183–8.

70. Stéphane David, 'Une communauté musulmane dans le Nord de la France' (1948), an unpublished report quoted in J.-J. Rager, *Musulmans Algériens en France*, p. 184.

71. G. Massard-Guilbaud, *Des Algériens à Lyon*, p. 309.

72. This is close to the 4 to 4.5 per cent of permanently settled Algerians in Lyons in the 1930s, see G. Massard-Guilbaud, *Algériens à Lyon*, p. 262.

73. A particularly detailed analysis of the Algerian petit-bourgeoisie is in K. Bouguessa, *Émigration et Politique*, pp. 105–32.

5 Life in the Enclave

1. On company housing during the inter-war period see R. Martial, *Traité de l'Immigration et de la Greffe Inter-Raciale* (Cuesmes-lez-Mons: Imprimerie Fédérale, 1931) pp. 256–8; G. Mauco, *Les Étrangers en France*, p. 254; H. Baroin, *La Main-d'Oeuvre Étrangère*, p. 48; R. Schor, 'Les conditions

de vie dès immigrés Nord-Africains dans la Meurthe-et-Moselle entre les deux guerres', *Cahiers de la Méditerranée*, No. 14 (June, 1977) 47; G. Cross, *Immigrant Workers*, p. 138; J. Ray, *Les Marocains en France*, p. 171, notes that the *Société des Mines de la Loire* housed 63 Moroccans in a hostel provided with a laundry, canteen, allotments and prayer room.

2. O. Carlier, 'Pour une histoire quantitative', p. 156; *Laroque Report*, pp. 37–8.

3. A. Pairault, *L'Immigration Organisée et l'Emploi de la Main-d'Oeuvre Étrangère en France* (Presses Universitaires de France, 1926) pp. 190–3; G. Cross, *Immigrant Workers*, pp. 80–4; R. Martial, *Traité de l'Immigration*, pp. 256–9; G. Mauco, *Les Étrangers en France*, p. 253.

4. A. Pairault, *L'Immigration Organisé*, pp. 186–7. See Table 8.1 and further discussion in Chapter 8.

5. The distinction between a paternalist social policy for European workers and neglect of North Africans is shown in M.-R. Santucci, 'La main-d'oeuvre étrangère dans les mines de La Grand-Combe', pp. 299–300; see also G. Cross, *Immigrant Workers*, pp. 137–40.

6. O. Depont, *L'Algérie du Centenaire*, p. 132; K. Bouguessa, *Émigration et Politique*, pp. 234–6.

7. Copigneaux and Besombes, *Note . . . sur le fonctionnement des centres d'hébergement des indigènes Nord-africains de Clermont-Ferrand, Marseille et Toulon*. Bibliothèque Administrative de la Ville de Paris (BAVP) Côte 1783, No. 141 (1926). The report of this delegation from the Paris City Council which visited *Michelin* served as a model for the hostels built by SAINA in Paris, see Chapter 9.

8. O. Depont, *Les Kabyles en France*, p. 48.

9. *Journal Officiel. Débats Parlementaires*, 17 December 1913, p. 3858.

10. O. Depont, *Les Kabyles en France*, p. 22.

11. Report of the Longwy commissaire de police, 7 April 1938, Archives Départementales de la Meurthe-et-Moselle 4 M 173, quoted in R. Schor 'Les Conditions de Vie', pp. 45–6.

12. J.-J. Rager, *Musulmans Algériens en France*, pp. 248–58.

13. M. Bennoune, *Impact of Colonialism and Migration*, p. 152. Another migrant from the same village was housed by railway contractors in old wagons, 'without any electric light, running water or heat', *Ibid.*, p. 218.

14. G. Mauco, *Les Étrangers en France*, pp. 294–5.

15. G. Mauco, *Les Étrangers en France*, p. 295. The Goutte d'Or quartier was the location of Emile Zola's *L'Assommoir* and provided Michel Tournier with the title for his novel on North African immigration, *La Goutte d'Or* (Gallimard, 1985). A detailed history of the formation of this Algerian enclave can be found in J.-C. Toubon, K. Messamah, *Centrale Immigrée: Le Quartier de la Goutte-d'Or* (Harmattan, 1990), 2 Vols.

16. In 1931 the total Algerian population of the Paris region was about 60 000, with two-thirds of them located in the suburbs. See C. Ben Fredj, *Aux origines de l'émigration*, p. 130. G. Cross, *Immigrant Workers*, p. 130 estimates that between 1921 and 1931 the city of Paris grew by 46 per cent, the suburbs by 146 per cent.

17. L. Massignon, 'Carte de la répartition des Kabyles dans la région

parisienne', *Revue des Études Islamiques*, No. 2 (1930), 166; J. Ray, *Les Marocains en France*, pp. 139–50.

18. H. Baroin, *La Main-d'Oeuvre Étrangère*.

19. C. Ben Fredj, *Aux origines de l'émigration*, p. 320.

20. G. Mauco, *Les Étrangers en France*, pp. 344–8. On the development of the squatter zones see N. Evenson, *Paris: A Century of Change, 1878–1978* (New Haven: Yale University Press, 1979).

21. J. Ray, *Les Marocains en France*, p. 103.

22. *Ibid.*, pp. 101–3, 162.

23. Lieutenant-Colonel Justinard, 'Les Chleuh dans la Banlieue de Paris', *Revue des Études Isalmiques* (1928) 479.

24. Commission du Conseil Municipal de Paris, 1927, quoted in J. Ray, *Les Marocains en France*, pp. 168–9.

25. Gennevilliers, and especially Les Grésillons, figured in a number of studies, for example O. Depont, *L'Algérie du Centenaire*, p. 136 and A. Bernard, 'Rapport sur la main-d'oeuvre dans l'Afrique du Nord', *Afrique Française. Renseignements Coloniaux* (May 1930) 301. Curious European 'tourists' visited Gennevilliers during a festival of the religious confraternity of the Gnaoua, an organisation of Blacks from southern Morocco who claimed descent from the black slave of Mahomet. They danced and sang grouped in a circle round a bull decorated in flowers and dressed in white. J. Ray, *Les Marocains en France*, p. 183.

26. P. Catrice and G. Buchet, 'Les Musulmans en France. Enquête. Gennevilliers: La Cité Arabe', *En Terre d'Islam* (1929) 336–48. By 1955 the housing conditions in Gennevilliers had changed little; see the investigation and photographs of cramped dormitories of a typical lodging house in A. and J. Belkhodja, *Les Africains du Nord à Gennevilliers*, Cahiers Nord-Africains No. 97 (1963) 59–63, 111.

27. J. Ray, *Les Marocains en France*, pp. 254–6; P. Catrice, 'Les Musulmans en France', pp. 345–6 describes in detail a visit to a Moroccan butchers.

28. For an excellent investigation of the later development of Gennevilliers, the growth of *bidonvilles* and ongoing social and spatial segregation, see A. El Gharbaoui, 'Les travailleurs maghrébins immigrés sans la banlieue nord-est de Paris', *Revue de Géographie du Maroc*, No. 19 (1971) 3–56.

29. J. Ray, *Les Marocains en France*, pp. 185–92 has details of typical migrant annual budgets which showed savings at about 45 per cent of income. Of the rest most went on food (30 per cent), clothing (10), rent and heating (2), and of 'other expenditure' (5) an infinitesimal sum went to tobacco, and café entertainment.

30. Quoted in B. Stora, *Ils Venaient d'Algérie*, pp. 20–1. For similar evidence see C. Ben Fredj, *Aux origines de l'émigration*, p. 209.

31. In the 1930s Radio-Paris Mondial was broadcasting in Arabic and Kabyle: see R. Faligot and R. Kauffer, *Le Croissant et la Croix Gammée* (Albin Michel, 1990) p. 121. J.-J. Rager, *Musulmans Algériens en France*, p. 289 notes that by 1949 the *Gouvernement Générale* was broadcasting four and a half hours a week programmes aimed specifically at Algerian workers in France.

32.   J. Ray, *Les Marocains en France*, pp. 181–2.
33.   APP. BA. 57, Police Report 30 October 1935. See also J. Zagoria, *Rise and Fall of Messali Hadj*, p. 95.
34.   G. Massard-Guilbaud, *Algériens à Lyon*, p. 446.
35.   G. Mauco, *Les Étrangers en France*, p. 175. Women constituted 14 per cent of Portuguese immigrants, 39 per cent of Poles and 42 per cent of Italians.
36.   T. Ben Jelloun, *La plus haute des solitudes. Misère affective et sexuelle d'émigrés nord-africains* (Seuil, 1977).
37.   *Le Peuple*, 23 September 1937, quoted in C. Ben Fredj, *Aux origines de l'immigration*, p. 210.
38.   J. Ray, *Les Marocains en France*, p. 203. R. Montagne referred elliptically to the dangers run by young migrants aged twelve to fifteen living, 'in the promiscuity of masculine groups deprived of women'. AOM. 762, *Rapport Provisoire*, p. 16. See also H. Marchand, *Les Mariages Franco-Musulmans* (Algiers: Vollot-Debacq, 1954) pp. 57–8, which claims that the so-called 'African vice' was 'extraordinarily widespread'. It is difficult to discern if such observations were another form of homophobic stereotyping of Arabs.
39.   C. Ben Fredj, *Aux origines de l'émigration*, p. 252.
40.   J. Ray, *Les Marocains en France*, pp. 192–7, notes that in Gennevilliers among those aged 20–39 years sixty per cent of deaths were caused by tuberculosis. Five out of seven Algerians admitted to the Beaujon hospital had the disease. See also J.-J. Rager, *Musulmans Algériens*, pp. 158–61; L. Muracciole, *Émigration Algérienne*, pp. 24–8, 109–11.
41.   The short article by the leading orientalist Louis Massignon, 'Cartes de Répartition des Kabyles dans la région Parisienne', had a big impact on the work of later scholars of migration. On Montagne's major study of 1952–4 see above, Chapter 2, endnote 6.
42.   A. Poitrineau, *Remues d'hommes. Essai sur les migrations montagnards en France*; R. Schor, *L'opinion française et les étrangers en France*.
43.   M. Bennoune, *Impact of Colonialism*, pp. 149–55.
44.   On the structure of family and fraction see R. Descloitres and L. Debzi, 'Système de parenté et structures familiales en Algérie', *Annuaire de l'Afrique du Nord* (1963) 23–59; R. Basagana and A. Sayad, *Habitat et Structures Familiales en Kabylie* (Algiers: SNED, 1974); J. Lizot, *Metidja. Un Village Algérien de l'Ouarsenis* (Algiers: SNED, 1973).
45.   J. Lizot, *Metidja*, p. 134.
46.   M. Khellil, *L'Exil Kabyle*, p. 60.
47.   AOM. 762. R. Montagne, *Rapport provisoire*, pp. 7–9.
48.   There is an excellent account of joint food-purchase by a group leader in J. Ray, *Les Marocains en France*, p. 179.
49.   M. Khellil, *La Kabylie ou l'Ancêtre sacrifié* (Harmattan, 1984) pp. 49–71.
50.   For group discipline see L. Muracciole, *Immigration Algérienne*, p. 108; J. Ray, *Les Marocains en France*, pp. 90, 134, 144–5, 159, 179; J.-J. Rager, *Musulmans Algériens en France*, pp. 240–1, 292; AOM. 762. R. Montagne, *Rapport Provisoire*, p. 11.
51.   R. Montagne, *Rapport Provisoire*, p. 10.

52. AOM. 9 H 113. Petition from E. Richer, solicitor, to Minister of the Interior, 16 February 1925. On the role of the SAINA police of the Rue Lecomte in 'intimidating' those who had abandoned their families in Algeria see N. Gomar, *Émigration Algérienne*, pp. 123–4; P. Godin, *Note sur le fonctionnement des Services de Surveillance, Protection et Assistance des Indigènes Nord-Africains* (Imprimerie Municipale, 1933) p. 11.
53. O. Depont, *Les Kabyles en France*, p. 27.
54. *Ibid.*, p. 30.
55. APP. BA. 67.
56. G. Massard-Guilbard, *Algériens à Lyon*, pp. 301–3, 313–16.
57. O. Carlier, 'Le Café Maure. Sociabilité masculine et effervescence citoyenne (Algérie XVII–XXe siècles)', *Annales. ESC* (July, 1990), 975–1003.
58. *Le Peuple*, 17 January 1931, 'Le Maghreb à Paris', quoted in C. Ben Fredj, *Aux origines de l'émigration*, p. 217.
59. A typical example is given in AOM. 762. R. Montagne, *Rapport Provisoire*, p. 8: 'Such is the small rural community of Guergour, composed of 128 members, which has 127 workers installed in a street of Levallois in a café run by one of their own number.'
60. On the historical development of café and shop ownership see M. Kerrou, 'Du colportage à la boutique. Les commerçants maghrébins en France', *Hommes et Migrations*, No. 1 105 (July, 1987) 26–34.
61. B. Stora, *Ils Venaient d'Algérie*, pp. 24–6. The history of the growth of the ENA in the émigré community in France has been the subject of extensive investigation. Space does not allow the detailed examination which it deserves, but this is well covered by the following: K. Bouguessa, *Émigration et Politique*; B. Stora, *Histoire Politique de l'Immigration Algérienne en France (1922–1962)*, Doctoral thesis, University of Paris XII (1991); B. Stora, *Messali Hadj*; J.D. Zagoria, *The Rise and Fall of Messali Hadj*; C.-R. Ageron *et al.*, *Les Mémoires de Messali Hadj, 1898–1938* (J.-C. Lattès, 1982).
62. APP. BA. 56; B. Stora, *Messali Hadj*, p. 105. The identity of many other militant café owners can be gleaned from B. Stora, *Dictionnaire Biographique des Militants Nationalistes Algériens (1926–1954)* (Harmattan, 1985) such as Ahmed Senhadji at Nanterre, Ismaïl Oufellah at Puteaux, Saïd Ould Hadj Ben Seddik in Lille, and Tahar Mezziani in the 5th arrondissement.
63. B. Stora, *Ils Venaient d'Algérie*, 'Batailles pour le contrôle des cafés', pp. 31–5.
64. APP. BA. 56. Police report 26 September 1936.
65. AOM. 762. R. Montagne, *Étude Sociologique*, Cahier No. 3.
66. AOM. 762. R. Montagne, *Rapport Provisoire*, pp. 4–5.
67. AOM. 762. R. Montagne, *Rapport Provisoire*, pp. 8–10; *Étude Sociologique* Cahier No. 3.
68. C. Ben Fredj, *Aux origines de l'émigration*, p. 792.
69. On the split between Chaouias of the Aurès, Kabyles and Arabs see B. Stora, *Ils Venaient d'Algérie*, pp. 360–1. In 1949 the 'crise berbériste' split the *Parti du peuple algérien* (PPA), the successor to the ENA, and boiled over into civil war after independence. B. Stora, *Ibid.*, pp. 107–

12; O. Carlier, 'La production sociale de l'image de soi. Note sur la "crise berbériste" de 1949', *Annuaire de l'Afrique du Nord*, Vol. 23 (1984); S. Chaker, *Berbères Aujourd'hui.*

70. J. Ray, *Les Marocains en France*, pp. 161–2.
71. P. Catrice and G. Buchet, 'Les Musulmans en France', p. 348.
72. A. Sayad, 'Les trois "âges"', p. 71.

6 Islam and the Village

1. G. Pervillé, *Les étudiants algériens de l'université française, 1880–1962* (CNRS, 1984) p. 278; see also G. Meynier, *L'Algérie révélée*, pp. 242–3.
2. Y. Turin, *Affrontements culturels dans l'Algérie coloniale*; F. Colonna, 'Cultural resistance and religious legitimacy in colonial Algeria', *Economy and Society*, Vol. 3 (1974) 233–52.
3. The number of naturalisations (mainly soldiers) averaged about 32 per year between 1865 and 1899 while in 1920 there were only 17. In 1935 the reformist journal *Sihab* stated, 'The five million Algerian Muslims . . . prefer to die in poverty, deprived of everything, blind and dumb, rather than to live by renouncing their faith', quoted in A. Merad, *Le Réformisme Musulman*, pp. 405–9.
4. A. Merad, *Le Réformisme Musulman*, pp. 58–76. For a more contemporary, anthropological study of *maraboutisme* see E. Gellner, *The Saints of the Atlas* (London: Weidenfeld and Nicolson, 1968).
5. For an excellent comment on how even universal religions only have 'meanings in a specific social location' see P. Lewis, *Islamic Britain*, p. 28.
6. L.H. Lees, *Exiles of Erin: Irish Migrants in Victorian London* (Manchester: Manchester University Press, 1979) Chapter 7 'The Reforging of an Irish Catholic Culture' provides a fascinating analysis of the ways in which a traditional peasant culture centred on local pilgrimages, holy wells, fertility rituals and the miraculous power of saints was transformed among migrants within an urban milieu. The role of the Catholic church was not unlike Islam for Algerian migrants, it 'drew the worshipper into a fervently nationalist piety that bridged the gap between the secular and the sacred, the political and the spiritual, and it provided an alternative to assimilation into the English working class', *Ibid.*, p. 164.
7. J. Horne, 'Immigrant Workers', 78–9. Another immigrant wrote, 'I work from morning to night with infidels who have no pity on us; they are the enemies of religion': quoted in T. Stovall, 'Colour-blind France?', p. 47.
8. O. Depont, *Les Kabyles en France*, p. 20. Kabyles in Paris also placed pressure on the municipality and the *Gouvernement Général* for a Muslim cemetery and provision by the abattoirs of halal meat. AOM 9 H 113, *Rapport sur l'émigration des indigènes* (1923), p. 22.
9. J. Ray, *Les Marocains en France*, p. 171. On similar provision of prayer rooms, *cafés maures*, and halal meat by major steel and mining companies in Moselle in 1949 see J.-J. Rager, *Musulmans Algériens en France*, pp. 256–7.

10. G. Meynier, *L'Algérie révélée*, pp. 238–9.
11. G. Meynier, *L'Algérie révélée*, p. 455; J. Ray, *Les Marocains en France*, p. 56.
12. N. Gomar, *Émigration Algérienne*, p. 25; R. Martial, *Traité de l'Immigration*, p. 187; J. Ray, *Les Marocains en France*, pp. 56–7.
13. P. Godin, *Note sur des Services Indigènes*, p. 16. N. Gomar, *Émigration Algérienne*, p. 133, viewed the Muslim hospital as, 'an instrument of propaganda among the Muslim masses in France'.
14. The most detailed treatment of the Paris Mosque is that of C. Ben Fredj, *Aux origines de l'émigration*, pp. 358–401; see also B. Stora, *Ils Venaient d'Algérie*, pp. 35–6; G. Kepel, *Les Banlieues d'Islam* (Seuil, 1987); A. Boyer, *L'Institut Musulman de la Mosquée de Paris* (La Documentation Française, 1992). On the Muslim Hospital, see below Chapter 9.
15. *Al Alam Al Ahmar* (No. 3. July 1926) quoted by C. Ben Fredj, *Aux origines de l'émigration*, p. 394.
16. AOM 9 H 113, 'Rapport sur l'émigration des indigènes' (1923), p. 21; N. Gomar, *Émigration Algérienne*, p. 25; P. Catrice and G. Buchet, *En Terre d'Islam* (1929) 347 note, 'On the whole they no longer practice their religion. The life of the factory, the promiscuity of their lodgings makes them stupid and debased. They are without religious support, driven desperate by poverty . . .'
17. J. Ray, *Les Marocains en France*, p. 201.
18. J. Ray, *Les Marocains en France*, p. 202 found that about half of the Moroccans drank alcohol, but in moderation. Such breaking of restrictions was justified on the grounds that it was normal to follow the customs of the land, or on the doctrinal ground that emigration, as with warfare in an infidel land, gave a dispensation from strict Islamic observation.
19. J.-J. Rager, *Musulmans Algériens en France*, p. 292.
20. G. Massard-Guilbard, *Algériens à Lyon*, p. 445. He was still active as a religious leader in Lyons in 1987.
21. L. Massignon, 'Carte de la répartition', 167. See also J. Ray, *Les Musulmans en France*, p. 202.
22. E. Dermenghem, 'Musulmans de Paris. Les Kabyles à Grenelle', *Grande Revue* (Dec. 1934) 15–21.
23. A. Boukhelloua, *L'Hôpital Franco-Musulman de Paris* (Algiers: Imprimerie Nord-Africaine, 1934), p. 25. In the village assemblies of the Aït-Mangellat in Kabylia it was customary to pray for the safe return of migrants and that none die in 'exile, in a foreign land': J. Morizot, *L'Algérie Kabylisée*, p. 155.
24. C. Ben Fredj, *Aux origines de l'émigration*, pp. 360–1.
25. J.-J. Rager, *Musulmans Algériens en France*, p. 297; J. Ray, *Les Marocains en France*, p. 204. For an account of a coffin arriving in the village of Tamazirt, tied on the roof of a bus, see M. Rémond, *Djurdjura. Terre de Contraste* (Algiers: Baconnier, 1940) p. 75. M. Miyaji, *Village Kabyle*, p. 58 provides a detailed account of a *Caisse d'Entraide et de Prévoyance* run by men from the Commune of Beni-Douala. Three coffins per year were sent in 1973–4 at the considerable cost of about 4750 francs each. See also C. Yassine, 'Pour une thanatologie maghrébine: les rapatriements de corps' in B. Etienne (ed.), *L'Islam En France* (CNRS,

1990) pp. 337–48; Y. Chaïb, 'Le lieu d'enterrement comme repère migratoire', *Migrations Société*, Vol. 6. Nos 33–4 (1994) 29–40.

26. In St Etienne a former miner who had been to Mecca served as the *ressat* (corpse washer). The Paris Mosque also had a *ressat* and organised the ritual burial of immigrants who died without any resources. J. Ray, *Les Marocains en France*, pp. 204, 357.

27. A. Boukhelloua, *L'Hôpital Franco-Musulman*, pp. 61–8. The cemetery, which still exists, was finally located on a patch of land located beside the marshalling yards of the SNCF in Bobigny.

28. J. Ray, *Les Marocains en France*, p. 204; P. Videlier, 'Espaces et temps de l'intégration des immigrés dans la région lyonnaise', in I. Simon-Barouh and P-J. Simon (eds), *Les Étrangers dans la Ville. Le regard des Sciences Sociales* (Harmattan, 1990) p. 303.

29. The *Étoile-Nord-Africaine* changed its name, after it was banned in January 1937, to the *Parti du Peuple Algérien*.

30. A. Merad, *Le Réformisme Musulman*, p. 399. Hence the celebrated motto of the Association: 'Algeria is my country, Arabic is my language, Islam my religion.'

31. B. Stora, *Ils Venaient d'Algérie*, pp. 71–3; A. Merad, *Le Réformisme Musulman*, pp. 428–30; AOM 8 H 62, *Laroque Report*, pp. 70–1.

32. B. Stora, *Messali Hadj*, pp. 108–18; J.D. Zagoria, *Rise and Fall of Messali Hadj*, pp. 158, 189, 202–7. Messali, during a period of exile in Switzerland in 1936, was much influenced by the religious leader and nationalist Chekib Arslan. See J. Bessis,'Chekib Arslan et les mouvements nationalistes au Maghreb', *Revue Historique*, Vol. 259 (1978) 467–89.

33. J.D. Zagoria, *Rise and Fall of Messali Hadj*, p. 189.

34. L. Massignon, 'Carte de la répartition', 168–9 states that 50 per cent of Kabyles stayed eight months, returning annually for Ramadan; 25 per cent for one and a half years and 25 per cent definitively. J.-J. Rager, *Musulmans Algériens en France*, pp. 50, 125–6 notes regional variations, with migrants from western Algeria returning annually for the harvest or Ramadan while workers from other parts stayed two to four years. See also L. Talha, *Le Salariat Immigré*, p. 116; N. Gomar, *Émigration Algérienne*, p. 57.

35. A. Sayad, 'Les trois "âges"', p. 61.

36. J. Van Velsen, 'Labor Migration as a positive factor in the continuity of Tonga tribal society', *Economic Development and Cultural Change*, Vol. 8 (1959) 265–78; W. Watson, *Tribal cohesion in a Money Economy* (Manchester: Manchester University Press, 1958); S. Stichter, *Migrant Laborers* (Cambridge: CUP, 1985).

37. B. Stora, *Histoire Politique de l'Immigration*, p. 177.

38. C.-R. Ageron, *Les Algériens Musulmans*, p. 1169.

39. AOM. 762. R. Montagne et al., *Étude Sociologique*, Cahier 9.

40. There is considerable evidence for the growth of economic and social inequalities in villages of emigration, mainly between those families which profited from emigration and those which remained trapped on the land in a cycle of deepening poverty and growing dependence on the 'new rich' for loans and access to land. See for example: A. Ben Younes, *Émigration et Société*, pp. 43–4; M. Bennoune, *Impact of Colonialism*, pp. 156, 226–7, 370–1; C. Lacoste-Dujardin, *Un village*

algérien, pp. 149–51; AOM. 762, R. Montagne, *Rapport Provisoire*, pp. 21–2.

41. K. Bougessa, *Émigration et Politique*, pp. 208–9.
42. J. Ray, *Les Marocains en France*, pp. 315–6; emphasis as in original. For evidence of a similar process of inflation and erosion in the value of savings leading to a further cycle of emigration among the Chleuh of Morocco, see L. Talha, *Le Salariat Immigré*, p. 97.
43. Letter from Fort-National, 15 October 1926, published in the Communist immigrant journal, *Al Lioua-Al-Ahmar*, No. 2 November 1926. Quoted in K. Bougessa, *Émigration et Politique*, Appendix, Document 16.
44. G. Massard-Guilbaud, *Algériens à Lyon*, pp. 271–2.
45. J. Morizot, *L'Algérie Kabylisée*, p. 110.
46. AOM. 8 H 62. *Laroque Report*, pp. 93–4. For other cases of agricultural decline see J.-J. Rager, *Musulmans Algériens en France*, pp. 139, 147; L. Talha, *Le Salariat Immigré*, 121–3; L. Muracciole, *Émigration Algérienne*, pp. 105–6; M. Bennoune, *Impact of Colonialism*.
47. F. Gourgeot, *Sept Plaies d'Algérie*, pp. 320–1. See also A. Merad, *Le Réformisme Musulmane*, p. 49.
48. See the photographs in F. Renaudot, *L'histoire des Français en Algérie, 1830–1962* (R. Laffont, 1979). During the twentieth century the traditional dress was increasingly mixed with elements of European clothing, especially jackets and trousers.
49. O. Depont, *Les Kabyles en France*, pp. 19–20, 27.
50. J.-J. Rager, *Musulmanes Algériens en France*, p. 261.
51. J. Ray, *Les Marocains en France*, p. 51; see J.-J. Rager, *Musulmans Algériens en France*, pp. 318–19 Annex 4 and 5 for the standard contracts of the Ministry of Labour and French Railways (SNCF).
52. The priests Paul Catrice and Georges Buchet on a visit to an Algerian café in Nanterre complimented an old worker on wearing a fez, but other migrants disagreed, ' "Him cap, good for work, fez fine, but not here". Yet a cap truly disfigures them. They wear it clumsily and this gives them the look of hooligans (*apaches*). But so what! They want to do like the others!', 'Les Musulmans en France', 22–3.
53. J.-J. Rager, *Musulmans Algériens en France*, p. 260; J. Ray, *Les Marocains en France*, p. 173.
54. Messali Hadj returned from exile in Switzerland in 1936 having changed his usual European suit for *burnous*, slippers, cap and beard. See J.D. Zagoria, *Rise and Fall of Messali Hadj*, p. 101. For graphic evidence of this shift see the photographs of Messali in C.-R. Ageron *et al.*, *Les Mémoires de Messali Hadj*, pp. 162–3.
55. A. Bernard, *L'Afrique du Nord Pendant la Guerre*, p. 13.
56. M. Rémond, *Djurdjura*, pp. 19–20. See L. Muracciole, *Émigration Algérienne*, p. 109; J.-J. Rager, *Musulmans Algériens en France*, pp. 136, 150–1, 259–61.
57. N. Gomar, *Émigration Algérienne*, pp. 57, 77; L. Muracciole, *Émigration Algérienne*, pp. 105–6; J.-J. Rager, *Musulmans Algériens en France*, p. 151; AOM. 762, R. Montagne, *Rapport Provisoire*, pp. 20–1.
58. R. Remond, *Au Coeur du Pays Kabyle* (Algiers: Baconnier, 1933) pp. 33–4. This also has a photograph of a typical new-style house at Azouza.
59. For an analysis of these changes see A. Ben Younes, *Émigration et Société*,

pp. 80–3; M. Côte, *L'Algérie*, pp. 24–8; R. Basagana and A. Sayad, *Habitat et Structures Familiales en Kabylie*.
60. P. Bourdieu and A. Sayad, *Le Déracinement. La crise de l'agriculture traditionnelle en Algérie* (Minuit, 1964), Chapters 4–7; see also C. Lacoste-Dujardin, *Un village algérien*, p. 78.
61. A. Ben Younes, *Émigration et société*, p. 48.
62. A. Sayad, 'Les trois "âges"', pp. 65–76; A. Gillette and A. Sayad, *Immigration Algérienne*, p. 82; M. Bennoune, *Impact of Colonialism and Migration*, pp. 387–92.
63. M. Bennoune, *Impact of Colonialism and Migration*, pp. 379–81; A. Ben Younes, *Émigration et société*, pp. 53, 87–90.
64. L. Muracciole, *Émigration Algérienne*, p. 107. See also J.-J. Rager, *Musulmans Algériens en France*, p. 152; J. Ray, *Les Marocains en France*, p. 282.
65. A. Merad, *Le Réformisme Musulman*, 53–76. The reformist movement had spread by 1935 primarily in the areas of emigration, especially Kabylia, *Ibid.*, pp. 192–6.
66. APP. BA. 56, [A. Godin], *Note sur l'activité de l'Étoile*; J.D. Zagoria, *Rise and Fall of Messali Hadj*, pp. 56–70.
67. B. Stora, *Histoire Politique de l'Immigration*, pp. 86–7.
68. B. Stora, *Ils Venaient d'Algérie*, p. 59
69. APP. BA. 56, [A. Godin], *Note sur l'activité de l'Étoile*, p. 157; B. Stora, *Dictionnaire Biographique*, pp. 88–9.
70. APP. BA 56, [A. Godin], *Note sur l'activité de l'Étoile*, p. 136. On the spread of nationalism into the village of El Akbia after the Second World War see M. Bennoune, 'The Introduction of Nationalism into Rural Algeria: 1919–1954', *The Maghreb Review*, Vol. 2, No. 3 (May–June 1977) 1–12.

7 Working-class Racism

1. R. Miles, *Racism* (London: Routledge, 1989) p. 71.
2. S. Hall quoted in R. Miles, *Racism*, p. 65. For an excellent discussion of *racisms* as the set of racialised exclusions that are manifold and situationally specific, see D.T. Goldberg, *Racist Culture. Philosophy and the Politics of Meaning* (Oxford: Blackwell, 1993).
3. T.A. van Dijk, *Elite Discourse and Racism* (London: Sage, 1993).
4. P. Weil, *La France et ses Étrangers*, p. 21 borrows the term 'secteur' from B. Jobert and P. Muller, *L'État en action* (PUF, 1987).
5. M.A. Schain, 'Policy and policy-making in France and the United States: models of incorporation and the dynamics of change', *Modern and Contemporary France*, No. 4 (1995) 410.
6. O. Depont, *Les Kabyles en France*, p. 19. When Moroccan troops arrived at Bordeaux on 17 August 1914, 'the inhabitants . . . crowded around a bizarre encampment installed on the paving of the Chartrons. They were drawn by the curious sight of the native soldiers who had installed their little tents there . . .'. Capitaine Juin quoted in J. Ray, *Les Marocains en France*, p. 222.
7. J.-J. Rager, *Musulmans Algériens en France*, p. 286.
8. R. Martial, *Traité de l'Immigration*, p. 256. For other examples of such a mix see J. Ray, *Les Marocains en France*, pp. 96–7, 106; G. Mauco,

Les Étrangers en France, pp. 214–312. In the Paris region in 1926, for example, the engineering industry (mainly cars) employed North Africans (6234), Italians (5196), Russians (3607), Belgians (3450), Spaniards (2480) and Poles (1680).

9. G.S. Cross, *Immigrant Workers,* p. 140. Cross argues that mixing of nationalities was a deliberate policy of employers in order to divide-and-rule.

10. G. Mauco, *Les Étrangers en France,* pp. 435–7, provides a graphic account of a visit to a multi-ethnic ghetto. 'All around Paris, at 20 minutes from the Opera, on a large part of the zone of the former fortifications, swarmed the living mass of the Spanish, Italian, Polish and Algerian "villages".'

11. O. Depont, *Les Kabyles en France,* p. 18.

12. O. Depont, *Les Kabyles en France,* pp. 14, 19, 28. A common demand after the First World War was that Algerians should be better treated after so many thousands had lost their lives fighting for France. At Toulon in about 1936, 'ex-servicemen from North Africa complained bitterly about the employment of foreign workers on a site involving the national defence, from which they were themselves excluded': *Laroque Report,* p. 66. This was still a source of complaint in 1947, see B. Stora, *Ils Venaient d'Algérie,* pp. 100–1.

13. O. Depont, *Les Kabyles en France,* pp. 28–9; R. Lopez and E. Temime, *Histoire de Migrations,* pp. 145–55.

14. A letter in the journal *Temps,* 8 December 1926, noted 'The "Sidis" is the name that has been invented by an instinctive and simplistic popular xenophobia to designate all the natives of North Africa, Kabyles and Arabs from Algeria, Tunisians and Moroccans . . .' See also J. Ray, *Les Marocains en France,* p. 359. As Meynier, *L'Algérie révélée,* p. 479 notes employers also used a range of confusing terms, for example 'les Kabyles' meaning all 'Algerians' or even 'les Kabyles arabes'.

15. W.H. Schneider, *An Empire for the Masses;* J.-H. Henry (ed.), *Le Maghreb dans l'imaginaire français. La colonie, le désert, l'exil* (Édisud, 1985).

16. W.H. Schneider, *Empire for the Masses,* pp. 175–92. Plates 41 and 42 show scenes in the Arab quarter, which include 'natives' in traditional dress. World Fairs were held in Paris in 1878 and 1889, the Marseilles Colonial Exhibition in 1906, and other major exhibitions in 1917 and 1922 (Marseilles), 1924 (Strasbourg), 1925 and 1931 (Paris). All had Algerian and, from 1917, Moroccan presentations. See J. Ray, *Les Marocains en France,* p. 253; H. Lebovics, *True France. The Wars over Cultural Identity, 1900–1945* (Ithaca: Cornell University Press, 1992) Chapter 2.

17. G. Meynier, *L'Alérie révélée,* pp. 105–9 gives a detailed analysis of textbooks.

18. H. Lebovics, *True France,* pp. 58–93.

19. Messali Hadj, *Mémoires* Ms. Cahier No. 13, pp. 4834–5, quoted in B. Stora, *Thesis,* p. 118.

20. O. Depont, *L'Algérie du Centenaire,* p. 116. F. Renaudot, *Histoire des Français,* pp. 128–9 has a photograph of Algerian infantrymen being welcomed in the streets of Paris in 1914.

21. For an excellent analysis of popular racism in Algeria see E. Sivan,

'Colonialism and Popular Culture in Algeria', *Journal of Contemporary History*, Vol. 14 (1979) 21–53. See also J. Berque, 'Recent Research on Racial Relations. The North of Africa', *International Social Science Journal*, Part 2 (1961) 177–96; P. Nora, *Les Français d'Algérie* (Paris: Julliard, 1961).

22. Charles Geniaux, *Sous les Figuiers de Kabylie* (1917), p. 40, quoted in G. Meynier, Doctoral thesis, p. 1240.

23. G. Meynier, *L'Algérie révélée*, p. 473. Interview with a skilled Kabyle worker, Mr Antoin Ould Aoudia.

24. G. Meynier, *L'Algérie révélée*, pp. 423, 437–9; J. Ray, *Les Marocains en France*, p. 224.

25. This is a major finding of G. Meynier's work; but see also T. Stovall, 'Colour-blind France?'.

26. G. Meynier, *L'Algérie révélée*, pp. 468–9; J. Horne, 'Immigrant Workers', 84–7.

27. G. Meynier, *L'Algérie révélée*, p. 469.

28. T. Stovall, 'Colour-blind France?', 50.

29. Police report, Le Havre, May 1917, quoted in J. Horne, 'Immigrant Workers', 85. G. Meynier, *L'Algérie révélée*, p. 470. At Pompey a young Kabyle was accused of, 'obscenely touching a woman in public', etc.

30. The most detailed investigation is that of K. Bouguessa, *Émigration et Politique*, but see also C. Ben Fredj, *Aux origines de l'émigration*, pp. 611–66 and B. Stora, *Ils Venaient d'Algérie*, pp. 24–5.

31. P. Celor, 'Les Travailleurs Coloniaux en France', *Cahiers du Bolchévisme* No. 36, 21 January 1926, p. 183, quoted in K. Bouguessa, *Émigration et Politique*, p. 240.

32. Report of Sous-Commission Nord-Africaine, 9 September 1926, quoted in K. Bouguessa, *Émigration et Politique*, p. 422.

33. *Ibid.*, pp. 252–3.

34. AOM. 9 H 112. Report of Prefect of Police to Minister of the Interior, 11 October 1923.

35. C. Ben Fredj, *Aux origines de l'émigration*, pp. 680–1.

36. A North African worker wrote, 'At the factory all the comrades despise and ill-treat us. They leave us the hardest tasks . . . they treat us like foreigners.' *En Terre d'Islam* (May 1932) 194, quoted in C. Ben Fredj, *Aux origines de l'émigration*, p. 662.

37. See below Chapter 9 and G. Massard-Guilbaud, *Algériens à Lyon*, p. 422.

38. G. Meynier, doctoral thesis, p. 1231.

39. G. Mauco, *Les Étrangers en France*, pp. 294–5.

40. *Le Petit Parisien*, 8 November 1923, p. 1.

41. *L'Humanité*, 9 November 1923.

42. *L'Echo d'Alger*, 9 November 1923.

43. *Le Matin*, 9 November 1923.

44. *Annales coloniales*, 20 November 1923, quoted in *Laroque Report*, p. 62. The right-wing *L'Action Française*, 9 November 1923, stated that the murders, 'present – yet again – the question of the "undesirable" Algerians who swarm in Paris . . . most of the Arabs who prowl in Grenelle live by their wits or by thieving, when they are not making play with a knife.'

45. As G. Meynier, *L'Algérie révélée*, p. 470 shows this racialisation of Algerians by the popular press began as early as 1916-7. For a more detailed examination of the links between racism and the press see R. Schor, *L'opinion française et les étrangers en France*; R. Schor, 'Racisme et xenophobie à travers la caricature française (1919-1939)', *Revue Européene des Migrations Internationales*, Vol. 4, 1-2 (1988) 141-55; F. Olivier, ' "L'Echo de Paris" et les étrangers (1921-1931)', *Ibid.*, Vol. 10, 2 (1994) 187-200; and R. Schor, 'L'Opinion Française et les Immigrés Nord-Africains (1919-1939). L'image d'un sous prolétariat', *Cahiers de la Méditerranée*, (1981) 51-67.

46. From the ENA newspaper *El Ouma*, December 1933, quoted in B. Stora, *Histoire Politique de l'Immigration*, p. 132.

47. C. Ben Fredj, *Aux origines de l'émigration*, p. 211. The targeting of single Algerians as a sexual danger during the early 1970s has been studied by T. Allal *et al.*, *Situations migratoires. La fonction-miroir* (Galilée, 1977) pp. 82-3.

48. L. Massignon, 'Carte de répartition des Kabyles dans la Région Parisienne', 168.

49. J. Ray, *Les Marocains en France*, pp. 197-201; see also M. Duplessis-Kergomard, 'Mariages Mixtes des Kabyles en France', *La France Méditerranéens et Africaine* (1938) 110-17; N. MacMaster, 'Sexual and Racial Boundaries: Colonialism and Franco-Algerian Intermarriage (1880-1962)', in M. Cross and S. Perry (eds), *France: Population and Peoples* (Cassell, forthcoming).

50. See for example Pierre Dubard's report on Les Grésillons, 'L'Afrique Au Bord de la Seine. Une grande ville arabe dans le Grand-Paris', *L'Intransigeant*, 2 February 1933.

51. M. Tribalat, *Faire France. Une enquête sur les immigrés et leurs enfants* (La Découverte, 1995) pp. 76-86. See further discussion of this issue in the Conclusion below.

52. *Le Petit Parisien*, 10 November 1923.

53. *L'Humanité*, 10 January 1925, quoted in C. Ben Fredj, *Aux origines de l'émigration*, p. 665. The racist term *Khouïa* or *Krouïa* may be a distortion of the name of the Berber people from the Aurès region, the Chaouia.

54. J. Ray, *Les Marocains en France*, p. 278.

55. 'Rapport sur l'organisation syndicale des travailleurs algériens au sein de la commission coloniale', (1924), quoted by K. Bouguessa, *Émigration et Politique*, p. 253.

56. *Laroque Report*, pp. 61-2. It is typical of Eurocentric commentary that the isolation of ethnic minorities was ascribed to their 'refusal' to integrate and become 'like us', overlooking the extent to which such segregation was an outcome of overt or institutional racism.

57. P. Catrice and G. Buchet, 'Les Musulmans en France' (1929), 337-8.

58. C.T. Husbands, *Racial Exclusionism and the City: The urban support of the National Front* (London: Allen and Unwin, 1983) pp. 52-6, provides an interesting analysis of the 'defended neighbourhood' in the East End of London, an inner-city area with a long history of immigration that is not dissimilar to Paris.

59. Archives municipales de Gennevilliers, *Registre des Délibérations du Conseil Municipal*, 8 November 1924. See also Côte 26/3 'Le Village algérien, 1922–1913'.

60. Mayor of Gennevilliers to Prefect of Police 18 November 1923. AOM Hors série Doc 5. 83/4. Plans to establish North African hostels were also blocked by local campaigns in the Rue Mouffetard and the Rue Monge, see J. Ray, *Les Marocains en France*, p. 345.

61. G. Massard-Guilbaud, *Algériens à Lyon*, pp. 220–1.

62. C. Ben Fredj, *Aux origines de l'émigration*, p. 211.

63. A. Boukhelloua, *L'Hôpital Franco-Musulman de Paris*, pp. 44–5.

64. Archives municipales de Bobigny, *Délibérations du Conseil*, 10 April 1930; and Côte W. 4433, W. 4434. J. Chevillard-Vabre, *Histoire de l'Hôpital Franco-Musulman*, Thesis for Doctorate in Medicine, Faculty of Medicine Saint-Antoine-Paris (1982), provides an excellent investigation of the procedures by which the project was forced onto the municipality.

65. Archives municipales de Bobigny, *Délibérations du Conseil Municipal*, 29 December 1932.

66. N. MacMaster, 'The *seuil de tolérance*: the uses of a "scientific" racist concept', in M. Silverman (ed.), *Race, Discourse and Power in France* (Aldershot: Avebury, 1991) pp. 19–20.

67. On the social psychology of 'visibility' as a reaction by the dominant French population towards a range of markers (of sound, smell, touch, etc.) that denote a disliked minority see A. Belbahri, *Immigration et Situation Postcoloniales* (Harmattan, 1987) p. 103.

68. *Laroque Report*, p. 63, 'Almost everywhere there is igorance but without malevolence, each group living its own life and having little contact with the neighbouring group.'

69. *Laroque Report*, p. 64. See also on the 'invasion' O. Carlier, 'Pour une histoire quantitative', 156.

70. *Laroque Report*, p. 64.

71. *L'Avenir Lorraine*, 6 February 1937.

72. G. Cross, *Immigrant Workers*, p. 143.

73. R. Schor, 'Les Conditions de Vie', 47.

74. *Laroque Report*, pp. 64–5; R. Schor, 'Les Conditions de Vie', 47.

75. See P. Foot, *Immigration and Race in British Politics* (Harmondsworth: Penguin, 1965); D. Dean, 'The Conservative government and the 1961 Commonwealth Immigration Act: the inside story', *Race and Class* Vol. 35 (Dec. 1993) 57–74.

8 Élite Racism and the Colonial Lobby

1. The articles on freedom of movement were probably lost from sight as part of a much larger revision of the *Code de l'indigénat* that was pushed through by liberal reformers led by Albin Rozet. The Governor General, Lutaud, opposed the law as a whole. See G. Meynier, *L'Algérie Révélée*, p. 49. The *Directeur de la Sûreté générale de l'Algérie* in a note to the *Gouverneur Générale* of 22 November 1923 hinted at the

'oversight' of 1914, 'I truly believe that the legislature in 1914 did not foresee the importance of the Kabyle emigration ...' G. Massard-Guilbaud, *Algériens à Lyon*, p. 117.

2. The archives of the *Gouvernement Générale* at Aix-en-Provence hold a rich deposit of the correspondence and reports of the administrators concerning emigration. Every month they were required to send an intelligence report on a printed form which included a section, 'Exode des indigènes vers la Métropole', see AOM. B3–167 Constantine. The most popular subject for the numerous dissertations written by officers trained in the *Centre de Hautes Études d'administration Musulmane* (CHEAM) was the impact of emigration on the communes to which they were posted (see Bibliography).

3. See A. Merad, *Le Réformisme Musulman*, p. 130 on the crucial importance of the DAI. Its directors, Dominique Luciani, Augustin Berque, Jean Mirante, Louis Milliot and Colonel Paul Schoën, were able to shape native policy according to their own personal view of the 'indigènes' and almost regardless of the purposes of the executive and legislative.

4. On Octave Depont, see above Chapter 3.

5. On Gérolami see P. Godin, *Note sur le fonctionnement des Services indigènes*, pp. 64, 69; the journal *Akbar*, 31 December 1926; K. Bouguessa, *Émigration et Politique*, Appendix Document 19; G. Massard-Guilbaud, *Algériens à Lyon*, pp. 135, 140.

6. On Pierre Godin see N. Imbert, *Dictionnaire National des Contemporains* (Editions Lajeunesse, 1939) Vol. 3; *Bulletin Municipal Officielle de la Ville de Paris*, 1925 (Vol. 3) p. 2936. Godin wrote an eulogy to O. Depont in the foreward to the latter's *L'Algérie du Centenaire*.

7. For example, the leading oriental scholar Louis Massignon based his influential 1930 study of migrants in Paris, 'Carte de la répartition des Kabyles dans la région parisienne' on data suppied by Gérolami.

8. See above Chapter 3.

9. APP. BA. 67. correspondence and reports of the Governor General, Paris Prefect of Police, and Ministry of the Interior.

10. O. Depont, *L'Algérie du Centenaire*, p. 121.

11. N. Gomar, *Émigration Algérienne*, p. 43.

12. Raymond Williams, *The Country and the City* (London: Chatto and Windus, 1973) has looked at this discourse in English literature. A similar tradition of thought was prevalent in France, as in the work of Rousseau.

13. *La Tunisie Française*, 18 November 1923, quoted in Ben Fredj, *Aux origines de l'émigration*, pp. 268–9.

14. G. Mauco, *Les Étrangers en France*, p. 485; H. Baroin, *La Main-d'Oeuvre Étrangère*, p. 161 estimated Algerian criminality to be ten times higher than that of the French.

15. This can be gleaned from detailed statistics of Algerians found guilty in Paris between 1 January 1920 and mid-1923. See AOM. 9 H 112. statistics of Paris Prefecture de Police. The deliberate exaggeration and manipulation of data on Algerian criminality has been examined

by C. Ben Fredj, *Aux origines de l'émigration*, pp. 253–78; K. Bouguessà, *Émigration et Politique*, pp. 220–1; G. Massard-Guibaud, *Algériens à Lyon*, pp. 97–100; J.-J. Rager, *Musulmans Algériens en France*, pp. 286–9.

16. On the press image of Algerians see especially R. Schor, 'L'Opinion Française en les Immigrés Nord-Africains', 51–67.

17. B. Stora, *Histoire Politique de l'Immigration*, pp. 118–19. In Jean Damase's novel, *Sidi de Banlieue* (Fasquette, 1937) pp. 82, 108, syphilis is noted as 'hereditary' in North Africa where it has 'infected the total population'. A doctor complains in anger at, 'the importation of international diseases . . . every filthy symptom of the whole world comes here . . . here you can carry out research on every disgusting colonial type'. Microbic invasion and propagation has been a constant of racist discourse in the twentieth century, as with J.-M. Le Pen's claim that AIDS has been spread into Europe by immigrants from Africa. A considerable specialist medical literature was devoted to North African migration and disease pathways; see R. Schor, 'L'Opinion Française', 55–6. The evidence suggests that fewer pathogens were introduced by migrants from North Africa than were carried back from the squalid slums of France. Isolated Algerian rural communities were devastated by tuberculosis transmitted in this way.

18. See W. Anderson, 'Excremental Colonialism: Public Health and the Poetics of Pollution', *Critical Inquiry*, 21 (Spring 1995) 640–69; A.M. Kraut, *Silent Travellers. Germs, Genes, and the "Immigrant Menace"* (Baltimore: John Hopkins, 1994).

19. Jean Damase, *Sidi de Banlieue*, p. 29.

20. G. Meynier, Doctoral thesis, pp. 1078–80.

21. A. Stoler, 'Rethinking Colonial Categories: European Communities and the Boundaries of Rule', *Comparative Studies in Society and History*, Vol. 13, No. 1 (1989) 134–61; E. Hyam, *Empire and Sexuality* (Manchester: Manchester University Press, 1992).

22. G. Meynier, *L'Algérie Révélée*, pp. 436–9. For a more detailed examination of this issue see N. MacMaster, 'Sexual and Racial Boundaries'.

23. Report of administrator of Ténès 1919. This and other reports below are from AOM. A. D. A 2 149 quoted in G. Massard-Guilbert, *Algériens à Lyon*, pp. 63–9.

24. Administrator of Mizrana.

25. R. Fonville, *De la Condition en France et dans les Colonies françaises des indigènes des protectorats français* (E. Duchemin, 1924) p. 10, argued that owing to miscegenation, 'Our prestige in Europe will be seriously damaged . . .' Octave Depont, *L'Algérie du Centenaire*, p. 117 noted that North African men showed off photographs of French women, 'as pictures of some of their innumerable mistresses. These photos are passed from hand to hand in the tribes, exciting laughter and derision'. J. Ray, *Les Marocains en France*, p. 283 recognised the links between devaluation of French women and the undermining of masculine colonial authority. 'The ex-emigrant no longer has for his European bosses, for the officer of Native Affairs who administers him – *and above all for the wife of the latter* – the respect which he had before departing' [emphasis as in original text].

26. Administrator of Boghari.
27. *L'Echo d'Oran*, 21 September 1923.
28. G. Massard-Guilbaud, *Algériens à Lyon*, p. 62. My emphasis.
29. He wrote a major work with X. Coppolani, *Les confréries religieuses musulmanes* (Algiers: 1897) and numerous articles, including 'Le panislamisme et la propagande islamique', *Revue de Paris*, November 1899. In 1915 he was sent to Sétif to investigate an attack by army deserters on a train and in 1917 prepared a detailed report on the Batna insurrection of 1916–17. See G. Meynier, Doctoral thesis, Appendix LXXXX–LXXXXIV, CLXV.
30. O. Depont, *L'Algérie du Centenaire*, pp. 144–8.
31. *Ibid.*, pp. 121, 180. The emir Khaled, grandson of Abdel Kader who led the revolt against French occupation between 1830 and 1847, became a focus for nationalist opposition to colonialism; see A. Koulakssis and G. Meynier, *L'Émir Khaled* (Harmattan, 1987).
32. At the annual general meeting of the *Afrique Française*, 2 June 1923 Depont gave a long speech on 'La Main-d'Oeuvre Indigène de l'Afrique du Nord en France'. The text is in *La Reforme Sociale*, September–October 1923, 654–73. Among the several thousand subscribers to the *Comité de l'Afrique* were General Lyautey, who in 1924 introduced measures to stop labour migration from Morocco; Albert Sarraut, Minister of the Colonies in 1921, who as Minister of the Interior introduced a decree (4 April 1928) which reinforced controls on Algerian emigration; and Camille Chautemps, who, as Minister of the Interior in 1924, also introduced controls on Algerian emigration. See below and G. Meynier, *L'Algérie Révélée*, pp. 39–40. On the *Comité de l'Afrique* see S.M. Persell, *The French Colonial Lobby 1889–1938* (Stanford: Hoover Institution Press, 1983) pp. 3, 15–17, 148.
33. S.M. Persell, *Ibid.*, p. 149.
34. C.-R. Ageron, *Algériens Musulmans*, p. 856.
35. O. Depont, *L'Algérie du Centenaire*, pp. 56, 194, 235.
36. *El Akbar*, 19 July 1917, 'Voeu des colons de l'arrondissement de Miliana, 31 mai 1917', quoted in G. Meynier, Doctoral thesis, Annex CCXI.
37. *Dépêche de l'Est*, 5 December 1918 quoted in G. Meynier, Doctoral thesis, Annex CV.
38. Text of resolution in N. Gomar, *Émigration Algérienne*, pp. 83–5; see also AOM. 9 H 113, *Rapport sur l'émigration des indigènes* (1923), p. 23; G. Massard-Guilbaud, *Algériens à Lyon,* pp. 109–11.
39. N. Gomar, *Émigration Algérienne*, pp. 84–5.
40. AOM. 9 H 112, Administrator of Aïn-Tagrout to Sous-Préfet of Sétif, 20 July 1923.
41. A large number of these returns are in AOM. 9 H 112. Some, like those for Sétif and Batna, include the name, age, date of departure and address in France and provide a valuable historical source on the pattern of emigration.
42. The returns from the Prefects are in AOM. 9 H 112. Other copies, along with further correspondence, have been located by historians in some departmental archives.
43. The typed report of twenty-nine pages was probably prepared by

M. Fabregoule and Mohamed Smati, a member of the *Conseil supérieur*, who were sent to France on a 'mission d'étude'; see G. Massard-Guilbard, *Algériens à Lyon*, p. 99. Although undated, it was probably written in late 1923. The report (AOM. 9 H 113) along with the Prefectoral returns (AOM. 9 H 112) provide one of the most important historical sources on early emigration.

44. On the murders see above Chapter 7. The report was completed shortly after this event.
45. AOM. 9 H 112. Letter of 14 November 1923.
46. G. Massard-Guilbaud, *Algériens à Lyon*, p. 117.
47. AOM. 9 H 113. Letter from Confédération des Agriculteurs to the Governor General, 4 December 1923.
48. The Commission which was first established in 1916 was made up of representatives from all the main ministries, on this occasion the Ministries of Interior, Health, Labour and Agriculture, and employer and union delegates. It worked out the detail of legislative proposals which were then reported back to the *Conseil National de la Main-d'Oeuvre*. See N. Gomar, *Émigration Algérienne*, p. 86; G. Mauco, *Les Étrangers en France*, pp. 110–17; M. Mercier, *Étude sur la Crise de la Main-d'Oeuvre en Algérie* (Algiers: J. Carbonel, 1929) pp. 14–15.
49. The full text is in N. Gomar, *Émigration Algérienne*, pp. 86–7.
50. Chautemps stated in the *Commission Interministérielle* the political importance of giving to the natives the 'impression that we do not wish through these regulations to protect ourselves against them, but to provide protection for them': N. Gomar, *Émigration Algérienne*, p. 90.
51. AOM. 9 H 11. Prefect of Constantine to Gouvernement Générale, quoted in G. Massard-Guilbaud, *Algériens à Lyon*, p. 127.
52. AOM. 9 H 113. Letter from *Michelin* to Governor General, 10 October 1924, requesting information on the new procedures.
53. M. Mercier, *Étude sur la crise*, p. 24.
54. AOM. 9 H 113. Report of Maraval, Chef de la sûreté départementale, Algiers, 13 October 1924.
55. For example, in December 1923 the *Gouvernement* rejected requests from the administrators of Touggourt and Biskra for a halt; see G. Massart-Guilbaud, *Algériens à Lyon*, pp. 117–18. Pierre Godin spelt out the government position in some detail in July 1924: the new 'left' majority in parliament (*Cartel des Gauches*) would not accept such a reactionary move as to abolish the 1914 law as this would damage the reputation of France among the natives. 'To place them again under the yoke of the most abhorrent measures of the past would run the risk of destroying in one blow the results obtained by the most generous and intelligent of policies.' P. Godin, *Proposition concernant la 'question Kabyle à Paris'*, BAVP Côte 1783, No. 95 (31 July 1924) p. 2.
56. AOM. 9 H 113. Comment written on a typed note from Algiers, *Direction des Affaires indigènes* to Ministry of Interior, Paris, 26 November 1927.
57. *Délégations financières* 13 June 1924, quoted in G. Massard-Guilbaud, *Algériens à Lyon*, pp. 114–5.

58. AOM. 9 H 113, note from *Directeur de la Sécurité Générale d'Algérie* to *Directeur des Affaires Indigènes*, 25 August 1924.
59. N. Gomar, *Émigration Algérienne*, pp. 90–1.
60. AOM. 9 H 113. Copy of the decision of the *Conseil d'État*, 18 June 1923.
61. The decree, while removing the need for a work contract, added two further requirements, a certificate to show that the migrant had no criminal record and a sufficient sum of money to subsist while looking for work in France. N. Gomar, *Émigration Algérienne*, p. 94.
62. G.S. Cross, *Immigrant Workers*, pp. 50–2.
63. M. Paon, *L'Immigration en France* (Payot, 1926), insisted on the need for a coherent 'French immigration policy' under a single authority; see also L. Pasquet, *Immigration et Main-d'Oeuvre Étrangère en France* (Rieder, 1927); A. Pairault, *L'Immigration Organisée*; J.-C. Bonnet, *Les Pouvoirs Publics Français et l'Immigration dans l'Entre-Deux-Guerres* (Lyon: Centre d'histoire économique et sociale de la région lyonnaise, 1976).
64. G. Cross, *Immigrant Workers*, pp. 67–8; on the fragmented ministerial control of colonial policy see J. Ray, *Les Marocains en France*, pp. 266–7.
65. G. Meynier, *L'Algérie révélée*, pp. 11–12.
66. On this decree, named after the Minister of the Interior, Albert Sarraut, see N. Gomar, *Émigration Algérienne*, pp. 97–9.
67. G. Massaud-Guilbaud, *Algériens à Lyon*, p. 141. The 1928 decree was very briefly suspended by the Popular Front government on 17 July 1936. However, this was almost immediately eroded by a series of health controls introduced by the Governor General and the Minister of Health between 14 October 1936 and 29 January 1937. See L. Muracciole, *Émigration Algérienne*, p. 20; J.-J. Rager, *Musulmans Algériens en France*, p. 20.
68. AOM. 9 H 113, Telegramme of 1927 from Ministry of Interior to administrators requesting them to be 'very strict' in the issue of identity cards. In 1930 Tardieu, the Minister of the Interior, instructed the Governor General that medical certificates should not only be refused to those with evident signs of illness but also those who, 'appear predisposed to contract . . . contagious diseases': G. Massard-Guilbaud, *Algériens à Lyon*, p. 139.
69. P. Catrice, 'Les Musulmans en France' (1929), p. 337.
70. The inter-war migration of Tunisians was so insignificant that it gave rise to very little debate.
71. N. Gomar, *Émigration Algérienne*, p. 61. On the racialised categorisation of primitives as incapable of sustained productive effort see S.H. Alatas, *The Myth of the Lazy Native* (1977).
72. L. Talha, *Le Salariat Immigré*, pp. 73–8 on *Renault* and the *Organisation Scientifique du Travail*.
73. A. Pairault, *L'Immigration Organisée*, pp. 188–9. Another survey of 1924 which assessed 60 000 foreign workers in the metal and engineering industry also placed North-Africans last; *Ibid.*, p. 187.
74. G. Meynier, *L'Algérie révélée*, p. 466.
75. N. Gomar, *Émigration Algérienne*, p. 37. Similar comments can be found in G. Mauco, *Les Étrangers en France*, p. 269; B. Nogaro and L. Weil, *La*

Main-d'Oeuvre Étrangère, p. 26; H. Baroin, *La Main-d'Oeuvre Étrangère*, p. 124 and elsewhere.

76. J. Ray, *Les Marocains en France*, pp. 146–7 states that the evidence for this can be found in Pairault, nine pages before the table, but these comments (p. 180) refer to an entirely different survey.

77. N. Gomar, *Émigration Algérienne*, p. 37.

9 Policing and Surveillance in France

1. The extent to which police officers, soldiers, administrators, educators and missionaries, strongly influenced by long periods of service in European empires, introduced colonial/racist attitudes and practices into Europe is of considerable interest. The best study for Britain is P. Rich, *Race and Empire in British Politics* (Cambridge: CUP, 1986). The institutional impact was much weaker than in France and related mainly to the control of 'colonial' seamen in the ports.

2. M. Foucault, *Surveiller et punir* (Gallimard, 1975); G. Noiriel, *La Tyrannie du National* (Calmann-Levy, 1991).

3. C.-R. Ageron, *Les Algériens Musulmans*, especially pp. 168–83.

4. *Ibid.*, p. 175.

5. On the *bureaux arabes* of the Second Empire see R.J. Perkins, *Qaids, Captains and Colons. French Military Administration in the Colonial Maghrib, 1844–1934* (New York: Africana Publishing Company, 1981); Jean Morizot, *Les Kabyles*, gives a personal account of the work of an enlightened administrator; for a wider perspective, W.B. Cohen, *Rulers of Empire: the French Colonial Service in Africa* (Stanford: Hoover Institute, 1971).

6. C.-R. Ageron, *Ibid.*, p. 175.

7. P. Godin, *Note sur le Fonctionnement des Services des Indigènes*, p. 69.

8. N. Gomar, *Émigration Algérienne*, p. 25.

9. *Ibid.*, p. 113.

10. AOM. 8 H 61. There are many reports of this kind, see for example J-C. Bonnet, *Les Pouvoirs Publics Français et l'Immigration*, p. 53.

11. N. Gomar, *Émigration Algérienne*, p. 24.

12. For an excellent analysis of such strategies, a feature of peasant, colonial and slave societies in which open rebellion may be almost impossible, see James Scott, *Domination and the Arts of Resistance*.

13. Quoted by B. Stora, *Les Sources du Nationalisme Algérien* (Harmattain, 1989) p. 50. Stora also quotes from Franz Fanon, 'faced with the occupier, the occupied learn how to hide themselves, to deceive'.

14. C.-R. Ageron, *Algériens Musulmans*, p. 995. In colonial Algeria when workers spoke among themselves in Arabic and the *colon* master, suspecting a 'little conspiracy', demanded to know what was being said, one would always say in a French-Arab patois, 'laisse le *ghâfel*' or 'leave him dumb', meaning 'don't say everything': see A. Belbahri, *Immigration et Situations Postcoloniales* (Harmattan, 1987) p. 122.

15. J. Ray, *Les Marocains en France*, pp. 140 fn. 35, 348, 377; AOM. 9 H 113, *Rapport sur l'émigration des indigènes*, pp. 28–9.

16. AOM. 9 H 112. Report of Prefect of Pas de Calais to Ministry of the Interior, 12 November 1923.
17. G. Massard-Guilbaud, *Algériens à Lyon*, pp. 91–3.
18. Besombes wrote immediately after the murders to the Prefect of Police asking for measures to protect citizens against the 'nocturnal aggressions' of Algerians. *Le Petit Parisien*, 10 November 1923.
19. P. Godin, *Note sur le fonctionnement des Services Indigènes*, pp. 3–4.
20. *Ibid.*, pp. 9–10.
21. *Ibid.*, p. 9.
22. On 24 March 1924 a special commission was established to consider 'the various problems presented by the Algerian exodus to France'. This was chaired by the Minister of the Interior and consisted of the Prefect of the Seine, the Prefect of Police, the director of the *Sûreté Générale* in the Prefecture of the Seine, and three city councillors, Godin, Besombes and Massard. See C. Ben Fredj, *Aux origines de l'émigration*, p. 286. Godin, *Note sur le fonctionnement des Services Indigènes*, p. 115 noted that SAINA received special support from the Ministers of the Interior (Chautemps, Albert Sarraut), the Prefects of Police (Morain, Chiappe), the Prefects of the Seine (Boujou and Renard), and André Cornu, *Directeur des Affaires algériennes* and later deputy.
23. Gérolami described his own position in 1932 as, 'Principal administrator of the *commune mixte* with special status, put by the Minister of the Interior at the disposition of the Prefects of the Seine and of the Police ... an Algerian functionary on secondment'; P. Godin, *Note sur le fonctionnement des Services Indigènes*, p. 69. This illustrates perfectly the fluidity of relations between the colonial and Paris administrations.
24. André-Jean Godin was born in Algiers in 1900. A senior career administrator, he joined the Ministry of the Interior in August 1928 where he served as second secretary to the Minister, André Tardieu, before being seconded to the Prefecture of Police in 1932. During the Second World War he organised a Resistance network in the police force. From 1946 to 1956 he was a Gaullist deputy for the department of the Somme and in 1978 president of the *Alliance des hommes libres*, a political organisation close to the right-wing Poujadist movement UDCA (*Union de défense des commerçants et des artisans*). See his obituary in *Le Monde*, 30 August 1989, p. 7.
25. G. Massard-Guilbaud, *Algériens à Lyon*, pp. 385–6.
26. The timing of Pierre Godin's first proposal for the SAINA to the city council on 20 December 1923 may, in addition to the Rue Fondary murders, have been prompted by the decision of the Ministry for the Colonies one week earlier (12 December) to create the *Service de Contrôle et d'Assistance en France aux Indigènes des Colonies* (CAI) the aim of which was to counter nationalist and revolutionary organisations of Indo-Chinese and Black African origin.
27. P. Godin, *Émigration Algérienne*, p. 33.
28. In 1929 the brigade made 1253 arrests. P. Godin, *Note sur le fonctionnement des Services Indigènes*, p. 10.
29. The Paris Police Archives (APP) – BA 56 and BA 57 contain a mass of documents on the surveillance of the ENA.

30. It was André Godin who wrote an anonymous, typed report, *Note sur l'activité de l'Étoile-Nord-Africaine depuis sa création jusque'au 15 Novembre 1934* (174 pp.), Archives PP – BA 56. This is the single most important source on the history and structure of the ENA. On the arrest and trial of 1934 see B. Stora, *Messali Hadj*, pp. 123–7.

31. *L'Humanité*, 29 August 1926.

32. G. Massard-Guilbaud, *Algériens à Lyon*, pp. 417–38.

33. P. Godin, *Note sur le fonctionnement des Services Indigènes*, p. 15.

34. *Ibid.*, p. 11.

35. *Ibid.*, p. 16.

36. A central ambiguity of the administrative lobby was that it aimed to educate migrants into the values of modernity while simultaneously preserving the traditional social structures of 'tribal' society. This was a classic paradox of most colonial regimes.

37. P. Godin, *Note sur le fonctionnement des Services Indigènes*, pp. 16–17.

38. *Ibid.*, p. 39, Edouard Renard report to the Paris City Council 1932.

39. APP. BA 57, police report 16 July 1935 on a meeting attended by 350 to 400 North Africans. An ENA leaflet headed 'Muslims of North Africa!', circulated in 1934, called for an end to SAINA, 'This *commune mixte* installed in the very heart of Paris in order to impose the odious Native Code ...' APP. BA 56. Report of Inspector Michel, 27 May 1934.

40. P. Godin, *Note sur le fonctionnement des Services Indigènes*, pp. 6, 26. This appears to have been also known as the *Commission des affaires nord-africaines*. In 1926 the Committee had twelve members which included seven city councillors (among them Godin, Besombes and Emile Massard); Cazée, the director of public health; Touzan, director for employment; Chaumet, deputy director to the Prefect of Police; Disert, first secretary to the Prefect of Police; and Gérolami, head of SAINA.

41. There are excellent photographs of the Rue Lecomte facilities and the Gennevilliers hostel in L. Milliot, 'Les Kabyles à Paris', *Revue des Études Islamiques*, Vol. 6 (1932) 162–74.

42. *Ibid.*, pp. 20–2.

43. N. Gomar, *Émigration Algérienne*, p. 121.

44. H. Baroin, *La Main-d'Oeuvre Étrangère*, pp. 134–40.

45. J. Azario, director of the Lyons service, proposing such an index noted it would list the address and exact identity of each migrant, avoid errors of homonymy common with Arab names, and track the movement of 'certain arab propagandists'. G. Massard-Guilbaud, *Algériens à Lyon*, p. 396.

46. See G. Noiriel, *La Tyrannie du National*, Part 2, 'Surveiller et Secourie', pp. 45–57.

47. M. Mercier, *Étude sur la crise de la main-d'oeuvre*, p. 14. On the expulsion of Moroccans by SAINA see J. Ray, *Les Marocains en France*, pp. 364–70.

48. G. Massard-Guilbaud, *Algériens à Lyon*, p. 140.

49. AOM. 9 H 113, Commissaire de Police of Bône to Sub-Prefect, 14 December 1926, criticising the action.

50. N. Gomar, *Émigration Algérienne*, pp. 112–13. During the 1930s depression functionaries constantly regretted the inability of the government

to resort to forced repatriation. See R. Schor, 'Les conditions de vie des immigrés Nord-Africains dans la Meurthe-et-Moselle', 43.

51. G. Cross, *Immigrant Workers*, p. 181, notes that expulsion of foreigners, particularly those who were active in left-wing politics or unions, was a standard practice. Between 1920 and 1932 some 93 131 immigrants were thus expelled by administrative means and without any right to judicial appeal.

52. Job applications to the bureau helped the Rue Lecomte to generate a further 7148 files by the end of 1929: see N. Gomar, *Émigration Algérienne*, p. 126.

53. G. Massard-Guilbaud, *Algériens à Lyon*, p. 408.

54. C. Ben Fredj, *Aux origines de l'émigration*, pp. 678–84. The strike-breaking functions of SAINA were exposed by the Communist councillor Emmanuel Fleury during a heated debate in the Paris council on 1 January 1937. He also accused SAINA of recruiting Algerians for fascist organisations, including the *Parti social français*, the *Solidarité fasciste* of Jean Renaud, and the *Croix de feu*. See *Bulletin Municipal Officiel de la Ville de Paris*, Council Debate 1 January 1937, pp. 27–45.

55. G. Massard-Guilbaud, *Algériens à Lyon*, pp. 398–407 on the 'Versille Affair' and the use of Algerian strike-breakers by other Lyons companies (*Vergne, Vuillod-Ancel*).

56. C. Ben Fredj, *Aux origines de l'émigration*, pp. 292, 550–60.

57. G. Massard-Guilbaud, *Algériens à Lyon*, pp. 408–10.

58. O. Depont, *L'Algérie du Centenaire*, pp. 131–2. The hostels were established by a *Comité d'assistance aux Indigènes Algériens* in Algiers founded by Louis Billiard, President of the Algiers Chamber of Commerce, and were funded by the *Gouvernement Général*.

59. AOM. 9 H 112. Letter from Chardenet to the President of the *Comité d'Assistance*, April 1923, detailed the problems in Paris where groups of natives were 'errants en quête d'un abri'.

60. J. Ray, *Les Marocains en France*, p. 346.

61. P. Godin, *Note sur le fonctionnement des Services Indigènes*, pp. 38–41, J. Ray, *Les Marocains en France*, pp. 346–8.

62. *Laroque Report*, pp. 300–3.

63. APP. BA 56. Police report 15 January 1934.

64. The ENA journal *El Ouma*, October 1933, quoted in C. Ben Fredj, *Aux origines de l'émigration*, p. 849.

65. B. Stora, *Messali Hadj*, pp. 105–7.

66. P. Godin, *Note sur le fonctionnement des Services Indigènes*, pp. 26–32; J. Ray, *Les Marocains en France*, pp. 351–3. The medical personnel were required to have a knowledge of Arabic or Berber.

67. The 'Moorish' façade of the original hospital gatehouse still exists as part of the modern Avicenne Hospital, renamed in 1978 to dissociate it from its colonialist origins and its associations with the '*bicots*'.

68. P. Godin, *Note sur le fonctionnement des Services Indigènes*, pp. 42–72. Although the hospital records were destroyed in the Second War there is a wealth of information on the hospital in O. Depont, *Les Berbères en France. L'hôpital franco-musulman de Paris et du département de la Seine*

(Lille: 1937); A. Boukhelloua, *L'Hôpital Franco-Musulman de Paris* and the thesis of J. Chevillard-Vabre, *Histoire de l'Hôpital Franco-Musulman.*

69. The project was, for example, supported by the Islamic scholar Louis Massignon, who was known for his liberal stance towards the Algerians.

70. P. Godin, *Note sur le fonctionnement des Services Indigènes*, p. 14. N. Gomar, *Émigration Algérienne*, pp. 131–2 described the hospital as, 'an instrument of propaganda among the Muslim masses in France', in the same was as 'colonial doctors have always been apostles of our influence'. On the ideological functions of colonial medicine see A. Marcovich, 'French colonial medicine and colonial rule: Algeria and Tunisia' in R. MacLeod and M. Lewis (eds), *Disease, Medicine and Empire* (London: Routledge, 1988) pp. 103–17.

71. O. Depont, *L'Algérie du Centenaire*, p. 137.

72. A. Boukhelloua, *L'Hôpital Franco-Musulman*, pp. 31–2, 97. Ahmed Boukhelloua, an educated francophile, shared these anxieties and referred to the 'ombre de la police'.

73. *Ibid.*, p. 90.

74. *Le Peuple*, 15 November 1937, quoted in C. Ben Fredj, *Aux origines de l'émigration*, p. 354.

75. APP. BA 56. Police report 22 September 1936; C. Ben Fredj, *Aux origines de l'émigration*, p. 352. Messali Hadj said that North Africans were isolated in the hospital, 'like an inferior race, plague victims'. Memoires Ms. Cahier No. 8, p. 1957, quoted in B. Stora, *Histoire Politique de l'Immigration*, p. 121.

76. P. Godin, *Note sur le fonctionnement des Services Indigènes*, pp. 16, 22–4.

77. J.-J. Rager, *Musulmanes Algériens en France*, p. 285.

78. G. Pervillé, *Les étudiants algériens*, pp. 52–5; P. Godin, *Note sur le fonctionnement des Services Indigènes*, p. 99.

79. On this dispute see P. Godin, *Note sur le fonctionnement des Services Indigènes*, pp. 89–105.

80. G. Pervillé, *Les étudiants algériens*, pp. 99–100. Soon after, in 1936, the *Cercle* in the Rue Gay-Lussac was closed down: see J. Ray, *Les Marocains en France*, p. 350.

81. J. Ray, *Les Marocains en France*, p. 343. The Director of the Saint-Etienne SAINA was a former Algerian administrator. There is a photograph of a *chikaïa* in session in the Rue Lecomte in L. Milliot, 'Les Kabyles à Paris', *Revue des Études Islamiques*, Vol. 6 (1932) 172.

82. Archives CHEAM, No. 3511. Commander Cunibile, *L'Assistance Technique aux Français Musulmans d'Algérie à la Prefecture de Police* (April 1961) pp. 53, 78–81.

83. G. Massard-Guilbaud, *Algériens à Lyon*, pp. 417–21, 445.

84. O. Depont, *L'Algérie du Centenaire*, pp. 140–1. Sarraut was strengthened in his resolve to extend the SAINA by a recent trip to Algeria.

85. *Laroque Report*, p. 218. In Saint-Etienne the director was Vauthier, an ex-administrator from Algeria, and in Lyons Julien Azario, ex-administrator from Morocco.

86. G. Massard-Guilbaud, *Algériens à Lyon*, pp. 384, 395–7. Between 1928 and 1934 the Lyons area was in principle served by the SAINA in Saint-Etienne. However, many of the functions of the *Service* were

carried out in Lyons during this period by a *Comité pour la protection des travailleurs nord-africain,* to which Julien Azario was secretary.

87. See the *Laroque Report,* pp. 219–21, which was highly critical of the failure of the SAINA.
88. APP. BA 56. *Note sur l'activité de l'Étoile-Nord-Africaine,* pp. 172–3.
89. J.D. Zagoria, *The Rise and Fall of Messali Hadj,* pp. 2, 355–7.
90. *Laroque Report,* p. 212.

10 Colonial Crisis and Emigration, 1930–54

1. Colonial writers recognised this spatial relationship between low emigration and zones of European settlement, but attributed it largely to the wonderful benefits of French civilisation and generous wages. Thus J.-J. Rager, *Musulmans Algériens en France,* p. 106, 'Emigration is insignificant from the regions of colonisation. The latter absorb local labour. The migratory phenomenon results essentially from demographic growth in the mountain regions and not, as certain tendentious thinkers try to claim, from expropriation of the land'. The pro-colonialist bias of the argument may have deterred neo-Marxist historians from exploring further the nature of this geographical distribution.
2. L. Talha, *Le Salariat Immigré,* p. 94.
3. The 1919 inquiry by the *Gouvernement Générale* on the adaptation of workers and soldiers who had returned from France after the war found that men from the 'Arab' zones like Boghari, Chélif, Aumale and Tablat had no wish to return, unlike those from Kabylia. G. Massard-Guilbaud, *Algériens à Lyon,* pp. 67–8.
4. Thus L. Talha, *Le Salariat Immigré,* p. 94 uses the following quotation from Rager, 'The arrondissement of Miliana has no migration to speak of. The majority of the 136 Muslims having left this administrative unit for France are demobilised soldiers.' This is a very low level of emigration. In such regions ex-soldiers carried little influence and were regarded with low esteem as uprooted misfits and wine drinkers who neglected religious duties. See G. Meynier, *L'Algérie révélée,* p. 91.
5. See above Chapter 3.
6. J. Connell, *Migration from Rural Areas,* in a review of the literature on migration argues that almost no research has been carried out on 'low-migration' villages as a control and to show what factors might work against mobility. *Ibid.,* pp. 39, 218.
7. J. Van Vollenhoven, *Essai sur le Fellah,* p. 250. See N. Gomar, *Émigration Algérienne,* p. 76, 'Too often the *colons* employ the natives during the day and, come the evening, even if their village is far away, send them away to spend the night no matter where.'
8. P. Carayol, 'Les Genres de vie Indigènes dans l'Atlas de Blida', *Revue Africaine,* Vol. 87 (1943) 239–65; G. Mutin, *La Mitidja: décolonisation et espace géographique* (CNRS, 1977) pp. 31–2.
9. X. Yacono, *La colonisation du Chélif.*
10. C.-R. Ageron, *Algériens Musulmans,* p. 754.
11. J. Lizot, *Metidja. Un Village Algérien,* p. 140. The *Laroque Report,* p. 94 noted, 'that the natives prefer to work near home rather than to go

to France if they are offered reasonable wages, even if they are well below those of the metropole'; L. Chevalier, *Le Problème Démographique*, p. 130 notes the same pattern. A.D. Goddard, 'Population movements and land shortages in the Sokoto close-settled zone, Nigeria', in S. Amin (ed.), *Modern Migrations in Western Africa* (1974) pp. 258–80 demonstrates a similar, 'clear inverse relationship between migration and local opportunities for earning cash incomes'.

12. The one major exception in Kabylia was the heavily colonised valley of the Soummam. G. Massard-Guilbaud, *Algériens à Lyon*, in an otherwise excellent thesis, also faces some difficulty in explaining why emigration was primarily from Kabylia. This, she argues, was due to the brutality of land seizure following the 1871 insurrection. The evidence is weak and does not square with the overwhelming evidence that Kabyle peasant society remained largely intact. However Massard-Guilbaud's own detailed evidence contradicts her thesis. In the valley floor of the Soummam there was little emigration from the *communes de plein exercise* where extensive colonisation led to proletarianisation of the natives. In the *communes mixtes* of the mountains bordering the valley, where there was a property-owning peasantry and little wage-labour, there was intensive emigration. *Ibid.*, pp. 178–88. This 'Kabyle anomaly' fits my argument perfectly.

13. C.-R. Ageron, *Algériens Musulmans*, pp. 505, 628, 653; C. Collot, *Les Institutions de l'Algérie*, pp. 298–9. G. Meynier, Doctoral thesis, p. LXXXXVI quotes oral evidence from a Kabyle who described the difficulty of inciting rebellion in the highly colonised Oran region during the First World War, 'Unlike the Kabyles, the people of the Oran region were as if in a cage; they worked from sunrise to sunset. Working for the *colon* one has no idea what's going on in the world and there are too many Europeans to allow a rising.'

14. The Prefect of Constantine, for example, in a letter to the Governor General, 27 August 1932, AOM. 9 H 113, complained of the terrible impact of repatriation by the Paris SAINA of Kabyle migrants. Back home agricultural wages were, 'undergoing a worrying deterioration', reaching three to four francs per day, totally insufficient to feed a family since grain prices were climbing. 'One can imagine, under these conditions, the terrible privations these men undergo but who have to still continue their back-breaking labour.'

15. H. Isnard, quoted in M. Côte, *L'Algérie*, p. 163.

16. M. Rouissi, *Population et Société au Maghreb* (Tunis: Cérès, 1983) p. 69.

17. J.H. Meuleman, *Le Constantinois entre les deux guerres mondiales. L'évolution économique et sociale de la population rurale* (Assen: Van Gorcum, 1985) p. 106.

18. J.H. Meuleman, *Le Constantinois*, p. 184. The increase was based on the difference between annual births per thousand, the fastest changing factor, and annual deaths per thousand, which were falling slowly.

19. AOM. 8 X 453, 'Sur les Hauts Plateaux Constantinois. La Commune Mixte des Eulma' (typescript, 1937), by the Deputy-Administrator, Roger Troussel. An abbreviated version was published in the *Revue Africaine*, Vol. 85 (1941) 230–57.

20. A Prenant, 'Facteurs du peuplement d'une ville de l'Algérie intérieure: Sétif', *Annales de Géographie* LXXII (Nov.–Dec. 1953) 434–51. On the similar pattern of migration into Algiers see R. Descloitres *et al.*, *L'Algérie des Bidonvilles. Le Tiers Monde dans la Cité* (Mounton, 1961); R. Lespès, *Alger. Étude de Géographie et d'Histoire Urbaines* (Alcan, 1930); and F. Benatia, *Alger: agrégat ou cité. L'intégration citadine de 1919 à 1979* (Algiers: SNED, 1980).

21. See above Chapter 3 on the distinction between 'closed' and 'open' villages. This pattern was particularly evident in the case of traditional internal migration from the Saharan Mozabite towns renowned for the stark, rigorist practice of the Abadite sect. See J.-J. Rager, *Musulmans Algériens en France*, pp. 26–30; J. Morizot, *L'Algérie kabylisée*, pp. 28–31.

22. M. Bennoune, *Impact of Colonialism*, pp. 142–54 provides much detailed evidence for the *douar* of El Akbia of the transition from internal labour migration (harvesting, mining, construction, dock work) to emigration.

23. M. Mercier, *Étude sur la Crise de la Main-d'Oeuvre*, p. 9, noted the spread of emigration into the region north of Sétif in 1928. See also J. Morizot, *L'Algérie kabylisée*, pp. 90–3.

24. AOM. 8 X 459, R. Troussel, *Sur les Hauts Plateaux*, p. 68.

25. AOM. 9 H 113 contains an extensive correspondence from landowner groups to government officials on the labour 'shortage'. It is interesting to note that farmers, including wealthy *caïds*, in the *commune mixte* of Jemappes in June 1927 placed pressure on the government not only to block emigration to France but also to restore the old permits required before 1914 to travel and work outside the commune.

26. J.H. Meuleman, *Le Constantinois*, pp. 104–5.

27. G. Massard-Guilbaud, *Algériens à Lyon*, pp. 162, 484 has established for the Lyons region an increase in migrants from the High Plains of Constantine from 3.1 per cent of all Algerians in 1923 to 16.2 per cent in 1926, 18.5 in 1931 and 27.9 in 1936.

28. J.H. Meuleman, *Le Constantinois*, pp. 179–83.

29. The *Laroque Report*, pp. 44, 89 had noticed the recent arrival of a few families in 1937–8 and raised the question whether emigration was entering a new phase.

30. G. Massard-Guilbaud, *Algériens à Lyon*, pp. 236–8, 247, 507–8.

31. *Laroque Report*, pp. 82–3.

32. Six months' residence in France gave Algerians the right to unemployment benefit, which was preferable to the terrible poverty facing men who returned home.

33. Decree of 1 August 1936. The *Laroque Report*, p. 93, noted by 1937–8 a 'plethora of labour'.

34. J.-J. Rager, *Musulmans Algériens en France*, pp. 71, 138; Morizot, *L'Algérie Kabylisée*, p. 96

35. B. Stora, *Ils Venaient d'Algérie*, p. 76. On the war period see also B. Hifi, *L'immigration Algérienne en France*, pp. 115–20.

36. J.-J. Rager, *Musulmans Algériens en France*, pp. 73–4.

37. The figures given by L. Chevalier, *Le Problème Démographique*, p. 184

and L. Muracciole, *Émigration Algérienne*, p. 114, of 15 to 20 000 mixed Algerian-European births seems exaggerated.

38. B. Stora, *Ils Venaient d'Algérie*, p. 79 gives a figure of 60 000, but this refers to only a partial census by the Labour Office, and derives indirectly from P. Berthod, *Le Problème de la Main-d'Oeuvre Nord-Africaine en France*, Doctorate, Faculty of Law, University of Paris (1946), pp. 13–26. Stora *Ibid.*, p. 40 agrees with most other authorities that there were about 120 000 men in France on the eve of the war. However, the balance of movement for 1940–2 (departures minus returns) was only –3036 (see Table A1). L. Muracciole's, *Émigration Algérienne*, p. 45, estimation of 120 000 Algerians in France at the Liberation seems most likely.

39. The native administrator of the *commune mixte* of Soummam wrote to the Prefect of Constantine in June 1943 that families of emigrants, receiving no more money, were 'in utter destitution and urgently need to be provided with aid'. J.-J. Rager, *Musulmans Algériens en France*, p. 96.

40. A. Horne, *A Savage War of Peace* (London: Macmillan, 1987 edition) p. 42.

41. L. Chevalier, *Le Problème Démographique*, pp. 77–96 provides a detailed analysis of the crisis. See also J.-J. Rager, *Musulmans Algériens en France*, pp. 111, 157.

42. By an ordonnance of 7 March 1944, De Gaulle extended to all Algerian Muslims the rights and duties of French citizens. Full citizenship, including the right to freedom of movement, was eventually confirmed in the Organic Law of 20 September 1947. See L. Muracciole, *Émigration Algérienne*, pp. 119–20.

43. L. Muracciole, *Émigration Algérienne*, pp. 22–3. J-J. Rager, *Musulmans Algériens en France*, pp. 81–2 notes that contract workers declined from 5.4 per cent of total Algerian emigrants in 1946 to 0.05 per cent in 1948.

44. R. Gallissot, 'Émigration Coloniale, Immigration Post-Coloniale', 31–49.

45. L. Chevalier, *Le Problème Démographique*, p. 143.

46. Details of the companies involved and the origin and size of each convoy of workers can be found in J.-J. Rager, *Musulmans Algériens en France*, p. 173; L. Chevalier, *Le Problème Démographique*, p. 149.

47. L. Muracciole, *Émigration Algérienne*, pp. 97–8. In 1949 there were more departures from the Department of Algiers by plane (33 000) than by ship (25 000).

48. J.-J. Rager, *Musulmans Algériens en France*, p. 80.

49. L. Muracciole, *Émigration Algérienne*, pp. 54–5; L. Henry *et al.*, *Les Algériens en France*, pp. 91–4.

50. J. Morizot, *L'Algérie kabylisée*, pp. 107–8 draws a sharp distinction between the traditional Kabyle forms of emigration and the new 'Arab' type, 'an emigration of fatalism and final rupture. It did not follow any pattern or tradition, quite at random, involving as it did people who were much more frustrated . . . and much more ignorant.'

51. AOM. 762. R. Montagne, *Rapport Provisoire*, pp. 12–13 notes work 'commandos' from the High Plains region who avoided the Kabyle bastion

of Paris. Montagne maps a spectacular 'conquest' of the Moselle steel towns by thousands of men from the Arab-speaking region of El-Milia, north-west of Constantine. M. Bennoune, *Impact of Colonialism* provides an excellent and detailed investigation of this type of 'new' emigration which started in 1946 from the *douar* of El Akbia near El-Milia, to Mulhouse.

52. L. Muracciole, *Émigration Algérienne*, pp. 28, 99–100.
53. L. Henry *et al.*, *Les Algériens en France*, pp. 58–60.
54. J.-J. Rager, *Musulmans Algériens en France*, pp. 261–74 on family groups in Champigny (Seine), Briey (Pas-de-Calais) and Aix-en-Provence; L. Henry *et al.*, *Les Algériens en France*, pp. 127–56 on families in Seine-et-Marne and Marseilles; and A. Girard, 'Familles Algériennes Musulmanes dans l'Agglomeration Parisienne', Chapter 2 in J. Stoetzel and A. Girard, *Français et immigrés*. Vol. 2, INED, Travaux et Documents, Cahier No. 20 (Presses Universitaires de France, 1954).
55. L. Muracciole, *Émigration Algérienne*, pp. 80–1, 103–5; J.-J. Rager, *Musulmans Algériens en France*, pp. 217–38.
56. A. Sayad, 'Les trois "âges"'.
57. L. Muracciole, *Émigration Algérienne*, pp. 15, 30. In early 1949 reports on Algerian migration to France were commissioned by the Ministries of the Interior, Labour, Finance, Defence, and Population and Public Health.
58. This list is by no means exhaustive. The CHEAM archives in Paris contain studies of North African emigration by M. Aldou (1948), Demondion (50), J. Etienne (50), M. Piquard (50), J. Vialatte de Pemille (51), Jean de Felix (51), A. Roche (51), Villey (52), N. Vadi (52), P. Vigo (52), Coste-Florat (54), Didier (54) and others.
59. L. Chevalier, *Le problème Démographique*, p. 180. The demographer Louis Henry estimated that the Muslim population of Algeria would increase from its 1948 level of seven and a half million to between ten and thirteen million by 1976.
60. L. Muracciole, *Émigration Algérienne*, p. 22. On the wider context of post-war planning see R. Kuisel, *Capitalism and the State in Modern France* (Cambridge: Cambridge University Press, 1981).
61. This was the standard theory of colonial crisis during 1945–54. Jacques Breil, a demographer working in the *Service Statistique de l'Algérie*, argued that 'the maximum population beyond which there would be a dangerous disequilibrium between population and resources has been passed in Algeria twelve years ago', quoted in J.-J. Rager, *Musulmans Algériens en France*, p. 96; L. Muracciole, *Émigration Algérienne*, p. 68 remarks that theories of 'demographic pressure' were 'à la mode', and seen as the 'cause of every problem Algeria faces!'
62. L. Muracciole, *Émigration Algérienne*, p. 89.
63. L. Muracciole, *Émigration Algérienne*, pp. 69–75. For Chevalier, *Le Problème Démographique*, p. 119, the impact of 'our African colonisation' in producing a huge population growth was, 'more of an embarrassing justification than a condemnation'. Rager, *Musulmans Algériens en France*, pp. 299–301 agreed that the 'disequilibrium' between population and resources followed from a gap between the success of public

health programmes and the failings of agriculture faced with adverse soil and climatic conditions.

64. J.-J. Rager, *Musulmans Algériens en France,* pp. 97–8.

65. Population pressure was thought to be so great that various controversial proposals were made for the resettlement of Algerians in Niger, Guyana and Madagascar. L. Chevalier, *Le Problème Démographique,* pp. 136–7; J.-J. Rager, *Musulmans Algériens en France,* p. 308.

66. L. Chevalier, *Le Problème Démographique,* p. 211.

67. In June 1940 the collaborator Richard Christmann, an ex-legionnaire and fascist supporter of Bucard's *Chemises bleues* during the Popular Front, was recruited to work for German counter-intelligence in Paris. He immediately seized the files of the SAINA in order to locate and organise Algerian nationalists opposed to France. On this and Algerian migrant collaborationism during the war see R. Faligot and R. Kauffer, *Le Croissant et la Croix Gammée.* J.-L. Einaudi, *La bataille de Paris. 17 Octobre 1961* (Seuil, 1991) p. 47 notes that the *Brigade nord-africaine* of the Rue Lecomte was known to have provided some of the principal French auxiliaries to the Gestapo. If the SAINA files still exist they would constitute the richest source on Algerian emigration and nationalist organisation before 1945.

68. J.-J. Rager, *Musulmans Algériens en France,* pp. 291–2. In a similar way in nineteenth century Europe, Christian revivalism in industrial-urban centres was seen as the antidote to the dissolving forces of materialism and atheism and the means to reconstruct a moral order based on face-to-face paternalism and an aristocratic hierarchy derived from rural society.

69. The study was undertaken by the *Bureau d'études des mouvements de main-d'oeuvre nord-africaine en France,* a unit established under the wing of the *Direction de l'action sociale musulmane* of the Ministry of the Interior. The *Bureau* went on to complete Montagne's study after his death in 1954. See A and J. Belkhodja, *Les Africains du Nord,* p. 23.

70. R. Montagne, 'L'Emigration Nord-Africaine en France', p. 366.

71. The official Laroque Report of 1938 was perhaps the first source to elaborate on a model of differential Berber and Arab zones of emigration.

72. For a critique of Montagne's theory see N. MacMaster, 'Patterns of Emigration'. On Montagne's anthropology see E. Gellner, *Muslim Society* (Cambridge: CUP, 1981), Chapter 8, 'The sociology of Robert Montagne (1893–1954)'; D. Seddon's Introduction to R. Montagne, *The Berbers: Their Social and Political Organisation* (London: Frank Cass, 1973).

73. M. Cornaton, *Les Regroupements de la décolonisation en Algérie* (Editions Ouvrières, 1967) p. 60.

11 Emigration and the Algerian War, 1954–62

1. The figures are from the table in A. Gillette and A. Sayad, *L'Immigration Algérienne en France,* pp. 258–9.

2. L. Henry *et al., Les Algériens en France,* pp. 144, 153–6.

3. A. Belbahri, *Immigration et Situations Postcoloniales*, pp. 84–5. Zoulika felt that there was more racism in the 1980s than during the Algerian war.

4. A. Michel, *Les Travailleurs Algériens en France*, pp. 152–3.

5. J.-J. Rager, *Musulmans Algériens en France*, pp. 288–9; L. Muracciole, *Émigration Algérienne*, p. 112.

6. J.-J. Rager, *Ibid.*, p. 289. P.-B. Lafont, 'La Criminalité Nord-Africaine dans la Région Parisienne', in *Esprit* (September 1953) 426–37, provides detailed statistics on crime rates for 1947–50 which shows that press reports exaggerated the seriousness of North African criminality and its rate of increase. Most infractions were relatively minor, and most acts of violence were not against Frenchmen but other North Africans.

7. On this and similar incidents, see A. Michel, *Les Travailleurs Algériens*, p. 161. See also T. Alall *et al.*, *Situations migratoires*, pp. 82–3.

8. Another case, from November 1966, illustrates the pattern. *Le Parisien Libéré*, 'It's like a jungle for women alone . . . At Bagneux, Luce (14 years) was sexually assaulted by four Algerians within 50 metres of a council block'. According to *France-Soir*, one held a knife to the throat of her younger sister Ariane. A few days later *Le Parisien Libéré* announced simply that the girl had lied. Even children were now able to manipulate the automaticity of responses and scapegoating. See J. Augarde, *La Migration Algérienne* (Hommes et Migrations, 1970) pp. 99–100.

9. J.-L. Einaudi, *La Bataille de Paris*, p. 47.

10. J.-J. Rager, *Musulmans Algériens en France*, p. 288.

11. At the end of the traditional Bastille Day demonstration of 14 July 1953 six Algerians were shot and killed by the police.

12. A. Michel, *Les Travailleurs Algériens*, pp. 155–6; report by Pierre Joffroy in *Paris-Match*, 20–7 August 1955. On the ghetto in general see J.-C. Toubon and K. Messamah, *Centralité Immigrée*; V. Vuddamalay, P. White and D. Sporton, 'The evolution of the Goutte d'Or as an ethnic minority district in Paris', *New Community*, Vol. 17 (Jan. 1991) 245–58.

13. *Le Monde*, 11 March 1956, quoted by A. Michel, *Les Travailleurs Algériens*, p. 157.

14. On conditions see M. Hervo and M.-A. Charras, *Bidonvilles* (Maspero, 1971); A. Sayad, *Un Nanterre algérien, terre de bidonvilles* (Éditions Autrement, 1995). There are interesting photographs of the Nanterre shantytowns in A. Tristan, *Le silence du fleuve* (Bezons: Au nom de la mémoire, 1991) pp. 14–23.

15. A. El Gharbaoui, 'Les travailleurs maghrébines immigrés dans la banlieue nord-est de Paris', pp. 15–17.

16. J.-L. Einaudi, *Le Bataille de Paris*, p. 35.

17. A. El Gharbaoui, 'Les travailleurs maghrébins', p. 51.

18. A. and J. Belkhodja, *Les Africains du Nord*, pp. 127–34.

19. A. El Gharbaoui, 'Les travailleurs maghrébins', p. 52; R. Grillo, *Ideologies and institutions in urban France*, pp. 130–7, has a detailed analysis of official theories of 'action socio-educative'.

20. See the photograph of a typical *cité*, barrack-like rows of prefabricated

huts, with a flag-pole to the fore, in A and J. Belkhodja, *Les Africains du Nord*, p. 121.

21. M. Ginesy-Galano, *Les Immigrés Hors La Cité. Le Système d'Encadrement dans les Foyers (1973–1982)*, (Harmattan, 1984) p. 29. SONACOTRA was part financed by the Algerian *Gouvernement Générale* and A. El Gharbaoui, 'Les travailleurs maghrébins', p. 53, notes that its promoters, 'are still profoundly imbued with colonial ideas'.

22. A. El Gharbaoui, 'Les travailleurs maghrébins', pp. 49–53.

23. N. MacMaster, 'The *seuil de tolérance*'; also 'Social tensions and racism in a "grand ensemble"', *Modern and Contemporary France*, No. 39 (Oct. 1989) 11–23.

24. The most detailed analysis of this civil war can be found in B. Stora, *Ils Venaient d'Algérie*, pp. 151–221, and in the book of a leading FLN organiser, Ali Haroun, *La 7e Wilaya. La Guerre du FLN en France, 1954–1962* (Seuil, 1986).

25. On FLN fundraising see B. Stora, *Ils Venaient d'Algérie*, pp. 162–9.

26. B. Stora, *Ils Venaient d'Algérie*, pp. 343–51.

27. On Papon see J.-L. Einaudi, *La Bataille de Paris*, pp. 39–57, and Papon's uninformative autobiography, *Les Chevaux du Pouvoir* (Plon, 1988). Since 1981 he has stood accused, and in January 1996 was indicted, for his role in the deportation of Jews from the Bordeaux region to the concentration camps in 1942–4. See M. Slitinsky, *L'Affaire Papon* (Alain Moreau, 1983); *The Guardian*, 2 January 1996.

28. One of the founding officers of the SAT, Commander Cunibile, wrote a detailed account of the organisation's structure and operations, *L'Assistance Technique aux Français Musulmans d'Algérie à la Prefecture de Police*, (April 1961), CHEAM archives, No. 3511.

29. Cunibile, *L'Assistance Technique*, pp. 67–8.

30. *Ibid.*, pp. 51–2, 84–7.

31. See B. Stora, *Ils Venaient d'Algérie*, pp. 303–6; P. Péju, *Les Harkis à Paris* (Maspero, 1961).

32. J.-P. Rioux and J.-F. Sirinelli (eds), *La Guerre d'Algérie et les intellectuels francais* (Brussels: Complexe, 1991); J.-F. Sirinelli, 'Les intellectuels dans la mêlée', in J.-P. Rioux (ed.), *La Guerre d'Algérie et les Français* (Fayard, 1990) pp. 116–30.

33. C.-R. Ageron, 'L'Opinion Française à travers les sondages', in J.-P. Rioux (ed.), *La Guerre d'Algérie*, pp. 25–44.

34. A. Frémont, 'Le Contingent: Témoignage et Réflexion' in J.-P. Rioux (ed.), *La Guerre d'Algérie*, pp. 84–5.

35. C.-R. Ageron, 'Les Français Devant la Guerre Civile Algérienne', in J.-P. Rioux (ed.), *La Guerre d'Algérie*, pp. 53–62.

36. A. Haroun, *La 7e Wilaya*, pp. 87–111.

37. *Ibid.*, p. 104.

38. On the October events see P. Péju, *Ratonnades à Paris* (Maspero, 1961), which was seized by the police; M. Levine, *Les Ratonnades d'Octobre. Un Meutre Collectif à Paris en 1961* (Ramsay, 1985); J.-L. Einaudi, *Le Bataille de Paris*; and A. Tristan, *Le silence du fleuve*, which has numerous photographs. On 13 July 1992 Channel 4 showed an excellent one-hour documentary on the massacre, 'Secret History: Drowning by Bullets'.

39. J.-L. Einaudi, *Le Bataille de Paris*, pp. 83–4, 250–2.
40. Speech in the National Assembly 30 October 1961, quoted in J.-L. Einaudi, *Le Bataille de Paris*, p. 258.
41. On those who gave clandestine support to the Algerians, including the movement of FLN funds, see H. Hamon and P. Rotman, *Les Porteurs de Valises. La Résistance Française et la Guerre d'Algérie* (A. Michel, 1979).
42. See the statement of Daniel Mayer, President of the League of Human Rights, quoted by J.-L. Einaudi, *Le Bataille de Paris*, p. 243.
43. On the erasure from French memory of key aspects of the Algerian War see B. Stora, *La gangrène et l'oubli*.
44. C. Ben Fredj, *Aux origines de l'émigration*, pp. 250–2; B. Stora, *Ils Venaient d'Algérie*, pp. 64, 370.
45. A. Horne, *A Savage War*, pp. 529–30.
46. M. Cornaton, *Les Regroupements*; K. Sutton, 'Population Resettlement – Traumatic Upheavals and the Algerian Experience', *Journal of Modern African Studies*, Vol. 15, 2 (1977) 279–300; and the classic study of Pierre Bourdieu and Abdelmalek Sayad, *Le déracinement*.
47. M. Bennoune, *Impact of Colonialism*, pp. 207–30 has much detail on the impact of war in accelerating emigration from El Akbia.
48. M. Harbi editorial, *Révolution Africaine*, No. 71, 6 June 1964, quoted in S. Adler, *International Migration and Dependence* (Farnborough: Saxon House, 1977) p. 156. A similar position was taken by the Algerian Trade Union Confederation, the UGTA, in 1962; see I. Brandell, *Les Rapports Franco-Algériens depuis 1962* (Harmattan, 1981) p. 109.
49. *El Moudjahid*, No. 165, 1 February 1964, quoted in S. Adler, *International Migration*, p. 158. See also B. Stora, *Ils Venaient d'Algérie*, pp. 420–1.
50. A. El Gharbaoui, 'Les travailleurs maghrébins', pp. 13–14; I. Brandell, *Les Rapports Franco-Algériens*, pp. 33–6; S. Adler, *International Migration*, pp. 75–9.
51. South Africa, for example, was able to bring great pressure on Mozambique since the income of migrants to the goldmines was vital to the impoverished socialist state. Ruth First, *Black Gold* (Brighton: Harvester, 1983).
52. S. Adler, *International Migration*, p. 134.
53. On the programme organised by the *Office National de la Main-d'oeuvre* (ONAMO) see the detailed study by M. Khandriche, *Développement et réinsertion. L'Exemple de l'Émigration Algérienne* (Publisud, 1982).
54. S. Adler, *International Migration*, p. 143.

Conclusion

1. Quoted in M. Tripier, *L'Immigration dans la Classe Ouvrière en France* (Harmattan, 1990) p. 300.
2. A. Jazouli, *Les Années Banlieues* (Seuil, 1992); P. Bourdieu (ed.), *La misère du monde* (Seuil, 1993); M. Wieviorka, *La France Raciste* (Seuil, 1992).
3. See R. Kuisel, 'The France We Have Lost: Social, Economic and Cultural Discontinuities', in G. Flynn (ed.), *Remaking the Hexagon. The New France in Europe* (Boulder: Westview Press, 1995) pp. 31–48.

4. For a typical example of the anxiety attached to the American 'model' see C. Jelen, *Ils feront de bons Français. Enquête sur l'assimilation des Maghrébins* (R. Laffont, 1991) pp. 48–50.

5. See for example, M. Khellil, *L'Intégration des Maghrébins en France* (Presses Universitaires de France, 1991).

6. M. Tripier, *L'Immigration dans la Classe Ouvrière*, p. 117.

7. For an excellent survey see N. Bancel *et al.* (eds), *Images et Colonies. Iconographie et propagande coloniale sur l'Afrique française de 1880 à 1962*, (Publications de la BDIC, 1993). M. Nasr, 'L'image des Arabes dans les manuels de lecture de l'enseignement primaire', *Mots*, No. 30 (March, 1992) 18–34, has shown how negative and colonialist stereotypes continue to be transmitted in primary-school reading books.

8. T.C. Holt, 'Marking: Race, Race-making and the Writing of History', *American Historical Review*, Vol. 100, No. 1 (February 1995) 1–20.

9. F. Batier, quoted in M. Tripier, *L'Immigration dans la Classe Ouvrière* pp. 186–7. Opinion polls invariably allocated North Africans to the bottom of the hierarchy. An INED survey carried out in late 1973 gave the lowest negative score to immigrants from Spain (5 per cent), then to Italy (8), Yugoslavia (10), Portugal (13), Turkey (15), Black Africa (23) with North Africa at the bottom (55 per cent). See the SOFRES poll of 1984 which also gave Algerians the most negative score, well below Turks, Moroccans, Black Africans and other groups: see A.C. Hargreaves, *Immigration, 'race' and ethnicity in Contemporary France* (London: Routledge, 1995) p. 155.

10. J.-F. Held 'Peut-On Vivre Avec des Arabes?', *Le Nouvel Observateur*, 3 September 1973, pp. 49–50.

11. *Paris-Match*, 3 September 1973, quoted in Y. Gastaut, 'La flambée raciste de 1973 en France', *Revue Européenne des Migrations Internationales*, Vol. 9, No. 2 (1993) p. 70.

12. *Le Méridional*, 26 August 1973. Domenech joined the *Front National* in 1985 and became editor of the rabid journal *Minute*.

13. B. Stora, *La gangrène et l'oubli*.

14. Y. Gastaut, 'La flambée raciste de 1973'. According to official Algerian sources, fifty Algerians were murdered and three hundred wounded in France during 1973.

15. *Le Monde*, 25–6 June 1926, quoted in Y. Gastaut, 'La flambée raciste de 1973', p. 63.

16. *Le Nouvel Observateur*, 3 September 1973, pp. 49–50; *Paris-Match*, 3 September 1973; *Le Nouvel Observateur*, 18 June 1973.

17. B. Stora, *La gangrène et l'oubli*, p. 293.

18. E. Temime, 'Marseille XXe siècle: de la dominante italienne à la diversité maghrébine', *Revue Européenne des Migrations Internationales* Vol. 11, No. 1 (1995) 12.

19. E. Plenel and A. Rollat, *L'effet Le Pen*, Chapter 6.

20. *Le Monde*, 18 December 1973, quoted in Y. Gastaud, 'La flambée raciste de 1973', p. 67.

21. *The Guardian*, 25 April 1995, p. 10. On the implantation of the FN in Provence see V. Rogers, 'The Front National in Provence-Alpes-Côtes d'Azur: a case of institutionalized racism?' in M. Silverman (ed.), *Race, Discourse and Power in France* (Aldershot: Avebury, 1991) pp. 84–97.

22. *Le Quotidien,* 13 November 1989.

23. J.-L. Einaudi, *La Bataille de Paris,* p. 284.

24. A. El Gharbaoui, 'Les travailleurs maghrébins', p. 48.

25. P. Jones, 'Race, discourse and power in institutional housing: the case of immigrant worker hostels in Lyons', in M. Silverman (ed.), *Race, Discourse and Power,* pp. 55–70; M. Ginesy-Galano, *Les Immigrés Hors la Cité.*

26. M. Tripier, *L'Immigration dans la Classe Ouvrière,* p. 143.

27. R. Grillo, *Ideologies and institutions,* pp. 117–18, 130–7.

28. M. Tripier, *L'Immigration dans la Classe Ouvrière,* p. 12.

29. M. Tripier, *Ibid.,* p. 311.

30. D. Joly, *The French Communist Party and the Algerian War* (London: Macmillan, 1991).

31. E. Todd, *Le Destin des Immigrés* (Seuil, 1994).

32. D. Joly, *The French Communist Party,* p. 88.

33. A.G. Hargreaves, *Immigration, 'race' and ethnicity,* p. 134.

34. J. Ponty, *Polonais Meconnus. Histore des travailleurs immigrés en France dans l'entre-deux-guerres* (Publications de la Sorbonne, 1988).

35. J. Ponty, *Ibid.,* pp. 123, 286.

36. See for example C. Jelen, *Ils feront de bons Français.*

37. N. MacMaster, *Sexual and Racial Boundaries.*

38. M. Tribalat, *Faire France,* p. 77. For a discussion of research in this field see Y. Rocheron, 'Families on the Front Line – Mixed Marriage in France', in M. Cross and S. Perry (eds), *France: Population and Peoples* (Cassells, forthcoming).

39. A.G. Hargreaves, *Immigration, 'race' and ethnicity,* p. 159. Jelen's thesis in *Ils feront de bons français* is that the true level of integration has been obscured by the activities of anti-racist organisations like SOS-Racisme which perpetuate a 'misérabiliste' image of Maghrebians as victims. This is a classic right-wing ploy, inverts the true power relationship and absolves the dominant social and political order for any responsibility for discrimination and racism.

Bibliography

ARCHIVE SOURCES

Archives municipales de Bobigny

W 617. *Délibérations du Conseil Municipal, 1930–2.*
W 4433–4. Papers on construction of the Franco-Muslim Hospital.

Archives municipales de Gennevilliers

Registre des délibérations du Conseil (1924)
Côte 26/3. Papers on construction of a hostel for North African workers (1924)

Archives Nationales, Paris

F7 – 13170, Propagande Communiste aux Colonies (1925–36).
F7 – 13518, Police Générale (1925).
F14– 11334, Procès-verbaux de la Conférence Interministerielle de la Main-d'Oeuvre (1917).

Archives Paris Préfecture de Police (APP)

BA. 56. – Police records on Étoile-Nord-Africaine (1926–34).
BA. 56. – [A. Godin], *Note sur l'activité de l'Étoile-Nord-Africaine depuis sa création jusqu'au 15 Novembre 1934.* Typescript.
BA. 57. – Police records on Étoile-Nord-Africaine (1928–36).
BA. 67. Foreign workers in France. 'Ouvriers Coloniaux' (1916–32).

Archives d'Outre Mer. Aix-en-Provence (AOM)

AOM. 762. R. Montagne et al., *Étude Sociologique de la Migration des Travailleurs Musulmans d'Algérie en Métropole,* 11 vols (1954–57). Cyclostyled.
AOM. 762. R. Montagne, *Rapport Provisoire sur l'Émigration des Musulmans d'Algérie* (1954). Cyclostyled.
B3. 167. Prefecture of Constantine. Emigration 1929.
8 H 61 – Le Haut Comité Mediterranéen.
8 H 62 – *Rapport de MM. Laroque et Ollive, Auditeurs au Conseil d'État. Sur la main-d'oeuvre Nord-Africains,* in 3 parts (1938). Cyclostyled.
9 H 112 – Gouvernement Générale papers on migration to France, 1923.
9 H 113 – as above 1923–40.
9 H 113. *Rapport sur l'émigration des indigènes* (1923).
10 H 66. Charavin, *Note sur la commune mixte de Fort-National* (1937).
10 H 88. M. Benet (Deputy Adminsitrator, Azazga), *De l'Immigration en France des Kabyles du Haute Sebaou et ses consequences* (Feb. 1937).

8 X 453 – R. Troussel, *Sur les Hauts Plateaux Constantinois. La Commune Mixte des Eulmas* (1937).

8 X 459 – P. Demondian, *L'Émigration de la Commune Mixte de Fort National* (1950).

9 X 58 – Report of M. Correard for Governor General on migration (c. 1949).

9 X 59 – P. Schoen, *Le Problème de la Main-d'Oeuvre Kabyle* (1940).

28 X 2. A. Roche, *Aspects de l'Émigration Algériennes* (Commune Mixte of Guergour), Mémoire ENA (Jan. 1951).

29 X 3. J.-C. Isnard, *Les Problèmes du Logement dans l'Agglomeration Algéroise*, Mémoire École Nationale d'Administration (Dec. 1949).

AOM Hors série. Doc. 5 – 83/4. Foyer indigène at Gennevilliers, 1924.

Bibliothèque Administrative de la Ville de Paris (BAVP)

Bulletin Municipale Officielle de la Ville de Paris Déliberations du conseil Municipale Côte 1783 contains numerous printed reports to the City Council on various aspects of the SAINA, policing of Algerians and related topics:

No. 141. Copineaux and Besombes, *Note . . . sur le fonctionnement des centres d'hébergement des indigènes Nord-africains de Clermont-Ferrand, Marseille et Toulon* (1926).

No. 178. P. Godin, Besombes, E. Massard, *Proposition tendant à créer à la Préfecture de police une section d'affaires indigènes nord-africaines* (1923).

No. 95. P. Godin, *Proposition concernant la 'question Kabyle à Paris'* (1924).

No. 125. P. Godin, *Proposition . . . à l'affection dans les cimetières en creation d'un emplacement pour les Musulmans* (1924).

No. 55. P. Godin, *Proposition . . . dénomination commune d'Algériens'* (1925).

No. 137. P. Godin, *Proposition . . . tendant à compléter l'organisation actuelle de la séction de surveillance* (1925).

No. 67. P. Godin, *Note au sujet des services de surveillance* (1930).

No. 117. P. Godin, *Proposition . . . création d'hôpitaux spéciaux pour étrangers* (1932).

No. 140. P. Godin, *Note sur les services Nord-africains* (1934).

No. 113. Le Provost de Launay, *Rapport sur le budget des services de protection des indigènes* (1935).

No. 153. Le Provost de Launay, *Rapport sur le budget des services de protection* (1936).

Bibliothèque Nationale, Algiers

No. 558980. J. Etienne, *L'Émigration vers la Métropole des Travailleurs Musulmans dans le département de Constantine*, Mémoire ENA (Jan. 1950).

Bibliothèque Nationale, Paris

Consultation of inter-war press, especially *Le Petit Parisien, L'Action Française, Le Matin, L'Humanité, L'Echo d'Alger, La Dépêche de Constantine, L'Oeuvre, La Voix de l'Est, Akhbar.*

Centre des Hautes Etudes sur l'Afrique et l'Asie Moderne (CHEAM)

No. 1410 – M. Aldou, *L'Émigration vers la métropole des travailleurs musulmans de la Commune Mixte de Nedroma* (1948).

No. 2036 – J. Vialatte de Pemille, *L'émigration des Nedromis en France* (1951).

No. 2156 – P. Vigo, *Le Problème de l'Emigration dans la Vallée de l'Oued Sahel (Commune Mixte d'Akbou)* (1952).

No. 2161 – N. Vadi, *Le Problème de l'Éxode des Populations Rurales vers la Métropole dans une Commune Mixte de Petite Kabylie* (CM of Soummam) (1953).

No. 2357 – A. Didier, *L'Exode en France dans la Commune Mixte des Rirha* (1954).

No. 3450 – J. Massoue, *L'Action Sociale en Faveur des Français Musulmans d'Algérie dans le Département de la Seine* (1960–1).

No. 3511 – Cunibile, *L'Assistance Technique aux Français Musulmans d'Algérie à la Préfecture de Police* (April, 1961).

No. 50108 – Jean de Felix, *Le problème de l'Immigration Algérienne en France* (Dec. 1951).

SECONDARY SOURCES

(The place of publication of all books is Paris unless otherwise stated.)

Abou-Zeid, A.H. 'Migrant labour and social structure in Kharga Oasis', in J. Pitt-Rivers (ed.), *Mediterranean Countrymen* (Mouton, 1963) pp. 41–53.

Adams, C. *Across Seven Seas and Thirteen Rivers. Life Stories of Pioneer Sylhetti Settlers in Britain* (London: THAP Books, 1987).

Adler, S. *International Migration and Dependence* (Farnborough: Saxon House, 1977).

Ageron, C.-R. 'La France a-t-elle eu un politique Kabyle?', *Revue Historique*, (April 1960), 311–52.

— *Les Algériens Musulmans et la France*, 2 Vols (Presses Universitaires de France, 1968).

— *Histoire de l'Algérie Contemporaine*, Vol. II (Presses Universitaires de France, 1979).

— 'La politique berbère sous le second Empire' in C.-R. Ageron, *L'Algérie algérienne de Napoleon III à de Gaulle* (Sindbad, 1980). pp. 37–71.

— 'L'Opinion Française à travers les sondages', in J-P. Rioux (ed.), *La Guerre d'Algérie*, pp. 25–44.

Ageron, C.-R *et al.* (eds), *Les Mémoires de Messali Hadj, 1898–1938* (J.-C. Lattès, 1982).

Allal, T. *et al. Situations migratoires. La fonction-miroir* (Galilée, 1977).

Amin, S. *The Maghreb in the Modern World* (Harmondsworth: Penguin, 1970).

Ananou, P. 'Les Populations Rurales Musulmanes du Sahel d'Alger', *Revue Africaine*, Vol. 97 (1953) 369–414; Vol. 98 (1954), 113–39.

Anderson, W. 'Excremental Colonialism: Public Health and the Poetics of Pollution', *Critical Inquiry*, Vol. 21 (Spring 1995) 640–69.

Andersson, C. *Peasant or Proletariat? Wage labour and peasant economy during industrialization. The Algerian experience* (Gothenburg: Almquist and Wiksell, 1985).

Ath-Messaoud, M and Gillette, A. *L' Immigration Algérienne en France* (Editions Entente, 1976). [Ath-Messaoud is a pseudonym for Abdelmalek Sayad. A slightly different second edition was published in 1984, see Gillette and Sayad, below]

Augarde, J. *La Migration Algérienne* (Hommes et Migrations, 1970).

Aujoulat. L, 'Chez les Kabyles du Nord de la France', *En Terre d'Islam* (May–June 1932) 190–8.

Baduel, P.-R. *Société et Émigration Temporaire au Nefzaoua (Sud-Tunisien)* (CNRS, 1980).

Ballard, R. and C. 'The Sikhs: the Development of South Asian Settlements in Britain', in J.L. Watson (ed.), *Between Two Cultures*, pp. 21–56.

Bancel, N. *et al.* (eds), *Images et Colonies. Iconographie et propagande coloniale sur l'Afrique française de 1880 à 1962* (Publications de la BDIC, 1993).

Baroin, H. *La Main-d'Oeuvre Étrangère dans la région Lyonnaise* (Lyon: Bosc Frères, 1935).

Baroli, M. *La Vie Quotidienne des Français en Algérie, 1830–1914* (Hachette, 1967).

Basagana, R. and Sayad, A. *Habitat et Structures Familiales en Kabylie* (Algiers: SNED, 1974).

Behr, E. *The Algerian Problem* (Harmondsworth: Penguin, 1961).

Belbahri, A. *Immigration et Situations Postcoloniales* (Harmattan, 1987).

Belkhodja, A. and J. *Les Africains du Nord à Gennevilliers*, Cahiers Nord-Africains. No. 97 (1963).

Benachenhou, A. *Formation du sous-développement en Algérie* (Algiers: Imprimerie Commerciale, 1978).

Benamrane, D. *L'Émigration Algérienne en France* (Algiers: SNED, 1983).

Benatia, F. *Alger: agrégat ou cité. L'intégration citadine de 1919 à 1979* (Algiers: SNED, 1980).

Benattig, R. *Migrations, emploi et revenus. Analyse de la situation dans deux régions montagneuses* (Algiers: Centre de Recherches en Économie Appliquée, 1981).

Bennoune, M. *Impact of Colonialism and Migration on an Algerian Peasant Community: a study in socio-economic change*, Doctoral thesis, University of Michigan (1976).

— 'The Introduction of Nationalism into Rural Algeria: 1919–54', *The Maghreb Review*, Vol. 2, No. 3 (May–June 1977) 1–12.

— *El Akbia. Un Siècle d'Histoire Algérienne, 1857–1975* (Algiers: Office des Publications Universitaires, c.1986?).

— *The making of contemporary Algeria, 1830–1987* (Cambridge: Cambridge University Press, 1988).

Ben Fredj, C. *Aux origines de l'émigration nord-africaine en France*, Doctoral thesis, University of Paris VII (1990).

Ben Jelloun, T. *La plus haute des solitudes. Misère affective et sexuelle d'émigrés nord-africains* (Seuil, 1977).

Bentahar, M. *Les Arabes en France* (Rabat: SMER, 1979).

Ben Younes, A. *Émigration et société: un village de Kabylie*, Dissertation for the diploma in Études Supérieures de Sciences Politiques, University of Algiers, June 1977.

Bernard, A. *L'Afrique du Nord Pendant la Guerre* (Presses Universitaires de France, 1926).

Bernard, A. 'Rapport sur la main-d'oeuvre dans l'Afrique du Nord', *Afrique Française. Renseignements Coloniaux* (May 1930) 297–311.
— *L'Algérie* (Larousse, 1930).
Berque, A. 'L'Habitation de l'Indigène Algérien', *Revue Africaine*, Vol. 78 (1936) 43–100.
Berque, J. 'Qu'est-ce qu'une tribu nord-africaine?', in *Eventail de l'histoire vivante: hommage à Lucien Fèbre*, Vol. 1 (A. Colin, 1953), pp. 261–71.
— *French North Africa. The Maghreb Between Two World Wars* (London: Faber, 1967).
— 'Recent Research on Racial Relations. The North of Africa', *International Social Science Journal*, Part 2 (1961) 177–96.
Berthier, C. *Activité, Chomage et Émigration dans l'Est Algérien*, Thesis in geography, University Louis Pasteur, Strasboug (1974).
Berthod, P. *Le Problème de la Main-d'Oeuvre Nord-Africain en France*, Doctorate thesis, Faculty of Law, University of Paris (1946).
Bessis, J. 'Chekib Arslan et les mouvements nationalistes au Maghreb', *Revue Historique*, Vol. 259 (1978) 467–89.
Betts, R.F. *Assimilation and Association in French Colonial Theory and Practice* (New York: Columbia University Press, 1961).
Boal, F.W. 'Ethnic Residential Segregation', in D.T. Herbert and R.J. Johnson (eds), *Social Areas in Cities*. Vol. 1. *Spatial Processes and Form* (London: J. Wiley, 1976) pp. 41–79.
Böhning, W.R. 'The Self-Feeding Process of Economic Migration', in P. Braham *et al.* (eds), *Discrimination and Disadvantage in Employment* (London: Harper and Row, 1981), pp. 28–41.
Bonn, C. 'Roman maghrébin, émigration et exil de la parole', in *Annuaire de l'Afrique du Nord*, Vol. XXIV (1985) 397–415.
Bonnet, J.-C. *Les Pouvoirs Publics Français et l'Immigration dans l'Entre-Deux-Guerres* (Lyons: Centre d'histoire économique et sociale de la région lyonnaise, 1976).
Bouguessa, K. *Émigration et Politique. Essai sur la formation et la politique de la communauté Algérienne en France à l'entre-deux-querres mondiales*, Doctoral Thesis, University of Paris V (1979).
Boukhelloua, A. *L'Hôpital Franco-Musulman de Paris* (Algiers: Imprimerie Nord-Africaine, 1934).
Bourdieu, P. *The Algerians* (Boston: Beacon Press, 1962).
— 'The attitude of the Algerian peasant toward time', in J. Pitt-Rivers (ed.), *Mediterranean Countrymen. Essays in the Social Anthropology of the Mediterranean* (Mouton: 1963) pp. 55–72.
— *Travail et Travailleurs en Algérie* (Mouton, 1963).
— *Outline of a Theory of Practice* (Cambridge: Cambridge University Press, 1992).
Bourdieu, P. and Sayad, A. *Le Déracinement. La crise de l'agriculture traditionnelle en Algérie* (Minuit, 1964).
— *La misère du monde* (Seuil, 1993).
Boyer, A. *L'Institut Musulman de la Mosquée de Paris* (La Documentation Française, 1992).
Boyer, P. 'L'Évolution Démographique des Populations Musulmanes du Département d'Alger, 1830–1948', *Revue Africaine*, Vol. 98 (1954) 308–53.

Braham, P. *et al.* (eds), *Discrimination and Disadvantage in Employment* (London: Harper and Row, 1981).

Brandell, I. *Les Rapports Franco-Algériens depuis 1962* (Harmattan, 1981).

Braudel, F. *The Mediterranean and the Mediterranean World in the Age of Philip II* (London: Fontana edition, 1975).

Brooks, D. and Singh, K. 'Asian brokers in British foundries', in S. Wallman (ed.), *Ethnicity at Work* (London: Macmillan, 1979) pp. 92–112.

Bundy, C. *The Rise and Fall of the South African Peasantry* (London: Heinemann, 1979).

Camus, A. *Actuelles III (Chroniques algériennes 1939–1958)*, in *Oeuvres complètes d'Albert Camus* (Gallimard, 1983), Vol. 5.

Carayol, P. 'Les Genres de Vie Indigènes dans l'Atlas de Blida', *Revue Africaine*, Vol. 87 (1943) 239–65.

Carlier, O. 'Pour une histoire quantitative de l'émigration algérienne en France dans la période de l'entre-deux-guerres', in J. Costa-Lascoux and E. Temime (eds), *Les Algériens en France* (Publisud, 1985) pp. 153–82.

— 'Aspects de rapports entre mouvements ouvriers émigré et migration Maghrébine en France dans l'Entre-Deux-Guerres', *Annuaire de l'Afrique du Nord*, Vol. XXI (1982) 50–67.

— 'La production sociale de l'image de soi. Note sur la "crise berbériste" de 1949', *Annuaire de l'Afrique du Nord*, Vol. 23 (1984).

— 'Le Café Maure. Sociabilité masculine et effervescence citoyenne (Algérie XVII–XXe siècles), *Annales. E.S.C.* (July, 1990) 975–1003.

Castles, S. *Here For Good. Western Europe's New Ethnic Minorities* (London: Pluto, 1984).

Catrice, P. 'Les Missions Protestantes et les Nord-Africains en France', *En Terre d'Islam* (1931) 200–3.

Catrice, P. and Buchet, G. 'Les Musulmans en France. Enquête', *En Terre d'Islam* (1929) 336–48 and (1930) 22–7.

Cesari, J. 'Les stratégies identitaires des musulmans à Marseille', *Migrations Société* No. 5–6 (1989), 59–71.

Chaïb, Y. 'Le lieu d'enterrement comme repère migratoire', *Migrations Société*, Vol. 6, Nos. 33–4 (1994) 29–40.

Chaker, S. *Berbères Aujourd'hui* (Harmattan, 1989).

Chapman, M. and Mansell Prothero, R. *Circulation in population movement. Substance and concepts from the Melanesian case* (London: Routledge, 1985).

Charnay, J.-P. *La vie musulmane en Algérie d'après la jurisprudence de la première moitié du XXe siècle* (Presses Universitaires de France, 1991).

Chatelain, A. 'Les Algériens dans la Région Parisienne', *Bulletin de la Société d'Etudes de la Région Parisienne*, Nos 91–2 (April–Sept. 1956) 23–9.

Chevalier, L. *Le Problème Démographique Nord-Africain*, Institut National d'Études Démographique, Travaux et Documents, Cahier No. 6 (Presses Universitaires de France, 1947).

— *Labouring Classes, Dangerous Classes* (London: Routledge, 1973).

Chevillard-Vabre, J. *Histoire de l'Hôpital Franco-Musulman*, thesis for doctorate in medicine, Faculty of Medicine, Saint-Antoine-Paris (1982).

Clément-Grandcourt, *Nos Indigènes Nord-Africains dans l'Armée Nouvelle* (Berger-Levrault, 1926).

Cohen, B.G. and Jenner, P.J. 'The Employment of Immigrants: A Case Study within the Wool Industry', in P. Braham *et al.* (eds), *Discrimination and Disadvantage in Employment* (London: Harper and Row, 1981), pp. 109–25.

Cohen, R. *The New Helots. Migrants in the International Division of Labour* (Aldershot: Gower, 1987).

Cohen, W.B. *Rulers of Empire: the French Colonial Service in Africa* (Stanford: Hoover Institute, 1971).

— *The French Encounter with Africans: White Response to Blacks, 1530–1880* (Bloomington: Indiana University Press, 1989).

Collot, C. *Les Institutions de l'Algérie durant la période coloniale (1830–1962)* (CNRS, 1987).

Colonna, F. 'Cultural resistance and religious legitimacy in colonial Algeria', *Economy and Society*, Vol. 3 (1974) 233–52.

— *Instituteurs algériens, 1883–1939* (Presses de la Fondation Nationales des Sciences Politiques, 1975).

— *Savants Paysans. Éléments d'histoire sociale sur l'Algérie rurale* (Algiers: Office des Publications Universitaires, 1987).

Commission Nationale Consultative des Droits de l'Homme, *1991, La Lutte Contre le Racisme et la Xenophobie* (La Documentation Française, 1992).

Connell, J. *et al. Migration from Rural Areas. The Evidence from Village Studies* (Delhi: Oxford University Press, 1976).

Corbin, A. 'Les paysans de Paris. Histoire des Limousins du bâtiment au XIXe siècle', *Ethnologie française*, Vol. 10 (1980) 169–76.

Cornaton, M. *Les Regroupements de la décolonisation en Algérie* (Editions Ouvrières, 1967).

Cornu, R. 'Quand les travailleurs maghrébins devinrent des travailleurs immigrés (1945–1962)', in *Annuaire de l'Afrique du Nord*, Vol. XX1 (1982) 69–83.

Costa-Lascoux, J. *De l'Immigration au Citoyen* (La Documentation Française, 1989).

Costa-Lascoux, J. and Temime, E. (eds), *Les Algériens en France. Genèse et devenir d'une migration* (Publisud, 1985).

Côte, M. *L'Algérie ou l'Espace Retourné* (Flammarion, 1988).

Cross, G.S. 'Toward Social Peace and Prosperity: the Politics of Immigration in France during the Era of World War I', *French Historical Studies*, Vol. XI, No. 4 (1980) 610–32.

— *Immigrant Workers in Industrial France. The Making of a New Laboring Class* (Philadelphia: Temple University Press, 1983).

Dahmani, M. *Économie et Société en Grande Kabylie* (Algiers: Office des Publications Universitaires, 1984)

Damase, J. *Sidi de Banlieue* (Fasquelle, 1937).

Dean, D. 'The Conservative government and the 1961 Commonwealth Immigration Act: the inside story', *Race and Class*, Vol. 35 (Dec. 1993) 57–74.

Depont, O. *Les Kabyles en France. Rapport de la Commission chargé d'étudier les conditions du travail des indigènes Algériens dans la Métropole* (Beaugency, 1914).

— 'La Main-d'Oeuvre Indigène de l'Afrique du Nord en France', *La Reforme Sociale* (September–October, 1923) 654–73.

— *Les Berbères en France. D'une meilleure utilisation de la main-d'oeuvre des Nord-Africains* (Comité de l'Afrique Française, 1925).

— *L'Algérie du Centenaire* (Bordeaux: Cadoret, 1928).

— *Les Berbères en France. L'hôpital franco-musulman de Paris et du département de la Seine* (Lille: 1937).

Dermenghem, E. 'Musulmans de Paris. Les Kabyles à Grenelle', *Grande Revue* (Dec. 1934) 15–21.

Descloitres, R. and Debzi, L. 'Système de parenté familiales en Algérie', *Annuaire de l'Afrique du Nord* (1963) 23–59.

Descloitres, R. et al. *L'Algérie des Bidonvilles. Le Tiers Monde dans la Cité* (Mouton, 1961).

Dine, P. *Images of the Algerian War. French Fiction and Film, 1954–1992* (Oxford: Clarendon Press, 1994).

Dixon, C. and Sutton, K. 'The Landscape of Colonialism. The Impact of French Colonial Rule on the Algerian Rural Settlement Pattern, 1830–1987', in C. Dixon and M.J. Heffernan (eds), *Colonialism and Development in the Contemporary World* (London: Mansell, 1991).

Dubet, F. *Immigrations: qu'en savons-nous?* (La Documentation Française, 1989).

Duplessis-Kergomard, M. 'Mariages Mixtes des Kabyles en France', *La France Méditerranéens et Africaine* (1938) 110–17.

— 'L'Émigration des Kabyles en France', *La France Méditerranéens et Africaine* (1938) 89–93.

Dyer, C. *Population and Society in Twentieth Century France* (London: Hodder and Stoughton, 1978).

Einaudi, J.-L. *Le Bataille de Paris. 17 Octobre 1961* (Seuil, 1991).

El Gharbaoui, A. 'Les travailleurs maghrébins immigrés dans la banlieue nord-est de Paris', *Revue de Géographie du Maroc*, No. 19 (1971) 3–56.

Engelbrekston, U.-B. *The Force of Tradition. Turkish Migrants at Home and Abroad* (Gothenburg: Acta Universitatis Gothenburgensis, 1978).

Evenson, N. *Paris: A Century of Change, 1878–1978* (New Haven: Yale University Press, 1979).

Faligot, R. and Kauffer, R. *Le Croissant et la Croix Gammée* (Albin Michel, 1990).

Fontaine, J. *Villages Kabyles et Nouveau Reseau Urbain*, Centre d'Etudes et de Recherches URBAMA (Tours: 1983).

Fontaine, L. 'Solidarités Familiales et Logiques Migratoires en Pays de Montagne à l'Époque Moderne', in *Annales E.S.C* No. 6 (Nov.–Dec. 1990) 1433–50.

Fonville, R. *De la Condition en France et dans les Colonies françaises des indigènes des protectorats français* (E. Duchemin, 1924).

Foot, P. *Immigration and Race in British Politics* (Harmondsworth: Penguin, 1965).

Foucault, M. *Surveiller et punir* (Gallimard, 1975).

Frémont, A. 'Le Contingent: Témoignage et Réflexion', in J.-P. Rioux (ed.), *La Guerre d'Algérie*, pp. 79–85.

Fryer, P. *Staying Power: The History of Black People in Britain* (London: Pluto, 1984).

Gainer, B. *The Alien Invasion. The Origins of the Aliens Act of 1905* (London: Heinemann, 1972).

Gallissot, R. *L'Économie de l'Afrique du Nord* (Presses Universitaires de France, 1978 edition).

Gallissot, R. 'Precolonial Algeria', *Ecomony and Society*, Vol. 4, No. 4 (1975) 418–45.

Gallissot, R. 'Émigration Coloniale, Immigration Post-Coloniale', in L. Talha (ed.), *Maghrébins en France*, pp. 31–49.

Gallissot, R. 'Aux origines de l'immigration Algérienne', in J. Costa-Lascoux and E. Temime (eds), *Les Algériens en France* (Publisud, 1985) pp. 207–23.

Gastaut, Y. 'La flambée raciste de 1973 en France', *Revue Européenne des Migrations Internationales*, Vol. 9, No. 2 (1993) 61–73.

Gates, H.L.G. (ed.), *'Race', Writing and Difference* (Chicago: University of Chicago Press, 1986).

Gellner, E. *Saints of the Atlas* (London: Weidenfeld, 1969).

— *Muslim society* (Cambridge: Cambridge University Press, 1981).

Gillette, A. and Sayad, A. *L'Immigration Algérienne en France*, 2nd edition (Entente, 1984).

Ginesy-Galano, M. *Les Immigrés Hors la Cité. Le Système d'Encadrement dans les Foyers (1973–1982)* (Harmattan, 1984).

Girard, A. Charbit, Y. and Lamy, M.-L. 'Attitudes des français à l'égard de l'immigration étrangère', *Population*, Vol. 29 (Nov.–Dec. 1974) 1015–69.

Girard, A. *et al.* (eds), *Les Immigrés du Maghreb. Etudes sur l'adaptation en milieu urbain*, INED, Travaux et Documents Cahier No. 79 (Presses Universitaires de France, 1977).

Goddard, A.D. 'Population movements and land shortages in the Sokoto close-settled zone, Nigeria', in S. Amin (ed.), *Modern Migrations in Western Africa* (London: Oxford University Press, 1974) pp. 258–80.

Godin, P. *Note sur le fonctionnement des Services de Surveillance, Protection et Assistance des Indigènes Nord-Africains* (Imprimerie Municipale, 1933).

Godin, P. and Marie, A. 'Le Problème des Malades Musulmans à Paris', *L'Hygiène Mentale* (Feb. 1934) 33–44.

Goldberg, D.T. *Racist Culture. Philosophy and the Politics of Meaning* (Oxford: Blackwell, 1993).

Gomar, N. *L'Émigration Algérienne en France* (Les Presses Modernes, 1931).

Gourgeot, F. *Les Sept Plaies d'Algérie* (Algiers: P. Fontana, 1891).

Grillo, R. *Ideologies and Institutions in Urban France: the Representation of Immigrants* (Cambridge: Cambridge University Press, 1985).

Halliday, F. *Yemeni Migrants in Urban Britain* (London: I.B. Tauris, 1992).

Hamon, H. and Rotman, P. *Les Porteurs de Valises. La Résistance Française et la Guerre d'Algérie* (A. Michel, 1979).

Hanoteau, A. and Letourneaux, A. *La Kabylie et les Coutumes Kabyles*, 3 Vols. (Imprimerie Nationale, 1872–3).

Hargreaves, A.G. *Immigration, 'race' and ethnicity in Contemporary France* (London: Routledge, 1995).

Haroun, A. *La 7e Wilaya. La Guerre du FLN en France, 1954–1962* (Seuil, 1986).

Heffernan, M.J. 'The Parisian Poor and the Colonization of Algeria during the Second Republic', *French History*, Vol. 3. No. 4 (1989) 377–403.

Henry, J.-H. (ed.), *Le Maghreb dans l'imaginaire français. La colonie, le désert, l'exil* (Édisud, 1985).

Henry, L. *et al. Les Algériens en France. Étude démographique et sociale*, Travaux et Documents de l'INED, Cahier No. 24 (Presses Universitaires de France, 1955).

Hervo, M. and Charras, M.-A. *Bidonvilles* (Maspero, 1971).

Hifi, B. *L'Immigration Algérienne en France. Origines et perspectives de non-retour* (Harmattan, 1985).

Holt, T.C. 'Marking: Race, Race-making and the Writing of History', *American Historical Review*, Vol. 100, No. 1 (1995) 1–20.

Horne, A. *A Savage War of Peace* (London: Macmillan, 1987 edition).

Horne, J. 'Immigrant Workers in France during World War I', *French Historical Studies*, Vol. 14, No. 1 (1985) 57–88.

Hufton, O.H. *The Poor of Eighteenth-Century France* (Oxford: Oxford University Press, 1979).

Husbands, C.T. *Racial Exclusionism and the City: The urban support of the National Front* (London: Allen and Unwin, 1983).

Hyam, R. *Empire and Sexuality* (Manchester: Manchester University Press, 1992).

Imbert, N. *Dictionnaire National des Contemporaines* (Editions Lajeunesse, 1939).

Isnard, H. *La Vigne en Algérie*, 2 Vols. (Gap: OPHRYS, 1951–4).

Jazouli, A. *L'Action Collective des Jeunes Maghrébins de France* (Harmattan, 1986).

— *Les Années Banlieues* (Seuil, 1992).

Jelen, C. *Ils feront de bons Français. Enquête sur l'assimilation des Maghrébins* (R. Laffont, 1991).

Joly, D. *The French Communist Party and the Algerian War* (London: Macmillan, 1991).

Jones, P. 'Race, discourse and power in institutional housing: the case of immigrant worker hostels in Lyons', in M. Silverman (ed.), *Race, Discourse and Power in France* (Aldershot: Avebury, 1991), pp. 55–70.

Julien, C.-A. *Histoire de l'Algérie Contemporaine (1827–1871)*, Vol. 1 (Presses Universitaires de France, 1964).

Justinard 'Les Chleuh dans la Banlieue de Paris', *Revue des Études Islamiques* (1928) 476–80.

Kepel, G. *Les Banlieues de l'Islam: naissance d'une religion en France* (Seuil, 1987).

Kerrou, M. 'Du colportage à la boutique. Les commerçants maghrébins en France', *Hommes et Migrations*, No. 1105 (July, 1987).

Khan, V. Saifullah. 'The Pakistanis: Mirpuri Villagers at Home and in Bradford', in J.L. Watson (ed.), *Between Two Cultures*, pp. 57–89.

Khandriche, M. *Développement et réinsertion. L'Exemple de l'Émigration Algérienne* (Publisud, 1982).

Khellil, M. *L'Exil Kabyle. Essai d'analyse du vécu des migrants* (Harmattan, 1979).

— *La Kabylie ou l'Ancêtre sacrifié* (Harmattan, 1984).

—— *L'Intégration des Maghrébins en France* (Presses Universitaires de France, 1991).

Kiernan, V.G. 'Foreign mercenaries and absolute monarchy', in T. Aston (ed.), *Crisis in Europe, 1560–1660* (London: Routledge, 1966) pp. 117–40.

Kobak, A. *Isabelle. The Life of Isabelle Eberhardt* (London: Chatto, 1988).

Kraut, A.M. *Silent Travellers. Germs, Genes and the 'Immigrant menace'* (Baltimore: Johns Hopkins University Press, 1994).

Kuisel, R. *Capitalism and the State in Modern France* (Cambridge: CUP, 1981).

—— 'The France We Have Lost: Social, Economic and Cultural Discontinuities', in G. Flynn (ed.), *Remaking the Hexagon. The New France in Europe* (Boulder: Westview Press, 1995) pp. 31–48.

Lacoste-Dujardin, C. *Un village algérien: structures et évolution récente* (Algiers: SNED, 1976).

Lafont, P.-B. 'La criminalité Nord-Africaine dans la Région Parisienne', *Esprit* (Sept. 1953) 426–37.

Larnaude, M. 'L'émigration temporaire des indigènes algériens dans la Métropole', *Revue de Géographie Marocaine* (1928) 45–51.

— 'Déplacements des travailleurs indigènes en Algérie', *Revue Africaine*, Nos 360–4 (1936) 207–15.

Lawless, R. 'Return Migration to Algeria: the impact of state intervention', in R. King (ed.), *Return Migration and Regional Economic Development* (London: Croom Helm, 1986) pp. 213–42.

Lawrence, E. 'Just plain common sense: the "roots" of racism', in P. Gilroy et al. (eds), *The Empire Strikes Back. Race and racism in 70s Britain* (London: Hutchinson, 1986) 47–94.

Lebovics, H. *True France. The Wars over Cultural Identity, 1900–1945* (Ithaca: Cornell University Press, 1992).

Lees, L.H. *Exiles of Erin: Irish Migrants in Victorian London* (Manchester: Manchester University Press, 1979).

Leroy-Beaulieu, P. *L'Algérie et la Tunisie* (Guillaumin, 1887).

Lespès, R. *Alger: Étude de Géographie et d'Histoire Urbaines* (F. Alcan, 1930).

Levine, M. *Les Ratonnades d'Octobre. Un Meutre Collectif à Paris en 1961* (Ramsay, 1985).

Lewis, M.D. 'One Hundred Million Frenchmen: The "Assimilation" Theory in French Colonial Policy', *Comparative Studies in Society and History*, Vol. 4 (1961) 129–53.

Lewis, P. *Islamic Britain. Religion, Politics and Identity among British Muslims* (London: I.B. Tauris, 1994).

Little, K.S. *Negroes in Britain* (London: Kegan Paul, 1947).

Lizot, J. *Metidja. Un Village Algérien de l'Ouarsenis* (Algiers: SNED, 1973).

Lopez, R. and Temime, E. *Migrance: Histoire des Migrations à Marseille*, Vol. 2 (Aix-en-Provence: Edisud, 1990).

Lorcin, P.E. *Imperial Identities. Stereotyping, Prejudice and Race in Colonial Algeria* (London: I.B. Tauris, 1995).

Lucas, P. and Vatin, J.C. *L'Algérie des Anthropologues* (Maspero, 1982).

MacKenzie, J.M. *Propaganda and Empire* (Manchester: Manchester University Press, 1984).

MacMaster, N. 'Social tensions and racism in a "grand ensemble"', *Modern and Contemporary France*, No. 39 (Oct. 1989) 11–23.

— 'The *seuil de tolérance*: the uses of a 'scientific racist concept', in M. Silverman (ed.), *Race, Discourse and Power in France* (Aldershot: Avebury, 1991) pp. 14–28.

— 'Patterns of Emigration, 1905–1954: "Kabyles" and "Arabs"', in A.G. Hargreaves and M.J. Heffernan (eds), *French and Algerian Identities from Colonial Times to the Present* (Lampeter: Edwin Mellen, 1993) pp. 21–38.

— 'The Rue Fondary Murders of 1923 and the origins of anti-Arab racism', in J. Windebank and R. Gunther (eds), *Violence and Conflict in the Politics and Society of Modern France* (Lampeter: Edwin Mellen Press, 1995) pp. 149–60.

— 'Labour Migration in French North Africa', in R. Cohen (ed.), *The Cambridge Survey of World Migration* (Cambridge: CUP, 1995) pp. 190–5.

— 'Sexual and Racial Boundaries: Colonialism and Franco-Algerian Inter-marriage (1880–1962)', in M. Cross and S. Perry (eds), *France: Population and Peoples* (Cassell, forthcoming).

Marchand, H. *Les Mariages Franco-Musulmans* (Algiers: Vollot-Debacq, 1954).

Marcovich, A. 'French colonial medicine and colonial rule: Algeria and Tunisia', in R. MacLeod and M. Lewis (eds), *Disease, Medicine and Empire* (London: Routledge, 1988) pp. 103–17.

Martial, R. *Traité de l'Immigration et de la Greffe Inter-Raciale* (Cuesmes-lez-Mons: Imprimerie Fédérale, 1931).

Masqueray, E. *Formation des cités chez les populations sédentaires de l'Algérie* (Aix-en-Provence: EDISUD, 1983 edition).

Massard-Guilbaud, G. *Des Algériens à Lyon, de la Grande Guerre au Front Populaire,* Doctoral thesis, University of Lyons II (1988).

Massignon, L. 'Carte de la répartition des Kabyles dans la région parisienne', *Revue des Études Islamiques,* No. 2 (1930) 161–9.

Mauco, G. *Les Étrangers en France* (A. Colin, 1932).

Meillassoux, C. *Maidens, Meal and Money. Capitalism and the Domestic Economy* (Cambridge: Cambridge University Press, 1991).

Merad, A. *Le Réformisme Musulman en Algérie de 1925 à 1940* (Mouton, 1967).

Mercier, M. *Étude sur la Crise de la Main-d'Oeuvre en Algérie* (Algiers: J. Carbonel, 1929).

Meuleman, J.H. *Le Constantinois entre les deux guerres mondiales. L'évolution économique et sociale de la population rurale* (Assen: Van Gorcum, 1985).

Meynier, G. *L' Algérie révélée* (Geneva: Droz, 1981).

—— *L'Algérie Révélée. La Guerre de 1914–1918.* Doctoral thesis, University of Nice (1979).

Michel, A. *Les Travailleurs Algériens en France* (CNRS, 1956).

Miles, R. *Racism* (London: Routledge, 1989).

Milliot, L. 'Les Kabyles à Paris', *Revue des Études Islamiques,* Vol. 6 (1932) 162–74.

Miyaji, M. *L'Émigration et le changement socio-culturel d'un village Kabyle,* Studia Culturae Islamica, No. 6 (Tokyo: 1976).

Montagne, R. 'L'émigration nord-africaine en France: son caractère familial et villageois', in *Eventail de l'histoire vivante: hommage à Lucien Fèbre,* Vol. 1 (A. Colin, 1953) pp. 365–71.

— *The Berbers: Their Social and Political Organisation,* with an Introduction by D. Seddon (London: Frank Cass, 1973).

Morizot, J. *L'Algérie Kabylisée* (J. Peyronnet, 1962).

—— *Les Kabyles: propos d'un témoin* (CHEAM, 1985).

Muracciole, L. *L'Émigration Algérienne. Aspects économiques, sociaux et juridiques* (Algiers: Ferraris, 1950).

Murray, C. *Families divided: the impact of migrant labour in Lesotho* (Cambridge: Cambridge University Press, 1981).

Mutin, G. *La Mitidja: décolonisation et espace géographique* (CNRS, 1977).

Nasr, M. 'L'image des Arabes dans les manuels de lecture de l'enseignement primaire', *Mots,* No. 30 (March 1992) 18–34.

Nelson, C. and Grossberg, L. (eds), *Marxism and the Interpretation of Culture* (Urbana: University of Illinois Press, 1988).

Noiriel, G. *Le Creuset Français. Histoire de l'immigration, XIXe–XXe siècles* (Seuil, 1988).

Noiriel, G. *La Tyrannie du National. Le droit d'asile en Europe (1793–1993)* (Calmann-Levy, 1991).

Nogaro, B. and Weil, L. *La Main-d'Oeuvre Étrangère et Coloniale Pendant la Guerre* (Presses Universitaires de France, 1926).

Nora, P. *Les Français d'Algérie* (Julliard, 1961).

Nouschi, A. *Enquête sur le niveau de vie des populations rurales constantinoises de la conquête jusqu'en 1919* (Presses Universitaires de France, 1961).

— 'Esquisse d'une histoire de l'immigration maghrébine', in M. Morsy (ed.), *Les Nord-Africains en France* (CHEAM, 1984) pp. 39–49.

Olivier, F. ' "L'Echo de Paris" et les étrangers (1921–1931)', *Revue Européene des Migrations Internationales*, Vol. 10, No. 2 (1994) 187–200.

Oualid, W. *L'Immigration Ouvrière en France* (Éditions SAPE, 1927).

Pairault, A. *L'Immigration Organisée et l'Emploi de la Main-d'Oeuvre Étrangère en France* (Presses Universitaires de France, 1926).

Palidda, S. 'Eurocentrisme et réalité effective des migrations', *Migrations Société*, Vol. 4, No. 2 (1992) 7–23.

Paon, M. *L'immigration en France* (Payot, 1926).

Papon, M. *Les Chevaux du Pouvoir* (Plon, 1988).

Park, T.K. 'Rural north-east Algeria, 1919–1938', *Peasant Studies*, Vol. 15 (Winter, 1988) 117–28.

Parry, B. 'Problems in Current Theories of Colonial Discourse', *Oxford Literary Review*, Vol. 9 (1987) 27–58.

Pasquet, L. *Immigration et Main-d'Oeuvre Étrangère en France* (Rieder, 1927).

Peach, C. *West Indian Migration to Britain. A Social Geography* (London: Oxford University Press, 1968).

Péju, P. *Les Harkis à Paris* (Maspero, 1961).

— *Ratonnades à Paris* (Maspero, 1961).

Perkins, K.J. *Qaids, Captains and Colons. French Military Administration in the Colonial Maghreb, 1844–1934* (New York: Africana Publishing Company, 1981).

Perotti, A. and Thépaut, F. 'L'affaire du foulard', *Migrations Société*, Vol. 2. No. 7 (Jan.–Feb. 1990) 61–82.

Perotti, A. and Toulat, P. 'Immigration et médias: Le Foulard surmédiatisé', *Migrations Société*, Vol. 2, No. 12 (Nov.–Dec. 1990) 9–45.

Persell, S. M. *The French Colonial Lobby, 1889–1938* (Stanford: Hoover Institution Press, 1983).

Pervillé, G. *Les étudiants algériens de l'université française, 1880–1962* (CNRS, 1984).

Philpott, S.B. *West Indian Migration: the Montserrat case* (London: Athlone Press, 1973).

Pieterse, J.N. *White on Black. Images of Africa and Blacks in Western Popular Culture* (New Haven: Yale University Press, 1992).

Plenel, E. and Rollat, A. *L'Effet Le Pen* (La Découverte, 1984).

Poitrineau, A. *Remues d'hommes. Les migrations montagnards en France, 17e–18e siècles* (Aubier-Montaigne, 1983).

Ponty, J. *Polonais Meconnus. Histoire des travailleurs immigrés en France dans l'entre-deux-guerres* (Publications de la Sorbonne, 1988).

Potter, L. *The World Labour Market. A History of Migration* (London: Zed Books, 1990).

Prenant, A. 'Facteurs du peuplement d'une ville de l'Algérie intérieure: Sétif', *Annales de Géographie,* Vol. LXXII (Nov.–Dec. 1953) 434–51.

Prochaska, D. 'La ségrégation résidentielle en société coloniale. Le cas de Bône en Algérie de 1872 à 1954', *Cahiers d'Histoire,* Vol. 25 (1980) 53–74.

——— *Making Algeria French. Colonialism in Bône, 1870–1920* (Cambridge: Cambridge University Press, 1990).

Rager, J.-J. *Les Musulmans Algériens en France et dans les Pays Islamiques* (Les Belles lettres, 1950).

——— *L'Émigration en France des Musulmans d'Algérie,* Documents Algériens No. 49 (July 1956).

Ranger, T. 'Growing from the Roots: Reflections on Peasant Research in Central and Southern Africa', *Journal of African Studies,* Vol. 5 (1978) 99–133.

Ray, J. *Les Marocains en France* (Syrey, 1938).

Reid, D. 'The Limits of Paternalism: Immigrant Coal Miners' Communities in France, 1919–45', *European History Quarterly,* Vol. 15 (1985) 99–118.

Rémond, R. *Au Coeur du Pays Kabyle* (Algiers: Baconnier, 1933).

——— *Djurjura. Terre de Contraste* (Algiers: Baconnier, 1940).

Renaudot, F. *L'histoire des Français en Algérie, 1830–1962* (R. Laffont, 1979).

Rex, J. and Tomlinson, S. *Colonial Immigrants in a British City. A Class Analysis* (London: Routledge, 1983).

Rich, P. *Race and Empire in British Politics* (Cambridge: Cambridge University Press, 1986).

Richardson, M.L. *French Algeria Between the Wars: Nationalism and Colonial Reform, 1919–1939,* Doctoral thesis, Duke University (1975).

Rioux, J.-P. (ed.), *La Guerre d'Algérie et les Français* (Fayard, 1990).

Rioux, J.-P. and Sirinelli, J.-F. (eds), *La Guerre d'Algérie et les intellectuels français* (Brussels: Complexe, 1991).

Roberts, H. *Algerian Socialism and the Kabyle Question* (Norwich: University of East Anglia, Monograph in Development Studies No. 8, 1981).

——— 'Notes on Relations of Production, Forms of Property and Political Structure in a Dissident Region of Algeria: Pre-Colonial Kabylia', University of East Anglia, Development Studies Discussion Papers No. 38 (Dec. 1978).

——— 'The Conversion of the Mrabtin in Kabylia', in E. Gellner *et al.* (eds), *Islam et Politique au Maghreb* (CNRS, 1981) pp. 101–25.

Rocheron, Y. 'Families on the Front Line – Mixed Marriage in France', in M. Cross and S. Perry (eds), *France: Population and Peoples* (Cassell, forthcoming).

Rogers, V. 'The Front National in Provence-Alpes-Côtes d'Azur: a case of institutionalised racism?', in M. Silverman (ed.), *Race, Discourse and Power in France* (Aldershot: Avebury, 1991) pp. 84–97.

Rosanvallon, A. *Les aspects économiques de l'émigration algérienne* (Grenoble: Unité des Sciences Sociales de Grenoble, 1974).

Rouissi, M. *Population et Société au Maghreb* (Tunis: Cérès, 1983).

Ruedy, J. *Modern Algeria. The Origins and Development of a Nation* (Bloomington: Indiana University Press, 1992).

Ruiz, D. *El Movimiento Obrero en Asturias* (Madrid: Jucar, 1979).

Saadia-et-Lakhdar, *L'aliénation colonialiste et la Résistance de la Famille algérienne* (Lausanne: La Cité, 1961).

Said, E. *Orientalism* (London: Penguin edition, 1987).
—— 'Representing the Colonized: Anthropology's Interlocutors', *Critical Inquiry* (1989) 205–25.
Sammut, C. 'La situation du prolétariat dans une entreprise coloniale française en Tunisie: La Compagnies des Chemins de Fer et Phosphate de Gasfa', *Revue d'Histoire Maghrébine* (July, 1977) 350–9.
Santucci, M.-R. 'La Main-d'Oeuvre Étrangère dans les Mines de la Grand-Combe jusque'en 1940', in *Mines et Mineurs en Languedoc-Rouissillon et régions voisines de l'Antiquité à nos jours* (Montpellier, 1977) 292–6.
Sari, D. *La dépossession des fellahs (1830–1962)* (Algiers: SNED, 1975).
Sayad, A. 'Les trois "âges" de l'émigration algérienne', *Actes de la Recherche en Sciences Sociales*, Vol. XV (1977) 59–79.
— 'L'Immigration Algérienne en Franc, une Immigration "Exemplaire"', in J. Costa-Lascoux and E. Temime (eds), pp. 19–49.
— *L'immigration ou les paradoxes de l'altérité* (Brussels: De Boeck-Wesmael, 1991).
— 'Aux origines de l'émigration Kabyle ou montagnarde', *Homme et Migrations*, No. 1179 (September, 1994) 6–11.
— *Un Nanterre algérien, terre de bidonvilles* (Éditions Autrement, 1995).
Schain, M.A. 'Policy and policy-making in France and the United States: models of incorporation and the dynamics of change', *Modern and Contemporary France*, No. 4 (1995), 401–13.
Schnapper, D. *La France de l'intégration* (Gallimard, 1991).
Schneider, W.H. *An Empire for the Masses. The French Popular Image of Africa, 1870–1900* (Westport: Greenwood Press, 1982).
Schor, R. 'Les conditions de vie des immigrés Nord-Africains dans la Meurthe-et-Moselle entre les deux guerres', *Cahiers de la méditerranée*, No. 14 (June, 1977) 41–51.
— 'L'opinion française et les immigrés nord-africaines, 1919–39. L'image d'un sous prolétariat', *Cahiers de la Méditerranée* (1981) 51–67.
— *L'Opinion Française et les Étrangers en France, 1919–1939* (Publication de la Sorbonne, 1985).
— 'Racisme et xénophobie à travers la caricature française (1919–1939)', *Revue Européene des Migrations Internationales*, Vol. 4, Nos 1–2 (1988) 141–55.
Scott, J.C. *Domination and the Arts of Resistance. Hidden Transcripts* (New Haven: Yale University Press, 1990).
Secrétariat Social d'Alger, *La Lutte des Algériens contre la Faim* (Algiers: Secrétariat Social d'Alger, 1955).
Seddon, D. *Moroccan Peasants: a century of change in the eastern Rif, 1870–1970* (Folkstone: Dawson, 1981).
Shaw, A. *A Pakistani Community in Britain* (Oxford: Blackwell, 1988).
Sherwood, M. 'Race, nationality and employment among Lascar seamen, 1660 to 1945', *New Community*, Vol. 17 (Jan. 1991) 229–44.
Singer-Kerel, J. 'Les Actifs Maghrébines dans les Recensements Français', in L. Talha (ed.), *Maghrébins en France. Émigrés ou Immigrés?* (CNRS, 1983) pp. 81–100.
Sirinelli, J.-F. 'Les intellectuells dans la mêlée', in J.-P. Rioux (ed.), *La Guerre d'Algérie*, pp. 116–30.

Sivan, E. 'Colonialism and Popular Culture in Algeria', *Journal of Contemporary History*, Vol. 14 (1979) 21–53.

Skelton, R. *Population Mobility in Developing Countries: A Reinterpretation* (London: Belhaven, 1990).

Slitinsky, M. *L'Affaire Papon* (Alain Moreau, 1983).

Smith, G. 'Jim Crow on the home front (1942–1945)', *New Community*, Vol. 8, No. 3 (Winter, 1980) 317–28.

Spivak, G.C. 'Can the Subaltern Speak?', in C. Nelson and L. Grossberg (eds), *Marxism and the Interpretation of Culture* (Chicago: University of Chicago Press, 1986).

Stichter, S. *Migrant Laborers* (Cambridge: Cambridge University Press, 1985).

Stoezel, J. and Girard, A. *Français et immigrés*, Vol. 2, INED, Travaux et Documents, Cahier No. 20 (Presses Universitaires de France, 1954).

Stoler, A. 'Rethinking Colonial Categories: European Communities and the Boundaries of Rule', *Comparative Studies in Society and History*, Vol. 13, No. 1 (1989) 134–61.

Stora, B. *Dictionnaire Biographique des Militants Nationalistes Algériens (1926–1954)* (Harmattan, 1985).

— *Messali Hadj (1889–1974). Pionnier du nationalisme algérien* (Harmattan, 1986).

— *Les Sources du Nationalisme Algérien* (Harmattan, 1989).

— *Histoire Politique de l'Immigration Algérienne en France (1922–1962)*, Doctoral thesis, University of Paris XII (1991).

— *La gangrène et l'oubli. La mémoire de la guerre d'Algérie* (La Découverte, 1991).

— *Ils Venaient d'Algérie. L'immigration algérienne en France, 1912–1992* (Fayard, 1992).

— *Aide-Mémoire de l'Immigration Algérienne* (Harmattan, 1992).

Stovall, T. 'Colour-blind France? Colonial Workers during the First World War', *Race and Class*, Vol. 35, No. 2 (1993) 35–55.

Sutton, K. 'Population Resettlement – Traumatic Upheavals and the Algerian Experience', *Journal of Modern African Studies*, Vol. 15, No. 2 (1977) 279–300.

Tabili, L. 'Keeping the Natives Under Control: Race Segregation and the Domestic Dimensions of Empire, 1920–1939', *International Labor and Working-Class History* No. 44 (Fall, 1993) 64–78.

— 'The Construction of Racial Difference in Twentieth-Century Britain: The Special Restrictions (Coloured Alien Seamen) Order, 1925', *Journal of British Studies*, No. 33 (January, 1994) 54–98.

Taguieff, P.-A. (ed.), *Face au racisme*, 2 Vols (La Découverte, 1991).

Talha, L. (ed.), *Maghrébins en France. Émigrés ou Immigrés?* (CNRS, 1983).

— *Le Salariat Immigré dans la Crise. La Main d'Oeuvre Maghrébine en France (1921–1987)* (Editions CNRS, 1989).

Temime, E. 'Marseille XXe siècle: de la dominante italienne à la diversité maghrébine', *Revue Européenne des Migrations Internationales*, Vol. 11, No. 1 (1995) 9–19.

Terrisse, A. 'Les Nord-Africains à Paris', *En Terre d'Islam* (1936) 228–36, 317–23, 374–9.

Tinker, H. *A New System of Slavery: the Export of Indian Labour Overseas, 1830–1920* (London: Oxford University Press, 1974).

Tlemcani, R. *State and Revolution in Algeria* (London: Zed Books, 1986).

Todd, E. *Le Destin des Immigrés* (Seuil, 1994).

Toubon, J.-C. and Messamah, K. *Centralité Immigrée: Le Quartier de la Goutte-d'Or*, 2 Vols (Harmattan, 1990).

Trebous, M. *Migration and Development. The Case of Algeria* (Paris: OECD Publications, 1970).

Tribalat, M. *Fair France. Une enquête sur les immigrés et leurs enfants* (La Découverte, 1995).

Tripier, M. *L'Immigration dans la Classe Ouvrière en France* (Harmattan, 1990).

Tristan, A. *Le silence du fleuve* (Bezons: Au nom de la mémoire, 1991).

Troussel, R. 'Note sur les Populations indigènes de la Commune mixte des Eulma', *Revue Africaine*, Vol. 85 (1941) 230–57.

Turin, Y. *Affrontements culturels dans l'Algérie coloniale. Écoles, médicine, religion, 1830–1880* (Maspero, 1970).

Valensi, L. *On the Eve of Colonialism: North Africa before the French Conquest* (New York: Africana, 1977).

Van Dijk, T.A. *Elite Discourse and Racism* (London: Sage, 1993).

Van Velsen, J. 'Labor Migration as a positive factor in the continuity of Tonga tribal society', *Economic Development and Cultural Change*, Vol. 8 (1959) 265–78.

Videlier, P. 'Espaces et temps de l'intégration des immigrés dans la région lyonnaise', in I. Simon-Barrouh and P.-J. Simon (eds), *Les Étrangers dans la Ville. Le regard des Sciences Sociales* (Harmattan, 1990) pp. 300–14.

Vollenhoven, J. Van, *Essai sur le Fellah Algérien* (A. Rousseau, 1903).

Vuddamalay, V.P. White and D. Sporton, 'The evolution of the Goutte d'Or as an ethnic minority district in Paris', *New Community*, Vol. 17 (Jan. 1991) 245–58.

Walvin, J. *Black and White: The Negro in English Society, 1555–1945* (London: Allen Lane, 1973).

Watson, J.L. (ed.), *Between Two Cultures. Migrants and Minorities in Britain* (Oxford: Blackwell, 1977).

Watson, W. *Tribal Cohesion in a Money Economy* (Manchester: Manchester University Press, 1985).

Weil, P. *La France et ses Étrangers* (Calmann-Lévy, 1991).

Wieviorka, M. *La France Raciste* (Seuil, 1992).

Wihtol de Wenden, C. *Les immigrés et la politique* (Presses de la FNSP, 1988).

— 'L'Immigration Maghrébine dans l'Imaginaire Politique Français', in B. Etienne (ed.), *L'Islam en France* (Editions CNRS, 1990) pp. 127–37.

Williams, P. and Chrisman, L. (eds), *Colonial Discourse and Post-Colonial Theory. A Reader* (London: Harvester Wheatsheaf, 1993).

Williams, R. *The Country and the City* (London: Chatto and Windus, 1973).

Winthrop, D.J. *White Over Black: American Attitudes Towards the Negro, 1550–1812* (Chapel Hill: University of North Carolina Press, 1968).

Wolf, E.R. *Peasant Wars of the Twentieth Century* (London: Faber, 1973).

Wolpe, H. 'Capitalism and cheap labour-power in South Africa', *Economy and Society*, Vol. 1, No. 4 (1972) 425–56.

Yacono, X. 'Peut-on évaluer la population de l'Algérie vers 1830?', *Revue Africaine*, Vol. 98 (1954) 277–307.

Yacono, X. *La colonisation des plaines du Chélif,* 2 Vols (Algiers: E. Imbert, 1955–6).

Yassine, C. 'Pour une thanatologie maghrébine: les rapatriements de corps', in B. Etienne (ed.), *L'Islam En France* (CNRS, 1990) pp. 337–48.

Zagoria, J.D. *The Rise and Fall of the Movement of Messali Hadj in Algeria, 1924– 1954,* Doctoral thesis, Columbia University (1973).

Index